DRAFTING LEGISLATION

In Memory of Sir William (Leonard) Dale KCMG (1906–2000)

Drafting Legislation
A Modern Approach

Edited by
CONSTANTIN STEFANOU
and
HELEN XANTHAKI
University of London, UK

Routledge
Taylor & Francis Group
LONDON AND NEW YORK

First published 2008 by Ashgate Publishing

2 Park Square, Milton Park, Abingdon, Oxon OX14 4RN
711 Third Avenue, New York, NY 10017, USA

Routledge is an imprint of the Taylor & Francis Group, an informa business

First issued in paperback 2016

British Library Cataloguing in Publication Data
Drafting legislation : a modern approach
1. Bill drafting
I. Stefanou, Constantin, 1961- II. Xanthaki, Helen
328.3'73

Library of Congress Cataloging-in-Publication Data
Drafting legislation : a modern approach / by Constantin Stefanou and Helen Xanthaki.
p. cm.
Includes index.
ISBN 978-0-7546-4903-8
1. Bill drafting. 2. Legislation. I. Stephanou, Constantine A. II. Xanthaki, Helen.

K3320.D73 2008
328.3'73--dc22

2008017341

ISBN 13: 978-0-7546-4903-8 (hbk)
ISBN 13: 978-1-138-26463-2 (pbk)

Contents

List of Figures

List of Contributors

Dr Helen Caldwell CB (MA, PhD) Parliamentary Counsel (UK).

Lydia Clapinska (LLB, MA) barrister of Gray's Inn and a member of the Government Legal Service, Criminal Law Division, Legal Directorate, Ministry of Justice.

Professor Dr Gerhard Dannemann (MA, Dr.jur.), Professor of English Law, British Economy and Politics at the Humboldt–Universität zu Berlin.

Professor Eileen Denza (LLB, LLM, MA) Visiting Professor, Department of Law, University College London and former Legal Counsel to the Foreign and Commonwealth Office.

Daniel Greenberg (BA) of Lincoln's Inn, Barrister; Parliamentary Counsel (UK).

Professor Dr Ulrich Karpen (Dr.jur.) Professor of Law, Law Faculty, University of Hamburg, Permanent Consultant in Legislation matters to the Council of Europe.

Alfred E. Kellermann (LLB) is a Senior Legal Policy Adviser at the T.M. Asser Institute in the Hague.

Stephen Laws CB (LLB) First Parliamentary Counsel (UK).

Justice Keith Mason (BA, LLB, LLM) New South Wales Court of Appeal (Australia).

Ian McLeod (LLB) is an Associate Senior Research Fellow, Sir William Dale Centre for Legislative Studies, Institute of Advanced Legal Studies, University of London, UK; Visiting Professor of Law, School of Social Sciences and Law, University of Teesside.

Dr Valsamis Mitsilegas (LLB, LLM, PhD) Reader in Law, Department of Law, Queen Mary University of London.

Zione Ntaba (LLB, LLM) Parliamentary Counsel (Malawi).

Richard C. Nzerem (LLB, LLM) Honorary Director, Sir William Dale Centre for Legislative Studies, Legal Consultant and former Director, Legal and Constitutional Affairs Division, Commonwealth Secretariat.

William Robinson (BA) is a coordinator in the Legal Revisers Group of the European Commission's Legal Service.

Hayley Rogers (LLB) Parliamentary Counsel (UK).

Alec Samuels (BA) JP Barrister, Councillor, Leader of Southampton City Council, formerly Reader in Law at the University of Southampton.

Professor Dr Giovanni Sartor (Cor. di pref., LLB, PhD) is Marie-Curie Professor of Legal informatics and Legal Theory at the European University Institute, Florence.

Professor Dr Ann Seidman (BA, MS, PhD) is Adjunct Professor of Law at Boston University.

Professor Robert B. Seidman (BA, LLM) is Emeritus Professor of Law and Political Science at Boston University.

Dr Constantin Stefanou (BA, MA, MPhil, PhD) is a Senior Lecturer and LLM Director at the Institute of Advanced Legal Studies, School of Advanced Study, University of London.

Dr Helen Xanthaki (LLB, MJur, PhD) is a Senior Lecturer and Academic Director of the Sir William Dale Centre at the Institute of Advanced Legal Studies, School of Advanced Study, University of London.

Chapter 1

On Transferability of Legislative Solutions: The Functionality Test

Helen Xanthaki

In 1997, Sir William Dale became the first Director of the Centre that bears his name. The aim of the Centre is to promote quality in legislation by identifying and disseminating best practices in legislation.[1] The logic is that one can and should learn from the experience of others, irrespective of the characteristics and intricacies of their own legal system, irrespective of the financial power of the borrowing legal system and irrespective of the level of development of the legal systems involved. In celebration of the 10th anniversary of the establishment of the Sir William Dale Centre for Legislative Studies at the Institute for Advanced Legal Studies of the School of Advanced Study of the University of London and in the memory of Sir William Dale, this chapter aims to put to the test the very essence of the Centre's philosophy. Can one really learn from others in the field of legislative drafting? Can legal texts, institutions and legislative solutions be transferred to other jurisdictions? And if so, under which conditions?

In answering this question, one cannot fail but question the essence of this publication. Are the essays generously contributed to this book in memoriam to Sir William Dale really useful as paradigms of best practices in aspects of legislative drafting and legislative studies? Or does this publication, and the Centre as a whole, continue a vain effort of a brilliant mind to teach what cannot be taught, to disseminate what cannot be transferred?

Transferability in Legislative Drafting

Transferability finds an eloquent supporter with Watson, the guru of transplants.[2] Watson, who focuses on the transferability of institutions, solutions and texts in the field of private law, claims that 'whatever their historical origins may have been, rules of private law can survive without any close connection to any particular

1 See Sir William Dale, 'The drafting of the norm' in U. Karpen and P. Delnoy (eds) *Contributions to the Methodology of the Creation of Written Law* (Baden-Baden: Nomos Verlagsgesellshcaft, 1996) pp. 35–8, at 35.

2 For an analysis of the term, see E. Öcürü, 'Critical Comparative Law: considering paradoxes for legal systems in transition' 59 (1999) *Nederlandse Vereniging voor Rechtsvergelijking*; also see E. Öcürü, 'Law as Transposition' 51 (2002) *ICLQ* pp. 205–23 at 206.

people, any particular period of time or any particular place'.[3] Watson could put an end to the questions posed by this chapter before any analysis takes place: if everyone can borrow from everyone else, then transferability can be useful even in an environment of anarchy by comparison. However, the liberal approach of Watson is rejected by Legrand,[4] Kahn-Freund[5] and the Seidmans,[6] who set conditions of transferability. It would be difficult to accept that national characteristics play no part in the transferability of legislative solutions, institutions or texts. It is therefore widely accepted that some prerequisites must be introduced when borrowing takes place. The question is what is the accepted criterion of transferability?

Gutteridge, Buckland and McNair accept the use of paradigms under the condition of similarity: like can only be compared with like.[7] Like is defined as countries in the same evolutionary stage.[8] Teubner and Allison support the conditionality of transferability but apply the exact opposite criterion, namely that of divergence: only differences enhance our understanding of law in a given society.[9] Schlesinger rejects the similarities versus differences debate and points out that 'to compare means to observe and to explain similarities as well as differences' [10] This seems to be the prevailing view. One can learn from similar and divergent legal systems and indeed one can borrow similarities and differences. But, if the criterion of transferability does not lie with the comparability of the legal systems involved, what is it?

---

3 See A. Watson, 'Legal Transplants and Law Reform' 92 (1976) *Law Quarterly Review* at 80; also see A. Watson, *Legal Transplants: An Approach to Comparative Law* (Edinburgh: Scottish Academic Press, 1974); A. Watson, 'Legal transplants and European private law' Ius Commune Lectures on European Private Law, No. 2, 4 (2000) 4 *Electronic Journal of Comparative Law* (www.ejcl.org/ejcl/44/44-2.html).

4 See P. Legrand, 'The Impossibility of Legal Transplants' (1997) *Maastricht Journal of European and Comparative Law* p. 111.

5 See O. Kahn-Freund, *On Uses and Misuses of Comparative Law*, 37 (1974) *Modern Law Review* at 7.

6 See A. Seidman and R. Seidman, *State and Law in the Developing Process: Problem Solving and Institutional Change in the Developing World* (London: Macmillan Publishers, 1994) pp. 44–6.

7 See H. Gutteridge, *Comparative Law* (Cambridge: Cambridge University Press, 1949) at 73; W.W. Buckland and A.D. McNair, *Roman Law and Common Law* (Cambridge: Cambridge University Press, 1936).

8 See C. Schmidthoff, 'The Science of Comparative Law' (1939) *Cambridge Law Journal* at 96.

9 See F. Teubner, 'Legal Irritants: Good faith in British law or how unifying law wends up in new divergences' 61 (1998) *Modern Law Review* at 11; also J.W.F. Allison, *A Continental Distinction in the Common Law: A Historical and Comparative Perspective on English Public Law* (Oxford: Clarendon Press, 1996) at 16.

10 See R.B. Schlesinger, 'The common core of legal systems: an emerging subject of comparative study' in K. Nadelmann, A. von Mehren and J. Hazard (eds) *XXth Century Comparative and Conflicts Law, Legal Essays in Honour of Hessel E. Yntema* (1961); Schlesinger, 'Research on the general principles of law recognised by civilised nations' 51 (1957) *American Journal of International Law* at 734.

The prevailing view in the theory of comparative law is expressed by Jhering, Zweigert and Kötz,[11] who view the question of comparability and subsequent transferability through the relative prism of functionality.[12] 'The reception of foreign legal institutions is not a matter of nationality, but of usefulness and need. No one bothers to fetch a thing from afar when he has one as good or better at home, but only a fool would refuse quinine just because it didn't grow in his back garden'.[13] It is the theory of functionality that seems to serve drafting teams in the current period of integrative legal globalisation,[14] although currently the use of social analysis in legislation is minimal.[15] Thus, legislative drafters can propose and apply policy, legal and legislative responses already tried elsewhere with unprecedented insight to the results produced in the legal system of origin. Does it really matter where these responses are borrowed from? Not in principle.

Functionality

A qualifier to Watson's liberal approach can be introduced via Zweigert and Kötz's functionality theory. The criterion for the transferability of institutions, solutions and texts is that of functionality. If the policy, concept or legislation of a foreign legal system can serve the receiving system well, then the origin of the transplant is irrelevant to its success.[16] As long as the transplant can serve the same social need, the transplant can work well in the new legal ground. In fact, it is this transfer of the transplant to national contexts that promotes indigenisation of positive transplants as a block to indiscrete globalisation and modern legal colonialism.[17]

But is there a unifying factor that can link all legal systems with a web of common functionality, thus justifying this publication and, perhaps more importantly, the existence of the Sir William Dale Centre? In other words, is there a concept which drives national legislative drafters in the performance of their tasks, which is detached from the national intricacies of the legal system, the national drafting style and the policy aims of each national law? Do drafters serve the same conceptual function when drafting legislation? Do they serve a higher virtue which acts as a conceptual

11 See K. Zweigert und H. Kötz, *Einführung in die Rechtsvergleichung*, 3. Neubearbeitete Auflage (Tübingen: J.C.B. Mohr, 1996).

12 See K. Zweigert and K. Sier, 'Jhering's influence on the development of comparative legal method' 19 (1971) *American Journal of Comparative Law* pp. 215–31.

13 See K. Jhering, *Geist des römischen Rechts* (1955, vol. 1) pp. 8–9.

14 See L.A. Mistelis, 'Regulatory Aspects: Globalization, Harmonization, Legal Transplants, and Law Reform – Some Fundamental Observations' 34 (2000) 3 *International Lawyer* at 1059.

15 See J. Brown, A. Kudan and K. McGeeney, 'Improving legislation through social analysis: a case study in methodology from the water sector in Uzbekistan' 5 (2005) *Sustainable Development Law and Policy* pp. 49–57 at 49.

16 See S. Zhuang, 'Legal Transplantation in the People's Republic of China: A Response to Alan Watson' (2006) *European Journal of Law Reform* pp. 215–36 at 223.

17 See R. Petrella, 'Globalization and Internationalization: The Dynamics of the Emerging World Order' in R. Boyer and D. Drache (eds), *States against Markets: the Limits of Globalization* (London and New York: Routledge, 1996) at 132.

framework applicable to all types of legal texts, in all types of legal systems and legislative environments? Of course, asking the drafter to select a single goal to serve in the complex task of drafting legislation has been criticised as simplistic; however, even those who accept the criticism also recognise that serving a single master focuses drafters' efforts and, consequently, is a better platform for success.[18] Irrespective of one's position on the debate, if such a single virtue exists, then it can serve as a functional glue that can justify transferability of texts, institutions, legislative solutions and, consequently, legislative techniques. Sir William's conviction that one can learn from the work and teachings of others will be proven, the Sir William Dale Centre will confirm its *raison d'être*, and this collection of essays will prove its usefulness for most national legislative environments.

In the search for the higher functionality concept in legislative drafting, one cannot avoid to explore the higher values, the virtues, promoted in the field: efficacy, effectiveness, efficiency, clarity, precision,[19] unambiguity, plain language[20] and gender neutral language. Could one of them, unrealisable as they may be,[21] serve as the functionality glue? And what is its relationship with the other concepts promoted in drafting manuals and legisprudence around the world?

Efficacy

Efficacy is defined as the ability to produce a desired or intended result.[22] Mader views efficacy as one of three criteria for the evaluation of legislation, namely effectiveness, efficacy and efficiency.[23] Mader provides the simpler yet most successful definition of efficacy as the extent to which legislators achieve their goal.[24] Delnoy draws the link between efficacy and quality in legislation in his definition of efficacy as the achievement of the least degree of litigation as a result of laws passed.[25] Thus, efficacy is achieved when the statute does not conflict with any other norm of the

---

18 See J. Stark, 'Should the main goal of statutory drafting be accuracy or clarity?' 15 (1994) *Statute Law Review* pp. 207–13 at 207.

19 See Sir W. Dale (1996) at 35.

20 See Jean-Louis Bergel, 'The drafting of the norm' in Karpen and Delnoy (1996) pp. 39–50 at 41.

21 See W. Cyrul, 'Lawmaking: between discourse and legal text', in L.J. Wintgens, *Legislation in Context: Essays in Legisprudence* (Aldershot: Ashgate, 2007) pp. 43–54 at 52.

22 See *Compact Oxford English Dictionary of Current English* (Oxford: Oxford University Press, 2005).

23 See L. Mader, 'Evaluating the effect: a contribution to the quality of legislation' 22 (2001) *Statute Law Review* pp. 119–31 at 126.

24 See ibid. at 126.

25 See P. Delnoy, *The role of legislative drafters in determining the content of norms* (Ottawa: The International Cooperation Group, Department of Justice of Canada, 2005) at 6, accessed at (www.justice.gc.ca/en/ps/inter/delnoy/index.html); L.E. Allen, 'Symbolic logic: a razor-edged tool for drafting and interpreting legal documents' 66 (1956–57) *Yale L.J.*, pp. 833–80 at 855.

same or higher hierarchical level and when the statute has no deficiencies.[26] In other words efficacy seems to reflect the quality of statutes that achieve their goal to such a degree that refuge to judicial interpretation is not necessary. In fact, Jones distinguishes between five types of inefficacy: failure of communication of the law's message; failure to enlist supportive action to the law; failure to forestall avoidance of the action required by the law; failure of enforcement; and failure of the law's moral obligations.[27] Is this the highest level of quality that a drafter can secure?

The achievement of a policy objective or purpose is not the sole task of the drafter. It is the task of a multi-level effort of policymakers, drafters, interpreters, applicators and enforcers of legislation.[28] This common effort is reflected in the many aspects of the policy process, of which the legislative process is a mere stage. It requires quality in the performance of the duties of all factors in the policy process. A drafter cannot possibly control the efficacy of the policy decided by the Cabinet Office and pushed forward by the Client Department, or the efficacy of the implementation of the legislation by the executive, or indeed the efficacy of its enforcement by the police.[29] If one accepts the multiplicity of actors in the policy process, clearly recognised in the prevailing vision of a drafting team, efficacy cannot be a goal set for the drafter alone.[30] As a result, despite acknowledging efficacy as the highest virtue in the policy process, efficacy cannot be viewed as the connecting function of drafters. A goal concrete to the work of the drafter, and consequently, achievable by the drafter must be sought.

Effectiveness

Quality of legislation is commonly attached to effectiveness rather than efficacy.[31] Effectiveness can be viewed as the drafter's contribution to the efficacy of the drafted legislation. It is widely accepted that drafters aim to be effective and efficient, 'effective' meaning that the norm produces effects, that it does not become a dead letter, and 'efficient' in the sense that the norm should produce the desired effects, should not have perverse effects and should so guide conduct as to achieve the desired objective.[32] Parkinson describes effective legislation as reasonable

---

26 See ibid. at 7.

27 See H.W. Jones, *The Efficacy of the Law* (Evanston: Northwestern University Press, 1969) pp. 18, 20, 32 and 34.

28 See U. Karpen, 'The norm enforcement process' in Karpen and Delnoy (1996) pp. 51–61 at 51; for the example of Switzerland, see L. Mader, 'Legislative procedure and the quality of legislation' in U. Karpen and P. Delnoy (1996) pp. 62–71 at 68.

29 See D. Hull, 'Drafter's Devils' (2000) *Loophole*, (www.opc.gov.au/calc/docs/calc-june/audience.htm).

30 See J.P. Chamberlain, 'Legislative drafting and law enforcement' 21 (1931) *Am. Lab. Leg. Rev.* pp. 235–43 at 243.

31 See H. Schäffer, 'Evaluation and assessment of legal effects procedures: towards a more rational and responsible lawmaking process' 22 (2001) *Statute Law Review* pp. 132–53 at 132–3.

32 See Delnoy (2000) at 3.

legislation.[33] Mader defines effectiveness as the extent to which the observable attitudes and behaviours of the target population correspond to the attitudes and behaviours prescribed by the legislator.[34]

Thus effectiveness seems to reflect the relationship between the effects produced by legislation and the purpose of the statute passed. It is different from efficacy in that it relates to the effect of the statute and not to the effect of the policy which the statute sets out to achieve. In other words, effectiveness can be described as the drafter's efficacy. The definition of effectiveness in legislation is rarely studied in literature in drafting terms. More often than not effectiveness of regulations and techniques is studied with reference to the nature of the specific regulation observed.[35] Thus, in international law effectiveness is related to treaties, where design and impact are critical to effectiveness.[36] In European Union law effectiveness appears to be at the forefront of lawmaking and is linked to minimum consultation standards applied by the Commission's departments: this leads to quality and equity of major political proposals which, in turn, guarantees the feasibility and effectiveness of the law-making operation.[37] Effectiveness is not simply the elaboration of legal doctrine.[38] It includes but is not limited to implementation, enforcement, impact and compliance.[39] Thus, effectiveness may include both the effects of legal norms and the following of such norms.[40]

However, one could distinguish in general between two prevailing models of effectiveness, often described as the positivist and the socio-legal models. In his positivist approach Jacobson links effectiveness to implementation and compliance.[41] In his socio-legal model of effectiveness, Jenkins relates the statute to the social reform attained.[42] Irrespective of which of the two models one favours, the fact of the matter is that drafters are in pursuit of effectiveness of the measure that they draft. And, although stating that a drafter can single-handedly achieve effectiveness in

33 See T.I. Parkinson, 'Functions of administration in labour legislation' 20 (1930) *Am. Lab. Leg. Rev.* pp. 143–54 at 144.

34 See L. Mader (2001) at 126.

35 See P. Birnie and A. Boyle, *International Law and the Environment* (Oxford: Oxford University Press, 2002) at 10.

36 See W.B. Chambers, 'Towards an improved understanding of legal effectiveness in international environmental treaties' 16(2003–04) *Geo. Int. Env. L. Rev.* pp. 501–32 at 503.

37 See Commission of the European Communities, 'Communication from the Commission: European Governance: Better lawmaking' COM (2002) 275 final, Brussels, 5 June 2002, at 3.

38 See F. Snyder, *New Directions in EC Law* (London: Weidenfeld and Nicholson, 1990) at 3.

39 See G. Teubner, 'Regulatory Law: Chronicle of a Death Foretold' (1992) *Social Legal Studies* pp. 451–75.

40 See F. Snyder, 'The Effectiveness of European Community Law: Institutions, Processes, Tools and Techniques' 56 (1993) *Modern Law Review* pp. 19–54 at 19.

41 See H. Jacobson, 'After word: conceptual, methodological and substantive issues entwined in studying compliance' 19 (1998) *Mich. J. Int. L.* pp. 569–80 at 573.

42 See I. Jenkins, *Social Order and the Limits of the Law: a Theoretical Essay* (Princeton: Princeton University Press, 1981) at 180; R. Cranston, 'Reform through legislation: the dimension of legislative technique' 73 (1978–79) *Nw.U.L.Rev.* pp. 873–908 at 875.

legislation would signify a complete ignorance of the interrelation between actors in the policy process, the truth of the matter is that the drafter can, and must seek, achieve attainment of the purpose and objectives set in the statute under construction.

Could effectiveness be the common functionality sought, one that can apply to the drafting of all legislation breaking the barriers of family of laws and bypassing national intricacies? Before drawing a conclusion, it is necessary to explore the other virtues sought in legislative drafting.

Efficiency

Efficiency is defined as working productively with minimum wasted effort or expense,[43] as the relation between costs and benefits of the legislative action,[44] as an economic analysis of what and how much input is required for an optimal output,[45] or as the extent to which perceived best practices are utilised in the process of the development of legislation.[46] Evaluating the efficiency of legislation means considering its costs[47] (namely direct financial costs of implementation and compliance with legal norms; non-material factors; and all negative effects of the legislation)[48] and the extent to which its goals have been achieved.[49] Efficiency is often perceived as a dual set of presumptions: the normative presumption is that the law should be efficient; the descriptive presumption is that the law is in fact efficient.[50]

Criteria for efficiency in legislation are borrowed from the theory of efficiency in economics and include the notions of productive efficiency, Pareto optimality, Pareto superiority, Kaldor-Hicks efficiency, and Posner's wealth maximisation.[51] Productive efficiency occurs when the economy is operating at its production possibility frontier:[52] thus productive efficiency in relation to legislation occurs

43 See *Compact Oxford English Dictionary of Current English* (Oxford: Oxford University Press, 2005).

44 See R. Posner, 'Cost Benefit Analysis: definition, justification, and comments on conference papers' 29 (2000) *The Journal of Legal Studies* pp. 1153–77.

45 See Government of the United Kingdom, *Efficiency and Effectiveness in the Civil Service, Government Observations on the Third Report from the Treasury and Civil Service Committee*, Session 1981–82, Cmnd 8616.

46 See P. Biribonwoha, 'Efficiency in the legislative process in Uganda' 7 (2005) *European Journal of Law Reform* pp. 135–64 at 138.

47 See L. De Alessi, 'Efficiency criteria for optimal laws: Objective standards or value judgements?' (2006) *Constitutional Political Economy* pp. 321–42.

48 See G. Regner, 'The view of the practical Swedish law-maker' in Karpen and Delnoy (1996) at 75–6.

49 See Mader (2001) at 126.

50 See L. Kornhauser, 'A guide to the perplexed claims of efficiency in the law' 8 (1979–80) *Hofstra Law Reiew* at 591.

51 See J. Coleman, 'Efficiency, utilisation and wealth maximalisation' 8 (1979–80) *Hofstra Law Review* at 512.

52 See P. Arestis, G. Chortareas and E. Desli, 'Financial development and productive efficiency in OECD countries: an exploratory analysis' 74 (2006) *The Manchester School* pp. 417–40.

when a legislative choice achieves the lowest cost possible in comparison with the costs incurred by all other legislative choices. Pareto superiority, as applied in legislative drafting, compares two legislative choices and puts forward as preferred the legislative choice which improves the welfare of at least one person while not diminishing the welfare of another. Pareto optimality, criticised as a valid criterion early on,[53] compares all possible legislative choices and promotes the choice which is superior among all others.[54] In the Kaldor-Hicks scenario, a legislative solution is efficient if those benefiting from it can fully compensate those whose welfare is diminished as a result of its application.[55] The Kaldor-Hicks criterion is rather popular as it allows one to make efficient judgements about the real world: 'to judge, for example, that Communism was inefficient or rent control is inefficient or piracy was inefficient'.[56] However, it is often criticised as 'actually grappling with the calculation problem'.[57] Wealth maximisation signifies the choice of rule that maximises total wealth, irrespective of who benefits.[58]

These choices are usually developed through the prism of utilitisation theory and are therefore criticised as contrary to fairness and equity. However, Zerbe Jr. suggests that the pure economic considerations of Kaldor-Hicks and Pareto efficiency need not be in direct conflict with equity, as equity can be considered as one of the values that they take into account when choices of solutions are made.[59] Nevertheless, the possibility of combining efficiency with equity in a single stage is doubtful.[60] Similarly, the choice between efficiency and fairness is a fallacy even if the traditional Coase Theorem does not serve the unified model well.[61]

Leaving the common ethical concerns arising from the actual choice between benefits for some and costs for others, one cannot depart from the realism of efficiency in legislative choices. When selecting a legislative choice, or indeed when supporting a policy choice, the drafter takes into account the financial and non-monetary costs of this choice to interest groups and to the State itself. In fact,

---

53 See H.M. Hochman and J.D. Rodgers, 'Pareto Optimal Redistribution' 59 (1969) The American Economic Review pp. 542–57.

54 See A. Sen, 'Liberty and Social Choice' 80 (1983) *The Journal of Philosophy* pp. 5–28.

55 See E. Stringham, 'Kaldor-Hicks efficiency and the problem of central planning' 4 (2001) *Quarterly Journal of Austrian Economics* pp. 41–50.

56 See B. Caplan, 'The Austrian Search for Realistic Foundations' 65 (1999) *Southern Economic Journal* pp. 823–38 at 835.

57 See G.O'Driscoll, 'Justice, Efficiency, and the Economic Analysis of Law: A Comment on Fried' 9 (1980) *Journal of Legal Studies* pp. 355–66 at 359.

58 See A. Seidman and R.B. Seidman, 'Drafting Legislation for Development: Lessons from a Chinese Project' 44 (1996) The American Journal of Comparative Law pp. 1–44 at 21.

59 See R.O. Zerbe Jr., 'An integration of equity and efficiency' 73 (1998) *Washington Law Review* pp. 350–61 at 361.

60 See R.B. Korobkin and T.S. Ulen, 'Efficiency and equity: what can be gained by combining Coase and Rawles?' 73 (1998) *Washington Law Review* pp. 329–48 at 348.

61 See M.I. Swyert and K.E. Yanes, 'A unified theory of justice: the integration of fairness into efficiency' 73 (1998) *Washington Law Review* pp. 249–327 at 327.

the essence of consultation is to identify such costs and interest groups as a means of completing the picture of conflicting benefits and damages incurring as a result of a legislative choice. Fairness and equity are driving forces behind this choice, either unconsciously or as formally recognised non- monetary criteria for making the choice. Calculation of the true cost of such factors is a hurdle that few policymakers, and far fewer drafters, are equipped to handle, especially in the case of substantive rather than procedural efficiency.[62] But at the end of the day, efficiency is a desired value that must be taken into account in legislative drafting. It is a tool which the drafter can use to achieve effectiveness: relatively cheap results are better than just results. However, efficiency, in the process or in the law, does not guarantee effectiveness: negotiating the less costly means for producing the objectives of legislation does not secure attainment of the law's objectives. In fact, one could support the view that efficiency, in the sense of extreme economy, may be adverse to effectiveness and may jeopardise results in the altar of cost minimisation. This need not be the case. In the hierarchy of values set for the drafter efficiency is one of the considerations that must be taken into account in the search for effectiveness as part of efficacy. The question then is, whether efficiency is the only tool that the drafter can utilise to achieve effectiveness?

Clarity, Precision, Unambiguity

Butt and Castle recommend that 'legal documents should be written in modern, standard English, namely in standard English as currently used and understood'.[63] Clarity, or clearness,[64] is defined as the state or quality of being clear and easily perceived or understood.[65] Clarity depends on the proper selection of words, on their arrangement and on the construction of sentences.[66] Clarity in the language of the law enhances understanding and transparency of legislation.[67] Ambiguity is defined as uncertain or inexact meaning.[68] Ambiguity exists when words can be interpreted in more than one way: for example, is a 'light truck' light in weight or light in colour? Thus, semantic ambiguity occurs when a single word has more than one meaning and is cured by defining any term that people might disagree about.[69] Syntactic ambiguity is the result of unclear sentence structure or poor placement of phrases or

62 See G. Tullock, 'Two kinds of legal efficiency' 8 (1979–80) *Hofstra Law Review* pp. 659–69 at 666.

63 See P. Butt and R. Castle, *Modern Legal Drafting* (Cambridge, 2001) at 129.

64 See Lord H. Thring, *Practical Legislation: The Composition and Language of Acts of Parliament and Business Documents* (London: John Murray, 1902) at 61.

65 See *Compact Oxford English Dictionary of Current English* (Oxford: Oxford University Press, 2005).

66 See Lord H Thring (1902) at 61.

67 See P. Wahlgren, 'Legislative techniques' in L.J. Wintgens (2007) pp. 77–94 at 84.

68 See *Compact Oxford English Dictionary of Current English* (Oxford: Oxford University Press, 2005).

69 See J. MacKaye, A.W. Levi and W. Pepperell Montague, *The Logic of Language* (Hannover: Dartmouth College Publications, 1939) ch. 5.

clauses.[70] Vagueness exists when there is doubt about where a word's boundaries are, or when a word has an open textured meaning:[71] if a law applies to the blind, which exactly is blind, and what degree of impairment counts? Legislatures sometimes choose to be vague or general and to let administrative agencies supply the specifics.[72] Thus, vagueness is often viewed as an indispensable tool for clarity and precision.[73] Legislatures rarely choose to be ambiguous. If legislation is drafted in terms which are wide and general, this is likely to give rise to different interpretations and inevitable challenge. Thus, clarity, in the sense of intelligibility and unambiguity, signifies that a document is not only easy to understand but that it conveys the same message to those who read it.[74]

At the other extreme, the more one tries to be exhaustive, the more vulnerable the legislation will be to omissions and potential challenge. Precision is defined as exactness of expression or detail.[75] Precision is traditionally viewed as the main aim of common law drafters who make the greatest effort to 'say all, to define all; to leave nothing to the imagination; never to presume upon the reader's intelligence' [76] So achieving a healthy balance between the two extremes represents a great challenge to any legislative drafter.

It is in this context that the Chief Parliamentary Counsel to the Government in Ireland warns against 'overdrafting':

> Precision in drafting is a worthy goal, but can be taken too far. It is frequently unnecessary to name every single thing you are forbidding or requiring. An overzealous attempt at precision may result in redundancy and verbosity. Drafting too precisely may create unintended loopholes.[77]

Equally he cautions against 'vagueness':

> Just as overdrafting can affect a provision in unforeseen ways, underdrafting is equally dangerous. Although it is often necessary or desirable to create a general or broad legislative standard or directive, beware of language that is so indefinite that it is meaningless or begs

---

70 For the distinction between semantic and syntactic ambiguity, see R. Dickerson, *The Fundamentals of Legal Drafting* (Boston: Little-Brown, 1986) at 101 and 104; for an application of rules of logic to resolve syntactic ambiguities, see Allen (1956–57) pp. 833–80.

71 See G.C. Christie, 'Vagueness and legal language' 48 (1963–64) *Minn. L. Rev.* pp. 885–912 at 886.

72 See Dickerson (1964) at 11.

73 See Christie (1963–64) at 912.

74 See G. Caussignac, 'Clear legislation' The International Cooperation Group, Department of Justice of Canada, 2001 [revised in 2005] (www.justice-canada.org/en/ps/inter/caussignac/index.html).

75 See *Compact Oxford English Dictionary of Current English* (Oxford: Oxford University Press, 2005).

76 See L-P. Pigeon, *Drafting and Interpreting Legislation* (Toronto-Calgary-Vancouver: Carswell, 1988) at 7.

77 Legislative Drafting Manual (Dublin, 2001) at para. 4.4. The Drafting Manual has not been published and is not available externally.

a challenge in court as invalid for vagueness. Generally, courts loathe declaring a law invalid on this ground, but careful drafting can eliminate the need for judicial scrutiny.

Why do we need clarity and precision? First, without clarity, precision and consistency the law lacks predictability. Second, democratic governments seeking to induce transformation require that the law is understood and followed by common people. Third, democracy requires clarity and precision: the rule of law requires that officers of the law understand and apply the law.[78] Fourth, there are high costs to inaccessible law related to enforcement, application and interpretation of texts whose meaning is under doubt.[79] Thus, clearer texts may cut the time spent by lawyers on them to half.[80] However, clarity and precision may not be needed when the policymakers utilise ambiguity to cover political disagreements; when a problem cannot be resolved by departmental legal officers and the drafters (in which case there might be scope for an intransitive bill which leaves way to ministerial regulation by delegation); or when the drafter wishes to introduce a degree of discretion for officials.[81]

Having established the definitions of clarity, precision and unambiguity and having proved that these are requirements for quality in legislation which need to be pursued by the drafter,[82] it is time to identify if one of these three notions is prevalent. An initial approach is introduced by Burrows who relates the style of drafting to the aim of the legislation, namely whether it is coercive or not. Thus, detailed, precision drafting is particularly suitable for criminal statutes, revenue law, business, commerce or when broad powers could infringe on basic human rights. On the other hand, precision is not equally vital when the drafter aims to introduce statements of general principle and leave the courts to work out their detailed application on a case by case basis.[83] A second approach views the debate with reference to the role of the particular provision in the text of the statute. Definitions require more precision than clarity.[84] A third approach views the matter *in abstracto*. Thus, Sutherland refers to the Renton Report and confirms that, when in conflict with simplicity, certainty must not be sacrificed.[85]

One cannot provide a generally applicable response to the question of the hierarchy between clarity, precision and unambiguity. It is true that certain types of legislation require more clarity, such as criminal laws, whereas others require more precision, such as rules of evidence. But the prism under which the choice is to be made rests

78 See A. Seidman, R. Seidman and N. Abeyesekere, *Legislative Drafting for Democratic Social Change* (The Hague: Kluwer Law International, 2001) at 255.

79 See S. Krongold, 'Writing laws: making them easier to understand' 24 (1992) *Ottawa Law Review* pp. 495–582 at 501.

80 See R.D. Eagleson, 'Taking the Gobbledegook out of Legal Language' 20 (1990) *Queensland Law Society Journal* pp. 103–15 at 115.

81 See A. Seidman, R. Seidman and N. Abeyesekere (2001) pp. 257–8.

82 See R. Dickerson, 'The diseases of legislative drafting' 1 (1964) *Harv. L.J.* pp. 5–15 at 5.

83 See Burrows, *Statute Law in New Zealand* (Wellington: Butterworths, 1992) at 63.

84 See Stark (1994) at 212.

85 See E. Sutherland, 'Clearer drafting and the Timeshare Act: 1992: a response from Parliamentary Counsel to Mr. Cutts' 14 (1993) *Statute Law Review* pp. 163–70 at 168.

in abstracto and relates to effectiveness.[86] Effectiveness is the virtue sought by the drafter and effectiveness must serve as the qualifier for a negotiation between clarity, precision and ambiguity. What matters is that the audience of the particular statute or legal text receives the message that the drafter attempts to communicate. If the audience of the particular text consists of mainly lay persons, then clarity, and unambiguity as part of clarity, must be put forward. If the audience consists of trained legal professionals, precision can prevail: a trained audience has a better chance to deal with implication[87] in order to receive the message communicated by the drafter.[88] If effectiveness is accepted as the qualifier for any choice made by the drafter, then the relationship between clarity, precision and unambiguity is a non-hierarchical one and these three virtues must be viewed as tools of effectiveness bearing equal gravitas and power. Vagueness is simply a tool for clarity and precision, provided that it is used consciously and as a legal rather than political tool.

Plain Language

Another tool for clarity, precision and unambiguity is plain language. The plain language movement evolved as a reaction to the incomprehensibility, remoteness and complexity of traditional legal language.[89] As plain language as a concept encapsulates a qualifier of language which is subjective to each reader or user,[90] the essence of the movement is not easy to identify. Eagleson describes plain language as 'clear, straightforward expression, using only as many words as are necessary. It is language that avoids obscurity, inflated vocabulary and convoluted sentence structure. It is not baby talk, nor is it a simplified version of the English language'.[91] Redish notes that 'plain English means writing that is straightforward, that reads as if it were spoken. It means writing that is unadorned with archaic, multi-syllabic words and majestic turns of phrase that even educated readers cannot understand. Plain English is clear, direct, and simple; but good plain English has both clarity and grace'.[92]

Thus, a plain language text is a passage that the intended audience can read, understand and act upon the first time they read it.[93] Plain language takes into account

---

86 See R. Dickerson (1964) at 5, where he refers to 'adequacy [of the legislative message] as a means of communication'

87 See ibid. at 15.

88 See D. Berry, 'Audience Analysis in the Legislative Drafting Process' (2000) *Loophole*, accessed at (www.opc.gov.au/calc/docs/calc-june/audience.htm).

89 See J. Barnes, 'The continuing debate about 'plain language' legislation: a law reform conundrum' 27 (2006) *Statute Law Review* pp. 83–132 at 97–9.

90 See R. Sullivan, 'Some implications of plain language drafting' 22 (2001) *Statute Law Review* pp. 145–80 at 149.

91 See R.D. Eagleson, *Writing in Plain English* (Commonwealth of Australia, 1990) at 4.

92 See J.C. Redish, 'The Plain English Movement' in S. Greenbaum, *The English Language Today* (New York: Pergamon Press, 1985) pp. 125–38 at 126.

93 See B. Bekink and C. Botha, 'Aspects of legislative drafting: some South African realities (or plain language is not always plain sailing) 28 (2007) *Statute Law Review* pp. 34–67 at 37.

design and layout, as well as language, and means analysing and deciding what information readers need to make informed decisions, before words, sentences or paragraphs are considered.[94] A plain language document uses words economically[95] and at a level that the audience of the particular text can understand. Sentence structure is tight. The tone is welcoming and direct. The design is visually appealing.[96] Although the terms plain language and plain English are often used interchangeably by commentators in this area, there is a difference between the two. Plain language is perhaps the broader term, and more suitable for jurisdictions that are bilingual. Plain language is broad as it reflects language as any method or means of communicating ideas and includes mathematical languages, flow charts and characters as well as words. English, on the other hand, is a particular type of language and is therefore a narrower term. Common problems identified by the plain language movement are long sentences; passive voice;[97] weak verbs; superfluous words; legal and financial jargon; abstract words; and unreadable design and layout.[98]

The plain language movement presents considerable advantages. First, the plain language movement can expose errors in drafting: in attempting to simplify the text, drafters identify errors of syntax or errors in the choice of words. Second, the plain language movement serves efficiency in that it ensures that legal texts are easier and faster to read.[99] Queries are therefore reduced. Third, plain language contributes to clarity and therefore serves effectiveness in drafting. Fourth, it serves democracy and the rule of law.[100]

However, a number of authors have expressed concerns. First, plain language may lower standards of good writing. This concern stems from the view that plain language consists of monosyllabic words, very short sentences and a complete rejection of complex words or sentence construction. If this were true of plain language then the criticism would be valid. It would certainly not be useful to draft statutes and legal documents in simplistic monosyllabic words. However, as other commentators have pointed out, this is to misunderstand plain language.[101] As the Law Reform Commission of Victoria note, plain language involves the use of plain, straightforward language, which avoids defects and conveys its meaning as clearly and as simply as possible, without unnecessary pretension or embellishment. It is

---

94 See B.A. Garner, *Legal Writing in Plain English* (Chicago: The University of Chicago Press, 2001) pp. 10–13.

95 See R. Wydick, *Plain English for Lawyers* (Durham, NC: Carolina Academic Press, 1998) pp. 9–24.

96 See ibid. pp. 121–34.

97 See Maine Manual in Legislative Drafting, ch. 1, section 7, accessible online at website, (www.janus.state.me.us/legis/ros/manual/Webdman-12.htm).

98 See Guidelines on Process and content of legislation 2001 (including the 2003 Supplement), May 2001, updated September 2003, Legislation Advisory Committee, Ministry of Justice, PO Box 180, Wellington, ISBN 0-477-07625-4.

99 See R. Wydick (1998) at 4.

100 See R. Sullivan, 'The Promise of Plain Language Drafting' 47 (2001) *McGill L.J.*, pp. 97–128 at 97.

101 See J. Kimble, 'Plain English: A Charter for Clear Writing' 9 (1992) *Thomas M. Cooley L.* pp. 19–22.

to be contrasted with convoluted, repetitive and prolix language. The adoption of a plain English style demands simply that a document be written in a style which readily conveys its message to its audience.[102] Second, plain language has given rise to a concern of intelligibility. Bennion believes that it may be positively dangerous to encourage non-lawyers to think they can understand legal texts unaided by expert advice:[103] it takes a lawyer to know whether simple words in what should be a technical text really carry their apparent simple meaning.[104] Third, the plain language movement has been criticised for its alleged sacrifice of certainty and an inevitable loss of precision and certainty.[105] Gowers feels that legislation must be unambiguous, precise, comprehensive and largely conventional: intelligibility is an advantage but it cannot justify the sacrifice of accuracy and clarity in the first reading.[106] However, the purposes of legislation are most likely to be achieved by the draftsman who is ardently concerned to be intelligible.[107] The irony is that in striving for precision at the expense of all other goals and especially at the expense of clarity, precision is lost. This irony has led Lord Campbell of Alloway to say that 'we should abandon that vain search for certainty in a statute, the cause of unintelligible and complex drafting which itself gives rise to uncertainty' [108] Fourth, plain language has given rise to concerns related to the loss of established meaning of words.[109] But plain language advocates delimit the circle of such words to very few and attribute most of the words used as examples for such a concern to meaningless jargon.[110]

Ultimately, the choice between plain language and other goals set for the drafter is a choice of simplicity against clarity, precision and unambiguity.[111] Simplicity is indeed a commendable goal for drafters as it promotes clarity which in turn leads to effectiveness and efficacy. Thus, simplicity and the plain language movement serves as a tool or a process[112] for clarity and in the hierarchy of goals to be set for the drafter the plain language movement can only be placed below clarity. Plain language is not necessarily clear language so,[113] when in conflict with plain

102 See Law Reform Commission of Victoria, *Plain English and the Law,* (Victoria, 1987) at 39.

103 See R. Sullivan (2001) at 180.

104 See F. Bennion, 'Don't Put the Law into Public Hands' *The Times*, 24 January 1995; see *contra* R. Sullivan (2001) at 120.

105 See M.L. Turnbull, 'Problems of Legislative Drafting' 7 (1986) *Statute Law Rev* pp. 67–77 at 70; Comment, 'Drafting Laws in Plain English, Can the Drafter Win' (1988) *NZLJ* pp. 25–8 at 26.

106 See Gowers, *The Complete Plain Words* (London: HMSO, 1986) at 7.

107 See G.C. Thornton, *Legislative Drafting* (London: Butterworths, 1987) at 49.

108 See Lord Campbell of Alloway, 'Law in Plain Language' (1983) *Law Society's Gazette* at 621.

109 On useful legal archaisms, see D. Greenberg (ed.) *Craies on Legislation* (London: Sweet and Maxwell, 2004) pp. 309–10.

110 See J. Kimble, 'A Plain English Primer' 33 (1987) *The Practical Lawyer* at 86.

111 See M.L. Turnbull (1986) at 67.

112 See J. Barnes (2006) at 122.

113 See B. Hunt, 'Plain language in legislative drafting: an achievable objective or a laudable ideal?' 24 (2003) *Statute Law Review* pp. 112–24 at 116.

language, clarity prevails. This does not by any means signify that plain language and simplicity are to be viewed as competing with clarity: simplicity assists clarity and in most circumstances works in parallel with it.[114] Since unambiguity is part of clarity, simplicity also works in parallel with it and is hierarchically inferior to it. However, one can envisage conflict between simplicity and precision. As precision was proven to be equal in standing with clarity and unambiguity, it is evident that precision prevails when in conflict with simplicity. The latter is a tool for precision[115] which subsides to it, if both cannot be achieved in parallel.[116]

Gender Neutral Language

Gender neutral language can be seen as a tool for accuracy, since it aims to promote gender specificity in the pronoun used when drafting legislation,[117] or even before the courts.[118] Gender neutral, or more appropriate gender specific,[119] language has gained momentum,[120] especially in the last few months after Jack Straw's statement that the government of the UK will endeavour to promote it when drafting legislation.[121]

Gender neutral language is therefore a formal goal set for the UK drafter. In the hierarchy of goals or virtues introduced here, the placement of gender neutral language is clear. It serves in parallel with plain language as an additional tool for the promotion of precision, clarity and unambiguity. Thus, it is not in conflict with these three concepts. However, if there is a choice to be made, clarity, precision and unambiguity prevail. After all, these three concepts serve effectiveness, which in turn, along with efficiency, promotes efficacy in the legislative process.

Conclusions

The Sir William Dale Centre for Legislative Studies was established by Sir William Dale as a forum for the promotion of quality of legislation primarily in the Commonwealth but also beyond. Sir William's enlightened conviction was that quality in legislation is affected directly by legislative techniques, which can be taught and learnt. These techniques break the barrier of common prejudices that

---

114 See D. St. L. Kelly, 'Legislative drafting and plain English' 10 (1985–86) *Adelaide Law Review* pp. 409–26 at 425.

115 See B. Bekink and C. Botha (2007) at 66.

116 See D. Greenberg (2004) at 307.

117 See Commentary, 'Avoidance of "sexist" language in legislation' 11 (1985) *Commonwealth L Bull* pp. 590–93 at 590.

118 See W.B. Hill Jr., 'A need for the use of nonsexist language in the courts' 49 (1992) *Wash. And Lee L. Rev.* pp. 275–8.

119 See S. Petersson, 'Gender-neutral drafting: recent Commonwealth developments' 20 (1999) *Statute Law Review* pp. 35–65 at 57.

120 See D. Schweikart, 'The gender neutral pronoun redefined' 20 (1998–99) *Women's Rts. L. Rep.* pp. 1–9, at 2.

121 HC Deb 8 March 2007 c. 146 WS, accessed online at (http://www.parliament.the-stationery-office.co.uk/pa/cm200607/cmhansrd/cm070308/wmstext/70308m0003.htm#07030896000015).

impose waterproof barriers between common and civil law systems, between developed countries and countries under development, between older and newer legal systems. It is precisely this universal approach to legislation that lies at the core of this publication, which is based on the belief that drafters and those dealing with legislation can and must learn from one another. But is it true that one can transplant best practices from one jurisdiction to another? Can we learn from each other, or is legislative drafting placed so solidly at the core of national legal and legislative systems, thus depriving it from the ability to benefit from the experience of others?

Legal transplants have been the subject of debate in comparative legal theory in the last few decades. Although Watson's liberal view seems to ignore the national intricacies of legal systems, which evidently affect the transferability of laws, institutions and legislative solutions, nevertheless drafters and legal systems actually do borrow from others. Under one requirement: functionality. Zweigert and Kötz's precondition of a functional link between lender and borrower is applicable in this case. In order to accept transferability of legislative techniques and doctrines it is imperative to identify a common factor, which can serve as a functionality glue allowing transferability between laws, institutions and legislative solutions. In the search for the functionality factor one must look at the goals set for the drafter in jurisdictions around the world. A higher virtue served by drafters can justify common ground fertile for transfers.

Efficacy is at the heart of legislative efforts. It orders all actors in the policy process to achieve the desired result. Thus, by definition efficacy refers to the common effort of those involved in the policy process, of which legislative drafting is only a small part. In view of the broad sense of efficacy, it cannot serve as the functionality glue for transferability in legislative drafting. In contrast to efficacy, effectiveness is focused on legislative drafting and can be assigned to the drafting team. As a result, effectiveness in legislative drafting can be identified as the virtue pursued by drafting teams in common and civil law jurisdictions, in developed and developing countries, in older and newer legal systems, in financially robust and financially vulnerable States. Effectiveness therefore is the connective factor that we set out to single out in this book. It applies to drafting around the world and it unifies legislative drafters under the umbrella of a common pursuit and a common search for quality in legislation.

But, if effectiveness is the platform of transferability of laws, institutions and legislative solutions, is efficiency irrelevant to legislative drafters? Efficiency, defined as the correlation between cost and effect, is an additional value served by the drafters of legislation. However, it is part of effectiveness, or it is a tool that contributes to effectiveness of legislation. Similarly, clarity, precision and unambiguity serve effectiveness as its tools. Efficiency, clarity, precision and unambiguity are inferior virtues to effectiveness and they must be applied with effectiveness as the defining criterion. Thus, is there is a conflict between clarity and effectiveness, clearly effectiveness will prevail and clarify must bow down. This hierarchical relation does not apply in the case of conflict between efficiency, clarity, precision and unambiguity, as these four values are of equal standing. If the drafter needs to make a choice between any of these four values, then the decision must be made with effectiveness as the deciding quality. In other words, in the case of such a conflict, the drafter must serve effectiveness using any of the four values that best serves the purpose in the particular circumstances.

Tools of clarity, precision and unambiguity are simplicity, as expressed by the plain language movement and gender neutral language. These are goals that the drafter must serve but only as instruments utilised to achieve clarity, precision and unambiguity. Thus, simplicity and gender neutral language are not at equal standing with clarity, precision and unambiguity; they bow down when in conflict with any of these values or virtues. If there is a conflict between gender neutral language and plain language, again the deciding factor is clarity, precision, unambiguity and ultimately effectiveness in legislation.

It is, therefore, evident that the highest virtue or value pursed by the drafter around the world is effectiveness. This prevails when in conflict with any other aim and also constitutes the deciding qualifier which settles any conflict between the other, inferior in hierarchy, values examined in this book. The identification of effectiveness as the common value of drafters leads to the acknowledgement of a common concept in the definition of quality in legislation, not only in the EU,[122] but in the Commonwealth and beyond. This common concept of quality in legislation, with effectiveness as its flagship, is promoted by drafters around the world. This is the functionality glue that allows drafters to learn from each other and to teach each other. It does not signify arrogance in the conviction that one's own solutions

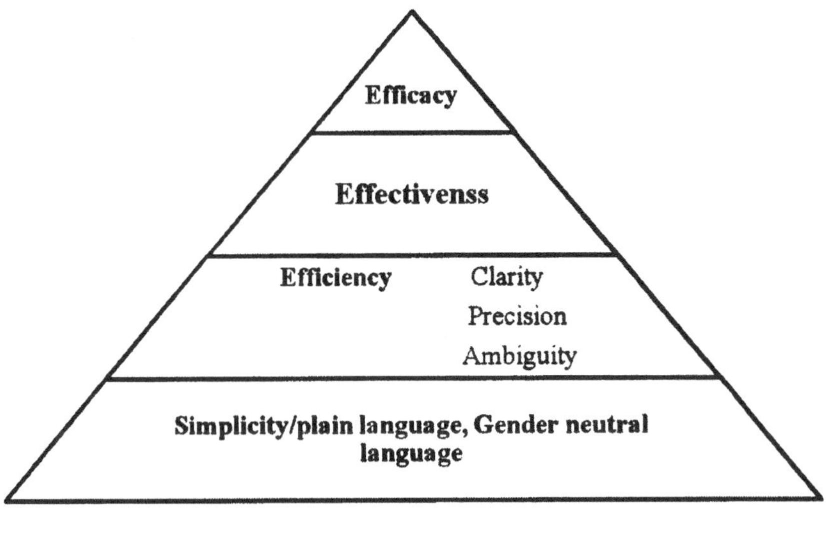

Figure 1.1 Diagram of the hierarchy of virtues served by the drafter

122 See H. Xanthaki, 'The Problem of Quality in EU legislation: what on earth is really wrong?' 38 (2001) *Common Market Law Review* pp. 651–76.

are superior; it simply reflects the increasing openness and transparency of national practices evident in recent years and also the growing willingness of drafters to exchange ideas and assist their colleagues around the world. Ultimately, it supports the view that legislative drafting can be taught and can be learnt. It provides proof of the *raison d'être* of the Sir William Dale Centre for Legislative Studies. And it offers the theoretical framework for this selection of essays in memoriam to Sir William. Without further ado, therefore, let us explore the valuable lessons offered by the distinguished experts who have kindly graced this book with sincere in-depth evaluation of their own professional experiences and best practices in legislative drafting.

Chapter 2

Drawing the Line[1]

Stephen Laws CB[2]

Introduction

It has often been claimed that it takes at least seven to eight years to 'train' a qualified and experienced lawyer to be a Parliamentary Counsel.[3] I am frequently asked how this can be – not least by those who are offering themselves as candidates to undergo the process. Surely, they say, the techniques and disciplines can be acquired more quickly than that. Do not qualified lawyers have many of the required skills already?

My answer is that it really takes much longer than seven or eight years to acquire the wisdom and to perfect the skills that are required, particularly the skill of 'drawing the line', which is unique to drafters and which I shall attempt to describe in detail in this chapter. Parliamentary Counsel are constantly developing and refining their skill, and acquiring new wisdom. There is no stage at which a Parliamentary Counsel finishes his or her training and becomes 'the finished article'. In this respect Parliamentary Counsel differ from their product, Acts of Parliament, which I describe below as having to be 'aimed' rather than 'steered'.[4] It is one of the joys of the job that it involves a constant process of discovering new ways of working, of continuously adapting and adjusting acquired techniques – and of improving on them. Each Bill is a new creative challenge, presents new problems and teaches new lessons.

So the practical differences between the different levels of seniority in the Office of the Parliamentary Counsel relate less to whether or not a particular stage of training has been completed and more to the level of supervision to which the

---

1 I am grateful to Sir George Engle KCB QC for suggesting this title (which he proposed as the ideal title for the autobiography of a Parliamentary Counsel). I am also grateful to Francis Coleman and Alexander Wharam for their contribution to the production of this chapter – any infelicities that remain are, of course, my own.

3 See, for example, the Memorandum by Sir Geoffrey Bowman KCB to the Select Committee on the Constitution (3 June 2004). The Memorandum is printed in the second volume of the *14th Report of the Select Committee on the Constitution: Parliament and the Legislative Process* (Session 2003–04, HL 173 – II).

4 See pp. 20-21. This is a distinction that is important in other contexts too. I first realised its importance in the course of learning to drive a car.

drafters are subject, and to the level of responsibility which they must accept both for the finished product and for the service provided to the instructing departments. To a large extent these things are dependent on the judgements for which the drafter is personally accountable. A relatively short initial period – but still at least two or three years – is required for familiarising able recruits with the basic techniques and knowledge needed to produce a piece of legislation that is competent from a purely technical point of view; but the honing of these techniques and the acquisition of the wisdom needed to do the job will take much longer.

So what we mean when we say that it takes seven or eight years to train a Parliamentary Counsel is that it is only after at least that amount of time that even a very able recruit to the Office is likely to have a sufficient grounding in the principles of legislation to take the lead in the production of a Government Bill. It is only after that amount of time that even the most able recruit is likely to be equipped with a sufficient range of experience of legislation, and of legislating, to be able to give authoritative advice with confidence on the major issues that are likely to be put to the drafter in the course of a legislative project. Even just producing the text of a piece of primary legislation in response to instructions – and the job is much more than that – requires drafters to have discovered, for example, how best in themselves to balance creativity with a rigid discipline in technical matters. That is a process that cannot be hurried.

The Work of Parliamentary Counsel

The case for a long period of preparation before a member of the Office is allowed to take responsibility for a Bill relates partly to the aspects of the job that involve the provision of an advisory service to the Office's departmental clients, and so goes beyond drafting. As well as producing legislative text, the Parliamentary Counsel have the function of being guides to the instructing departments through the process of legislating. They are not just wordsmiths; they are also counsel, who advise the instructing department on a whole range of matters, including some that may be intimately entwined with the process of policy formulation.

This advisory role involves giving advice on both the Parliamentary process and the related processes within the Government. Departments often need to rely on their Parliamentary Counsel – as someone who is involved with the legislative process continuously from year to year over a substantial period – for advice and assistance in the planning and management of their legislative projects. Only someone who has built up a significant body of relevant experience can meet that need.

However, the long period of preparation is also attributable to the necessity of acquiring the experience and wisdom on which a Parliamentary Counsel can draw when making the many subtle judgements that have to be made in the course of producing the legislative text itself. So, even the 'wordsmith' aspects of the role require a lengthy apprenticeship. The judgements that have to be made about the text are important and must be justifiable and sound. There is no room for any risks to be taken with whether a drafter is equipped to take responsibility for a piece of legislative text. And there are at least two reasons why the soundness of the drafter's judgement is vital.

Bills often take several months to draft; and typically they also take several months to pass through Parliament. When they are eventually launched as Acts of Parliament they need to be effective and clear. Once launched they cannot be 'steered' to the right target: they have to have been well aimed before having been launched. There is hot competition within Government for places in the legislative programme because there is only a finite amount of Parliamentary time available each Session for legislation. If an Act misses its target, it may take at least a couple of years to put things right. In the meantime, the government's policy will not be delivered[5] and the law may be producing the wrong result in case after case. Furthermore, if a Bill is obscure and requires litigation to clarify its effect, the result will be the imposition of a very considerable extra and wasteful burden of expenditure on those involved in the litigation and, conceivably, more generally on one or more sectors of the national economy.

Bills also need to be well constructed because their passage through Parliament forms a significant part of the national political process – as well as being a condition for their becoming law. The government's legislative programme sets the agenda for much of the national political debate, both in Parliament and in the country. Every year it represents a very significant part of the work carried out by the main democratic institution of the nation. So Bills have to be drafted 'to pass, no less than razors ... [are] made to sell'.[6] The judgements Parliamentary Counsel make when drafting a Bill are capable of having a significant impact on the smoothness of a Bill's passage through Parliament, and thus on events in the world of politics generally.

These two reasons alone require that the judgements that are made in producing a Bill are made only by those who have had the opportunity to acquire a comprehensive understanding of what is involved in legislating. It is worth acknowledging that, while a Parliamentary Counsel in drafting a Bill will receive plenty of comments on it and advice from departmental clients and from others and, very importantly, will also be able to draw on the wisdom and experience of colleagues in the Office of the Parliamentary Counsel, the judgements about how competing interests or objectives are resolved in the case of a particular Bill need, in the last resort, to be personal, professional judgements made by the one person, the drafter, who as the creator of the text has the most intimate and comprehensive understanding of it.

What follows is a discussion of the nature of the more important of the different judgements that are required to be made in order to get a legislative text right, both

---

5 In the words of the Note on the Preparation of Bills issued by the Treasury for official use in March 1948, 'All who are parentally concerned with Parliamentary Bills should recall Tristram Shandy's warning to "mind what they are about". The admonition is neither impertinent nor superfluous, for however clear may be their perception of what they wish to accomplish they will need to bear constantly in mind that *what they are about* is the fashioning of something whereby the King-in-Parliament will bring into being a new law.'

6 See Sir Henry Thring KCB, *Simplification of the Law: Practical Suggestions* (London: Bush, 1875) at 13.

for Parliament and for the courts, but also for all the other interests involved. In doing this, I touch briefly on elements of the advisory aspects of the role of Parliamentary Counsel; but most of what follows is confined to the more obvious part of the task: producing Bill text that will be acceptable to Parliament and can then also serve as the text of an Act that implements the intended policy effectively.

Drawing the Line

An important component of the answer to why the development of a trained lawyer into a Parliamentary Counsel is a lengthy process relates to the unique context in which judgements have to be made when drafting primary legislation. The work of a lawyer practising in a field other than practical legislation[7] is entirely different from what a drafter of primary legislation does when producing a legislative text. A lawyer in a conventional legal practice is employed by the client to 'find' a line. The line the lawyer has to find is the line the law has drawn. The client may want to be sure not to cross it – or perhaps to be advised on how to get as close to it as is safe – or the client may need help with understanding and managing the consequences of having crossed the line. But all the work, including any drafting, that is done by lawyers outside government is constrained by the lines already drawn by the law. It is for this reason that such lawyers, when they draft, tend to rely so heavily on precedents. The precedents have already been found to have a particular effect within the existing law and the lawyer who is not a Parliamentary drafter is required to select the desired effects only from those for which the law already provides.[8]

By contrast, a Parliamentary Counsel is not concerned with finding a line; it is the function of a Parliamentary Counsel to 'draw' the line, and effectively to draw

---

7 *Practical Legislation* is the title of the book on Parliamentary drafting written by Lord Thring, last published in 1902, see Lord Thring, *Practical Legislation: The Composition and Language of Acts of Parliament and Business Documents* (London: John Murray, 1902). As Sir Henry Thring, he was the first person to hold the Office of the Parliamentary Counsel, from which the present Office of the Parliamentary Counsel originates (on which see Sir George Engle KCB, QC, 'The Rise of the Parliamentary Counsel' (1996) 16 *Parliaments, Estates and Representation* 193).

8 I remember that, as a very new member of the Parliamentary Counsel Office, I was asked to set up a fund to be used by its administrator for supporting a particular activity to the benefit of a particular industry. My first instinct was the natural one for a trained lawyer. I looked in the existing law for the mechanism that could most easily be made to fit what I was asked to do (a trust for the statutory purposes, I thought). I then tried to apply that concept to my case with the appropriate modifications. It soon appeared that I was leading myself into a maze of complexity by attracting the whole of trust law, much of which I then had to disapply or modify. The answer, it became clear, was to start from scratch and to set up the fund and the mechanism for administering it as a purely statutory creature. The concept of a trust was unnecessary and unhelpful. The purely statutory scheme was much clearer; but, at least for the inexperienced drafter, it initially exposed me to the need to make more decisions about what I needed to say and what I could leave unsaid.

it on a blank piece of paper.[9] Parliamentary Counsel have to work with a potentially infinite number of permutations of hypothetical facts to create new laws; and they can change and manipulate the laws to fit their hypotheses. Other lawyers tend to work with a limited number of known, or at least assumed, facts within existing parameters which have to be accepted as having been fixed by the law. Although the drafters of primary legislation have to know and understand how other lawyers will approach the construction of legislation – because that will determine how their drafts are construed –they themselves have to put aside their knowledge of the constraints of existing legal structures in order, when drafting, to accommodate a shifting kaleidoscope of possibilities.

It is the scope for creativity and flexibility that makes drafting an art not a science: a conclusion also reached by my predecessor, Sir Geoffrey Bowman.[10] It is the challenge posed by the freedom the drafter has that makes drawing the line such a complex matter. There is a relative absence of clear rules about how and where the line should be drawn, and there is no fixed starting place for the line. The facts and the law are both fluid to start with, and the drafter must choose where to begin.

The doctrine of Parliamentary sovereignty gives the drafter a very free hand but, although the line that has to be drawn has to be drawn free-hand, there are, as I shall show, various principles that affect how that freedom is exercised. The problem for the drafter is that the principles are imprecise and often conflicting, so that their application requires the making of sophisticated judgements by experienced practitioners.

The Parliamentary Counsel does have the existing law and departmental instructions to guide their drafting. In the UK the convention is for the instructions to take the form of a narrative description of the desired outcomes. But beyond that the drafter is alone. So, with the assistance of the instructions the job is:

- to analyse what is needed to give effect to the instructions;
- to devise a structure for the new provisions which is consistent with the policy objectives of the instructing team and which facilitates Parliamentary debate of what is proposed;
- to produce provisions that make the legal objectives clear to users of the statute book, as well as to Parliament, and which are effective when tested in the courts.

This process involves balancing a number of competing interests and objectives; and it is finding the right balance for the Bill in question that requires such a high quality of judgement from the drafter.

---

9 In this respect, I do not accept that Parliamentary Counsel is required to conform to Winston Churchill's rule that 'The English never draw a line without blurring it.' Hansard HC vol. 458 col. 221 (16 November 1948).

10 See Sir Geoffrey Bowman KCB, 'The Art of Legislative Drafting' (2006) 7 *European Journal of Law Reform* 3.

Different Audiences

It is well recognised[11] that one of the main balancing exercises a drafter of legislation has to carry out is the balancing of the interests of the different audiences for the legislation.

There may be many audiences that the drafter has to consider. The drafter's clients, the potential users of the legislation, members of Parliament and peers and the courts are all important; but those categories may also divide into smaller groups (e.g. into lay users and professional, legally qualified users or, in the case of the lay users of housing legislation, into existing and prospective landlords, agents and tenants).

Some of the different interests of different audiences and of different groups within those audiences are discussed below. However, it will also become clear from that discussion that the idea of different audiences is often only a metaphor for different, competing objectives for the legislative drafter.

The drafter has two main objectives. The Bill must be drafted to pass and it must work as intended when it becomes an Act. If a Bill is to pass, it has to be in a form that is acceptable to a majority of the members in each House of Parliament, and if an Act is to be effective it has to be given the meaning intended for it by the Government when it is construed by the highest court of appeal (the Judicial Committee of the House of Lords or, in due course, the Supreme Court). That, though, is only the minimum requirement. There are subsidiary objectives that also need to be considered.

In 1975, the Renton Report recommended[12] that 'in principle the interests of the ultimate users should always have priority over those of the legislators: a Bill, which serves a merely temporary purpose, should always be regarded primarily as a future Act'. This principle is now the one that governs how legislation is drafted. But the contrast is rarely as clear-cut as the principle suggests and the drafter cannot disregard his or her first objective. The Bill that the clients want, or at least a Bill that they are content with, must pass.

Furthermore, when it comes to the Act, the tasks of identifying the 'ultimate' users and of identifying their interests can often be extremely complex.[13] In the final analysis no Act of Parliament is ever ambiguous. It will, eventually, have its meaning authoritatively fixed by the court of ultimate appeal. So, for the purposes of effectiveness, the court of ultimate appeal is the drafter's most important audience – the ultimate user. However, it is not necessarily a definition of success for an Act

---

11 See e.g. *The Preparation of Legislation: Report of a Committee appointed by the Lord President of the Council* (1975) Cmnd 6053 (referred to in the rest of this chapter as 'the Renton Report'): paras. 7.6–7.16 and Bowman 7 *European Journal of Law Reform* 3. (2006).

12 The Renton Report, para. 10.3; and paras. 11.13 and 13.17.

13 The Renton Report recognised this when it said '... in most spheres the ultimate users of the Act will include not only the professionals, but also the ordinary citizen who is bound by, and presumed to know about, the provisions of the Act of Parliament; and ... the conflict is not only between the needs of the legislators and those of consumers: it is also between differing needs of consumers on different occasions.' (ibid. para. 10.1).

eventually to be given the intended construction on appeal to the House of Lords. Every drafter is ultimately seeking to produce a provision that is clear enough for even opposing parties to understand it in the intended sense without unnecessary litigation,[14] and its attendant costs for litigants and the economy generally.

The main objectives concentrate on relatively narrow audiences and that is why there are subsidiary objectives. If an Act is going to work well, to be understood and accepted in the form of widespread compliance and to be implemented and operated efficiently and economically, it is necessary (subject to the two main objectives) to ensure that the different needs of the other different audiences are also all met so far as possible. Where conflicts arise in meeting either the main objectives or the subsidiary ones, the drafter needs to exercise judgement about how best to reconcile them and what follows describes some of the issues that arise.

Abstract Understanding *v* Practical Understanding

One element of meeting the needs of different audiences is the judgement the drafter often has to make between the reader of the Bill who wants to obtain an understanding, in the abstract, of the body of law with which it deals and the reader who is seeking to discover how the law applies to a particular case.

Parliamentarians usually fall within the first category and legal professionals will normally fall, at least in the long run, within the second. But much will depend on the circumstances. The lay person often falls between the two, wanting to understand how the law works in the normal case (expecting to have such a case) and to be able to identify areas of uncertainty, but also understanding that the services of a lawyer will bw required, where the case is on the borderline.

There are some provisions that will only ever be capable of being understood when applied to a particular case. One example is the definition of 'a connected person', in section 839 of the Income and Corporation Taxes Act 1988. The concept captured by that definition seems to me to be one that is incapable of being fully understood by someone who wants to read the section and to understand the concept in its entirety. No ordinary person can hold the concept in the mind with all its permutations. It can only make sense in any real way to a person who is confronted with a particular case and wants to answer the question whether two or more people involved in that case are 'connected'.

This means that when it comes to drafting a definition like the definition of 'connected person', the drafter can only frame the provision by methodically working through each of the permutations and connections that the instructions say need to be caught, together with those that are to be excluded, then testing them against the words the drafter uses. Then the drafter has to chip away at the draft, like a sculpture, to achieve the desired result.

---

14 Nor, of course, is it a definition of failure for the construction of a provision to be litigated up to the ultimate court of appeal. There are many reasons why the construction of a provision may reach that appeal court, including that Parliament intended the application of the provision in particular cases to be worked out by the courts according to relatively general statutory principles.

On the other hand, there are propositions that present the drafter with a choice between the person who wants to read them for an overview and the practitioner. Explaining the idea and facilitating its practical application require different drafts.

A good example is, perhaps, a case where the drafter has the option of using a mathematical formula. The concept that finds its most common practical example in a repayment mortgage is familiar to most educated laymen, although it is not particularly easy to describe: an arrangement that produces the total repayment of an interest-bearing debt over a specified fixed period by regular payments of the same sum, with each payment being made up of interest on the capital outstanding and of a contribution towards the reduction of the capital. The details of the arrangement will specify the period for repayment, the rate of interest, the times when interest is calculated and added to the fund and the frequency with which the regular payments are to be made. The amount of each of the regular payments can then be worked out.[15]

The mechanism for calculating the amount of the regular payment required to repay a debt in that way over a particular period can be expressed either by a description like the one in the last paragraph or by a mathematical formula. The description, though not easy to keep simple, may still be much better at explaining the principle of a sinking fund to those who want to know what the policy is; but it does not facilitate the calculation of the amount of the regular payment in a particular case. The mathematical formula for calculating that amount provides the best way of calculating it in a particular case; but, except to someone with a relatively sophisticated understanding of mathematics, it does not help ordinary readers to understand that the mechanism for calculating it is the one with which they are already likely to be familiar.

Describing the Route *v* Describing the Destination

A similar judgement arises for the drafter where there is a choice between describing the change that a Bill makes and describing the law as it will stand after the change has occurred. The sole purpose of every Act of Parliament is to change the law;[16] but it is common, these days, for the change to be enacted by means of the repeal of the existing law and the enactment of provisions to give effect to the new policy.

The Renton Report endorsed in 1975 what was then the growing practice of using textual amendment, rather than non-textual amendment, for modifying the effect of an existing provision; and it did this in the interests of the eventual user.[17] This practice is now the practice of all UK Parliamentary Counsel in the overwhelming number of cases. The rule is departed from only for good reason.

---

15 For these purposes I have disregarded the further complications that can arise where the interest rate, and therefore the amount of the repayments, may change during the repayment period.

16 There is an exception of course for Acts that are expressly intended to consolidate the law, but the Bills for such Acts are subject to special Parliamentary procedures.

17 See The Renton Report, para. 13.17.

However, the application of the rule needs sophisticated judgement. The rule does not require every addition to the existing law to take the form of an amendment of some existing Act. Difficult questions can arise about whether a new proposition should be inserted as a new provision in an existing Act or enacted as a 'free-standing' provision in the Bill under construction.[18] How is the integrity of the statute book best served? Will an insertion in the existing Act attract incidental provisions that would otherwise have to be spelt out or would it require such provisions to be disapplied?

Where what a textual amendment does is to modify existing propositions, a textual amendment enables the reader to construct the law as it will be after the law has changed; but it is less revealing about what the change is because it requires the reader to compare the law as it was with the new law. Also it may need to be supplemented by separate transitional provisions that deal with cases that are pending when the change is made. It is usual for drafters to seek to overcome the tension here by various devices (e.g. the form of some parenthetical description of the amended provision) that will give the reader a basic understanding of the change without having to take himself off to a law library; but the balance between the usefulness of these devices and their potentially confusing or obscuring effect is a subtle one.

The form of a textual amendment may also be affected by a judgement about whether it is more important to put an emphasis on the change or on the new law. Does the drafter substitute only the minimum number of words necessary to effect the required change? Or does the drafter leave out enough other words to insert a provision the effect of which is clear when read in the context of the amendment? The latter approach, while making the new law clear, may tend to disguise how much of the law has been left unchanged.

The drafter's approach to the choice between describing the destination and explaining the route may also depend on the target audience. When I was in charge of drafting Finance Bills, I used to receive comments on their drafting from tax professionals. It was usually possible to guess which of these had been prepared by trainees and adopted by the firm's tax partner and which had been prepared by the partner himself. The former would often complain about any provision that operated on an existing legislative scheme by a series of textual amendments and would suggest that the revised law should have been set out in its entirety. The latter would criticise any provision that re-enacted an existing code with modifications (particularly if established section numbering changed as a result), on the grounds that it would have been clearer if the draft had confined itself to the minimum changes to the existing scheme. So the drafter needs to balance the interests of those who are

---

18 It is the practice in some jurisdictions (e.g. in Australia and the US) to have major Acts on particular topics that are frequently reprinted with authority. In those jurisdictions it is common to fit whole new parts into the Act on a particular topic, even if the subject-matter of the new provisions does not appear. In the UK this may be appropriate and can happen in certain codes (e.g. tax and social security), where there has been a consolidation of all the relevant existing law, but in other cases it may be thoroughly misleading e.g. if the Act that would be amended was itself originally enacted with the emphasis on changing the law rather than stating it.

coming fresh to the area of law on which the text operates against the interests of those who are already steeped in its intricacies.

The subject matter of a Bill may be relevant to this judgement and may also affect other cases where a drafter has a choice whether to frame the provision with a view primarily to illustrating the change or to setting out the law that will emerge. The Communications Act 2003 changed the licensing regime for the provision of television and radio services. Often, where an Act changes a licensing regime, it is appropriate to set out the licensing regime for new applications and then to deal with existing licensees as transitional cases in a Schedule. In the case of the licences for Channel 3 services however, there were only ever going to be relatively few licences and the next licensing round was not scheduled to take place until 2014. It was appropriate to draft the provisions with particular emphasis on how the proposed changes affected the existing licensees.[19] That change was of more immediate relevance and interest to everyone than the licence regime that would be operated 11 years after the Act had passed. Of course many cases present a choice that is more evenly balanced than this.

Innovation and Progress *v* Consistency

Another dilemma often confronts the drafter, particularly when drafting textual amendments. Should the drafting be made to fit the linguistic register of the amended Act or should it adopt whatever is the best and most modern way of expressing the ideas?

Drafters are constantly seeking to keep the language they use up to date and to take appropriate account of the latest developments in plain language techniques. It is important that developments and innovations that improve the quality of legislative language are allowed to take place: the fewer inhibitions that are imposed on the process the better. However, adopting a different way of expressing ideas carries an inherent risk of prejudicing the construction of provisions which expressed the same ideas in different terms in the past — the closer the provisions to each other, the greater the risk of prejudice. The assessment of the risk in a particular case is likely to be complex.

Similar issues also arise in relation to the substance of provisions. It is not uncommon for a set of provisions to be devised for a relatively straightforward case. Similar provisions are subsequently required for a more complex case and are refined to fit it.[20] This process may continue through several different sets of provisions. In due course, the complexity of one of the cases creates an argument for setting out a proposition that it was thought unnecessary to mention in the initial case. The judgement for the drafter is to balance the risk of prejudicing the initial

19 See s 215 of the Communications Act 2003.

20 A process of this sort can be followed through the various privatisation Acts of the 1980s and early 1990s for the establishment of the successor company or companies of the statutory corporation and the transfer to the company or companies of the corporation's property, rights and liabilities. (Compare the Civil Aviation Act 1980 with, for example Part 1 of the Coal Industry Act 1990).

case by having something express in the later case against the argument for having that express provision in the more complex context of that later case.

Incidentally, these issues also arise for the leader of a drafting office, at the general level of deciding the extent to which the office should seek to impose requirements of consistency on its members.

Flexibility *v* Certainty

The question of how much detail should be inserted in a legislative provision and how much should be left to a discretion to be operated in practice is primarily a question of policy for those who instruct the drafter. But it is not a question in which the drafter can or should be uninvolved.

The expertise of the drafter is often called on to set the parameters for any discretion. In doing that the drafter has to decide to what extent those parameters need to be tightly drawn in order to secure that the discretion will be exercised in the manner intended. The drafter's skill is required to assess whether the nature of the questions that are left to be answered by an administrative authority, or by the courts, makes them questions which are capable of being decided using the chosen decision maker or methodology.[21]

The drafter also needs to consider whether the structure of the legislative scheme that has been asked for is still clear enough, once the required element of flexibility has been introduced. And the drafter will also often be asked to draw on their experience of legislation to assess whether the minister in Parliament is likely to be put under pressure to make express provision to deal with the cases that the policymakers are willing to see dealt with under the discretion, or to particularise how the discretion will be exercised in particular cases.

The process of Parliamentary debate on proposed statutory discretions can sometimes create a paradox under which the discretion becomes politically acceptable only if the outcome of its exercise in particular cases can be guaranteed first. This reasoning also often leads to a request for the production before a power is accepted of a draft of the first set of regulations that will be made under the power.[22]

---

21 *In re S (Minors) (Care Order: Implementation of Care Plan); In re W (Minors) (Care Order: Adequacy of Care Plan)* [2002] UKHL 10, [2002] 2 AC 291. There may be difficulties for example in asking a court to assess a balance between the rights of an individual and the resources available for protecting them (see *R. v North and East Devon Health Authority, ex parte Coughlan* [2001] 1 QB 213).

22 During the lengthy passage of the Bill for what became the Financial Services and Markets Act 2000, numerous drafts of orders and regulations to be made under the powers to be conferred by the Bill when enacted, and containing key features of the new system of financial regulation, were published. Paradoxically, it is possible for a decision to leave matters to subordinate legislation to result in even more detail having to be settled while the Bill is passing through in the form of draft regulations than if the Bill had sought to spell out only the main features of the required detail.

It is the function of the drafter to ensure that the structure of a Bill is not rendered incoherent by the legislation dealing with some decisions in a very general way, while related decisions are supervised by the legislation in great detail.[23]

Simplicity *v* Certainty and Comprehensiveness

Another conflict which the drafter often needs to resolve is that between clarity through simplicity, on the one hand, and clarity through certainty and comprehensiveness on the other hand. Modern courts assert a principle of purposive construction[24] and it has in any event, always been the case that courts construe provisions 'in their context' (whether they are purporting to do so by purposive canons or literalist canons). To what extent is the drafter of legislation entitled to rely on these principles or wise to do so?

For the drafter the initial response would probably be to say that words are the drafter's only tool; and so the only way to make sure the meaning is clear is by setting it out with complete literalist accuracy. If the drafter gets it right, the courts will not need to resort to purposive construction to find out what is meant. However, it does not take long trying to draft a provision to realise that this approach has its limitations.

First, of course, it is important to ensure, given the courts' preference for purposive construction, that the literalist approach does not tend to camouflage the purpose which will be employed to construe the provision if an ambiguity is found. The drafter must take account of that possibility and must ensure the purpose too can be found in the context.

Second, excessive literalism tends to undermine the simplicity of a draft; and simplicity can be as great a contributor to understanding as absolute literal certainty.

---

23 So it might be inappropriate to insert a great deal of detail defining exactly the circumstances when a person is a fit and proper person to be granted a licence if the decision whether or not to grant a licence is intended to be subject to a broad discretion permitting a great many factors to be taken into account, including whether the applicant is a fit and proper person.

24 See Lord Wilberforce in *Fothergill v Monarch Airlines* [1981] AC 251, HL – 'Consideration of the purpose of an enactment is always a legitimate part of the process of interpretation ...'; see also Lord Bingham of Cornhill in *R (Quintivalle) v Secretary of State for Health* [2003] UKHL 13 at [8], [2003] 2 A.C. 687 – 'The basic task of the court is to ascertain and give effect to the true meaning of what Parliament has said in the enactment to be construed. But that is not to say that attention should be confined and a literal interpretation given to the particular provisions which give rise to difficulty ... The court's task, within the permissible bounds of interpretation, is to give effect to Parliament's purpose. So the controversial provisions should be read in the context of the statute as a whole, and the statute as a whole should be read in the historical context of the situation which led to its enactment.'; see also Lord Steyn at [21]. For a general discussion of literal and purposive interpretation, see D. Greenberg (ed.) *Craies on Legislation*, 8th edn (London: Sweet and Maxwell, 2004), ch. 18. For an interesting discussion of the way in which a 'system of purposive interpretation' may 'facilitate [a] statute's adaptation to changes in the conditions of existence' see A. Barak *The Judge in a Democracy* (Princeton NJ and Oxford, 2006) pp. 3–8.

So, for example, it used to be the practice to ensure that every sentence in a statute was self-contained and its connection to every other sentence clearly pinned down. If subsection (1) provided for the service of a notice, subsection (2) would refer to 'a notice served under subsection (1)'. A modern draft is much more likely to refer just to 'the notice' assuming that the context itself identifies the notice, as in that case it clearly does. However, there are many cases in which the decision whether to rely on the context to make things clear is far from easy.

It is not uncommon, in the early years of a drafter's career, to be subject to two apparently conflicting criticisms. On the one hand, the drafter will be told that it is not necessary to complicate the draft with cumbersome precision. On the other hand, the drafter will be told that, just because the courts could not mistake Parliament's intention there is no reason not to spell it out, even if to do so will only spare the reader a few moments confusion.[25]

It is drafter's lore that 'excess matter in Bills, as in people, tends to go septic' [26] So that and the clarifying effect of keeping provisions simple lead the drafter towards provisions that are sparse. Bills do not use repetition or elegant variation in saying the same thing: for fear that the unnecessary provision, or the unnecessary variation, will lead the court to infer that a different meaning was intended for each. Similarly, Bills do not often spell out the legal consequences of a proposition if they would follow in any event. Transitional provisions, for example, have to be drafted starting from an analysis of what the law would be if no provision were made.

However, this theory produces a principle that lacks certainty in its application. The need for a transitional provision may depend on whether the courts will construe a provision as applying to proceedings (and, therefore, applicable to past cases that are subject to pending proceedings)[27] or to the substance (and, therefore, inapplicable to past cases by reason of the presumption against retrospection).[28] The drafter must choose and must make a choice that ensures not only that the provision being drafted will not be misconstrued but also that similar provisions already on the statute book are not misconstrued because of the assumptions made by the solution in question. Very often there is no clear-cut answer. A very subtle balancing of different risks has to be achieved.

---

25 For an example of how easy it is to get this wrong see *R (on the application of the Crown Prosecution Service) v Bow Street Magistrates' Court (James and others, interested parties)* [2006] EWHC 1763 (Admin), [2007] 1 WLR 291, a case in which the court found no difficulty at all in identifying Parliament's purpose, but still found, despite persuasive arguments (including an apparently applicable provision of the Interpretation Act 1978) for construing the provision in accordance with that purpose, that the drafter had erred and Parliament's intention could be implemented by applying the rule which permits the courts to correct what they regard as an obvious 'slip' on the part of the drafter: *Inco Europe Ltd. v First Choice Distribution (a firm)* [2000] 1 W.L.R. 586.

26 Quoted by Sir Geoffrey Bowman KCB, 'Why is there a Parliamentary Counsel Office?' (2005) 26 *Statute Law Review* at 69, 77.

27 See *Yew Bon Tew alias Yong Boon Tiew v Kenderaan Bas Mas* [1983] 1 A.C. 553; also *R. v Makanjuola* [1995] 1 W.L.R. 1348.

28 See *Lauri v Renad* [1892] 3 Ch. 402; *Sunshine Porcelain Potteries Pty. Ltd. v Nash* [1961] A.C. 927.

Both simplicity and comprehensive literalism are ways of achieving a degree of certainty and therefore effectiveness. It is possible that they each have different appeals for different legislative audiences; but a context of purposive construction and the impatience of both Parliamentarians and judges with texts that are either impenetrable or cryptic means that the drafter's line has to be drawn carefully to find the relatively narrow path between the two.

Additionally, it should be noted that the tensions described here also have their parallels in policy formulation in areas which shade into those within the domain of the drafter. The drafter is often asked to contribute professional advice on these matters. Tax legislation, for example, is often subject to pressure to make it more complex, either to stop up avoidance mechanisms or to achieve fairness between different categories of taxpayer (which may be the same thing if the categories are the rich well advised taxpayer and the ordinary taxpayer 'on the Clapham omnibus'). The drafter has a role in helping the department to judge when succumbing to these pressures will produce a provision that is so complex that it runs a risk of not achieving its main purpose.

Today *v* Tomorrow

The choice between drafting for today and drafting for tomorrow underlies a number of the matters I have already discussed (such as the choice between setting out the destination or the route).[29] However, there is one aspect of this to which I want to draw particular attention.

It is the function of Parliamentary Counsel to be the advocates within the Governmental system for maintaining and securing the integrity of the statute book, something that is the policy of all Governments. The constitutional settlement between Parliament and the Executive (on the one hand) and the courts (on the other), under which Parliament and the Executive cooperate in making legislation and the courts interpret the result depends crucially on there being no debasement of the coinage of communication between the two. The effectiveness of legislation generally to give effect to Government policy and the intention of Parliament relies on the courts' assumptions about the language and disciplines that are applied in its making.

The drafter needs to secure the long-term maintenance of the system in order to be able to continue to operate it effectively. In short, bad drafting, or even ill-judged drafting, can pollute the system and make the job more difficult for succeeding generations of drafters.

The rule against unnecessary material, which I have already mentioned,[30] is part of this and so is a rule to protect the integrity of the statute book. An unnecessary provision departs from the convention of communication that the courts expect. It can have one of two effects which could in the long term undermine the effectiveness of Government legislation. There is a risk that the courts will infer that the unnecessary

29 See pp. 26-28.

30 Quoted by Sir Geoffrey Bowman KCB, 'Why is there a Parliamentary Counsel Office?' (2005) 26 *Statute Law Review* at 69, 77.

material must have some effect, even though none is intended; and there is also a risk that the courts, having recognised the redundancy of the provision, will be misled into assuming that other provisions, which are intended to have an effect, are also mere window dressing. These implications can go beyond the Bill in question.

However, the line between what is necessary and what is not is a matter of judgement in the circumstances and sometimes today's more pressing considerations (such as the need to get the Bill passed) cannot be ignored when making the judgement. The drafter has to balance the risks. There is no denying that legislating is a political process – and so it should be in a democracy – but the application of legislation by the courts is a more objective process. The reconciliation of these competing interests is seldom easy.

This is only one example of the way the drafter has to protect the government's long-term interests by taking account of what the courts expect in legislation. The drafter may also have to frame a provision in a way that takes account of rules of construction and the wider constitutional principle sometimes described as the 'rule of law' [31] That too is all part of the process of protecting the integrity of the statute book and constitutional balance – something that has also required drafters to adapt to the new context created by the Human Rights Act 1998.

Sometimes the rules of construction, the rule of law or the Human Rights Act may require the drafter to question whether the proposed policy conforms to the government's own legal policy; but more often the task will be to frame the provision in a way that adequately explains how the government believes it to be in conformity with general principle. This can create yet another factor to balance against others, such as simplicity, clarity and effectiveness that the drafter has to take into account when deciding where and how to draw the line that has been asked for.

The need to get these judgements right, is another and important reason why it is necessary to ensure that Parliamentary Counsel are made solely responsible for a Bill only after they have had a thorough grounding in the whole practice of legislation and can make the required judgements with the authority of experience. In resolving issues between today's concerns and tomorrow's the legislative drafter has in his or her hands not only the fate of a particular government policy. The decisions that are made potentially have a long-term effect on the development of the constitution.

Conclusion

This chapter set out to explain the special role of Parliamentary Counsel and the reason why a long apprenticeship is required to take on the role. I have concentrated on the drafting side of the job rather than the advisory or consultancy service that the drafter provides to the instructing department to help them through the process. I may perhaps have taken the acquisition of the necessary linguistic skills and techniques too much for granted. They too need experience and dedication to master. What

31 See an interesting example and description of the rule of law as it applies to construction of legislation in *FP (Iran) v Secretary of State for the Home Department* [2007] EWCA civ. 13 at [59] – [60] and [74] –75] per L.J. Arden; see Lord Bingham of Cornhill's Sir David Williams Lecture, 16 November 2006 'The Rule of Law' (2007) 66 *CLJ* 67.

I think is clear is that drafting legislation, 'drawing the line', as opposed to just finding it, is a unique skill that requires long experience and accumulated authority. Choosing the words for a statute can often involve subtle and difficult judgements to be made in circumstances in which long experience is the only guide.

Chapter 3

Legislative Intention

Ian McLeod

Introduction

It would be difficult to deny that, in the context of the day to day realities of legislative and judicial practice within a liberal democracy, the legislature and the courts function in some sort of partnership with each other. As Payne says:

> The proper office of a judge in statutory interpretation is ... that of a junior partner in the legislative process, a partner empowered and expected within certain limits to exercise a proper discretion as to what the detailed law should be.[1]

The fact, which Payne recognises, that the partners are by no means equal does not avoid the need to establish the legitimacy of allowing judges to ascribe authoritative meanings to legislative texts, especially when those authoritative meanings deviate from the plain words of the texts.[2] The most obvious, and satisfactory, way of establishing the requisite legitimacy is by way of arguing that the courts are implementing the intention of the legislature because this clothes the courts' interpretative activities with democratic legitimacy, even if only on a vicarious basis.

This chapter discusses the problem of the sense (if any) in which a legislature can be said to have an intention, before identifying a credible explanation of what such an intention (assuming that it exists) may be taken to be, and how it may inform the process of interpretation in specific cases. It begins with some judicial and academic comments on the problem of legislative intention in general, before considering both subjective and objective versions of the concept. It then shows how the idea of legislative intention may, especially when linked to the ideas of political integrity and delegation, provide an account of the interpretative process which is both accurate and constitutionally acceptable. Finally, there is the conventional formality of a conclusion.

---

1 See D. Payne, 'The Intention of the Legislature in the Interpretation of Statutes' (1956) *Current Legal Problems* 96, 105.

2 See *Kammins Ballrooms Co Ltd v Zenith Investments Ltd* [1970] 2 All ER 871.

Some Judicial and Academic Comments on Legislative Intention

Although courts and commentators often use phrases such as 'legislative intention' and 'the intention of Parliament',[3] it must be acknowledged that there is substantial disagreement as to the nature – and even the existence – of legislative intention.

> Intention of the Legislature' is a very slippery phrase, which, popularly understood, may signify anything from intention embodied in positive enactment to speculative opinion as to what the legislature intended probably would have meant, although there been an omission to enact it.[4]

Cross, Bell and Engle, in a phrase which makes up in elegance what it lacks in apparent meaning, say the intention of Parliament is 'not so much a description as a linguistic convenience'.[5] More helpfully, they quote an American commentator who asserted that legislative intention could be both fictitious and useful.

> Of course we use a fiction if we speak of the legislature as if it were a being of one mind. But so durable a fiction endures because it has a use validated by experience. This formula reminds all who deal with a statute that they are operating in a field of law in which they are not free to define public policy simply according to their own judgment.[6]

Clearly, therefore, the idea of legislative intention is intrinsically controversial. Rather than dwelling on this fact, however, the purposes of this chapter will be better served by assuming that legislative intention does exist (even if some sceptics would insist that this assumption should be made only *de bene esse*), in order to enable the discussion to focus on what its nature might be.

Subjective and Objective Approaches to Legislative Intention

There are both subjective and objective approaches to the nature of legislative intention. We will consider each of them in turn.

---

3 To take a single example, in *Ealing London Borough Council v Race Relations Board* [1972] 1 All ER 105 Lord Simon said (at 113) 'It is the duty of a court so to interpret an Act of Parliament as to give effect to its intention.' This proposition has been described as 'one of the most ancient principles of the law of England and Wales'; see D. Greenberg, 'The Nature of Legislative Intention and Its Implications for Legislative Drafting' (2006) *Statute Law Review* 15.

4 See *Lord Watson, Saloman v Saloman & Co Ltd* [1897] AC 22, 38.

5 See R. Cross, J. Bell and G. Engle, *Statutory Interpretation*, 3rd edn (Oxford: Oxford University Press, 1995) at 28.

6 See J.W. Hurst, *Dealing With Statutes*, (New York: Columbia University Press, 1982) at 33, quoted in Cross, Bell and Engle (1995) at 29. The problems of the mind of the legislature and the effect of legislative intention as a restraining influence on interpreters are both addressed below.

The Subjective (or Speaker's Meaning) Approach

The subjective, or speaker's meaning approach, emphasises that legislation is an act of communication in which the legislature 'speaks' to the 'hearers', who are the users of legislation; and from this, it is argued that what really matters is the speaker's meaning. This simple model in which *a speaker + a hearer = communication,* may often fit the everyday realities of social intercourse between individuals, where the intended meaning of words may reasonably be presumed to reflect the intention (or, in other words, the state of mind) of the speaker. However, it is deeply problematic in the context of legislation.

First, although autocratic lawmakers have existed (and still do exist) in some legal systems, it is a matter of common observation that legislatures in developed societies typically take the form of some sort of assembly. Beyond this, it is difficult to generalise, since some legislatures are unicameral and some bicameral, while in either case the legislative process may or may not include an additional actor, such as a president, a monarch or a Governor General. However, even in the most straightforward case of a unicameral legislature functioning as the sole actor in the legislative process, there will be a multiplicity of members. It follows from this that, if we focus on the membership of the assembly, we immediately encounter both a multiplicity of minds, and, crucially, a multiplicity of intentions. Shifting the focus to the assembly itself is equally fruitless because a multi-member body does not have a mind; and without a mind it cannot have a state of mind; and without a state of mind, it cannot have an intention in any ordinary sense of the word.

Furthermore, while all members who vote for a measure must be taken as having at least the minimal intention that that measure should become law, their number will commonly include some members who have no intention whatsoever in relation to the measure's merits. Members will inevitably vary as to the extent of their interest in – and perhaps even their understanding of – different topics. In some cases, therefore, some members may well, in effect, delegate to their colleagues the task of evaluating the merits of a proposed measure, after which they are content simply to vote in the same way as those colleagues. In other cases, some members may be simply accepting their party's discipline.[7]

Second, the members of multi-member legislatures cannot, without recourse to fiction, claim to be speaking (in the everyday sense of articulating thoughts) since it is the drafter (albeit acting on instructions from the relevant government department) who composes the texts which will be debated and, at the option of the legislature, may be amended or approved, or both.[8] As Dworkin puts it:

7 See W.S. Gilbert's account of how Sir Joseph Porter became First Lord of the Admiralty:

'I always voted at my party's call,
And I never thought of thinking for myself at all.
I thought so little they rewarded me,
By making me the Ruler of the Queen's Navee!'
(*HMS Pinafore*, Act 1.)

8 Even if a single member proposes an amendment which is subsequently incorporated into the text as enacted, the 'speaking' will have been done only by that member and not by

> [The member] is ... not like someone choosing to communicate some thought or idea or wish. He occupies a position intermediate between speaker and hearer. He must decide what thought the words on the paper before him are likely to be taken to express and then decide whether he wishes that message to be sent ... given the only realistic alternative of sending no message at all ... he treats the document, not himself or any other person, as the author of the message he agrees to send.[9]

Similarly, any attempt to treat the minds of its members as being, in some way or other, the mind of the legislature is too far removed from reality to be taken seriously.

Furthermore, it can also be argued that, in many cases, it would be difficult to the point of impossibility to identify the membership of the legislature, since this would have to be done not only as at the date of the statute's enactment, but also for the remainder of that legislature's period of office and for each succeeding legislature which has allowed the statute to continue in force without amendment. However, the analysis presented in this chapter places relatively little reliance on the subjective view of legislative intention, so the introduction of tacit legislation as another layer of argument would be merely an unnecessary complication.

Some attempts to circumvent the difficulties we have just identified rely on viewing the drafter of the legislation as the speaker, so that the drafter's intention becomes the legislative intention. Mac Callum puts the argument thus:

> The judgment of ... persons ... authorised by the legislature may stand for the judgment of the legislature ... Thus our discovery of what these persons intended ... is a discovery of intentions that the legislature stood behind, wished us to attend to, wished us to regard as authoritative as their own – indeed wished us to regard as their own. These intentions may therefore be taken as, and in fact are, the intentions of the legislature.[10]

However, clear judicial authority warns of the danger of relying on the intention of its drafter. In *Hilder v Dexter*,[11] Lord Halsbury abstained from contributing to the decision on the ground that he had been 'largely responsible for the language' of the statute which was before the court:

> I have more than once had occasion to say that in construing a statute I believe the worst person to construe it is the person who is responsible for its drafting. He is very much disposed to confuse what he intended to do with the effect of the language which in fact has been employed.[12]

---

the assembly.

9 See R. Dworkin, *Law's Empire* (Cambridge Mass: Harvard University Press, 1986) at 322.

10 See G.C. Mac Callum, 'Legislative Intent' 75 (1966) *Yale Law Journal* at 754 and 782.

11 See [1902] AC 474, 477–8.

12 But it has not always been so. In 1305 C.J. Hengham rebuked counsel thus, 'Do not gloss the Statute; we understand it better than you do, for we made it'. (Modernised language, YB 33–5 Edw 1 (RS) 82.)

In *Stock v Frank Jones (Tipton) Ltd*,[13] Lord Simon, viewing the matter in the most basic constitutional terms, made substantially the same point (even though he fell into obvious error while doing so):

> In a society living under the rule of law, citizens are entitled to regulate their conduct according to what a statute has said, rather than by what it was meant to say, or by what it would have otherwise said if a newly considered situation had been envisaged.[14]

Since comments such as these constitute assertions of the objective approach to the intention of Parliament, it will be convenient at this stage to consider that approach in its own right.

The Objective (or Reasonable Meaning) Approach

The reasonable meaning approach emphasises the importance of taking the enacted text (rather than the putative state of mind of the lawmaker) as a starting point. This approach can be classified as objective, in the sense that it seeks to identify what the enacted words can reasonably be taken to mean. There is little doubt that this is the prevailing view among the modern English judiciary. In addition to the comments of Lord Halsbury and Lord Simon which we have already noted,[15] there is the leading statement of Lord Reid:

> We often say that we are looking for the intention of Parliament, but that is not quite accurate. We are seeking the meaning of the words which Parliament used. We are seeking not what Parliament meant but the true meaning of what they said.[16]

More recently, Lord Nicholls emphasised the objective approach thus:

> The phrase [*sic* the intention of Parliament] is a shorthand reference to the intention which the court *reasonably* imputes to Parliament in respect of the language used. It is not the subjective intention of the minister or other person who promoted the legislation. Nor is it the subjective intention of the draftsman, or of individual members or even

13 See [1978] 1 All ER 948, 953.

14 The obvious error into which Lord Simon fell is simply that in many cases the courts will have no alternative to filling a gap in a legislative scheme. In these cases, from the point of view of preserving at least a semblance of constitutional legitimacy, the most obvious approach – and perhaps the only realistic one – is to consider what the legislature would have said if the point before the court had been considered during the legislative process. As the American Realist, John Chipman Gray said, 'The fact is that the difficulties of so-called interpretation arise when the legislature had no meaning at all; when the question which was raised on the statute never occurred to it; when what the judges have to do is, not to determine what the legislature did mean on a point which was not present to its mind, but to guess what it would have intended on a point not present to its mind, if the point had been present.' (*The Nature and Sources of the Law*, 2nd edn (New York: Columbia University Press, 1921) s 370.

15 See *Hilder v Dexter* and *Stock v Frank Jones (Tipton) Ltd*, respectively.

16 See *Black-Clawson International Ltd v Papierwerke Waldhof-Aschaffenburg AG* [1975] 1 All ER 810, 814.

> of a majority of individual members of either House. These individuals will often have widely varying intentions. Their understanding of the legislation and the words used may be impressively complete or woefully inadequate. Thus, when courts say that such-and-such a meaning 'cannot be what Parliament intended', they are saying only that the words under consideration cannot *reasonably* be taken as used by Parliament with that meaning.[17] (emphasis added)

While the objective approach avoids the problems which flow from its subjective counterpart, it creates two new ones.

First, reasonableness is a very broad concept. After all, reasonable people may – and commonly do – reasonably disagree, as evidenced, for example, by the readily observable fact that dissenting judgments are a feature of English judicial practice. In the present context, therefore, once we accept that reasonable minds may come to different conclusions in respect of the same material, we must accept that the objective approach, in itself, offers no guarantee of producing a single meaning for the words in question. In many cases this truth may be obscured because all the judges in a case agree on a single meaning; but there remain many cases where the objective approach can do no more than produce a range of legally credible meanings.

Second, once judges adopt the idea of reasonable meanings instead of attempting to identify and articulate the subjective intention of the legislator, they are (at least to some extent) becoming legislators themselves. In a democratic system which falls short of having an elected judiciary, this immediately raises the question of legitimacy. Nevertheless, as the remainder of this chapter will seek to show, it is possible to formulate cogent responses to both these objections. We will begin by considering the possibility of balancing the subjective and objective approaches in individual cases.

Balancing the Subjective and Objective Approaches

The fact that neither a subjective nor an objective approach, when taken individually, can yield a satisfactory answer does not mean that either or both must be discarded. What it does mean is that the courts must have regard to both, so that they may weigh each against the other, in order to arrive at a single, balanced view of *the* intention of Parliament, in a form which will be useful in resolving specific problems of interpretation. Bennion speaks of the 'duplex approach' to interpretation, which has 'due regard' to the fact that the text has been 'produced by a fallible drafter who is not a legislator but possesses an intention taken to be adopted by the legislator', and that the text has been 'validated by a legislature' some of whose members 'may in fact have disagreed with, or been unaware of, some or all of the Act's provisions'.[18]

The remainder of this chapter will suggest that the English judiciary generally undertakes this process of weighing and balancing by exercising its discretion

---

17 See *R v Secretary of State for the Environment, Transport and the Regions ex parte Spath Holme Ltd* [2001] 2 AC 349, 396.

18 See *Statutory Interpretation*, 4th edn (2002) at 412.

in this context (as it does in so many others, although almost always without acknowledgment) in accordance with Dworkin's idea of 'political integrity'.[19]

The Idea of Political Integrity

If it is self-evident that the State ought to act consistently throughout the formulation, enactment and application of a coherent body of law, there is no difficulty in accepting Dworkin's proposition:

> We have two principles of political integrity: a *legislative* principle which asks lawmakers to try to make the total set of laws morally coherent, and an *adjudicative* principle, which instructs that the law be seen as coherent in that way, so far as possible.[20] (emphasis added)

However, since our discussion concerns the way in which the courts adjudicate in cases arising from legislation, thus fusing the two categories of legislative and adjudicative integrity into one, it follows that the distinction between those two categories need not be pursued here.

It is important to realise that Dworkin claims to be offering no more than a way of thinking about the problem: he makes no claim whatsoever that the application of political integrity will yield definitive answers in all cases (although, of course, it may do so in some). A straightforward case will provide an appropriate starting point.

In *Re Sigsworth*[21] the court held that the property of a woman who had been murdered by her son (who had then committed suicide) could not pass to the son's estate on her intestacy, even though the application of the plain words of the Administration of Estates Act 1925 would have required it to do so.[22] The decision reflects the common law principle (or requirement of public policy) which prohibits gaining advantage from wrongdoing.

The results of more complicated cases may vary according to the timescale which is used to identify the requirement of moral coherence. In other words, the result in a specific case may depend on whether the court applies general and long-term values of the community (such as judicial deference to Parliament and respect for individual rights) or more immediate concerns (such as the climate resulting from contemporary legislation). Dworkin himself emphasises the importance of the contemporary context.

> Integrity does not require consistency in principle over all historical stages of a community's law ... It commands a horizontal rather than a vertical consistency of principle across the range of legal standards the community now enforces ... Law as integrity ... begins in

19 See Dworkin (1986); and, more particularly, see ch. 6 and 7.

20 See ibid. at 176.

21 See [1934] All ER Rep 113.

22 Section 46 of the 1925 Act provides that an intestate's property 'shall be distributed' in accordance with the section.

> the present and pursues the past only so far as and in the way its contemporary focus dictates.[23]

Three cases arising from same sex relationships are instructive.

First, in *Harrogate Borough Council v Simpson*,[24] a lesbian couple, who regarded themselves as husband and wife, lived in a council house. The tenancy (which was technically known as a 'secure tenancy') was in the sole name of one of the partners, and on her death the question arose as to whether the survivor was entitled to inherit the tenancy on the ground that she and her partner had been living together as husband and wife.[25] She failed in both the county court and the Court of Appeal.

Responding to the argument that the survivor should be allowed to rely on the corresponding statutory provisions governing rights of succession to protected tenancies in the private sector and, in particular, the way in which those provisions had been interpreted in earlier cases concerning unmarried heterosexual couples, Watkins L.J. felt that the difference in sexual orientation and lifestyle made the earlier cases clearly distinguishable:

> If Parliament had wished homosexual relationships to be brought into the realm of the lawfully recognised state of a living together of man and wife for the purpose of the relevant legislation, it would plainly have so stated in that legislation, and it has not done so ... It would be surprising in the extreme to learn that public opinion is such today that it would recognise a homosexual union as being akin to a state of living as husband and wife. The ordinary man and woman ... would in my opinion not think even remotely of there being a true resemblance between those two very different states of affairs.[26]

Why did Watkins L.J. not conclude that respect for adjudicative integrity requires homosexual and heterosexual couples to be treated in the same way in relation to security of tenure? The answer seems to be that although ordinary people might feel that all couples should be treated equally in terms of security of tenure, the wider priority which was then given to heterosexuality over homosexuality would be sufficient to displace this feeling in cases arising from same sex relationships.

It may not be wholly irrelevant that this case was decided at a time when the law was inclining somewhat against homosexuals, as evidenced by s 28 of the Local

23 See Dworkin (1986) at 227.

24 See [1986] 2 FLR 91.

25 The relevant statutory provisions were contained in the Housing Act 1980, s 30 of which provided:

(1) Where a secure tenancy is a periodic tenancy and, on the death of the tenant, there is a person qualified to succeed him, the tenancy vests by virtue of this section in that person ...

(2) A person is qualified to succeed a tenant under a secure tenancy if he occupied the dwelling house as his only or principal home at the time of the tenant's death and either (a) he is the tenant's spouse; or (b) he is another member of the tenant's family and has resided with the tenant throughout the period of twelve months ending with the tenant's death.

The relevant part of the definition of 'family' was to be found in s 50 (3), 'A person is a member of another's family ... if she is his spouse ... or if they live together as husband and wife.

26 See ibid. at 95.

Government Act 1988, which introduced a general prohibition on local authorities intentionally promoting homosexuality, and a specific prohibition on the teaching in State maintained schools of 'the acceptability of homosexuality as a *pretended* family relationship' (emphasis added).[27] Nevertheless, whatever the wider context of the decision may have been, it remains true that Miss Simpson's choice of a lesbian lifestyle as an essential element of 'the good life' resulted in her being denied a right which she would have enjoyed if her orientation and lifestyle had been heterosexual. In other words, even if s 28 of the 1988 Act is treated as evidence of a prevailing climate of lawful discrimination against homosexuals, and therefore as helping to justify the decision in terms of political integrity, it remains strongly arguable that if a concern for the protection of human rights and fundamental freedoms had been the operative factor, the judicial decision would have been different.

The issue of whether a same sex partner may succeed to a tenancy on the death of the tenant came before the Court of Appeal again in *Fitzpatrick v Sterling Housing Association Ltd.*[28] The facts involved gay men while the law related to the private sector tenancies,[29] but the issue of political integrity which arose on the death of the tenant was indistinguishable from that in *Harrogate Borough Council v Simpson.*

All three judges in the Court of Appeal were plainly sympathetic to the survivor. Thus, Roch L.J.said that to allow the survivor to succeed 'would ... be consistent not only with social justice but also with the respect accorded by modern society to those of the same sex who undertake a permanent commitment to a shared life' [30] However, both he and Waite L.J. concluded that the case raised an issue which was within the sole remit of Parliament. On the other hand, Ward L.J., in a dissent which Roch L.J. described as 'interesting and elegant', had no such constitutional qualms.

> To exclude same-sex couples from the protection of the 1977 Act proclaims the inevitable message that society judges their relationships to be less worthy of respect, concern and consideration than the relationship between members of the opposite sex. The fundamental human dignity of the homosexual couple is severely and palpably affected by the impugned distinction. The distinction is drawn on grounds relating to their personal characteristics, their sexual orientation. If the law is as my Lords state it to be, then it discriminates against a not insignificant proportion of the population who will justly complain that they have been denied their constitutional right to equal treatment under the law.[31]

Two points may be noticed in passing. First, Ward L.J. approved Dworkin's comment that '... [the judge] interprets not just the statute's text but its life, the process that begins before it becomes law and extends far beyond that moment ... [the judge's]

27 The provision which became s 28 was originally introduced into Parliament in early 1987, but when a general election was called it was withdrawn along with a number of other provisions in order that other non-contentious material contained in the same Bill could be enacted before the dissolution of Parliament.

28 See [1997] 4 All ER 991.

29 Under the Rent Act 1977.

30 See [1997] 4 All ER at 1021.

31 See ibid.

interpretation changes as the story develops'.[32]

Second, just as the climate of opinion which gave rise to the enactment of s 28 of the Local Government Act 1988 formed part of the contemporary context of the decision in *Harrogate Borough Council v Simpson*, so s 145 of the Criminal Justice and Public Order Act 1994, which reduced the age of consent for homosexual acts between consenting males from 21 to 18, may have contributed to the sympathy of the majority, and the support of the minority, in the Court of Appeal, in *Fitzpatrick*.

Against this background, it is worth noticing that when the Appellate Committee of the House of Lords dealt with the case,[33] the Commons and the Lords were engaged in a protracted wrangle. Briefly, a proposal to reduce the age of consent still further (to 16), was passed by the House of Commons as a private member's amendment to the Bill which became the Crime and Disorder Act 1998, but was rejected by the House of Lords. The Commons did not press the issue, and therefore the provision did not appear in the Act itself. However, in late 1998 the proposal returned to the Commons as a government measure in the form of the Sexual Offences (Amendment) Bill. The Commons passed it again by a large majority but, on 13 April 1999, the Lords, also by a large majority, effectively rejected the Bill by voting to postpone its second reading for six months.

Meanwhile, on 13 and 14 April 1999, the Appellate Committee heard argument in *Fitzpatrick*. When the Appellate Committee gave judgment, on 28 October 1999, Lord Nicholls, in the majority of three to two in favour of allowing the appeal, said:

> In one respect of crucial importance there has been a change in social attitudes over the last half-century. I am not referring to the change in attitude toward sexual relationships between a man and a woman outside marriage or toward homosexual relationships. There has been a widespread change in attitude toward such relationships, although differing and deeply felt views are held on these matters. These differing views are to be recognised and respected. The crucial change to which I am referring is related but different. *It is that the morality of a lawful relationship is not now regarded as relevant when the court is deciding whether an individual qualifies for protection under the Rent Acts.* (emphasis added)[34]

On the other hand, Lord Hutton (a member of the minority), in addition to being against the survivor on the merits, also took the view that the whole matter was one for Parliament and not for the courts.[35] Similarly, Lord Hobhouse (Lord Hutton's companion in the minority) took the view that '... the developments for which [counsel for the surviving partner] contend involve developments of social policy and fall far outside the proper ambit of statutory construction'.[36]

It is difficult to avoid the conclusion that the Lords' second rejection of the measure, which clearly represented the continuing will of the Commons, must have

32 See ibid. at 1020; and see Dworkin (1986) at 348.
33 See [1999] 4 All ER 705.
34 See ibid. at 722.
35 See ibid. at 742.
36 See ibid. at 750.

had at least some impact on the minds of the Appellate Committee, even if the impact varied from one mind to another.

Almost finally, it may be worth recording that, having been reintroduced in the following session of Parliament, in February 2000 the Bill was again passed by the Commons. This time the Lords accepted the Bill but only subject to an amendment which stipulated a differential age of consent to anal sex. Because the House of Lords had not accepted the Bill in the form in which it had been approved by the House of Commons, they had rejected it for the purposes of the Parliament Acts 1911 and 1949. Accordingly, under the terms of the 1911 and 1949 Acts, the Bill was able to receive the Royal Assent and become the Sexual Offences (Amendment) Act 2000.

The House of Lords returned to the issue of homosexual partners' rights of succession to tenancies in *Ghaidan v Mendoza.*[37] On this occasion, taking the final step beyond *Fitzpatrick*, the House held (by a majority of 4:1) that for the purposes of the Rent Act 1977, a homosexual partner may be more than merely a *member of the tenant's family* and may fall within the meaning of the word *spouse*. (The effect of this decision was that the surviving partner would inherit the more advantageous *statutory tenancy*, rather than the less advantageous *assured tenancy*.) More particularly, the House held that there was no reason to exclude the survivors of stable homosexual relationships from the statutory protection which would clearly have applied to the survivors of identical heterosexual relationships; and that, therefore, the denial of that protection constituted unjustifiable discrimination against homosexuals.

The House was not bound by *Fitzpatrick* because that decision pre-dated the interpretative obligation imposed by s 3 of the Human Rights Act 1998. (Section 3 requires courts to read and apply legislative provisions in such a way as to make them compatible with Convention rights under the Act, where it is possible to do so. The Convention rights which arose for consideration in *Ghaidan* are contained in articles 8 and 14 of the ECHR, relating respectively to respect for the home and the grounds on which discrimination is prohibited.) In passing, and pursuing the contextual nature of the foregoing discussion, *Ghaidan* was decided after the general climate of legislative opinion in relation to gay and related rights had moved on in at least three respects.

First, the Local Government Act 2003 had repealed s 28 of the Local Government Act 1988. Second, the Sexual Offences Act 2003, which had largely replaced the Sexual Offences Act 1967, had totally abolished the offences of buggery and gross indecency between consenting male adults. Third, the enactment – on 1 July 2004 – of the Gender Recognition Act 2004, which enables transsexuals to obtain legal recognition of their acquired gender, was imminent. (The decision in *Ghaidan v Mendoza* was handed down on 21 June 2004.)

It is clear, therefore, that the application of political integrity will not necessarily solve every problem arising from attempts to identify and apply the intention of Parliament in specific cases. However, it is equally clear that thinking in terms of political integrity does help to refine the objective approach by specifying a starting point for the reasonable exercise of discretion; and, in practice, this will sharpen

---

37 See [2004] 3 All ER 411.

the focus of the judicial mind, thus narrowing the likely range of legally credible meanings.

Is Parliament Really Delegating Legislative Functions to Drafters and the Courts – and, if so, Does it Matter?

The only reasonable conclusion to be drawn from the discussion so far is that Parliament delegates legislative (or at the very least, quasi-legislative) functions to drafters and judges. While this analysis causes no particular difficulty in relation to drafters, whose words are always subject to Parliamentary endorsement, it can be seen as raising a problem in terms of legitimacy in relation to judges. However, this problem is more apparent than real, and rests on a misapprehension as to the nature of delegation in English law.

The leading case is *Huth v Clarke*,[38] where a local authority which was responsible for controlling diseases of animals appointed an executive committee, which in turn appointed local subcommittees. When the subcommittees took no action under the Rabies Order 1887, the executive committee itself made appropriate regulations. The question arose as to whether the executive committee had retained the power to make the regulations.

Answering this question in the affirmative, the High Court held that delegation involved a sharing, rather than a transfer, of power.

Additionally, it must be remembered that an act of delegation is subject to an implied power of revocation.[39] In the context of a judicial decision which the legislature regards as wayward, the equivalent would clearly be for the legislature to pass amending legislation, couched in sufficiently unequivocal terms to ensure that no later courts would fall into the same 'error'. Overall, therefore, the idea of delegation not only explains but also legitimises the judicial role in law-making within the context of legislative interpretation. If this causes concern based on the proposition that the rule of law requires the exercise of official discretion to be subject to legal control, it is only necessary to recall that the legislative supremacy of Parliament remains as a long stop; and, moreover, that Parliamentary 'correction' of judicial 'errors' may even operate retrospectively.[40]

38 See (1890) 25 QBD 39.

39 See *Manton v Brighton Corporation* [1951] 2 All ER 101.

40 See the War Damage Act 1965, effectively overruling and reversing the decision of the House of Lords in *Burmah Oil v Lord Advocate* [1964] 2 All ER 348 that the Crown could be liable to pay compensation in respect of damage caused by the British Army's scorched earth tactics while retreating in the face of a Japanese advance during the Second World War. The fact that legislation, such as the 1965 Act, raises other issues in relation to the rule of law is beyond the scope of this chapter.

Conclusion

A substantial degree of uncertainty surrounds the idea of the intention of Parliament, but, assuming it is not simply a fiction, it can be analysed into both subjective and objective elements. Deciding the relative weight to give to each element in the context of an individual case may be problematic. However, in practice, the idea of political integrity provides a way of thinking this problem through, and, in some cases, it may even provide clear answers. Once the nature of the process of legislative interpretation has been appreciated, it can easily be seen in terms of delegation to both the drafter and the court. Delegation to the drafter is unproblematic. On the other hand, delegation to the court may appear to raise a question of constitutional legitimacy but once the nature of delegation in English law is appreciated, that question may be easily answered.

Chapter 4

Legislator's Intent: How Judges Discern it and What They do if They Find it

Justice Keith Mason

In *Roe v Russell*[1] *L.J. Scrutton* lamented that he could not order costs to be paid by the draughtsmen of the Rent Restrictions Acts, and the Members of the Legislature who passed them, whom he considered responsible for the obscurity of the legislation.

The sometimes jaundiced experience of judges needs, like statutes themselves, to be understood in context. Statutes are read and applied thousands of times a day across the country. Genuine problems of ambiguity in meaning or difficulty of application are really few and far between, and they come into sharp focus in adversary litigation. We judges should in fact marvel at how few difficulties arise in practice. We should also bear in mind that provisions we find either vexing or too clear for argument may, to other judges higher up the ladder, reveal our own short-sightedness.

Courts must resolve every dispute brought within their jurisdiction. Judges therefore take up the strain of finding meaning in the relevant text and applying that meaning to the situation presented. We do not have the option of telling litigants that 'it is too hard' or 'no answer to your problem is available' or 'the matter is remitted to Parliament to have a second attempt at explaining itself'. Statutes must always fit one with the other because the bedrock principle that the law is a coherent unity means that 'the legislature cannot speak with a forked tongue'.[2]

Chief Justice Willmott wrote in 1767 that 'words are only pictures of ideas on paper'.[3] Sometimes the picture is unclear because the idea (or legislative policy) was also fuzzy. Sometimes the word painters (or Parliamentary Counsel) had inadequate instructions or insufficient time to complete the portrait to their fullest satisfaction. Judges need at least to remind themselves that legislative drafters often work to produce gold from dross within very short time frames. From personal experience, they know that the discipline of writing a reserved judgment can itself expose problems requiring further attention. Alas for Parliamentary Counsel, there may not always be time for a further draft. And the attention span of those giving instructions

1 See *Roe v Russell* [1928] 2 KB 117 at 130.
2 See *Waugh v Kippen* [1986] 160 CLR 156 at 165.
3 See *Roe d Dodson v Grew* (1767) Wilm 272 at 278; 97 ER 106 at 108.

may sometimes be limited. Sometimes too, distorting amendments are inserted in Committee, on the run, and by persons not completely au fait with the big picture.

In any event, it is vain to think that those involved in preparing legislation will foresee all problems, solve all foreseen problems or never create fresh problems by their own tampering.

Once again, this should not surprise our judges. The common law has been wrestling to declare itself with clarity and coherence for centuries, with courts being assisted by counsel and the writings of legal scholars. Yet basic principles still lack or defy pellucid enunciation. *Donoghue v Stevenson*[4] proved more of a beginning than an end. There are whole areas in the law of obligations that lie uneasily one against the other, like the tectonic plates of the earth's crust, apparently stable in the centre yet mobile at the points of overlap and liable to shift catastrophically from time to time. L.J. Diplock once remarked that:

> … the law is nearly always most obscure in those fields in which the judges say: 'the principle is plain, but the difficulty lies in its application to particular facts' [5]

Anyone who has been involved in law reform will know that clear proposals often need radical surgery in light of the questions that accompany early drafts of the Bill intended to become an appendix to the final report.

The exigencies of the drafting task and the constancy of human imperfection guarantee that hard problems of statutory interpretation will always be with us. Parliamentary Counsel will never have to adopt the work practices of the rug weavers of Qum who deliberately insert a mistake into their handiwork because only Allah is perfect. Those who write judgments are similarly placed.

You may have observed that I have so far said nothing about the foresight, competency or motives of our legislators. I can assure you that my silence on this topic does not stem from Article 9 of the Bill of Rights which provides that 'the freedome of speech and debates or proceedings in Parlyament ought not to be impeached or questioned in any court or place out of Parlyament'.[6]

Pepper v Hart[7] reversed a well-established rule of statutory interpretation that can be traced back to the mid-eighteenth century and had only been modified in the late nineteenth century to permit reference to White Papers and the like in the context of the mischief rule.[8] The Law Commissions in 1969[9] and the Renton Committee in

4 See *Donoghue v Stevenson* [1932] 1 AC 562.

5 See *Ilkiw v Samuels* [1963] 2 All ER 879 at 889; [1963] 1 WLR 991 at 1004.

6 See Bill of Rights 1688 (UK).

7 See *Pepper (Inspector of Taxes) v Hart* [1993] 1 AC 593; [1993] 1 All ER 42.

8 See *Eastman Photographic Materials Co. Ltd v Comptroller-General of Patents, Designs and Trade Marks* [1898] AC 571.

9 The Law Commission and the Scottish Law Commission, 'The Interpretation of Statutes', Law Com No. 21 and Scot Law Com No. 11 [1969] at 31–6.

1975[10] had recommended against change. The Hansard exclusionary rule had been restated emphatically by the House of Lords in 1975[11] and again in 1981.[12]

Pepper was a hard case in which the Revenue propounded an interpretation of a taxing statute that flew in the teeth of assurances, illustrated by examples, repeatedly given by the Financial Secretary to the Treasury when promoting the legislation through the Commons. Yet, if ever there were an idea whose hour had come by 1992, it was the legitimacy of referring to Hansard for at least some purposes in construing legislation. The law was already moving away from the 'austere judicial literalism'[13] of Lord Simonds. The notion of a purposive construction was emerging, pushing the boundaries of the ancient mischief rule stemming from Heydon's Case.[14] Access to travaux preparatoires had become the acceptable method for construing international treaties and the growing body of municipal legislation giving them effect. Some judges were troubled (in the way their predecessors were not) by the discordance between a rule banning consideration of this material for any purpose and their own practice of taking the odd peek at Hansard for assistance.[15] And, by 1992 the House of Lords had declared itself able to revisit its earlier decisions, thereby reflecting the post-modern uncertainties of our current age.

As acknowledged in Pepper, there were already decisions (some of them pre-dating confirmatory legislation) in Australia and New Zealand that gave effect to principles similar to those that were to be adopted by the Law Lords. The exclusionary rule has also been abandoned in Canada,[16] India[17] and Singapore,[18] some of the cases in those jurisdictions having preceded Pepper. American law is to similar effect, not without its critics, most notably Justice Antonin Scalia of whom more later. On my researches, only the Supreme Court of Ireland has rejected Pepper.

I do not suggest that any Pepper principle is applied uniformly in the different jurisdictions.[19] Quite the contrary. Professor Vogenauer's review of the English jurisprudence, published in the 2005 Oxford Journal of Legal Studies,[20] shows that the

10 See Renton Committee Report, *The Preparation of Legislation – Report of a Committee Appointed by the Lord President of the Council*, Cmnd 6053, (London: HMSO, 1975).

11 See *Black-Clawson International Ltd v Papierwerke Waldhof-Aschaffenburg AG* [1975] AC 591 at 598.

12 See *Fothergill v Monarch Airlines Ltd* [1981] AC 251 at 278 per Lord Diplock.

13 The Right Hon Sir Nicholas Lyell QC MP, '*Pepper v Hart: The Government Perspective*' 15 (1994) *Statute Law Review* pp. 1–9.

14 See *Heydon's* case (1584) 3 Co Rep 7a; 76 ER 637 at 638. See *Pepper (Inspector of Taxes) v Hart* [1993] 1 AC 593 at 617 per Lord Griffiths.

15 See *Pepper (Inspector of Taxes) v Hart* [1993] 1 AC 593 at 618.

16 See R. Sullivan and E. Driedger, *On the Construction of Statutes*, 4th edn (Markham, Ont: Butterworths, 2002) at 485.

17 See *K.P. Varghese v Income Tax Officer AIR* [1981] SC 1922.

18 See *Tan Boon Yang v Comptroller of Income Tax* [1993] 2 SLR 48; also The 'Seaway' [2005] 1 SLR at 435.

19 *Crilly v T & J Farrington* [2001] 3 IR 251.

20 See *S. Vogenauer, 'A Retreat from Pepper v Hart? A Reply to Lord Steyn'* 25 (2005) 25 Oxford Journal of Legal Studies pp. 629–74.

reasons given for the rule of exclusion tended to be pragmatic rather than principled until the 1970s. The source materials were neither dependable nor accessible until 1909, when Hansard became comprehensive and authoritative in this country. Online searching was only coming into vogue around the time Pepper was decided. Other pragmatic reasons, including the transactional costs of searching for needles in haystacks and the unlikelihood of finding them were weighed in Pepper and (over the dissent of Lord Mackay) found not to be determinative.

As happens in life, appeals to principle often come to the fore only when people start questioning an ancient practice. And, as also happens in life, defenders of the status quo may advance untenable grounds for holding the line. (Some of the arguments belatedly advanced against the enfranchisement or ordination of women have borne these two qualities.) Sometimes too, those exercising the newly found liberty fail to avoid abuses stemming from their own misunderstanding of the reasons that ought to set the proper boundaries of the new dispensation. The debate about *Pepper v Hart* and the sometimes casual attitude to its stringencies in this country, as documented by Professor Vogenauer, illustrate these phenomena.

One argument of principle was raised and easily despatched in Pepper itself, but it was already unfashionable by 1992. This was the suggestion that Article 9 of the Bill of Rights might prohibit courts from consulting Hansard to construe legislation.

Before moving away from pragmatism, I should emphasise the reasons for caution about relying upon what is said and done in Parliament in aid of construction of statutes. The idea picks up the thinking in Bismarck's attributed aphorism that those who like law and sausages should never watch either being made. It is advanced most convincingly by those with direct experience in the cut and thrust of parliamentary law-making. Sir Nicholas Lyell QC, who was Attorney General at the time of *Pepper v Hart* and leading counsel for the Crown in the case itself, has pointed out that parliamentarians are not and cannot be equipped to consider nuances of language used by promoters of a Bill in the course of debate. It is therefore most unlikely that they will consult the text of earlier legislation or indeed any extraneous material before voting for a Bill as it emerges sausage-like from the churn of proceedings in Parliament.[21] Professor Baker has reminded us that these considerations are multiplied when it is borne in mind that the Members of one chamber of a bicameral legislature can hardly be expected to be on top of the speeches made in the other chamber.[22]

Now these matters should not be taken too far, lest judges apply different standards to Parliament than the Members require of themselves. Modern legislatures have extremely tight schedules. Lots of material is taken as read, as it were. Attendance at Parliament is not compulsory. Party discipline is a reality. In these circumstances, it may be too precious and ultimately counter-democratic for judges to refuse in a proper case to infer that Members did not assent to principles and policies advanced by the mover, incorporating them into their decision to vote for the Bill to pass.

---

21 See The Right Hon Sir Nicholas Lyell, QC, MP *'Pepper v Hart: The Government Perspective'* 15 (1994) *Statute Law Review* pp. 1–9.

22 See J.H. Baker, 'Case and Comment: Statutory Interpretation of Parliamentary Intention' 52 (1993) *Cambridge Law Journal* pp. 353–7.

Often it will be wrong to infer anything beyond courtesy from those listening silently or anything beyond preoccupation from those absent from the chamber during the critical debate.[23] But surely not always. Can I seek to make the point negatively, by asserting that no one today would defend the pre-Pepper law on the basis that the Queen's assent is necessary to pass a law and by arguing that Her Majesty was not privy to the proceedings in Parliament. Yet this was a reason given for the exclusionary rule when first promulgated in 1769.

A clear statement in a second reading speech or explanatory memorandum that is replicated in each House may cast genuine light on the text to which it is addressed. The same cannot as easily be said for speeches made in Committee as to a perceived state of affairs, including remarks about the meaning of a clause or the current state of the common law. I confess to real difficulty in making a bridge between such statements and the meaning of the finished legislative product, especially where the statement is used to head off an amendment proposed in Committee in only one House of the Parliament. The readiness of Courts in this country to use such material appears to be a real point of distinction between your jurisprudence and that with which I am more familiar.

From the outset, Pepper attracted critics who began to invoke fundamental, sometimes constitutional, principles to turn back the clock. Lord Steyn, in particular, voiced such concerns on and off the bench,[24] some of which appear to have persuaded the House of Lords to apply the Pepper with a good pinch of salt. Since Pepper is a common law principle of statutory interpretation in this country, the debates have taken place in the time-honoured ways. Sometimes they have involved attempts to 'explain' Pepper by finding a different ratio decidendi to that which would have occurred to (dare I say have been intended by) the bench that decided the supposedly authoritative case. I shall pass over Francis Bennion's assertion that the Law Lords in Pepper misapplied the very principle they brought into being.[25] Professor Vogenauer suggests (with a question mark)[26] that there has been a retreat from Pepper, although he does not, I think, point to any case in which there was majority support for retreat, apart from the Spath Holme decision.[27] He summarises that case in the following terms:

> ... for the purpose of statutory interpretation, Pepper is confined to cases where the court is concerned with the meaning that is given to the words used in legislation. As a matter of principle, reference to Hansard is inadmissible if the policy and objects of an Act have to be ascertained for the purpose of identifying the scope of a discretionary power. This

---

23 See *A. Kavanagh, 'Pepper v Hart and Matters of Constitutional Principle'* 121 (2005) 121 *Law Quarterly Review* at 105.

24 See The Right Hon Lord Johan Steyn, *'Pepper v Hart; A Re-Examination'* 21 (2001) 1 *Oxford Journal of Legal Studies* pp. 59–72; The Right Hon Lord Johan Steyn, 'The Intractable Problem of the Interpretation of Legal Texts' 25 (2003) 1 *Sydney Law Review* pp. 5–19.

25 See F.A.R. Bennion, *Statutory Interpretation*, 4th edn (London: Butterworths, 2002) at 53.

26 See S. Vogenauer (2005) pp. 629–74.

27 See *ex parte* Spath Holme Limited [2001] 2 AC 349; [2001] 1 All ER 195.

> may only be done in exceptional cases where the minister gave a categorical assurance to Parliament that the discretionary power would not be used in a given situation.[28]

If I may be permitted an aside, and it is not a new point, I would have thought that resort to Hansard to find legislative policy was more defensible than resort to it for finding the meaning of particular words. It would defy common sense to spurn the bridge of Hansard if one was left speculating whether Parliament was responding to the mischief identified in say a law reform commission report or a decided case. My own experience, for what it is worth, is that discovering the policy of an Act as an aid to a purposive construction is the only area where reference to Hansard has ever proved the slightest bit helpful. Perhaps the distinction between mischief, on the one hand, and policy or objects, on the other, is somewhat less categorical than suggested in the summary of Spath Holme I have quoted.

Others have criticised Pepper for betrayal of private law principles touching the interpretation of written contracts.[29] Their views are also overstated, in my respectful opinion. The law does at times receive evidence going to the meaning of a text from things done or said during its creation. Thus, with contracts, help will occasionally (and I stress occasionally) be drawn from evidence as to the mischief or context revealed during the drafting stage from the discussion of the negotiating parties or even snippets of text considered and rejected for not embodying their common intent. With contracts as with statutes, the search is for the so-called objective meaning of the final product. But it is not possible to demonstrate a *priori* that such meaning can never be discerned from travaux preparatoires. Lord Nicholls has recently suggested that the law is moving in this area.[30] The parol evidence rule is riddled with so many exceptions and qualifications that Professor Fridman has suggested that the rule itself may be the potential cause of injustice.[31]

I cannot refrain from some comments about in *R v A* (No. 2)[32] while recognising that several later cases appear to adopt a less controversial approach to the application of s 3 of the Human Rights Act 1998.[33] The House of Lords was faced with a carefully crafted 'rape-shield' law that had been enacted after the Human Rights Act. The law set up a clear and detailed regime restricting the right to cross-examine a complainant as regards previous sexual relations with the accused. Most of their Lordships acknowledged that the text was intractable if one applied the ordinary canons of statutory interpretation, including the rules about promoting the legislative purpose and leaning in favour of the accused. Nevertheless, the unfairness of the

28 See S. Vogenauer (2005) at 653.

29 See J.H. Baker, 'Case and Comment: Statutory Interpretation of Parliamentary Intention' 52 (1993) *Cambridge Law Journal* pp. 353–7.

30 See The Right Hon Lord Nicholls, 'My Kingdom for a Horse' 121 (2005) *Law Quarterly Review* pp. 577–91; also *Codelfa Construction Pty Ltd v State Rail Authority of NSW* (1982) HCA 24; [1982] 149 CLR 337.

31 See G.H.L. Fridman, The Law of Contract in Canada, 4th edn (Scarborough, Ont.: Carswell, 1999) at 481.

32 See *R v A* (No. 2) [2002] 1 AC 45; [2001] UKHL 25.

33 See A. Kavanagh, 'The Elusive Divide Between Interpretation and Legislation under the Human Rights Act 1998' 24 (2004) *Oxford Journal of Legal Studies* at 259.

legislative restrictions, in the eyes of the Court, saw the judges substituting their own views of fairness and relevance for the closely crafted intentions of Parliament. They did so in 2001 by invoking Parliament's broadly expressed intention about Convention principles, stated in 1998, to trump Parliament's particular statement in 1999. In Lord Steyn's words, 'while the [rape-shield] statute pursued desirable goals, the methods adopted amounted to legislative overkill'.[34] The 1999 Act was found to have made an excessive inroad upon the unqualified Convention right to a fair trial.

I wish to say nothing about the ultimate judgment call as to the link between common law relevance and Convention fairness. The House of Lords ultimately concluded that a broad brush reading down s 41 of the Youth Justice and Criminal Evidence Act 1999 was a 'possible' interpretation of the statute in light of the Convention. This country has chosen to arm its judges with the right to make that decision. The majority invoked s 3 of the Human Rights Act which, as you know, provides that:[35]

> So far as it is possible to do so, primary legislation and subordinate legislation must be read and given effect in a way which is compatible with the Convention rights.

I venture to suggest that *R v A* (No. 2) shows the capacity of s 3 to become the judicial equivalent of a Henry VIII clause in Convention matters.[36] To this observer, it does seem to have been a most strained view of the concept of interpreting or 'reading' a statute to see that case being determined by reference to s 3 rather than by a frank declaration of incompatibility.

The forensic outcome of A's case also suggests that it is not always correct to view resort to s 3 as the lesser intrusion, the remedy that gives greater deference to the so-called true intention of Parliament.[37] As I understand it, the reasons given by their Lordships in *R v A* (No. 2) would have been immediately binding on the parties in the yet unfinished rape trial, not to mention its impact on the rights of the complainant, in a way different to the impact of a declaration of incompatibility. The latter remedy would have returned the statute to Parliament to do what it wished in response, whether or not that involved repeal, amendment in a more specific direction than the interpretation offered by their Lordships or no change at all to the status quo. Parliament would also have been free to make its call as to the transitional aspects of any response to the Court's ruling on the Convention issue. I have not overlooked the European Court of Human Rights in this gallop through the options open to the litigants and the courts.

---

34 See *R v A* (No. 2) [2002] 1 AC 45 at [67], [43].

35 See Human Rights Act 1998 (UK).

36 In Dr Kavanagh's more nuanced words, a 'transformative interpretation' under s 3 is 'the same as those types of legislative amendment which change a statute by inserting a word or a phrase. So it seems that section 3 authorizes a form of judicial amendment of statutory material.' A. Kavanagh, 'The Elusive Divide Between Interpretation and Legislation under the Human Rights Act 1998' 24 (2004) *Oxford Journal of Legal Studies* pp. 259 at 283.

37 See S. Fredman, 'From Deference to Democracy: The Role of Equality Under the Human Rights Act 1998' 122 (2006) *Law Quarterly Review* pp. 53–81 at 79.

To adapt *Lord Hoffmann in R (Wilkinson) v Inland Revenue Commissioners*,[38] the outcome in A's case may have come as a surprise to the Members of the Parliament which enacted the 1999 rape-shield law. In his Lordship's words:

> ... in that sense the construction may have been contrary to the intention of Parliament'.

In my respectful view, it is not easy to detect any sense in which the reasoning in *R v A* (No. 2) accords with the traditional understanding of that guiding concept of statutory interpretation. The Law Lords' acknowledgment of the intractability of the later statute embodying the rape-shield provisions suggests, to this observer, that Dicey's bedrock principle about the supremacy of a later Parliament over its predecessor, in any battle of competing statutory wills, seems now to need qualification in the field of human rights in this country. In cases dealing with enactments passed after the Human Rights Act there is, to my perception, an unresolved tension between two propositions stated a couple of paragraphs apart by Lord Bingham in re S, when he said that s 3 is 'a powerful tool whose use is obligatory' and that s 3 is the means whereby the Human Rights Act 'seeks to preserve parliamentary sovereignty'.[39] Are there not (I ask) some constitutional limits upon the manner in which Parliament can tell judges how to go about their core business of interpreting statutes, particularly recent ones? But these fascinating constitutional issues are far too large for me to dwell upon in this chapter.

In *R v A* (No 2), Lord Steyn invoked *Pepper v Hart* when placing reliance upon a statement by the Lord Chancellor that 'in 99% of the cases that will arise, there will be no need for judicial declarations of incompatibility'.[40] The linkage between this prediction made in the third (and I emphasise third) reading speech on the Human Rights Act and the meaning of s 3 of that Act is not at once apparent. Nor is it clear to me how this approach fits with Lord Steyn's estoppel-based interpretation of Pepper itself, given that the matter in issue was the scope of s 3 of the Human Rights Act.

When I differed from Professor Vogenauer as to the extent of the retreat from Pepper, I had the benefit of material coming into existence after the time he wrote his article.[41] This said, my reading of the cases here suggests that judges seldom find any crock of gold in Hansard.

Lord Steyn's proposed alternative ratio of Pepper,[42] involving private law notions of estoppel and admissions by the Executive against interest, as well as what strikes me as the untenable corollary that an Act could have a different meaning depending on who invokes it, has been (in my respectful view) answered convincingly in the

---

38 See *R v Her Majesty's Commissioners of Inland Revenue* (Respondents) *ex parte* Wilkinson (FC) (Appellant) [2005] 1 WLR 1718.

39 In re S (Minors) (Care Order: Implementation of Care Plan) [2002] 2 AC 291 at [37], [39]; [2002] UKHL 10; [2002] 2 AC 291 at [37], [39].

40 See *R v A* (No. 2) [2002] 1 AC 45 at 68 [44].

41 See also P. Sales, *'Pepper v Hart: A Footnote to Professor Vogenauer's Reply to Lord Steyn'* 26 (2006) *Oxford Journal of Legal Studies* pp. 585–92.

42 See *R v A* (No. 2) [2002] 1 AC 45 at 68 [45]; *McDonnell v Congregation of Christian Brothers Trustees & Ors* [2004] 1 AC 1101 at [29]; [2003] UKHL 6.

academic literature.[43] It has not, to my knowledge, been endorsed by other than Lord Hope in *R v A* (No. 2)[44] and somewhat tentatively by Lord Hobhouse in Wilson.[45]

Lord Nicholls spoke against the 'sidelining' of Pepper in Jackson's Case[46] and his remarks were recently endorsed by Lord Carswell.[47]

Several clouds of doubt appear to have lifted in the recent decision of Harding *v* Wealands.[48] There it was held that the 'damages-capping' provisions of the New South Wales Motor Accidents Compensation Act 1999 did not apply to tort claims arising out of accidents in New South Wales that are litigated in this country. The local statute in question was the Private International Law (Miscellaneous Provisions) Act 1995. Their Lordships in Harding were not troubled by invoking Pepper in private litigation that had nothing to do with governmental rights. Significant too, was their readiness to examine a statement by the Lord Chancellor in the nature of a blanket assurance about how English courts would continue to deal with the assessment of damages with regard to foreign torts. The Chancellor was then the head of the judiciary, but he was on any view dealing with a complex aspect of the evolving common law.

The Lord Chancellor's statements in Committee deflected an amendment that would have put the matter beyond doubt. There was, however, no reference in the reasons for judgment in Harding as to what might have been said in the Commons where, on my researches, the Bill passed without any debate (admittedly later than the legislative proceedings in the House of Lords).

The reasoning in Harding and the specific endorsements of Pepper have well and truly brought the original case back into the sunshine, perhaps also into the glare of its opponents.

Some of Pepper's fiercest critics have, in my view, overstated their case and therefore not assisted in the search for those variants of Pepper that are worth retaining in the judicial kitchen. I include three matters in this context. The first are statements from Francis Bennion, Lord Steyn, Dr Aileen Kavanagh and others to the effect that ministers' statements may, under Pepper, operate to bind the courts or serve as a 'trump card' in litigation, allowing the Executive to legislate through ministerial assertion.[49] This is not a fair reading of the speeches in Pepper,

---

43 See A. Kavanagh (2005) pp. 116–18; Vogenauer (2005) pp. 629–74; Sales (2006) pp. 585–92.

44 See *R v A* (No. 2) [2002] 1 AC 45 at [81].

45 See *Wilson v First County Trust Ltd* (No. 2) [2004] 1 AC 816 at 865 [140]; [2003] UKHL 40.

46 See *R (on the application of Jackson) v A-G* [2006] 1 AC 262 at [65]; [2005] UKHL 56.

47 See *Harding v Wealands* [2007] 2 AC 1; [2006] UKHL 32; [2006] 3 WLR 83.

48 See *Harding v Wealands* [2006] 2 AC 1 at 25 [81]; [2006] UKHL 32; [2006] 3 WLR 83.

49 See Bennion (2002) at 547; The Right Hon Lord Steyn, *'Pepper v Hart; A Re-Examination'* 21 (2001) 1 *Oxford Journal of Legal Studies* pp. 59–72 at 64–70; Kavanagh (2005) at 100–101.

as Professor Vogenauer and Lord Nicholls among others have pointed out.[50] It is Parliament's legislated intention alone that counts.

The law is very clear in Australia that a minister's understanding of the effect of a statute or the state of the common law cannot give the Bill he or she is promoting an effect inconsistent with its terms as construed by the court.[51] In Re Bolton; *Ex parte* Beane,[52] the High Court of Australia went further in refusing to give any weight to a minister's unambiguous second reading speech that contradicted the text. C.J. Mason, Wilson and J.J. Dawson stated:[53]

> The words of a Minister must not be substituted for the text of the law ... It is always possible that through oversight or inadvertence the clear intention of the Parliament fails to be translated into the text of the law. However unfortunate it may be when that happens, the task of the Court remains clear. The function of the Court is to give effect to the will of Parliament as expressed in the law.

These three justices were former Solicitors General.

The words of a minister can be definitive in the sense of resolving a particular dispute as to the meaning of an ambiguous text,[54] but they are never 'authoritative' in the sense sometimes advanced by the critics of Pepper.[55]

My second example of overreaction to Pepper is related to the first. Dr Kavanagh has recently taken up Lord Steyn's proposition that *Pepper v Hart* offends the principle of the separation of powers, a doctrine she describes as forbidding Members of the executive or the legislature to interpret the law as well as make it. She invokes Lord Wilberforce's spectre of courts sinking to the level of being 'a reflecting mirror of what some other interpretation agency might say'.[56] This, with respect, is fallacious on two counts, because it misstates the interpretative functions of both the agencies and of the courts.

It would be an intolerable state of affairs if all agencies of government were not constantly involved in interpreting the laws by which they and citizens are governed. And there is nothing at all wrong with MPs forming their own views about the meaning of Bills and Acts as they go about their work. Courts alone can construe legislation authoritatively and the separation of powers doctrine requires their rulings to be followed by everyone unless and until Parliament speaks again. There is a world of difference between listening to someone's views and being bound to give them effect. A judge who takes account of evidence and listens to counsel does not abdicate the responsibility of judgment.

---

50 See *Wilson v First County Trust Ltd* (No. 2) [2004] 1 AC 816 [58]–[59].

51 See *Plaintiff S157/2002 v Commonwealth of Australia* (2003) 211 CLR 476 at 499 [55]; [2003] HCA 2 at [55].

52 See re Bolton; *ex parte* Beane (1987) 162 CLR 51; [1987] HCA 12.

53 See re Bolton; *ex parte* Beane (1987) 162 CLR 514 at 518; [1987] HCA 12.

54 See *Insurance Commission of Western Australia v Container Handlers Pty Ltd & Ors*(2004) 218 CLR 89 at 103 [33] per J. McHugh; [2004] HCA 24 at [33].

55 See Kavanagh (2005) at 98.

56 See ibid. at 102 and 103, citing *Black-Clawson International Ltd v Papierwerke Waldhof-Aschaffenburg AG* [1975] AC 591 at 629.

Pepper v Hart has nothing to do with the separation of powers, except in the entirely different sense that judges who are reluctant to give effect to ministerial statements (in general or in the particular) are emphasising the separation between the Executive and Parliament as regards law-making competence.

Third and most curious of all, are the concerns expressed about the impact of Pepper upon the practices of Parliament itself. The voicing of these matters by judges and academics lies uneasily with the separation of powers arguments coming from the same sources.[57] Now it is undoubtedly true that Pepper has led, in this country, to practices whereby Members of Parliament ask the promoter of a Bill to give particular assurances, sometimes expressly referring to *Pepper v Hart* in case the minister has not got the message.[58] Sometimes these questions may have been planted (we call them 'Dorothy Dixers' in Australia). And it is undoubtedly the case that ministerial statements are occasionally used in preference to further drafting, or worse still, to preclude a clarifying amendment in Committee. I have experienced the former situation myself when I was Solicitor General for New South Wales, where Pepper is nothing like the industry it is in this country.

But surely judges can be trusted not to be duped or overborne. They are capable of ensuring that the loud voice of an unambiguous text is not drowned out by the tiny voice of its promoter. This is an area where Article 9 of the Bill of Rights and separation of powers principles ought themselves to have some sway. Judges should leave Parliament to enforce its own best practice. They should also recognise that Hansard records statements made in a forum where meaningful debate and attempts at persuasion still sometimes occur. Parliament is the place to discipline the ministerial assurance that is untrue, sloppy or mispredictive. Courts do not need to wander down this path and Pepper does not require it.

Slanted statements by legislators are an art form in the United States, but judges there are not fooled, certainly not J. Scalia. In the recent Guantanamo Bay case of *Hamdan v Rumsfeld*,[59] he railed against the use made by the majority of his colleagues on the Supreme Court who selectively quoted what the Americans call 'floor statements' to support a contentious point of statutory interpretation. J. Scalia warned against indulging in 'the fantasy that Senate floor speeches are attended (like the Philippics of Demosthenes) by throngs of eager listeners, instead of being delivered (like Demosthenes' practice sessions on the beach) alone into a vast emptiness'

This leads me briefly to the philosophical debate about the intention of Parliament or the intention of the Members whose votes are responsible for the passage of a

57 See The Right Hon Lord Steyn (2001) at 69; Kavanagh (2005) at 106–107; *Pickin v British Railways Board* [1974] AC 765.

58 Based on a casual electronic stroll through 2006 Hansard in the House of Lords.

59 See *Hamdan v Rumsfeld* 548 U.S. 557 (2006).

Bill.[60] At one level, the matter is a non-issue for, as Lord Reid pointed out,[61] we are always looking for the meaning of the words which Parliament has used in its solemn enactment. The motives or beliefs of those who vote for a measure, even their beliefs as to its meaning, may cast little or no light on the meaning of the text and may, in any event, prove extremely difficult to establish in point of fact.

Some, like Lord Steyn[62] and J. Scalia attack the whole notion of the intent of the legislature as unprovable and spurious. J. Kirby has described the concept as a 'polite but unacceptable fiction'.[63] J. Scalia has observed that:

> We are governed by laws, not by the intentions of legislatures.
>
> Our task is not to enter the minds of the Members of Congress – who need have nothing in mind in order for their votes to be both lawful and effective – but rather to give fair and reasonable meaning to the text.

Similar points about the minds of politicians were made by Lord Nicholls and Lord Hobhouse in *Wilson v First County Trust Ltd* (No. 2), but without I think denying the basal idea of Parliament's intention. Lord Nicholls said delicately that '... it should not be supposed that members necessarily agreed with the minister's reasoning or his conclusions' Lord Hobhouse was blunter in stating (with the concurrence of Lord Rodger) that it was a 'fundamental error of principle to confuse what a minister or a parliamentarian may have said (or said he intended) with the will and intention of Parliament itself' [64]

Sometimes legislative intention is explained as an objective concept, an idea that is in turn difficult to pin down from a philosophical point of view. It has been critically examined in the writings of Daniel Greenberg, Parliamentary Counsel and the author of the much improved latest edition of Craies on Legislation.[65] I shall mask my ignorance by not venturing into these philosophical debates.

To me, it is significant and sufficient that our highest courts explicitly recognise that Parliament can have an intention that may be hidden behind the opacity of its statutory language, or even demonstrably misstated in that language. We have all seen examples of this, just as we have seen wills that make perfect and obvious sense if the word 'not' is read into a clause or if a legacy to a non-existent 'daughter' is read

---

60 See 'The Principle of Legality and the Clear Statement Principle' Opening Address by the Honourable J.J. Spigelman AC, Chief Justice Of New South Wales, to the New South Wales Bar Association Conference 'Working With Statutes' Sydney, 18 March 2005 for a recent discussion; see Vogenauer (1997) 235–43.

61 See *Black-Clawson International Ltd v Papierwerke Waldhof-Aschaffenburg AG* [1975] AC 591 at 613.

62 See The Right Hon Lord Steyn (2001) at 64–6.

63 See *R v Hughes* (2000) 202 CLR 535; [2000] HCA 22.

64 See *Wilson v First County Trust Ltd* (No. 2) [2004] 1 AC 816 at [66], [178], [139] respectively.

65 See D. Greenberg, 'The Nature of Legislative Intention and Its Implications for Legislative Drafting' 27(1) *Statute Law Review* pp. 15–28; see also S. Vogenauer, 'What is the Proper Role of Legislative Intention in Judicial Interpretation?' 18 (1997) 3 *Statute Law Review* pp. 235–43.

as going to the testator's son. Every Interpretation Act sets out rules to be applied 'unless the contrary intention appears'.

In Pepper, the Law Lords worked on the premise that there is such a thing as the 'intention of the legislature'. They spoke in these very terms[66] and it is, I suppose, proper to have regard to their speeches to determine what they were intending to convey. Alas, there is little point in asking them personally because, as Lord Hoffmann remarked very recently in the Deutsche Morgan case:[67]

> Once a judgment has been published, its interpretation belongs to posterity and its author and those who agreed with him at the time have no better claim to declare its meaning than anyone else.

Beyond the semantics, the philosophical debates and the empirical points about difficulty of proof lies the important constitutional message that judges are endeavouring to convey when they use this language of intention.[68] Fairness, accessibility to law and the primary rules of statutory interpretation all direct us to the ordinary and grammatical sense of the enacted words read in context. We are also required nowadays to avoid absurdity and to construe enactments purposively. In your system this reference to purposive construction is found in the case law. For us in Australia, it is a statutory rule of interpretation. In either case, 'purpose' implies unexpressed intention in the sense of something anterior to and not discovered directly from the text itself.

Bennion is surely correct in describing the suggestion that there can be no true intention behind an Act of Parliament as 'anti-democratic'.[69] When judges invoke the intention concept they are in the same breath acknowledging the supremacy of statute over common law and the reality that legislators and those assisting them (being human) do not always express their meaning clearly when signing off on the legislative text. 'Legislative intention' is thus more than a polite fiction. As C.J. Gleeson put it, the concept expresses the constitutional relationship between the legislature and the judiciary.[70]

We fool ourselves if we think that, in every case, a single 'true' meaning will emerge if we wrestle long enough with the text. It follows that we should welcome all the help we can get in resolving genuine ambiguities that emerge, so long as we remember that the task remains that of determining what Parliament meant by

66 See Vogenauer at 654.

67 See *Deutsche Morgan Grenfell Group Plc v Inland Revenue & Anor* [2007] 1 AC 558.

68 See *Singh v The Commonwealth* [2004] 222 CLR 322 at [19]; [2004] HCA 43 at [19] for a sustained defence of the concept by C.J. Gleeson.

69 See Bennion (2002) at 409.

70 See also J. *French in NAAV and Ors v Minister for Immigration and Multicultural and Indigenous Affairs* (2002) 123 FCR 298 at 411, describing the concept as a 'legitimising and normative term'

the words it used, not what it was intending to say.[71] Judges must never assume a particular intention and then proceed to find it in Hansard or anywhere else.[72]

Hansard may occasionally provide useful and legitimate clues. But not often, for myriads of reasons many of which I have already touched upon. There are others. Sometimes the people involved in statute-making were themselves uncertain about where they were aiming. Sometimes they deliberately chose to confer a broad discretion, or to use woolly or fuzzy language or language that was obviously always speaking. These latter methods of drafting are occasionally used with deliberate but undisclosed intent on the Executive's part. The Executive in Parliament may be content to let the courts work matters out by trial and error, even or especially if that leaves the judges taking the flack in particular classes of case. Lord Browne-Wilkinson was surely smiling when he wrote in Pepper that 'Parliament never intends to enact an ambiguity'.[73]

We would fool ourselves if we thought that even sharper rules of statutory interpretation could iron out ambiguity or avoid hard choices in statutory construction. If our prescient legislators may be taken to recognise this truth of nature, then it is to me inconceivable that Parliament would not want judges to look at all available material that might cast genuine light upon what it was seeking to convey. In several countries, including my own, Parliament has decided to spell out this mandate to the judges by enacting rules similar to those expounded in Pepper.

In 1946, Lord MacMillan, having detected the purpose of an Act, remarked that: 'The legislature has plainly missed fire'.[74] Lord Diplock's extra-judicial riposte in 1978 was that: 'if ... the Courts can identify the target of Parliamentary legislation their proper function is to see that it is hit: not merely to record that it has been missed'.[75] This latter sentiment better captures the true role of judges when interpreting legislation in a parliamentary democracy.[76]

The concept of the intention of Parliament expresses an important constitutional principle rooted in political reality and judicial prudence. Because of it, the principles in *Pepper v Hart*, properly understood and cautiously applied, should continue to guide our courts.

---

71 See *Black-Clawson International Ltd v Papierwerke Waldhof-Aschaffenburg AG* [1975] AC 591 at 645 per Lord Simon.

72 See *Richardson v Austin* (1911) 12 CLR 463 at 470 per C.J. Griffith; [1911] HCA 28.

73 See *Pepper (Inspector of Taxes) v Hart* [1993] 1 AC 593 at 634.

74 See *Inland Revenue Commissioners v Ayrshire Employers Mutual Insurance Association Ltd* [1946] 1 All ER 637 at 641 cited in *Kingston & Anor v Keprose Pty Ltd* (1987) 11 NSWLR 404 at 424.

75 See Lord Diplock 'The Courts as Legislators' in The Lawyer and Justice (London: Sweet and Maxwell, 1978) at 274 cited in *Kingston & Anor v Keprose Pty Ltd* [1987] 11 NSWLR 404 at 424.

76 See *Kingston & Anor v Keprose Pty Ltd* [1987] 11 NSWLR 404 for chapter and verse for these two quotes.

Chapter 5

The Techniques of Gender-neutral Drafting

Daniel Greenberg[1]

Introduction

Gender-neutral drafting has been the norm for some years in many jurisdictions which use the English language to draft legislation. For United Kingdom statutes it is an innovation. The need to implement at short notice a ministerial decision to adopt gender-neutral drafting has occasioned consideration of a variety of techniques. This article explores the advantages and disadvantages of different techniques that can be adopted by drafters who are required (or who voluntarily determine) to abandon the practice of using masculine pronouns in reliance on the implicit inclusion of their feminine equivalent.

The UK History

In 1850 an 'Act for shortening the language used in Acts of Parliament'[2] enacted 'That in all Acts Words importing the Masculine Gender shall be deemed and taken to include Females, ... unless the contrary as to Gender ... is expressly provided' This provision has been replicated in the two Interpretation Acts since that time and still has effect.[3]

The earlier traditional practice was to use 'he or she' or something along those lines in any provisions which might reasonably be expected to apply both to males and females.[4] Of course, in those times in many official and commercial contexts

1 Views of the author are not necessarily those of the Government. This article draws on ideas discussed at a series of seminars on gender-neutral drafting held in the office of the Parliamentary Counsel, London in 2007. I am particularly grateful to Catherine Lister and Saira Salimi, both of that Office, for their comments and assistance.

2 See 13 and 14 Vict. c. XXI (10 June 1850) s IV.

3 Interpretation Act 1889 (c. 63), s 1(1)(a) 'words importing the masculine gender shall include females'; Interpretation Act 1978 (c. 30), s 6(a) 'words importing the masculine gender include the feminine' The 1978 Act introduced (s 6(b)) the reciprocal rule that 'words importing the feminine gender include the masculine', as recommended by the Law Commissions in Recommendation 2 of the Appendix to their Report on the Interpretation Bill, April 1978.

4 For examples, see Habeas Corpus – Imprisonment Act 1679 (31 Chas. 2 c. 2) s 15 'Provided also that if any person or persons ... shall have committed any capital offence in

it was reasonable for the statute to assume that only men would be concerned (however unreasonable it may have been for the social situation to be such as to support that assumption); and so one finds a number of places where 'he' is used alone without qualification, apparently on the basis of some such assumption.[5] (And indeed there were some contexts in which even a gender-neutral word would be construed as restricted to the male.)[6] Shortly before the passage of the 1850 Act the traditional approach had become modified to the extent that it had become common for individual Acts to include a specific interpretation provision of the kind that was eventually codified in the 1850 Act.[7]

From 1850 until 2007, Acts of the Westminster Parliament habitually relied on the general interpretation provision and used 'he', 'him' and 'his' with the intention of including reference to males and females (and, often, bodies corporate or unincorporate).[8] This practice was challenged from time to time, and with increasing frequency, in both Houses of Parliament, not on grounds of legal efficacy[9] but on grounds of taste, propriety and social policy.[10]

Scotland ... where he or she ought to be tried for such offence ...'; Gaming Act 1739 (12 Geo. 2 c. 28) s 5 'Provided always ... that if any person or persons shall think him or her or themselves aggrieved by the judgment or determination of any justice ...'; Ecclesiastical Corporation Lands Act 1832 (2 & 3 W. IV c. 80) s III '... it shall and may be lawful to and for the said Lessee or Lessees ... his, her or their Heirs ...'

5 There are, however, cases where one wonders whether any such assumption has been made or whether the use of the masculine gender alone was inadvertent: compare, for example, the opening and closing passages of section IV of the Half Pay Receipt Act 1832 (2 & 3 W. IV c. 106) the former of which includes express reference to the feminine and the latter of which does not.

6 The most obvious example being that of the franchise; so in *Nairn v University of St Andrews* [1909] AC 147 HL (Sc.) the House of Lords construed 'persons' as applying only to men, both despite the contrast with the express use of 'man' in earlier sections of the same Act and also despite the fact that Lord Loreburn LC agreed 'that the word "persons" would prima facie include women'(!); see also *Viscountess Rhondda's Claim* [1922] 2 AC 339 HL (E) Committee for Privileges.

7 For examples, the Indictable Offences (Ireland) Act 1849 (12 & 13 Vict. c. 69) s XXXIII 'That in the Interpretation of this Act, unless there be something in the Subject or Context repugnant to such Construction ... Words denoting a Male shall be deemed to include a Female also ...'; Cruelty to Animals Prevention Act 1849 (12 & 13 Vict. c. 92) s XXIX 'And, subject to the Context and to the Nature of the Subject Matter ... Words denoting the Masculine Gender are to be understood to apply also to Persons and Animals of the Feminine Gender.'

8 Interestingly, it was never thought necessary to provide that masculine pronouns included the neuter: but the word 'person' as used in Acts has, since the enactment of section 19 of the Interpretation Act 1889, included bodies corporate and unincorporate.

9 Although there were of course instances in relation to which it was unclear whether the inclusion of the other gender was intended or was rebutted by contrary intention: for an early interesting example, see *Chorlton v Lings* LR 4 CP 374, 388, in which J. Willes dismissed a claim to the franchise by a woman in reliance on 'man' as sought to be construed in accordance with the 1850 Act.

10 See, for example, the speech of Jean Corston MP on a motion for the introduction of a Bill 'to eliminate sexism in the language of future Acts of Parliament and other instruments'

The Government consistently resisted these challenges for many years.[11] The policy underlying this resistance was explained in a 'Written Answer' given to the House of Commons by the Prime Minister in 1998[12] in the following terms:

> The most important objectives in the language used in legislation are clarity and legal certainty. In general, the use of gender-specific language is not necessary to meet these objectives. But there are occasions when, for example, the use of gender-specific pronouns makes it possible for legislation to be expressed more simply, and so more clearly, than it otherwise could be. In these cases, section 6 of the Interpretation Act 1978 applies. It provides that, unless the contrary intention applies, words importing the masculine gender include the feminine, and vice versa.[13]

That remained the Government's policy until a change in 2007, announced in a Written Ministerial Statement made by the Leader of the House of Commons:[14]

> For many years the drafting of primary legislation has relied on section 6 of the Interpretation Act 1978, under which words referring to the masculine gender include the feminine. In practice this means that male pronouns are used on their own in contexts where a reference to women and men is intended, and also that words such as chairman are used for offices capable of being held by either gender. Many believe that this practice tends to reinforce historic gender stereotypes and presents an obstacle to clearer understanding for those unfamiliar with the convention.

– 'All legislation passed by Parliament is drafted in a form that assumes that the male gender defines humanity ... We cannot have actions that are equitable without language that is equitable. Language is the mirror of society. Women must be able to see themselves in that mirror.' HC Deb 9 May 1995 cc. 580–81; see also the Oral Question at HL Deb 29 June 1995 cc. 868–70 and the Adjournment Debate at HC Deb 20 January 2000 cc. 1094–100.

11 See, for example, HC Deb 14 July 1995 WA 833.

12 HC Deb 29 October 1998 WA 241.

13 The point is expanded slightly in a letter sent by the then First Parliamentary Counsel, Sir Christopher Jenkins KCB, QC to The Women's Unit on 18 September 1998, 'There is no technical reason why legislation should not be drafted in a way that avoids gender-specific pronouns ... The only reason why we continue to use these pronouns is that they seem to us to help in achieving simplicity, and therefore clarity and certainty (which is an essential feature of good legislation). Simplicity is always elusive, but one way of making progress towards it is to use words sparingly, omitting any that are unnecessary. The use of 'he or she' and other phrases to overcome the objection to the use of 'he' alone adds a complication which is bound on occasion to make the meaning of a provision less easy to ascertain. There will frequently be ways round the problem, such as the repetition of a noun or the use of the plural ... But it is inevitable that there will remain some occasions when a provision will be less simple, and therefore less clear, if the drafter has to take account of a factor aimed at other objections. One of the ways of avoiding the use of masculine pronouns without loss of simplicity would, of course, be to switch to using feminine pronouns instead. I do not know whether it would be regarded as unsatisfactory by all those who object to the present system, but from the drafter's point of view it would be equally effective.'

14 See HC Deb 8 March 2007 c. 146 WS.

> I have worked with colleagues in Government to secure agreement, that it would be right, where practicable, to avoid this practice in future and, accordingly, Parliamentary Counsel has been asked to adopt gender-neutral drafting.
>
> From the beginning of next Session, Government Bills will take a form which achieves gender-neutral drafting so far as it is practicable, at no more than a reasonable cost to brevity or intelligibility. This policy already applies to tax law rewrite Bills and is consistent with the practice in many other jurisdictions in the English-speaking world.
>
> The Government recognise that, in practice, Parliamentary Counsel will need to adopt a flexible approach to this change (for example, in at least some of the cases where existing legislation originally drafted in the former style is being amended).

There were doubtless a number of reasons that brought about this change of policy. Among them was presumably the fact that very few English language jurisdictions were still drafting in gender-specific terms,[15] and the Westminster Parliament appeared to be increasingly out of step not only with foreign Governments but even with other sources of legislation within the United Kingdom.[16]

The Basic Aim: Reducing the 'Cost' of Gender-neutrality

If the best practice in drafting involves the most flexible and creative use of all possible linguistic techniques, it is inevitable that any policy that denies the drafter the use of a particular technique carries a risk of reducing the simplicity, clarity or

15 Most of the largest English language jurisdictions adopted a gender-neutral policy some time ago (in some cases, but not all, adopting 'he or she' as an acceptable alternative) including New Zealand, Canada, Ireland, South Australia and South Africa. In New South Wales, for example, the move to a gender-neutral approach in legislative drafting was approved by the Attorney General in 1983. New Zealand adopted a formal gender-neutral policy in the mid-1980s at the direction of its Attorney General. And although there are still a small number of English language jurisdictions (such as Bermuda) that use gender-specific terminology, there is increasing resistance even at a legal or quasi-legal level towards the approach: note, for example, Recommendation No. R (90)4 adopted by the Committee of Ministers of the Council of Europe on 21 February 1990 'on the elimination of sexism from language, by bringing the terminology used in legal drafting and public administration into line with the principle of sex equality'. For an account of the history of gender-neutral drafting in different jurisdictions see Sandra Petersson, 'Gender-Neutral Drafting' 20 (1999) 1 *Statute Law Review* pp. 35–65.

16 In a paper entitled *Equality Strategy: Working together for Equality* published on 18 May 2005 the Scottish Executive wrote, 'The language of legislation is also an important signal of the Executive's commitment to greater equality. When drafting Acts of the Scottish Parliament and Scottish Statutory Instruments, the Executive will do so in gender neutral terms whenever practicable. It will not be possible to avoid gender specific terms completely where existing legislation, which has not been drafted in gender neutral form, is being amended, but these will be kept to a minimum.' And the Tax Law Rewrite Project announced in its Annual Plan 2004–05 the intention to 'attempt to achieve gender neutral drafting so far as it is practicable to do so at reasonable cost to brevity and intelligibility': in fact, the products of that project have been almost entirely gender-neutral.

elegance of the final product. That would be true of any policy, but it is especially so of a policy that seriously constrains the use of pronouns, which are probably the part of speech most used in vernacular communication for improving the flow and conciseness of both spoken and written statements.

So ministers and others must start by accepting that there will inevitably be a cost of implementing the policy of gender-neutral drafting.[17] It is, of course, for politicians to determine, as they have in this case, that the cost is worth incurring in order to secure the social benefit conferred (or to reduce the social disadvantage imposed on women by masculine legislative drafting). That accepted, it becomes the job of the drafter to set about implementing the policy in a way that limits the damage as much as possible.

Ideally, however, drafters can approach a new requirement to draft in gender-neutral style in a more positive spirit than seeing its implementation only as an exercise in damage limitation. Anything that causes us to overhaul our drafting techniques, and that challenges our ingrained habits, is capable of being seen as an opportunity for rejuvenation and improvement. That must be welcome in the environment of legislative drafting, in which considerable reliance on precedent is inevitable and often desirable, a factor which inevitably introduces a resistance to change into legislative language and makes it prone to archaism.[18] So one of the purposes of this article is to discuss whether certain of the techniques used to implement gender-neutral drafting can result in a product that is better than what one had before, not merely as little worse as possible.

Repetition

Manuals on legislative drafting which deal with gender-neutrality often offer repetition as the standard way of dealing with the problem.[19] It is of course the most obvious way of avoiding 'he' in 'The Secretary of State may collect snurkles if he thinks ...' to opt for 'The Secretary of State may collect snurkles if the Secretary of

---

17 In which context it is interesting to note that the original provision allowing masculine pronouns to be used on the implicit assumption of the feminine was part of an Act 'for shortening the language used in Acts of Parliament'; making it clear that any policy which, in effect, determines not to rely on that provision, is likely to lengthen Acts, however marginally.

18 Not all of which is necessarily undesirable, of course: see, for example, D. Greenberg and M.J. Goodman (eds), *Craies on Legislation*, 8th edn. (London: Sweet and Maxwell, 2004) para. 8.1.9 'Useful Legal Archaisms'.

19 See, for example, First Parliamentary Counsel, *Drafting Direction No. 2.1*, 1 May 2006, Australian Government (www.opc.gov.au/about/drafting_series/DD%202.1.pdf -) 'A masculine personal pronoun in a Bill must always be accompanied by a feminine personal pronoun (and vice versa) except in the very rare case of legislation intended to apply to people of one sex but not the other (e.g. maternity leave legislation). Drafters should use their discretion in deciding, in individual cases, whether it would be better to avoid the use of pronouns altogether by repeating the relevant noun instead.'; or the *Texas Legislative Council Drafting Manual*, c. 7, Style and Usage, para. 7.26, accessed online at (www.tlc.state.tx.us/legal/dm/sec726.htm).

State thinks ...' And it is a reasonably familiar technique for drafters and readers alike, as we have been adopting for a long time in sentences containing two actors, 'The Secretary of State may confiscate a person's hippopotamus if the Secretary of State thinks ...'[20]

As well as being the most obvious technique, however, repetition is also necessarily the one that tends to produce the longest drafts, and those that are the most dissonant for the reader.

In the traditional use of repetition, as described above, to avoid ambiguity in a sentence with two actors, we have always accepted dissonance as the reasonable price of clarity, reminding ourselves that we are writing law not poetry and that certainty must always be preferred to elegance or brevity.[21] The potential for ambiguity in the vernacular use of pronouns has been a concern long before the advent of gender-neutral drafting, and repetition was always encouraged as an obvious method of avoiding doubt. An early writer on legislative drafting, and to this day one of the most authoritative, Sir Alison Russell, wrote as follows:[22]

> If any conceivable ambiguity is caused by the use of a pronoun, 'he', 'him' or 'his', the noun to which it refers should be repeated. A draftsman should never be afraid of repeating a word as often as may be necessary in order to avoid ambiguity.[23]

Despite the dissonance of repetition, it is the most certainly effective technique, and it also requires no structural readjustment. It is therefore regarded by some as the first port of call in the search for gender-neutrality. It is, however, better seen as a necessary last resort where one has failed to find a more brief and elegant, but equally unambiguous solution.

Omission

The first alternative to repetition which the drafter may wish to consider is simple omission. The imposition of a requirement of gender-neutrality and the consequent reconsideration of drafting techniques have shown many of us, who thought we were already drafting in as plain and simple English as possible, that we were still

20 Although, of course, a useful way of making that proposition more elegant and concise – 'If the Secretary of State thinks ... he may confiscate a person's hippopotamus' – will no longer be available in the gender-neutral regime.

21 'Repetition of the same word is never a fault in business composition, if an ambiguity is thereby avoided.' Lord H. Thring KCB, *Practical Legislation* (London: John Murray, 1902) at 82.

22 See Sir A. Russell, *Legislative Drafting and Forms*, 4th edn (London: Butterworths, 1938) at 103.

23 This is also very much in line with the important statement of the '*Renton Report*', *The Preparation of Legislation*, Cmnd 6053, May 1975, para. 11.5 – 'On the other hand, the draftsman must never be forced to sacrifice certainty for simplicity, since the result may be to frustrate the legislative intention. An unfortunate subject may be driven to litigation because the meaning of an Act was obscure which could, by the use of a few extra words, have been made plain.'

including a number of superfluities. For example, a search for the phrase 'due from him' in UK statutes presently in force revealed 120 instances of the expression: in none of them do the words 'from him' appear to add anything to the meaning (or at least nothing that could not instantly be supplied by the reader's sense without distracting from the flow of the provision). They are inserted because they complete the thought at little or no cost to the flow of the provision: but once the cost would be expanded by a requirement to repeat the noun, they would more conveniently be simply dispensed with.

UK statutes regularly include redundancies that could be eliminated by a more rigorous reliance on the application of a naturally contextual construction, an approach with which the UK courts have neither theoretical nor practical difficulty.[24] Although these redundancies are generally individually small, the collective effect of their omission could be significant not only on the length of statutes but also on the ease with which the reader absorbs them. And there is now a particular reason to omit those, like 'due from him', that include a personal pronoun and would therefore now require to include repetition of the noun.

Nor are all common redundancies in legislative drafting so small in their individual effect. One of the most welcome casualties of the technique of omission with particular reference to gender-neutral drafting would be phrases of the kind 'if he thinks fit'. I remember the glee with which I heard my overbearing pupil–master rebuffed by a Deputy High Court Judge, to whom he was rather condescendingly dictating the terms of an order which we were seeking during the recess, and which he finished with a self-satisfied flourish of 'the court deeming it fit so to order' 'Mr X,' came the snapped response of a judge who, however junior and temporary, had finally determined to put up with no more bullying from Counsel, however senior and successful, 'I have no intention at all of saying that – it adds absolutely nothing – if I didn't think it fit to make the order, I wouldn't make it, would I?' Flourishes of this kind abound in legislative drafting as in commercial drafting, and are usefully excised not only for reasons of gender-neutrality but for reasons of simplicity. They add nothing and, however elegant or euphonious they may appear on their own (which like all matters of taste is debatable), the product overall is undoubtedly improved by their omission.

So, 'If the Lord Chancellor thinks fit to do so, having regard to such matters as he thinks appropriate, he may appoint a Chief Snurkle-Boggler' becomes simply 'The Lord Chancellor may appoint a Chief Snurkle-Boggler'; and nothing is lost (except possibly the snurkle).

Similarly 'If a person is aggrieved by a decision of the Referee of Snurkle-Boggling he may appeal against it to the High Court' can become simply 'A person may appeal to the High Court against a decision of the Referee of Snurkle-Boggling.' To paraphrase the Deputy Judge in the anecdote above, if people were not aggrieved

---

24 See D. Greenberg, 'All Trains Stop at Crewe: the Rise and Rise of Contextual Drafting' *European Journal of Law Reform* 7 (2005) 1/2 pp. 31–46.

it can be presumed that they would not wish to appeal, and if they seek to appeal it can reasonably be inferred that they must be aggrieved.[25]

Reorganisation

Omission will, of course, help only to a limited extent, and an attempt to avoid gender-specific pronouns without either omitting necessary material or resorting to lengthy and inelegant repetition is likely to begin by considering various ways of reorganising the sentence in order to dispense with pronouns. Changing a proposition from the active voice to the passive can be a neat way of gender-neutralising a proposition, in certain cases. So, for example:

> Where a person gives a notice to the Chief Snurkle-Boggler on a Tuesday, he[26] must give the notice on pink paper and by pigeon post.

could become:

> A notice given to the Chief Snurkle-Boggler on a Tuesday must be given on pink paper and by pigeon post.

Traditionally, those training legislative drafters exhorted them to use the active voice in preference to the passive wherever reasonably possible, on the grounds that the

---

25 It might be objected that the reference to being aggrieved is a restriction of the right of appeal to those who are properly aggrieved by it, in the sense of being affected by it (see the cases construing the term as an applied restriction set out in: J. Burke, P. Allsop, Stroud, *Stroud's Judicial Dictionary*, 7th edn (London: Sweet and Maxwell, 2006) pp. 88–90. Those cases show, however, that the concept of being aggrieved is uncertain in most contexts, and where the policy is to restrict a right of appeal to a certain class it will generally be both possible and necessary to describe the concept more helpfully than by this rather outdated expression; see, for example, section 206 of the Gambling Act 2005 (c. 19). In the case of an appeal from a decision of a court or tribunal, the intended restriction will often be to parties to the original decision, in which case it can be stated more clearly and simply by saying, 'A party to proceedings before ... may appeal'; or it may be thought appropriate to state the right of appeal without any restriction in reliance on the fact that an appeal is unlikely to be brought by someone without a sufficient interest or, if it were brought, is likely to be dismissed swiftly. Incidentally, the form used in Article 230 of the Treaty establishing the European Community is, 'Any natural or legal person may, under the same conditions, institute proceedings against a decision addressed to that person or against a decision which, although in the form of a regulation or a decision addressed to another person, is of direct and individual concern to the former.' That seems wide but reasonably clear and helpful.

26 A purist (for which read tiresome pedant) might argue that there is a technical ambiguity here which would in any event prevent the use of the personal pronoun: it takes, however, not so much a contextual construction as a modicum of common sense to conclude that any construction of 'he' as referring to the Chief Snurkle-Boggler would be perverse and can therefore safely be ignored (and therefore should be ignored in the interests of brevity and clarity).

active is normally shorter and slightly simpler.[27] That traditional approach will now have to be qualified by the observation that where gender-neutrality would otherwise require a repetition or other relatively cumbersome structure, the passive may be an acceptable resort amounting to the lesser of two evils. Interestingly, that is precisely how the point is put in a document relating to one of the UK legislatures that led the way in gender-neutral drafting within the UK.[28]

Another form of syntactic reorganisation that avoids the use of gender-specific personal pronouns involves the use of the relative pronoun. So, 'A person who drives on the pavement commits an offence' is an entirely acceptable (and in some senses preferable) replacement for, 'A person commits an offence if he drives on the pavement.'

This is certainly a profitable technique for gender-neutral drafters, but it has its limitations. In particular, it works very well in a short proposition, but much less well in a long proposition with subordinate clauses. So, for example, 'A person commits an offence if he drives on the pavement on a Tuesday while he has a hippopotamus in the back of his car' is relatively easy to assimilate, because one part of the story has been told in its entirety (a person commits an offence) before the sentence proceeds to list the conditions precedent. This does not translate so easily into a proposition beginning, 'A person who ...' because the reader is launched into the list of conditions without knowing what they are conditions for, and is let down with a bump by the abrupt 'commits an offence' at the end: a significant loss not merely of elegance but of clarity and ease of absorption.

Reorganising propositions by dividing them into a number of shorter sentences can lessen, or at least disguise, the inelegance of repetition or of the use of the relative pronoun. And this is a popular and attractive technique because there is general consensus that shorter sentences are to be preferred in legislative drafting. But as with all techniques this too has its limitations. A staccato series of short sentences can be longer and less pleasing than a single sentence which develops a single story intuitively, and through which the subordinate clauses flow so naturally as to aid rather than impede rapid comprehension. As with all legislative techniques, no rule of thumb is helpful in determining the proper limits of abbreviation: a drafter who is driven not by dogma but by the desire to present the material clearly and simply will be able to spot those occasions on which the division of a thought into separate sentences obstructs comprehension rather than assisting it.

---

27 See, for example, G.C. Thornton, *Legislative Drafting*, 4th edn (London: Butterworth, 1996) at 60, 'The advantage of the active voice is that the subject of the sentence names the performer of the action stated in the verb. The passive form either omits, or reduces the emphasis on, the person performing the action ... Expression in the passive voice may lead to a lack of directness.'

28 See The Scottish Executive, *Plain Language and Legislation*, accessed online from 2006 (www.scotland.gov.uk/Publications/2006/02/17093804/4).

Alternative Pronouns

Since reorganising the statutory material to avoid a pronoun will sometimes result in a displeasing or less pleasing product, the drafter must at least consider the possibility of using alternative pronouns which are acceptably gender-neutral and which do not interfere, or not so much, with the optimal drafting structure.

For example, some people have suggested that in order to facilitate gender-neutral drafting the word 'they' should become an honorary singular pronoun (but still taking a plural verb form). As in:

> A person may submit an application only if they think ...

Most people regard this as abhorrent both on grounds of being incorrect grammar and also on grounds of euphony; while some who do not especially revile the idea simply do not accept that it is likely to command widespread acceptance.[29] Whatever one may wish to say about correct usage, it is certainly true that in vernacular conversation the word 'they' is used in precisely this way frequently (perhaps with such increasing frequency that its grammatical incorrectness is already debatable and will sooner or later become unarguable).

The strongest objection to this technique at present, however, is that, although it is used considerably in the vernacular, as a rule it is used most naturally and unaffectedly in the kind of long and rambling sentence in which 'they' sounds natural only because one cannot remember who the subject was. A sentence of that kind has no place in legislative drafting, and in any event the technique becomes less comfortable when the sentence is written down, because the eye is drawn back to discover that the subject was singular. That explains why the technique is used frequently in conversation but much less frequently in writing.

It is, however, both possible and entirely unobjectionable to make greater use of the plural pronoun if one makes greater use of plural nouns. There is nothing wrong with the following:

> Persons may submit applications only if they think ...[30]

The possibility of this solution requires an examination of the reason why traditional advice to drafters has been to draft in the singular in preference to the plural, and to rely on section 6(c) of the Interpretation Act 1978 for implied inclusion of the plural. The preference may have something to do with simplicity, but there is also a

---

29 See, for example, P.T. O'Conner, 'Speech Crimes' *New York Times*, Sunday Book Review, 11 March 2007 – 'Much as I admire both Crystal and Yagoda, I can't believe the singular 'they' will become accepted in educated writing in our lifetime. Of course, I could be wrong. In the words of Fats Waller, "One never knows, do one?"'

30 Perhaps one should even throw caution to the winds, along the lines of regarding gender-neutrality as an inspiration to greater simplification and improvement of legislative language, and recognise that the vernacular has a simple plural for the word 'person' that grates less against most people's ears than does 'persons' – 'People may submit applications only if they think ...'

point of construction at issue. If it is against the law to hunt one fox with one dog, it will certainly be against the law to hunt two foxes with two dogs. But the fact that Parliament have seen fit to prohibit the hunting of foxes with 'dogs' does not necessarily mean, in the known context of a law aimed at preventing traditional fox-hunting packs, that it was intended also to prohibit the use of a single dog in hunting. The presumption in section 6(c) of the Interpretation Act 1978 is rebuttable by the appearance of contrary intention, it being possible to conceive of reasons why Parliament would accept the need to allow a gamekeeper to use a single dog while banning the use of packs.[31]

So in adopting the plural in order to found an unobjectionable gender-neutral use of 'they' the drafter will have to exercise caution to avoid an indication contrary to the application of section 6(c) of the Interpretation Act 1978. That said, it is likely that in the vast majority of cases it will be sufficiently clear that there is no reason why the singular should not be implied: and the point will of course become increasingly safe if and when it becomes more normal, for reasons of gender-neutrality, to find provisions drafted in the plural.

There being no rules of good drafting other than the rule that there are no rules of good drafting, it is impossible to ignore entirely the possibility that the use of 'he or she' will sometimes provide the most appropriate solution to gender-neutral drafting, requiring no restructuring at all. There are, however, a number of objections to this technique.

First, we have fallen into the comfortable habit of using the masculine personal pronoun in relation to a 'person' despite the fact that Schedule 1 to the Interpretation Act 1978 defines a person as including 'a body of persons corporate or unincorporate'.[32] We say 'a person who wishes a licence to sell snurkles must satisfy the Chief Snurkle-Boggler that he has taken all reasonable steps to ensure the safety of snurkles at the hands of the purchaser', without worrying that the vendor will in the vast majority of cases be a body corporate. But the possibility of 'he or she' as a relatively brief and simple alternative to 'he' on its own recalls one to the need to reflect the possibility of corporate and unincorporate persons: and '... must satisfy the Chief Snurkle-Boggler that he, she, it or they has or have taken ...' would be substantively baffling and stylistically repulsive. So 'he or she' will be available only in the comparatively rare case of provisions directed exclusively to individuals.

Second, 'he or she' may be a relatively brief way of avoiding causing offence, but it introduces a minor additional complexity into the sentence, whereas some of the other methods discussed above and below are capable of presenting the proposition in gender-neutral form without at all reducing the ease of flow of the language.

Third, 'he or she' is, of course, strictly speaking not gender-neutral at all, but merely inclusive of both genders; as such, sooner or later its widespread use would be likely to prompt the objection that it puts the masculine routinely before the feminine and is therefore, in its own way, as offensive as the practice of relying on

---

31 Indeed, some of the exemptions in Schedule 1 to the Hunting Act 2004 (c. 37) refer to the number of dogs used.

32 Slightly confusingly, given that the latter does not for general legal purposes have personality.

'he' alone. The use of 'he or she' might avoid that objection, but it might be thought artificial and, therefore, offensively patronising. One could try to alternate 'he or she' and 'she or he', but the result would be confusing and inelegant (even without taking into account the complexities of applying the rule to textual amendments).

It is not impossible that there might be occasions on which the word 'one' could be used to replace a gender-specific pronoun. But a sentence such as, 'When one submits one's tax return one must ensure that the details of one's name and address are given prominently' would nowadays be thought a little forced and precious in conversation; and it will anyway be rare for a legislative proposition to be able to operate entirely in the abstract without specifying the subject more precisely. Moreover, once the drafter has mentioned the subject expressly – as in, 'A person may not ...' – it becomes unacceptably strained to continue by reference to 'one'.

In commercial contexts considerable advances have been made in the use of plain English by the use of second-person drafting. Consumer contracts are frequently drafted nowadays by way of addressing the consumer as 'you', generally with great advantage of clarity. This technique has not escaped the notice of the legislative drafter, and a number have toyed with the idea of using it; in general, however, it has not been received with enthusiasm.[33]

Although use of the technique may be worth additional consideration on the grounds that its utility in the cause of gender-neutrality is obvious, it is unlikely that it will ever be appropriate to use the technique widely. It is rare that provisions of legislation are addressed to a single class of person; a proposition about directors' liability, for example, is not addressed exclusively to the directors, but has such critical implications for the behaviour and situation of others that it cannot sensibly be seen merely as an instruction to directors, but as a statement addressed to the public generally about the effect of certain things done or not done by directors.

Tagging

A technique that has been used long before the advent of gender-neutral drafting as a way of avoiding an unhelpful degree of repetition is the assignment to a noun of a tag that can then be used for the rest of the provision or enactment to refer to the noun without either repeating it or substituting a pronoun. This is an effective technique which, while like all techniques it has its limitations, can result in a pleasing product that is relatively easy for the reader to absorb.

33 For example, the Tax Law Rewrite Project canvassed views on second-person drafting in a consultation document in 1996 and found, '3.9 there was less agreement on the use of second-person drafting. Most respondents found the examples we published in October attractive, but they were concerned that second-person drafting will not work in certain areas, such as where legislation addresses more than one taxpayer or where the taxpayer is not an individual. Some were prepared to accept second-person drafting where it works and third-person drafting where it does not. But most would prefer a consistent approac. We accept that mixing the drafting style in this way will not be helpful and our current intention is not to use second-person drafting in any part of the rewrite.' – *Plans for 1997*, c. 3.

There are a number of different kinds of tag that can be used. In particular, the drafter has to choose between tags consisting of whole words and tags consisting merely of letters. There is much to be said for each, in its place.

As a rule, the use of a whole word as a tag helps the sense to flow through the proposition to a degree that is not attainable with letters alone: a proposition about what A does to B in the presence of C becomes difficult to follow after the fifth mention of C, requiring constant reference back to the place where the tag C was assigned. Whereas a short tag can preserve the meaning of the noun which it replaces: as in, '(1) This section applies where a property–investment partnership ("the vendor") disposes of land to a partnership ("the purchaser") which has a principal place of business in the United Kingdom. (2) The vendor …' In some cases the tag can even add useful flavour to the provision as a whole:[34] but the drafter needs to be sure not to use a tag which has such a pronounced flavour that it might be used by the courts to influence the construction of the provision in some unintended way.[35]

Single letter tags can be perfectly intuitive in some contexts, and can even have the advantage of more closely matching the practice of the outside professional world in their use of examples: so, in a provision about stamp duty land tax the use of P and V to connote purchaser and vendor is sufficiently intuitive not to disrupt the reader's flow of comprehension at all, and will actually advance it for a professional who is thoroughly used to expounding points by reference to P and V. And single letter tags assist euphony more than do whole word tags: for example, 'P must resign if P …' is considerably less clumsy to read than, 'A person must resign if the person'

A Technical Afterthought: Interpretation Act 1978, s 6(a) and (b)

Section 6(a) and (b) of the Interpretation Act 1978 read as follows:

> In any Act, unless the contrary intention appears,–
> (a) words importing the masculine gender include the feminine;
> (b) words importing the feminine gender include the masculine;

Are these provisions still required in a gender-neutral drafting world, and can their continued existence actually cause harm? The answer to some extent depends on whether statutory instruments come to be written wholly in gender-neutral form: since section 6 of the 1978 Act applies to them,[36] it will continue to have importance while they continue to be drafted using gender-specific masculine pronouns in reliance on section 6. And it will certainly continue to be required for the construction of pre-2007 Acts.

---

34 See, for example, the use of the tag 'foreign criminal' in the automatic deportation provisions of the UK Borders Act 2007.

35 For example, the Texas manual cited above suggests, 'A judge may not lend the prestige of *judicial* (rather than "his") office to private interests': but there is nothing neutral about the tag 'judicial' inserted in place of the pronoun, and it could be relied upon either as widening or narrowing the proposition.

36 By virtue of section 23.

While it might be tempting to leave section 6(a) and (b) alone so that they can apply to new Acts to cope with occasional cases of inadvertence, it must be very doubtful whether in a gender-neutral drafting world a slip would not be bound to be construed by the courts as amounting to a contrary indication. Once 'he' or 'his' is no longer used routinely, having been abandoned in accordance with a public Ministerial pronouncement, it would be very difficult to argue that the drafter had not used it deliberately as intending a gender-specific reference. At least, that would certainly be so in a case where a respectable argument could be mounted that only men (or only women) were meant: and in the majority of cases, where no such argument were possible and the gender-specificity were an obvious error, section 6(a) and (b) would add nothing to the court's ability[37] to rectify obvious drafting errors.[38]

Conclusion

In common with other technical artists, legislative drafters are able to deliver whatever the customer requires. Our Ministerial customers now require gender-neutral legislation, and we will certainly be able to deliver it. It comes with a price of a slight loss of simplicity and elegance, but we will do what we can to keep the price to the minimum; and that will require a flexible consideration of all the techniques, discussed above, in order to find the best tool for the job on each occasion.

37 For a recent example, see *R (Crown Prosecution Service) v Bow Street Magistrates' Court* [2006] EWHC 1763 (Admin).

38 Consistently with this approach, the New Zealand Interpretation Act 1999 restricts its provision deeming the masculine to include the feminine (s 31) to 'enactments passed or made before commencement of this Act' in reliance on the by then firmly established practice of gender-neutral drafting for new Acts.

Chapter 6

Drafting Legislation at the Tax Law Rewrite Project

Hayley Rogers[1]

Background to the Tax Law Rewrite Project

The Tax Law Rewrite project (TLR) is part of HM Revenue and Customs (formerly the Inland Revenue). It was established in 1996 in response to a growing unease among tax professionals at the ever increasing complexity of UK tax law. The project was originally set up as a tax *simplification* project, but it soon became clear that in order for the project to stand a realistic chance of making progress it needed to focus on rewriting tax law rather than simplifying it. The gains from rewriting the law (in terms of making it clearer and easier to understand for users) were viewed as of value in themselves.

TLR now expresses its overall aim as, 'to rewrite primary direct tax legislation to make it clearer and easier to use, without changing the law'. The main features of TLR, its achievements to date, and its future plans, are set out in more detail in its annual Report and Plans document (*Report and Plans 2008/09*, published May 2008 and available at www.hmrc.gov.uk/rewrite). I discuss the approach and techniques used in rewriting tax law in more depth below. Before I do so it is worth saying a little about how TLR works.

The Project Team at TLR

There are around 30 full-time members of the team at TLR. Team members come from a variety of backgrounds. Some are from different parts of HM Revenue and Customs. Others are recruited from the private sector, with experience in aspects of the wider tax profession. The team includes parliamentary drafters. These are either on secondment from the Office of the Parliamentary Counsel in Whitehall or are former members of that office. I led the drafting team within TLR from April 2005 to March 2007. The diversity of the TLR team, and the fact that the drafters are very much part of the team, is viewed as one of the strengths of TLR.

1 This chapter was written by Hayley Rogers of the Office of the Parliamentary Counsel. It is published with the permission of the Controller of HMSO and the Queen's Printer for Scotland.

The TLR Committees

TLR is overseen by a Steering Committee, which provides strategic guidance and monitors the work undertaken. The Steering Committee brings together a wide range of talents and experience. Its members are drawn from both Houses of Parliament, the judiciary, the legal and accountancy professions, consumer and business interests. The Steering Committee is currently chaired by Lord Newton of Braintree. There is also a standing Consultative Committee, with members drawn from the legal, tax and accountancy professions, whose role is to ensure continuous consultation on the rewritten law. The Consultative Committee is chaired by the TLR Project Director.

The Consultation Process

Underpinning the work of TLR is the process of consultation on the rewritten law. When a batch of draft clauses has been prepared within TLR, the normal process is for them to be published on its website with a commentary which explains the existing law from which they are derived, the approach taken to rewriting the existing law and (in some instances) proposes minor changes to the law. Comments are invited by the end of a specified period (usually 12 weeks). The clauses may then need to be revised in the light of comments received. The revised versions are then published again, in the context of a draft Bill which pulls together published clauses on a number of topics. Following a further 12-week consultation period the Bill's provisions will be further revised, with a view to getting the Bill ready for introduction into Parliament. This process is supplemented on occasion by consultation on particular topics with specialist groups. This took place, for example, in connection with rewritten clauses on life insurance gains and tax relief for venture capital investments. The consultation process is of vital importance to TLR. It means that by the time clauses appear in a Bill, they will normally have been the subject of critical analysis by a range of tax professionals on at least two occasions.

The Parliamentary Process

TLR Bills are the subject of a special expedited parliamentary process, similar to that which applies for consolidation Bills. The justification for this process is the fact that TLR Bills (unlike the annual Finance Bill) do not change the law, except in minor identified respects, and have been the subject of extensive prior consultation.

Under this process, a TLR Bill is introduced into the House of Commons. Its second reading is taken in a Second Reading Committee rather than on the floor of the House of Commons. It is then committed to a Joint Committee of both Houses. The committee calls witnesses (including members of TLR) and looks in particular at whether the Bill rewrites the existing law without making changes, except those identified. It also examines the changes to ensure that they are not so substantial that they ought to be effected in a Finance Bill in the usual way.

Changes in the Law

As stated above, the remit of TLR is to rewrite existing tax law to make it clearer and easier to use, without changing its effect. Often the most difficult aspect of rewriting a provision in a way that makes it clearer for users is to ensure that, in doing so, its effect has not been changed inadvertently. A concern that was often expressed in the early days of TLR was that, in changing the words of a provision, or even the way it was laid out, TLR would inevitably produce a different legal effect. TLR has taken this risk seriously. Rewritten provisions are carefully analysed to try to ensure that, so far as possible, the law is not changed inadvertently. TLR relies on consultees who are experienced in working with a particular area of existing tax law to examine the rewritten version to check that changes have not crept in.

That said, each TLR Bill has included a number of changes in the law identified as such. For the Bill that became the Income Tax Act 2007 ('ITA 2007'), these are set out in Annex 1 to the Explanatory Notes. The aim of these changes is normally to bring consistency or clarification to the language of the rewritten law, or to bring the law into line with established practice. Where a change is proposed, its effect is examined within TLR to see if it could have an adverse effect on taxpayers (by leading to a potential increase in tax liability). The TLR Committees, and the Joint Committee on Tax Law Rewrite Bills, take particular interest in these 'taxpayer-adverse' changes to see whether they can be justified. If a change is likely to make a real difference to someone's tax liability the committees would be likely to take the view that it should be effected by means of a provision in a Finance Bill, so that it is subject to the usual scrutiny to which the House of Commons subjects changes in taxation.

Drafting Approach and Techniques

The approach and techniques used in rewriting legislation at TLR have developed with each Bill produced. The aim of all the techniques used is to make the legislation clearer and easier for readers to understand, while still maintaining the technical effect of the original legislation.

Structure

Tax legislation has developed in a piecemeal fashion over the last 200 years. From time to time it has been consolidated. Before TLR Bills started to be enacted, the last major consolidation of the legislation on income tax and corporation tax was the Income and Corporation Taxes Act 1988 ('ICTA 1988'). That Act has been substantially amended by subsequent Finance Acts. In addition, some Finance Acts have made provision on particular topics, not by means of amending the consolidation Act, but by means of free-standing provision. As loopholes or new cases have emerged in particular areas, further amendments have been made to address them.

All this has made the structure of tax law very complex. So the first job in rewriting an area of tax law has been to take an overview of the topics involved and try to arrange them in a more logical order, grouping similar rules together and making an attempt to tell the 'story' of how tax liability is calculated. This high-level restructuring is a key respect in which TLR Bills can make tax law clearer and easier to understand.

An early decision on the structure of the rewritten legislation was to split income tax and corporation tax and deal with them in separate Bills. ICTA 1988 reflected the development of the two taxes. Corporation tax was introduced in 1965 and applies many of the calculation rules used for income tax. So the provisions about the two taxes were intertwined in ICTA 1988, with some provisions applying to both taxes (even if expressed only in terms of income tax).

In rewriting the provisions about income tax, it was felt that it would be clearer for users if the corporation tax rules were addressed separately. When this approach has been fully worked through (following the rewrite of both the income tax and corporation tax provisions in separate Acts) the rewritten legislation on income tax and corporation tax will be considerably longer than it was before the rewrite process began, as many of the corporation tax provisions will repeat those for income tax. The view has been that the increased length will be more than outweighed by the gains in clarity.

Once the decision had been made to separate income tax and corporation tax, the next decision on structure related to the division of material between Bills. It was felt that the income tax rules about tax on earnings and pensions were of relevance to the greatest number of taxpayers and so they were rewritten first. The Bill containing this material became the Income Tax (Earnings and Pensions) Act 2003. The next severable group of rules were those relating to income tax on income from trades, property rentals and other types of income. The Bill containing these rules became the Income Tax (Trading and Other Income) Act 2005 ('ITTOIA 2005'). The third Bill on income tax was used to cover the rules on the rates at which income tax is charged, the calculation of income tax, a variety of relieving provisions (such as the rules about relief for losses) and administrative rules about the deduction of income tax at source. This Bill became ITA 2007. It is intended to rewrite corporation tax in two Bills, the first of which was published in draft in February 2008.

There are also benefits to be gained in terms of increased clarity in the way provisions are structured within Bills. This might involve, for example, grouping together all the rules about calculating trade profits. This was done in Part 2 of ITTOIA 2005. Within a Part, rules which do similar things can be grouped together. For example, Chapter 4 of Part 2 of ITTOIA 2005 groups together rules restricting a deduction from being made in the calculation of trade profits.

Drafting Style

There is no single style that is suited to rewriting all tax legislation. As with any legislative drafting, it is a question of expressing propositions in a clear and logical way. How that is achieved will differ depending on the nature of the proposition that needs to be expressed. Some tax law is extremely complex and so, however clearly the propositions about it are expressed, users may still take some time to understand how it works. There are, though, a few fairly straightforward principles that can help achieve TLR's aim of legislation that is clearer and easier to understand.

Modern Language

Some tax law is very old. The original provisions about income tax can be traced back to the early part of the nineteenth century. The language used reflects that in some instances. Even more recently drafted provisions often use language that is no longer in everyday use. At TLR, the aim is to use clear colloquial English where possible and avoid archaic language. Obvious archaisms are words such as 'hereunto', 'hereinbefore' and 'aforesaid' Other apparently archaic expressions have, however, been the subject of judicial interpretation and so to replace them would risk changing the law. In such cases, TLR retains the original expressions. An example might be a reference to a '*donatio mortis causa*' This expression appears in section 472(4)(a) of ITA 2007.

Shorter Clauses and Sentences

The piecemeal development of tax law, with layers of refinement and special provision added to sections by successive Finance Acts, has resulted in some very long sections. Within a section, individual subsections are sometimes so long as to be almost impenetrable on a first reading. One of the main benefits that can be achieved on a rewrite is to break up long sections (sometimes into as many as four or five new clauses) and at the same time to split long subsections (for example, by replacing a single subsection with two or three new subsections or by paragraphing material within a subsection).

Formulas and Method Statements

By its nature, much tax law turns on the calculation of particular amounts. This can lead to difficulties, as traditionally words have been used to describe the calculation that is required to be made. Tax professionals, such as accountants, often find it easier to understand a calculation that is expressed as a formula, rather than solely in words. So sometimes TLR has used a formula to replace or supplement some of the words of an existing provision. Some calculations involve taking steps in a particular order. To convey this, an alternative to a formula is to use what is known at TLR as a 'method statement'. Rather like the 'method' set out for a recipe, this involves breaking down a calculation into a series of 'steps', which are then set out in order. An example of this is section 23 of ITA 2007, which sets out the steps to be taken in calculating a taxpayer's liability to income tax for a tax year.

Definitions

An aspect of existing tax law which is prone to cause confusion among users is the use of different terms to mean the same thing (or very nearly the same thing). TLR Bills try to use a single term consistently, so far as is possible. This may occasionally give rise to a minor change in the law, but the gain in terms of ease of understanding for users is normally seen as making such changes worthwhile. An example in ITA 2007 is the use of the term 'repo' in Part 11. 'Repo' (defined in section 569 of ITA 2007) is used instead of terms such as 'sale and repurchase arrangement' or 'sale and repurchase agreement' which appear in the legislation from which Part 11 is derived.

TLR Bills also try to use informative definitions and labels, so far as possible. Tax law often uses labels such as the 'relevant amount' or 'relevant period' which, on their own, do not convey a flavour of why an amount or period is likely to be relevant. It is sometimes possible to replace these with labels, such as 'relievable amount' or 'holding period', which give a more immediate indication of their likely meaning.

Signposts and Overviews

Tax law is very long. The three rewritten Acts on income tax together contain more than 2,500 sections. However clear the structure of these Acts, it is difficult for users to be aware of other provisions that might be relevant, or to have an overview of how the provisions fit together.

TLR Bills therefore contain provisions which point readers to other related provisions (both in the same Bill and in other Acts). These provisions are known as 'signposts' They are popular among consultees but there are risks attached to their use. A 'signpost' provision needs to make clear that it is not operative law. For example, a provision which says, 'Relief for expenditure within this section may also be granted under section x' could be read as conferring entitlement to relief under section x. That might give rise to confusion, because relief under section x might depend on a further range of conditions being satisfied. A signpost which says something like, 'Section x also makes provision about relief for expenditure within this section' is sometimes preferable, in that it is more obvious that it merely points to another provision but is not itself conferring entitlement to relief.

A further risk with the use of signposts is that a signpost has the potential to mislead if the provision or provisions signposted are not the only ones that are relevant. It is not always easy to be sure that a list of signposted provisions is exhaustive – and the alternative of having a 'sweep-up' signpost referring to other (unidentified) provisions is not particularly helpful to readers.

Within a TLR Bill, it is viewed as helpful to give readers a 'bird's-eye view' of the provisions of a particular Bill. An example is section 2 of ITA 2007, which lists the Parts into which the Act is divided. In the case of ITA 2007 (which completed the work of TLR on income tax), it was also viewed as useful to give an overview of the main Acts which made provision about income tax. Section 1 provides this overview. Overviews are also viewed as helpful within a Part (and sometimes within a Chapter), again in order to help readers to get to grips with what is going to be dealt with in the Part or Chapter more quickly. An example is section 33 of ITA 2007.

Since an overview is intended to be no more than a useful guide to the provisions of a Chapter, Part or Bill and is therefore not in itself operative law, it is important to ensure (so far as possible) that a clause describing itself as an overview does not also contain operative provisions (such as definitions).

A risk with both signposts and overviews is that subsequent amendments to TLR Acts will mean that the signposts and overviews become inaccurate or incomplete. This could happen if a signpost or overview provision was not amended in consequence of, for example, the addition of a new Part to an Act or a new Chapter to a Part, or the creation of a new relief that was not included in a list of reliefs. This is a real risk, because an amendment to a non-operative provision, such as a signpost or overview, is not needed to make the operative provision (for example, the new relief) work as intended and can easily be overlooked when the operative provisions are drafted. It is, however, a risk that TLR has been prepared to take, on the basis of the welcome given by users to signposts and overview provisions.

Before and After Examples

The examples in Appendix A are intended to demonstrate some of the challenges faced in rewriting tax legislation, and also some of the possible drafting solutions.

The provisions of ICTA 1988 are in the form they were in immediately before enactment of ITA 2007 in March 2007. The provisions of ITA 2007 are in the form they were in when TA 2007 was enacted. They do not take account of subsequent amendments.

Example 1

In Example 1, the 'before' text sets out subsections (2) to (4) of section 1 of ICTA 1988. The 'after' text sets out sections 4, 6, 10, 20 and 21 of ITA 2007. Those sections rewrite the material in section 1(2) to (4) of ICTA 1988.

The first point to note on Example 1 is how much longer the rewritten material is than the source material. As more tax law has been rewritten by TLR, it has become evident that the process of restructuring and rewriting it results in longer legislation, with a greater number of sections and subsections. This results from the process of trying to tease out individual propositions from a complex and densely-drafted existing provision.

This process of teasing out propositions is illustrated in Example 1. In the opening words of section 1(2) of ICTA 1988, the words, 'Where any Act enacts that income tax shall be charged for any year' have become section 4(1) of ITA 2007, which states as a separate proposition that, 'Income tax is charged for a tax year only if an Act so provides'.

In section 1(2) of ICTA, paragraphs (aa), (a) and (b) do three separate things: (1) they establish that there are to be rates of income tax called the starting rate, basic rate and higher rate; (2) they say that those rates are to be set by Parliament; and (3) they set the boundaries (or 'bands') of income to which each of those tax rates is to apply. The closing words of section 1(2) provide that the provisions of the subsection providing for particular income to be charged at the starting, basic or higher rate have effect subject to other provisions by virtue of which income tax is charged at different rates.

Section 1(2) of ICTA 1988 is rewritten in sections 6, 10 and 20 of ITA 2007. Section 6(1) sets out that income tax is charged at three 'main' rates: the starting rate, basic rate and higher rate. Section 6(2) provides for those rates to be set by Parliament for a tax year. Section 6(3) is a signpost pointing to the fact that income tax is also charged at other rates in some circumstances.

Section 10(1) to (3) set out the 'bands' of income that are subject to the starting rate, basic rate and higher rate. Section 10(4) provides that the preceding provisions have effect subject to sections 12 and 13 (which tax particular types of income at different rates) and also 'any other provision' charging particular income at a different rate. This 'sweep-up' provision is needed to ensure that the closing words of section 1(2) are fully addressed. It may not be possible in all cases to give an exhaustive list of the provisions to which a particular rule is subject.

Section 10(5) is a signpost to section 20, which sets out the starting rate limit and basic rate limit, referred to in section 10(1) to (3). Section 20(1) and (2) sets out what those limits are. Section 20(3) is a signpost to provisions under which the basic rate limit is increased in some circumstances.

Section 1(4) of ICTA 1988 sets out a mechanism for automatically increasing the limits between the 'bands' of income charged at the starting rate, basic rate and higher rate, in line with increases in the retail prices index. The opening words of the subsection are lengthy and difficult to understand on an initial reading. Section 1(4) is rewritten in section 21 of ITA 2007. Section 21 makes use of a simple method statement to set out the mechanism for automatic uprating of the limits. It deals separately with the starting rate limit and the basic rate limit. The result of the rewrite is a substantially longer provision but one that is viewed as making it clearer and easier for readers to understand how uprating works.

Example 2

In Example 2, the 'before' text sets out extracts from sections 730A(1), 730B(3) and 737B(1) of ICTA 1988. The 'after' text sets out section 569 of ITA 2007. Section 569 rewrites the material in the extracts from ICTA 1988. A point to note here is the use of the term 'repo' in the rewritten legislation to replace the 'this section applies where …' approach in section 730A(1) of ICTA 1988. This approach enables other provisions in Part 11 of ITA 2007 (for the purposes of which section 569 applies) to refer to a case in which there is a repo, which is viewed as being clearer than referring to a case in which a particular provision applies. The term 'repo' is one that is used and understood by tax professionals accustomed to applying this area of law.

Section 730A(1)(a) of ICTA 1988 is in terms of a transfer of 'securities'. Section 730B(3) of ICTA 1988 provides for 'securities' in section 730A to have the same meaning as in section 737A of that Act. Section 737B(1) of ICTA 1988 provides for 'securities' in section 737A to mean United Kingdom equities, United Kingdom securities or overseas securities. So to discover the wider meaning of 'securities' in section 730A it is necessary to look at three other provisions. In contrast, although section 569(1) and (2) of ITA 2007 are still in terms of 'securities', section 569(3) tells you that the securities must be UK shares, UK securities or overseas securities. There is no need to go elsewhere for the full meaning of 'securities' in this context. This is viewed as making the definition easier for users to understand.

Example 3

In Example 3, the 'before' text sets out subsections (4) to (6) of section 587B of ICTA 1988. The 'after' text sets out section 434(1) of ITA 2007. That subsection rewrites section 587B(4) to (6) of ICTA 1988. The main point to note here is the use of a formula in the rewritten provision. In section 587B of ICTA 1988, subsection (4)(a) defines the 'relevant amount', in a case where a disposal to a charity takes the form of a gift, as the value of the net benefit to the charity at a particular time. But this is qualified by subsection (6), which requires the relevant amount to be increased by the amount of the incidental costs of making the disposal, and subsection (5), which requires the relevant amount to be reduced by the value of any benefit received by the person making the gift (or a connected person).

The rewritten provision conveys the same meaning by using a simple formula: V+IC–B. It is of course then necessary to define 'V', 'IC' and 'B' in terms that reflect the words used in section 587B(4) to (6) of ICTA 1988. But the use of the formula enables a reader to grasp the essence of how the relievable amount is calculated more quickly than the use of words alone. Another point here is the use of 'relievable amount' as the label for the amount concerned in the rewritten section, compared with 'relevant amount' in the original. 'Relievable amount' conveys the idea that the amount concerned is likely to qualify for tax relief.

Conclusion

I hope I have given you some idea of the challenges faced in rewriting tax law. There is no single drafting approach that can be used for rewriting all types of tax legislation; but with imagination and ingenuity there is a great deal that can be done to make even the most complex legislation clearer and easier to understand.

Appendix

Drafting Legislation at the Tax Law Rewrite Project: Before and After Examples

Example 1

Before:

Income and Corporation Taxes Act 1988

Section 1(2) to (4): The charge to income tax

(2) Where any Act enacts that income tax shall be charged for any year, income tax shall be charged for that year—

(aa) in respect of so much of an individual's total income as does not exceed £2,150, at such rate as Parliament may determine to be the starting rate for that year;
(a) in respect of any income which does not fall within paragraph (aa) above or paragraph (b) below, at such rate as Parliament may determine to be the basic rate for that year;
(b) in respect of so much of an individual's total income as exceeds £33,300, at such higher rate as Parliament may determine;
but this subsection has effect subject to any provision of the Income Tax Acts providing for income tax to be charged at a different rate in certain cases.

(2A) The amount up to which an individual's income is by virtue of subsection (2) above chargeable for any year at the starting rate shall be known as the starting rate limit.

(3) The amount up to which an individual's income is by virtue of subsection (2) above chargeable for any year at the starting rate or the basic rate shall be known as the basic rate limit.

(4) If the retail prices index for the month of September preceding a year of assessment is higher than it was for the previous September, then, unless Parliament otherwise determines, subsection (2) above shall apply for that year as if for each of the amounts specified in that subsection as it applied for the previous year (whether by virtue of this subsection or otherwise) there were substituted an amount arrived at by increasing the amount for the previous year by the same percentage as the percentage increase in the retail prices index and—

(a) if the result in the case of the amount specified in subsection (2)(aa) above is not a multiple of £10, rounding it up to the nearest amount which is such a multiple, and
(b) if the result in the case of the amount specified in subsection (2)(b) above is not a multiple of £100, rounding it up to the nearest amount which is such a multiple.

After:

Income Tax Act 2007

Section 4: Income tax an annual tax

(1) Income tax is charged for a year only if an Act so provides....

Section 6: The starting rate, basic rate and higher rate

(1) The main rates at which income tax is charged are—
(a) the starting rate,
(b) the basic rate, and
(c) the higher rate.

(2) The starting rate, basic rate and higher rate for a tax year are the rates determined as such by Parliament for the tax year.

(3) For other rates at which income tax is charged see—
(a) section 7 (savings rate),
(b) section 8 (dividend ordinary rate and dividend upper rate), and
(c) section 9 (trust rate and dividend trust rate).

Section 10: Income charged at the starting, basic and higher rates: individuals

(1) Income tax is charged at the starting rate on an individual's income up to the starting rate limit.
(2) Income tax is charged at the basic rate on an individual's income above the starting rate limit and up to the basic rate limit.
(3) Income tax is charged at the higher rate on an individual's income above the basic rate limit.
(4) This section is subject to—
section 12 (income charged at the savings rate),
section 13 (income charged at the dividend ordinary and dividend upper rates: individuals), and
any other provisions of the Income Tax Acts which provide for income of an individual to be charged at different rates of income tax in some circumstances.
(5) See section 20 for the starting rate limit and the basic rate limit.

Section 20: The starting rate limit and the basic rate limit

(1) The starting rate limit is £2,150.
(2) The basic rate limit is £33,300.
(3) The basic rate limit is increased in some circumstances: see—

(a) section 414(2) (gift aid relief), and

(b) section 192(4) of FA 2004 (relief for pension contributions).

Section 21: Indexation of the starting rate limit and the basic rate limit

(1) This section applies if the retail prices index for the September before the start of a tax year is higher than it was for the previous September.
(2) The starting rate limit for the tax year is the amount found as follows.

Step 1
Increase the starting rate limit for the previous tax year by the same percentage as the percentage increase in the retail prices index.

Step 2
If the result of Step 1 is a multiple of £10, it is the starting rate limit for the tax year.
If the result of Step 1 is not a multiple of £10, round it up to the nearest amount which is a multiple of £10.

That amount is the starting rate limit for the tax year.

(3) The basic rate limit for the tax year is the amount found as follows.

Step 1
Increase the basic rate limit for the previous tax year by the same percentage as the percentage increase in the retail prices index.

Step 2
If the result of Step 1 is a multiple of £100, it is the basic rate limit for the tax year.

If the result of Step 1 is not a multiple of £100, round it up to the nearest amount which is a multiple of £100.

That amount is the basic rate limit for the tax year.

Example 2

Before:

Income and Corporation Taxes Act 1988

Section 730A: Treatment of price differential on sale and repurchase of securities

(1) ... this section applies where—
(a) a person ('the original owner') has transferred any securities to another person ('the interim holder') under an agreement to sell them; [and]
(b) the original owner or a person connected with him—
(i)is required to buy them back in pursuance of an obligation imposed by, or in consequence of the exercise of an option acquired under, that agreement or any related agreement, or
(ii) acquires an option to buy them back under that agreement or any related agreement which he subsequently exercises;...

Section 730B: Interpretation of section 730A

(3) In section 730A ... 'securities' has the same meaning as in section 737A.

Section 737B: Interpretation of section 737A

(1) In section 737A ... 'securities' means United Kingdom equities, United Kingdom securities or overseas securities;

After:

Income Tax Act 2007

Section 569: Meaning of 'repo'

(1) For the purposes of this Part there is a repo in respect of securities if conditions A, B and C are met.

(2) Condition A is that a person ('the original owner') has agreed to sell the securities to another person ('the interim holder').

(3) Condition B is that the securities are UK shares, UK securities or overseas securities.

(4) Condition C is that the original owner or a person connected with the original owner—

(a) is required to buy back the securities by the agreement or a related agreement,
(b) is required to buy back the securities as a result of the exercise of an option acquired under the agreement or a related agreement, or
(c) exercises an option to buy back the securities which was acquired under the agreement or a related agreement.

Example 3

Before:

Income and Corporation Taxes Act 1988

Section 587B: Gifts of shares, securities and real property to charities etc

(4) Subject to subsections (5) to (7) below, the relevant amount is an amount equal to:
(a) where the disposal is a gift, the value of the net benefit to the charity at, or immediately after, the time when the disposal is made (whichever time gives the lower value);
(5) Where there are one or more benefits received in consequence of making the disposal which are received by the person making the disposal or a person connected with him, the relevant amount shall be reduced by the value of that benefit or, as the case may be, the aggregate value of those benefits;
(6) Where the disposal is a gift, the relevant amount shall be increased by the amount of the incidental costs of making the disposal to the person making it.

After:

Income Tax Act 2007

Section 434: The relievable amount

(1) If the disposal is a gift, the relievable amount is given by the formula—

$$V + IC - B$$

where—
V is the value of the net benefit to the charity at, or immediately after, the time when the disposal is made, whichever is less,
IC is the amount of the incidental costs of making the disposal to the individual making it, and
B is the total value of any benefits received in consequence of making the disposal by the individual making the disposal or a person connected with the individual.

Chapter 7

Retrospectivity in the Drafting and Interpretation of Legislation

Lydia Clapinska[1]

Overview

Time is crucial in the drafting and interpretation of legislation. However, as Lord Rodger of Earlsferry has commented extra judicially, 'For the most part when you are simply applying the law in a routine fashion, you scarcely think of matters of time. But when something draws the question to your attention, all of a sudden you see the issue everywhere you look'.[2] Unlike some of our continental neighbours, who use the term 'intertemporal law' to denote a body of law on this topic, English legal tradition has not recognised an identifiable body of law relating to the treatment of legal changes over time.[3] Time can wreak revenge when problems with a temporal dimension arise, creating uncertainty for the users of legislation and leaving the courts to interpret and determine its relationship with the law.

The purpose of this chapter is to unravel one aspect of the knotty relationship between time and the law – the retrospective effect of legislation. The chapter aims to provide an introductory overview of the concept of retrospectivity. The chapter will start by explaining the origin and justification for the presumption against retrospectivity in legislation. There is one fundamental concept, but different terminology used in the United Kingdom, European Union, United States and Canada can lead to confusion. The different terms are examined and explained to equip the reader with an awareness of their meanings in different jurisdictions.

The focus will then turn to the operation of the presumption in England and Wales. Retrospective legislation will be considered in a number of contexts including differences in procedural and substantive changes to the law, criminal law and civil law. Further analysis brings out the different rules that apply in relation to legislation and judge-made law and considers whether prospective overruling by the courts is a suitable solution to the iniquities that can be caused by retrospective decisions. The final evaluation emphasises the concept of fairness as the key to the interpretation

1 The views expressed in this chapter belong to the author alone and do not represent the views of the UK Government or any other organisation.

2 Lord Rodger of Earlsferry, 'A Time for Everything Under The Law: Some Reflections on Retrospectivity' 121 (2005) *Law Quarterly Review 2005* at 59.

3 See ibid. at 60.

of legislation when determining whether retrospective effect was intended and describes the best practice of drafters.

The Origins of the Presumption Against Retrospectivity

The true principle is that *lex prospicit non respicit* – the law looks forward not back,[4] a principle which has also been expressed as *nova constitutio futuris formam imponere debet, non praeteritis* – a new statute ought to prescribe form to future acts, not past.[5] However, it has long been recognised that, 'this general rule, which is one of construction only, will yield to a sufficiently expressed intention of the legislature that the enactment should have a retrospective operation'.[6] The principle finds modern expression and explanation in Bennion on Statutory Interpretation,

> Retrospectivity is artificial, deeming a thing to be what it was not. Artificiality and make-believe are generally repugnant to law as the servant of human welfare. So it follows that the courts apply the general presumption that an enactment is not intended to have retrospective effect. As always, the power of Parliament to produce such an effect where it wishes to do so is nevertheless undoubted.[7]

It is of course the doctrine of parliamentary sovereignty that allows Parliament to make law with retrospective effect.

As Lord Mustill has expounded, the basis of the principle against retrospectivity 'is no more than simple fairness, which ought to be the basis of every legal rule'.[8] In the English legal system, this rule – which has been described as a 'fundamental rule of English law'[9] – is commonly known as the 'presumption against retrospectivity'. It is important to remember that as it is a presumption – albeit a strong presumption – rather than an absolute rule, there are circumstances in which legislation with retrospective effect is perfectly permissible, and even desirable, as is illustrated below. In English law, the general presumption is a rule born of the common law and is not expressed in statute although the Human Rights Act 1998 does enshrine the rule with respect to certain aspects of the criminal law. The general principle also appears in the US and other Constitutions around the world.

---

4 See F. Bennion, *Statutory Interpretation*, 4th edn (London: Butterworths, 2002) at 265.

5 See F.J. Stimson, *Glossary of Technical Terms, Phrases and Maxims of the Common Law*, (New Jersey: Lawbook Exchange Ltd, 1999) at 217.

6 See per B. Alderson, *Moon v Durden* [1848] 2 Ex. 40.

7 See Bennion (2002) at 266.

8 See *L'Office Cherifien des Phosphates v Yamashita-Shinnihon Steamship Co Ltd* [1994] 1 AC 486, *per* Lord Mustill at 525.

9 See P. Maxwell, *Interpretation of Statutes*, 12th edn (1969) at 215.

Retrospectivity in Comparative Context

It is worth considering whether there is any practical difference between the terms 'retrospectivity' and 'retroactivity' in the light of the use of both terms in academic literature and judicial citation. The answer to this question depends upon the jurisdiction under consideration. The following section gives an overview in order to equip the reader with an awareness that the terms have been interpreted in different ways in different jurisdictions.

England and Wales

In England and Wales, the terms 'retrospective' and 'retroactive' both have the same meaning. Craies suggests the following definition:

> Legislation is retrospective if it has effect in relation to a matter arising before it was enacted or made.[10]

A more complex definition previously received judicial approval, 'A statute is deemed to be retrospective, which takes away or impairs any vested right acquired under existing laws, or creates a new obligation, or imposes a new duty, or attaches a new disability in respect to transactions or considerations already past'.[11]

Traditionally, the word 'retrospective' was used almost exclusively. This is evidenced by the presence of an entry for 'retrospective' in Stroud's Judicial Dictionary[12] and the absence of an entry for 'retroactive'. In the English legal context, there is no difference in meaning between the two terms and they are often used synonymously. The House of Lords judgment in *Wilson v First County* Trust (No. 2)[13] provides an example of synonymous judicial use of the terms. A small empirical study has revealed that 'retrospective' is still the preferred judicial term and has been used in 826 instances in House of Lords decisions between 1900 and 2006 while retroactive occurs only 167 times in the same period.[14] However, the preference for "retrospective' in the UK is gradually disappearing; it may be that this can be attributed to the usage by the European Court of Justice, the general usage in North America of the word 'retroactive' to mean statutes that alter the past and the adoption by the Canadian courts of a specific meaning for each of the two words.[15]

---

10 See D. Greenberg (ed.) *Craies on Legislation* (London: Sweet and Maxwell, 2004) at 299.

11 See ibid., The judicial approval was given by the Court of Appeal in *L'Office Cherifien des Phosphates v Yamashita-Shinnihon Steamship Co Ltd* [1993] 3 All ER 686 at 692 CA ; and by the House of Lords in the same case ([1994] 1 Al ER 20 HL).

12 See D. Greenberg (ed.) *Stroud's Judicial Dictionary of Words and Phrases*, 7th edn (London: Sweet and Maxwell 2006) at 2406.

13 See [2004] 1 AC 816.

14 See C. Bobbett, 'Retroactive or Retrospective? A Note on Terminology' 1 (2006) *British Tax Review* pp. 15–18 at 17.

15 See ibid. at 17–18.

The Canadian Approach

The Canadian attempt to define 'retrospectivity' and 'retroactivity' as two distinct concepts with different meanings is particularly interesting, if not confounding. A recent decision of the Canadian Federal Court reviews the development and downfall of the distinction.[16] The distinction was emphasised in the second edition of Driedger on the *Construction of Statutes*[17] where 'retroactive' describes legislation that changes the past legal consequences of completed transactions, and 'retrospective' describes legislation that changes the future consequences of completed transactions by imposing new liabilities or obligations.

The distinction was effectively abandoned in the third edition of Driedger on the *Construction of Statutes*[18] with the following explanation:

> Some years ago, in an effort at refinement, a distinction was drawn between 'retroactive legislation', defined as legislation that changes the *past* legal consequences of completed transactions, and 'retrospective legislation', defined as legislation that changes the *future* consequences of completed transactions by imposing new liabilities or obligations. The legislature was presumed to eschew both retroactive and retrospective applications, both of which were distinguished from interference with vested rights, a less serious matter. Although this analysis has been adopted by courts on many occasions, it is not always clearly understood and the result has been a growing confusion around the term 'retrospective' in Canadian case law. The term is used in three different ways: (1) as a synonym for 'retroactive', to describe legislation that applies to past facts; (2) in the special sense explained above, to describe legislation that attaches new prejudicial consequences to closed transactions; and (3) most frequently perhaps, to describe legislation that if applied immediately and generally would attach new prejudicial consequences to ongoing facts.

The Canadian approach cannot be reconciled with cases and commentary from other jurisdictions, especially the UK.[19] In the context of UK legislation, each of the two terms can be used as a synonym of the other to define legislation which is made operative at a time prior to its enactment. This corresponds to the Canadian definition of retroactivity. There has been some indirect judicial support in the UK for the notion that the Canadian understanding of retrospectivity – future action in relation to past events – has no correlation with the UK meaning. For example, in an English case, an Act which enabled an order to be made disqualifying a person from acting as a solicitor's clerk in the future when some past event was the reason for

---

16 *Incremona-Salerno Marmi Affini Siciliani (I.S.M.A.S.) s.n.c. v Castor (The) (T.D.)* [2001] FCT 1330.

17 See E.A. Driedger, *Construction of Statutes*, 2nd edn (Toronto: Butterworths, 1983).

18 See R. Sullivan, *Driedger on the Construction of Statutes*, 3rd edn (Toronto: Butterworths, 1994) at 511, as cited in *Incremona-Salerno Marmi Affini Siciliani (I.S.M.A.S.) s.n.c. v Castor (The) (T.D.)* [2001] FCT 1330 at [13].

19 See G.T. Loomer, 'Taxing out of time: Parliamentary supremacy and retroactive tax legislation' 1 (2006) *British Tax Review* pp. 64–90 at 66.

the making of the order was held not to be retrospective.[20] The reason was that the Act did not affect anything done by the appellant in the past even though it referred to past events. This case would arguably have fallen into the Canadian definition of 'retrospectivity' although it was actually found to be prospective by an English court. This example illustrates that it would not be helpful in the UK context to distinguish separate meanings of retroactivity and retrospectivity. However, it is important to be equipped with an awareness that in the Canadian, North American and European contexts, distinct meanings for the terms have emerged.[21] When the word 'retrospective' appears in a UK context, it can generally be taken to mean 'retroactive' in the Canadian sense and when 'retrospective' is used in the Canadian sense, it may actually mean 'prospective' in a UK context.[22]

USA

The rule against retrospective legislation is enshrined in the United States Constitution. Art. I, s. 9, cl. 3 – which concerns the limits on legislative power – simply states that 'no ex post facto law shall be passed' The US Supreme Court recently enunciated that, 'the Ex Post Facto Clause raises to the constitutional level one of the most basic presumptions of our law: legislation, especially of the criminal sort, is not to be applied retroactively'.[23] In the US context it may be seen that the word 'retroactive' is judicially preferred.

In general terms, the retroactive application of civil statutes is disfavoured. Statutory provisions do not apply to events which pre-date enactment unless there is clear congressional intent that they so apply.[24] This presumption can, as in the UK context, be rebutted by clear legislative intent. In *Landgraf v USI Film Products*,[25] the US Supreme Court stated that, 'requiring clear intent assures that Congress itself has affirmatively considered the potential unfairness of retroactive application and determined that it is an acceptable price to pay for the countervailing benefits' However, the prohibitions on *ex post facto* laws effectively impose a constitutional bar to retroactive application of penal laws.[26]

20 *Re A Solicitor's Clerk* [1957] 3 All ER 617, 619 QBD, as cited in Greenberg (2004) at 391.

21 See Bobbett (2006) at 18.

22 An additional distinction that may be drawn, in the context of existing rights interference, is discussed below.

23 See *Johnson v United States*, 529 US 694, 701 [2000].

24 Congressional Research Service Report for Congress on Statutory Interpretation: General Principles and Recent Trends (March 2006).

25 See *Landgraf v USI Film Products*, 511 US 244, 265 [1994].

26 Congressional Research Service Report for Congress on Statutory Interpretation: General Principles and Recent Trends (March 2006).

Existing Rights Interference

An added complication is the distinction between retrospectivity and the concept of existing rights interference. This concept has been considered in the UK, Canadian and US contexts.

In the UK, the distinction has been illuminated by L.J. Buckley in *West v Gwynne*.[27] In that case, the question was whether an 1892 enactment affected the parties' rights from 1909 with respect to a lease commencing in 1874. The defendant urged that the statute should not be applied retrospectively. Lord Justice Buckley held that the statute had no such operation – it merely altered existing rights, which virtually any statute would do:

> As a matter of principle an Act of Parliament is not without sufficient reason taken to be retrospective. There is, so to speak, a presumption that it speaks only as to the future. But there is no like presumption that an Act is not intended to interfere with existing rights. Most Acts of Parliament, in fact, do interfere with existing rights.[28]

The following observation implicitly recognises the reality of interference with existing rights in the United States, 'Because legislative enactments cannot help but have retroactive consequence, both intended and unintended, the issue of retroactivity is particularly difficult. If every change in the law with a negative impact for someone were invalid because retroactive, government would indeed cease to function'.[29]

In Canada, there is a presumption against interference with vested rights, albeit a weaker presumption than that against retroactivity and retrospectivity. The Supreme Court considered the issue in the case of Gustavson Drilling:[30]

> The rule is that a statute should not be given a construction that would impair existing rights as regards person or property unless the language in which it is couched requires such a construction ... The presumption that vested rights are not affected unless the intention of the legislature is clear applies whether the legislation is retrospective or prospective in operation. A prospective enactment may be bad if it affects vested rights and does not do so in unambiguous terms. This presumption, however, only applies where the legislation is in some way ambiguous and reasonably susceptible of two constructions. It is perfectly obvious that most statutes in some way or other interfere with or encroach upon antecedent rights, and taxing statutes are no exception.

European Union

In European Community law, the preferred term is retroactivity and the concept is inextricably bound with principles of legal certainty and legitimate expectation. It has been observed that the main field of application of the principles of legal

27 See *West v Gwynne* [1911] 2 Ch 1, 11 CA.

28 See ibid.

29 See J.L. Huffman, 'Retroactivity, the Rule of Law, and the Constitution' 51 (1999–2000) *Alabama Law Review* at 1116.

30 See *Gustavson Drilling (1964) Ltd. v M.N.R.* [1977] 1 S.C.R. 271.

certainty and of the protection of legitimate expectations is the review of rule-making acts from the point of view of retroactivity.[31] The European Court of Justice ('ECJ') drew out the implications for retrospective measures in the case of *Racke*[32] where it held that although in general the principle of legal certainty precludes a Community measure from taking effect from a point in time before its publication, it may exceptionally be otherwise where 'the purpose to be achieved so demands and where the legitimate expectations of those concerned are duly respected'

The ECJ has found that there is 'actual retroactivity' where a rule is to be introduced by the legislature in respect of events which have already been concluded.[33] There is also a notion of 'apparent retroactivity' which is deemed to be the applicability of legislative acts to events which originated in the past but which have yet to be definitively concluded. This notion has been identified by Schwarze and although the ECJ has yet to use the term 'apparent retrospectivity' itself, it has in one case referred to 'a regulation having no retrospective effect in the proper sense of the expression'.[34] An English lawyer might translate this conclusion to mean that the regulation was, in fact, prospective. The ECJ has occasionally upheld the validity of retroactive measures, particularly in the agricultural sphere where they were necessary to ensure market stability; however, the normal presumption is against the validity of retroactive measures.[35] And in substantive terms, the court will strike down measures that have a retroactive effect where there is no pressing Community objective which demands this temporal dimension, or where the legitimate expectations of those affected by the measure cannot be duly respected.[36]

Operation of the Presumption Against Retrospectivity

The following sections provide an overview of how the presumption against retrospectivity operates in an number of different contexts. The emphasis is on English law but comparative examples are also drawn on for the purpose of illustration.

Procedural and Substantive Law

English law distinguishes between the retrospective operation of procedural provisions and substantive provisions, providing an exception to the presumption for

31 See J. Schwarze, *European Administrative Law*, Revised 1st edn, (Thompson, Sweet and Maxwell, 2006) at 1119.

32 See case 98/78, *Firma A Racke v Hauptzollanmt Mainz* [1979] ECR 69 as cited in P. Craig and G. De Burca, *EU Law – Text, Cases and Materials*' 4th edn, (Oxford: Oxford University Press, 2007) at 380.

33 See Case 1/73 *Westzucker GmbH v Einfuhr und Vorratsstelle fur Zucker* [1973] ECR 733 at 738, as cited in Schwarze (2006) at 1120.

34 For a detailed discussion on actual and apparent retroactivity in European Community law, see ibid. at 1122. The case referred to is Case 74/74 *CNTA v Commission* [1975] ECR 533 at 548.

35 See Craig and De Burca (2007) at 552.

36 See ibid.

procedural enactments. In R*e Athlumney*, it was held that 'a retrospective operation is not to be given to a statute so as to impair an existing right or obligation, otherwise than as regards a matter of procedure'.[37] Bennion has explained that this is because a procedural change is expected to improve matters for everyone concerned, (or at least to improve matters for some, without inflicting detriment on anyone else who uses ordinary care, vigilance and promptness).[38] Furthermore, as was pointed out by Lord Brightman in *Yew Bon Tew Alias Yong Boon Tiew v Kenderaan Bas Mara*,[39] in the case of a statute which is purely procedural, 'no person has a vested interest in any particular course of procedure, but only a right to prosecute or defend a suit according to the rules for the conduct of an action for the time being prescribed'.

It is not always easy to distinguish substance from procedure and Craies suggests the better approach is 'consideration of the substance of the provision concerned and, taking all the circumstances into account, considering what results the legislature can reasonably be assumed to have wanted or not wanted to achieve'.[40]

Criminal Law and Civil Law

A distinction must be drawn between civil and criminal law with regard to retrospective legislation. This is underpinned by the procedural/substantive distinction described above. Thornton explains that a criminal law enacted ex post facto cannot fulfil the primary purpose of all penal legislation – it cannot deter what is already done.[41] Thornton's explanation clearly refers to substantive criminal law, rather than law relating to criminal procedure. By contrast with substantive criminal law, civil law can operate retrospectively to fulfil its primary purpose. This is best illustrated by example. In the case of validation of marriages which would otherwise be held void owing to some technical defect in the ceremony, legislative proposals to validate retrospectively the marriages would confer benefits on private persons without imposing corresponding obligations.[42] In this example, the legislation would be retrospective if it validated the marriages from the date of marriage, i.e. from a date prior to the coming into force of the legislation. If the marriages were validated from the date of validation onwards, so that the status of the marriages before that date was unchanged, the legislation would not have retrospective effect. It is less likely that there will be objection to retrospective legislation in a non-criminal context so long as it is fair, certain and general in character. This echoes the reasoning in relation to the procedural/substantial distinction discussed earlier. Conversely the application

37 R*e Athlumney* [1898] 2 QB 547, *per* J. Wright at 551–2, cited in Bennion (2002) at 270.

38 See ibid.

39 See *Yew Bon Tew alias Yong Boon Tiew v Kenderaan Bas Mara* [1983] 1 AC 553, 557 PC.

40 See Greenberg (2004) at 394.

41 See G.C. Thornton, *Legislative Drafting*, 4th edn (London: Butterworths, London, 1996) at 136.

42 See ibid.

of retrospective rules may be extremely damaging in commercial circumstances, upsetting the presuppositions on which transactions have been based.[43]

Retrospective Legislation in the Civil Context

In 1965, the UK Parliament enacted the War Damage Act which had a deliberate retrospective effect. The Act was passed in order to overrule the House of Lords decision in *Burmah Oil Ltd v The Lord Advocate*.[44] The effect of the legislation was to deprive Burmah Oil of the compensation to which they were entitled following the House of Lords decision, for damage to their oil installations by British troops during the Second World War. However, the 1965 Act also prevented the burden of compensation having to be met by the British taxpayer.[45] Section 1 of the War Damage Act 1965 states, 'No person shall be entitled at common law to receive from the Crown compensation in respect of damage to, or destruction of, property caused (whether before or after the passing of this Act, within or outside the United Kingdom) by acts lawfully done by, or on the authority of, the Crown during, or in contemplation of the outbreak of, a war in which the Sovereign was, or is, engaged.' The 1965 Act is a rare example, but serves as a reminder that Parliament can enact retrospective legislation if it so wishes as long as express words – such as those in section 1 above – are used to convey the legislative intent.

In the field of taxation, retrospective legislation is not unusual. However, as for all legislation intended to have retrospective effect, clear wording must be used to convey the intended effect. The most common use of retrospective tax legislation is the practice of making annual budget proposals effective from the date of announcement. The announcement is usually made in the Chancellor's Budget speech and set out in the annual Finance Bill. The Budget speech is followed by House of Commons' resolutions giving temporary effect to tax measures pending enactment of the Finance Act. The resolutions have temporary statutory authority by virtue of the Provisional Collection of Taxes Act 1968. Furthermore the annual Finance Act usually declares that certain provisions are deemed to be effective from the date of announcement. Thus the application of new or amended tax measures during the time between announcement and enactment is retrospectively validated.[46] A justification is that, if the new law were not applied retrospectively, taxpayers and their advisers would have a window of opportunity to undertake tax avoidance measures before the new law became effective.[47] This backdating does not lead to unfairness provided that the announcement is given due publicity[48] and is sufficiently detailed. Furthermore, Lord Diplock has argued that this practice of backdating does not weaken the presumption against retrospectivity where there is no express

43 See Craig and De Burca (2007) at 552.

44 [1965] AC 75.

45 See G. Slapper and D. Kelly, *The English Legal System*, 6th edn (London: Cavendish Publishing Limited, 2003) at 188.

46 The process as described by Loomer (2006) at 67–9.

47 See ibid.

48 See Greenberg (2004) at 396.

provision in the statute to that effect; he commented that, 'rather it serves to confirm that the reason for the presumption is that in a civilised society which acknowledges the rule of law individual members of that society are entitled to know when they embark upon a course of conduct what the legal consequences of their doing so will be, so that they may regulate their conduct accordingly'.[49]

Human Rights Act

The Human Rights Act 1998 formally incorporated the European Convention on Human Rights into UK law. Section 3 of the Act concerns the interpretation of legislation and provides that, 'so far as it is possible to do so, primary legislation and subordinate legislation must be read and given effect in a way which is compatible with the Convention rights'.[50] Section 3(2) states that section 3 applies to primary and secondary legislation whenever enacted. Some commentators have argued that as the Human Rights Act is not criminal legislation and is not penal in character, it should be capable of retrospective application.[51] However, the Canadian Charter of Rights and Freedoms and the New Zealand Bill of Rights Act 1990 have been held not to have retrospective effect.[52] UK judges have decided the same in respect of the Human Rights Act. In *Wilson v First County Trust* (No. 2),[53] Lord Nicholls of Birkenhead reasoned that the principle of interpretation in section 3(1) Human Rights Act 1998 does not apply retrospectively because if it did, it would change the interpretation and effect of existing legislation and may well produce an unfair result for one party or the other.[54]

Criminal Law

Retrospective application of the criminal law requires special attention. Lord Reid observed in *Waddington v Miah*[55] that, 'it is hardly credible that any government department would promote, or that Parliament would pass, retrospective criminal legislation'.[56] This reasoning resonates well beyond the boundaries of English law. Judge Rosalyn Higgins, President of the International Court of Justice:

> The retrospective application of the criminal law has very special overtones. The principle of *nullum crimen, nulla poena sine lege* [no crime, no penalty without law] is indeed so

---

49 *Inland Revenue Commissioners v Joiner* [1975] 1 WLR 1701, 1714 HL as cited in ibid.

50 See Section 3(1), Human Rights Act 1998, ch. 42.

51 See R. Glover, 'Retrospectivity and the Human Rights Act 1998' 4 (2003) *Web Journal of Current Legal Issues* pp. 1–17 at 9–10.

52 See ibid.

53 See [2003] 3 WLR 568 HL.

54 Ibid., see discussion of this case in Greenberg (2004); see also *Re McKerr* [2004] UKHL 12 and *R (on the application of Christine Hurst) v The Commissioner of the Metropolitan Police* [2007] UKHL 13.

55 See [1974] 1 WLR 683.

56 See ibid. at 694.

widely accepted that it may properly be described as a general principle of law – that is, one common to all developed legal systems and thus itself a source of international law.[57]

This principle is enshrined in Article 15(1) of the UN International Covenant on Civil and Political Rights and Article 7(1) of the European Convention on Human Rights. The first part of these two provisions is the same and reads as follows, 'No one shall be held guilty of an offence on account of any act or omission which did not constitute a criminal offence, under national or international law, at the time when it was committed' [58] The second part of Article 7(1) of the European Convention on Human Rights prohibits a heavier penalty being imposed than the one that was applicable at the time the criminal offence was committed.

There is no distinct corresponding right to Article 7 in the civil sphere.[59] There is an express exception to Article 7(1) created by Article 7(2) which states that Article 7 shall not prejudice the trial and punishment of any person for any act or omission which, at the time when it was committed, was criminal according to the general principles of law recognised by civilised nations.[60] The exception was intended to allow for the application of legislation to punish war crimes.[61] Even so, legislation of this type, such as the UK War Crimes Act 1991, has been drafted narrowly and with great caution.[62]

The European Court of Justice has specifically given the prohibition of the retroactivity of penal provisions the status of an autonomous principle of European Community law.[63] In the case of *Regina v Kent Kirk*,[64] the court had to decide whether a Council Regulation of 25 January 1983 by which, with retroactive effect from 1 January 1983, national measures contravening community law prohibitions on discrimination were approved by way of transitional arrangements, could also retroactively validate penal provisions. Without embarking on an examination of the general legality of the Regulation, the court held that it was sufficient that 'such retroactivity may not, in any event, have the effect of validating ex post facto national measures of a penal nature which impose penalties for an act which, in fact,

---

57 See Judge Rosalyn Higgins, 'Time and the law: international perspectives on an old problem' 46 (1997) 3 *International and Comparative Law Quarterly* pp. 501–20 at 507–508.

58 Article 15(1) UN ICCPR: accessed online at (www.hrweb.org/legal/cpr.html); Article 7(1) ECHR: online at (www.hri.org/docs/ECHR50.html#C.Art7).

59 See Lord Rodger of Earlsferry, 'A Time for Everything Under The Law: Some Reflections on Retrospectivity' (2005) *Law Quarterly Review* pp. 57–79 at 64.

60 See Article 15(2) of the UNICCPR is worded in a very similar way; see previous note 25.

61 See A. Lester and D. Pannick, *Human Rights Law and Practice* 2nd edn (London: Lexis Nexis Butterworths, 2004) at 260.

62 For a discussion of the drafting of the UK 1991 War Crimes Act, see Higgins (1997) at 509.

63 See J. Schwarze, *European Administrative Law*, Revised 1st edn (London: Thompson, Sweet and Maxwell, 2006) at 1122.

64 See Case 63/83 *Regina v Kent Kirk* [1984] ECR 2689 as described in Craig and De Burca (2007) at 553.

was not punishable at the time at which it was committed'.[65] The court emphasised that, 'the principle that penal provisions may not have retroactive effect is one which is common to all the legal orders of the Member States and is enshrined in Article 7 of the European Convention of Human Rights and Fundamental Freedoms as a fundamental right; it takes its place among the general principles of law whose observance is ensured by the Court of Justice'.

Just as the principle against retrospectivity in the criminal context generally operates to prevent the criminalisation of past conduct, if an Act of Parliament decriminalises conduct, it is presumed to have prospective effect only. If a statutory offence is repealed, section 16(1)(d) Interpretation Act 1978 provides that where an Act repeals an enactment, the repeal does not, unless the contrary intention appears, affect any penalty, forfeiture or punishment incurred in respect of any offence committed against that enactment. In other words, the repeal will not affect previous convictions for conduct which is no longer an offence as a result of the repeal.

The rule against retrospective legislation in relation to criminal conduct appears to be quite clear. However, it must be remembered that the rule only applies to legislation. Unlike statutes, judicial decisions can have retrospective effect. Two situations arise here. The first is the construction of a piece of legislation where the court declares what the legislation means (and has always meant). For example, the ECJ has explained recently that, 'the interpretation which, in the exercise of the jurisdiction conferred on it by Article 234 EC, the Court gives to a rule of Community law clarifies and defines where necessary the meaning and scope of that rule as it must be or ought to have been understood and applied from the time of its entry into force. It follows that the rule as thus interpreted may, and must, be applied by the courts even to legal relationships which arose and were established before the judgment ruling on the request for interpretation'.[66] However, the court's declaration does not operate at any point earlier than when the legislation was passed. The second situation with regard to judicial decisions is the peculiarly common law doctrine of the court declaring, not simply what the law has always *meant*, but what the law has always *been*, which is particularly objectionable in the case of criminal offences.

In *R v R*,[67] the House of Lords abolished a husband's common law immunity against criminal liability for rape within marriage which had meant that a husband could not be guilty of raping his wife.[68] The effect of the House of Lords decision was to deem, retrospectively, marital rape an offence when at the time the act was committed, it was not an offence. As Ashworth has expounded, there are many convincing reasons why the law should have been thus changed but the relevant question is whether it should have been changed by a judicial decision which operated

65 See Case 63/83 *Regina v Kent Kirk* [1984] ECR 2689 at [21].

66 See Case C–262/96 *Surul v Bundesastalt fur Arbeit* [1999] ECR I–2685, [2001] 1 CMLR 4 at para. 1.07, as cited at ibid., note 1.

67 See [1992] 1 AC 599.

68 For a full discussion of the development of the common law in this area, see G. Slapper and D. Kelly, *The English Legal System*, 6th edn (London: Cavendish Publishing Limited, 2003) at 189.

retrospectively on the defendant, rather than prospectively by the legislature.[69] The husband in *R v R* was duly convicted of rape and complained to the European Court of Human Rights that the UK had violated Article 7 of the European Convention on Human Rights. In what has been described as 'a distinctly common-law method of reasoning, undoubtedly affected by the subject matter'[70] the European Court said that criminal law could be applied retrospectively, provided that the development of criminal liability was reasonably foreseeable.[71]

This decision is in line with the 'thin ice' principle developed by Lord Morris, 'he who skates on thin ice can hardly expect to find a sign which will denote the precise spot where he will fall in' [72] As Ashworth explains, as a counterpoint to retrospectivity, the arguments in favour of this principle combine a moral element: criminal law ought to penalise conduct widely regarded as immoral, and a political element: those indulging in immoral activities ought to know that there is a risk of criminal liabilities extending to those activities. However, these arguments negate the fairness principle and as such Article 7 should not be trumped by the 'thin ice' principle.[73] However, cases like the marital rape case demonstrate that there is some leeway and that Article 7 can make allowances for the 'gradual clarification' of the rules of criminal liability through judicial interpretation from case to case, provided that the resulting development is consistent with the essence of the offence and could be reasonably foreseen.[74]

Prospective Overruling

One technique which can be used in order to combat the injustice of retrospective application of judicial decisions is prospective overruling, by which a court limits the retrospective effect of its decision. For example, a court could indicate that its decision applies to future cases only. Lady Justice Arden has discussed the advantages and disadvantages of this technique.[75] On the one hand, it has the advantage that the effect of a change in the law can be limited so as not to disturb past transactions, on the other hand, it may not give the benefit of any change to the claimant in the present case. Prospective overruling has been rejected in Australia and Canada but it is a technique used by the European Courts, India and Israel.[76] The UK courts are generally against the idea and some judges have denounced it as denial of

69 See A. Ashworth, *Principles of Criminal Law*, 3rd edn (Oxford: Oxford University Press, 1999) at 72.

70 See Higgins (1997) at 508.

71 The case was called *SW and CR v United Kingdom* [1995] 21 EHRR 363.

72 See *Knuller v DPP* [1973] AC 435 as cited in Ashworth (1999) at 75.

73 See Ashworth (1999) at 76.

74 See A. Lester and D. Pannick, *Human Rights Law and Practice*, 2nd edn, (London: Lexis Nexis Butterworths, 2004) at 257.

75 See Lady Justice Arden, 'Prospective Overruling' 120 (2004) *Law Quarterly Review* pp. 7–11 at 7.

76 See ibid. at 8.

the constitutional role of the courts.[77] Lady Justice Arden has pointed out that the question of whether there should be relief in respect of past breaches of an Act of Parliament must be a matter for Parliament itself.[78]

Fairness as the Key to Interpretation

In the final analysis, Craies suggests that the question of whether a statute is intended to have retrospective effect should be answered not by the application of any rigid criteria of distinctions between classes of enactment, but by considering, in the light of all the circumstances of each case the following factors:

> What degree of unfairness (if any) might be thought to be suffered if the provision were applied with retrospective effect, and
>
> That the greater the unfairness the stronger the presumption that Parliament would not have intended it, and therefore the greater the clarity of language required to rebut it.[79]

The approach by Craies, distilled from Lord Mustill's reasoning in *L'Office Cherifien des Phosphates*[80] accords with a general trend of the courts away from the rigid application of formulaic presumptions and towards the application of common sense in the search for the legislative intention in each context, by having regard to all relevant circumstances.[81]

Best Practice of Drafters

Bennion warns that, 'doubt as to whether an enactment is intended to be retroactive is usually caused by bad drafting. It is the duty of the drafter to supply appropriate transitional provisions so as to make clear whether, and if so to what extent, the enactment has a retrospective effect'.[82] As a matter of general principle in drafting, Thornton states that, 'legislation intended to regulate human conduct ought to deal with future acts and ought not to change the character of past transactions carried on upon the faith of the then existing law'.[83]

Thornton describes five stages of the drafting process: 1) understanding; 2) analysis; 3) design; 4) composition and development; and 5) scrutiny and testing.[84] Drafters have a particular responsibility when it comes to proposals for retrospective

77 See discussion by F. Bennion, 'Consequences of an Overrule' (2001) *Public Law* pp. 450–6 at 454.

78 See Arden (2004) at 11.

79 See Greenberg (2004) at 392.

80 See *L'Office Cherifien des Phosphates v Yamashita-Shinnihon Steamship Co Ltd* [1994] 1 AC 486.

81 See Greenberg (2004) at 392.

82 See Bennion (2002) at 273.

83 See Thornton (1996) at 135.

84 See ibid. at 128.

legislation, which Thornton identifies as a potential danger area and which should ideally be considered at the second stage of the drafting process which is 'analysis' Drafters should bear in mind that the presumption against retrospection is not a technicality, it is a general rule of justice not dependent on forms of words.[85] Where it is necessary to convey a legislative intent of retrospection, a clear form of words should be used. Bennion cautions, 'the drafter needs to think very carefully about this, visualising just how the legislative scheme will work out in practice'.[86] It may be necessary to state explicitly in the legislation that, for example, there is an intention to allow future action to be influenced by pre-commencement events.[87] Drafters always need to judge what is reasonable in the circumstances, 'if legislative proposals are patently unreasonable or shock the drafter's sense of justice, the drafter must advise the sponsors of the proposal of his or her opinion and draw attention to the inequity or breach of fundamental principle involved'.[88]

Conclusion

Charting a course through retrospectivity, retroactivity and prospectivity in the drafting and interpretation of legislation is quite a daunting challenge. This chapter has given an introductory overview of how the concepts are applied in different ways and it is clearly important to understand and distinguish them in order to avoid confusion and omissions in drafting. A number of distinctions must be drawn, between procedural and substantive law, criminal law and civil law, legislation and judge-made law. In drafting, all of the considerations must be understood and borne in mind in order to avoid the temporal dimension of legislation in the form of retrospectivity causing difficulties in interpretation for the users of legislation and the courts alike.

---

85 See *per* Lord Pearce in *Customs and Excise Comrs v Gallaher Ltd* [1971] AC 43 at 66, quoted in Thornton (1996) at 135.

86 See F. Bennion 'Threading the Legislative Maze – 7' (1998) document 1998.015, at 2, accessed online at (www.francisbennion.com).

87 This was done in s 4(4) of the Nationality, Immigration and Asylum Act 2002 (ch. 41), see Greenberg (2004) at 392.

88 See Thornton (1996) at 136.

Chapter 8

Repealing or Amending Legislation by Non-Legislative Means

Alec Samuels

Introduction

There is far too much legislation; it is too detailed; the drafting may not always measure up to the highest standards; too often legislation is of the vague enabling variety; the statute, or parts of it, may not stand the test of time, it may be becoming inappropriate or obsolete, it may be casting an oppressive burden upon individuals, society or a section of society, such as business, especially small business, and the public service. All society is over regulated. The cost to society of bad laws has been estimated at £100 billions a year. There is a widespread view that repeal or amendment is necessary or desirable. Deregulation is imperative. So why not repeal or amend the offending legislation, either by primary or indeed perhaps by secondary means, or indeed any other means properly available.

There are a variety of ways of approaching or tackling or challenging the problem. The statute may be invalid, which is normally very unlikely, though the chance of the statute being struck down by the European Court of Human Rights or the European Court of Justice is increasingly likely.[1] The statute may provide for its own start and termination, instead of the normal presumption of an indefinite or perpetual life. Judicial activism may virtually transform the meaning of a statute from what Parliament manifestly intended on enactment, though perhaps many years earlier. It is possible that the statute has fallen into obsolescence or desuetude, though this is not an overt judicial principle of interpretation. A statute may, or purport to be, non-repealable, though again this would be contrary to traditional principle, though in practice repeal may be impossible or almost impossible, especially where international dimensions obtain. The process of repeal may be greatly helped not only if legislation is carefully drafted before enactment but also carefully and systematically reviewed and scrutinised after enactment so as to facilitate repeal

1 The Merchant Shipping Act 1988 was struck down as contrary to EU law in the Factortame cases, summarised in *R v Secretary of State ex parte Factortame* [2000] 1 AC 524, 530B, 547C and 552C. *Wilson v First County Trust* [2004] 1 AC 816, paras. 61–7, 116–8, 140–45, admissibility of ministerial statements and parliamentary debates. *OT Computers* (2004) ch. 317. *Pepper v Hart* [1993] AC 593, Practice Direction (Hansard: citation) [1995] 1 WLR 192. *Three Rivers DC v Bank of England* (No. 2) [1996] 2 All ER 363. *Thoburn v Sunderland City Council* [2002] EWHC 195 (Admin), [2003] QB 151, para. 63.

or amendment where experience or changing requirements make this necessary or desirable.

Implied Repeal by Subsequent Statute

The legislature does not always sufficiently consider the possible effects of a new statute upon an old statute. The issue of implied repeal (intentional or unintentional) may arise. The Local Government Act 1972 section 123 authorises a local council to dispose of land held by them, but provided that they obtain best consideration. The Local Government Act 2000 section 2 empowers a local council 'to do anything' which they consider likely to promote economic, social or environmental well-being, including apparently disposing of land for less than best consideration. Although in principle where there is a conflict or potential conflict a later statute prevails over an earlier statute, the legislature would have done better expressly to clarify the relationship between the old and the new law.

Invalid Statute

To be valid a statute must be passed in the required constitutional manner or it is invalid. Invalidity is most unlikely to arise. The judges are always scrupulous not to intrude upon the procedure and privilege of Parliament. The issue was raised over the validity of the Parliament Act 1949 which purported to amend the Parliament Act 1911, and the consequent validity of statutes passed under the 1949 Act, for example, the Hunting Act 2004. The House of Lords did consent to the restriction on its powers in 1911, but did not consent to the further restriction on its powers in 1949, by the House of Commons altering the 1911 Act in 1949. However, this cogent argument was rejected.[2]

Consolidation

Consolidation is a most useful process, and we need much more. Care must always be taken when any change of wording is made that no unintentional change of meaning is made.[3]

2 See *R (Jackson) v Attorney-General* [2005] UKHL 56, [2006] 1 AC 262; see Lord Steyn, paras. 80, 87–8, and 91. Alec Samuels, 'Is the Parliament Act 1949 valid? Could it be challenged?' 24 (2003) *Statute Law Review* pp. 237–42. Richard Ekins, 'Acts of Parliament and the Parliament Acts' 123 [2007] LQR 91–115. The judges will not entertain a challenge to a statute changing the *Statute of Westminster Manuel v Attorney-General* [1983] ch. 77, CA. *Pickin v British Railways Board* [1974] AC 765.

3 See *IRC v Joiner* [1975] 1 WLR 1701, HL. Alec Samuels, 'Consolidation: A plea' 26 (2005) *Statute Law Review* pp. 56–63.

The Statute Provides for Start and Finish: Sunrise and Sunset Clauses

The contemporary statute nearly always provides for the minister to bring it into force by means of a commencement order or orders, and such orders usually are made, in due course, often irregularly. Suppose the statute has not been brought into force after a very long delay: is there any remedy? The answer appears to be that, subject to any express provision to the contrary, the minister has a discretion whether or not to make an order but, nonetheless, he is under a duty to keep the situation under review, for example, where the statute says that the statute 'shall come into force' when the minister decides to make an order. For example, it would be an abuse of power to discontinue a former non-statutory compensation scheme and not bring into force the new statutory compensation scheme which was intended by Parliament to replace it.[4]

Where a statute is directed to a mischief which is perceived as temporary or time limited, or is a particularly sensitive or controversial matter, then Parliament may insist upon a 'sunset' section, requiring the termination of the statute after a specified time. The Prevention of Terrorism (Temporary Provisions) Act 1989 indicated in its very title that it was temporary. The Prevention of Terrorism Act 2005 section 13, control orders, provides specifically for a limited duration of 12 months, but by statutory instrument, subject to the affirmative procedure, the minister may repeal, revive or continue the statute in force, for another year at a time, a very considerable power, albeit subject to parliamentary approval. Also the minister must review and report upon the operation of the statute.

Judicial Activism: Statute Extended or Restricted by Reinterpretation

A statute may be in effect changed, altered, extended, restricted or repealed by way of judicial construction and interpretation, perhaps robust, forceful, vigorous or radical construction and interpretation, for instance, judicial activism. Though the concept of implied repeal by judicial constitution might be seen as a potentially dangerous constitutional situation.

Where the tenant of a statutory or protected tenancy dies, a surviving spouse or a member of his family residing with him for two years immediately before his death is entitled to succession to the tenancy. The statutory provision had existed since 1915 and 1920. A survivor of a same-sex relationship sought succession. The House of Lords held[5] that he did not qualify as a spouse, but he did qualify as a member of the family. The word family is undefined in the statute. The way we live today and the perceptions we have have changed. Social attitudes, opinions and habits have changed. Relationships other than by blood (consanguinity) or marriage (affinity) are recognised, even respected, for example, homosexual relationships. A refusal to recognise the reality of the situation would be unattractive and unacceptable.

---

4 See *R v Secretary of State for Home Department ex parte Fire Brigades Union* [1995] 2 AC 513, [1995] 2 All ER 244.

5 See *Fitzpatrick v Sterling Housing Association* [2001] 1 AC 27. See Alec Samuels 22 (2001) *Statute Law Review* pp, 154–6, setting out all the arguments.

This may be a matter for concern or for congratulation. Anyway, morality is not the criterion to apply to a landlord and tenant legal issue.

Subsequent to the decision the jurisprudence of the European Court of Human Rights and article 8, the Civil Partnerships Act 2004, the Equality Act 2006 section 81 and the Equality Discrimination Regulations 2007 have further strengthened the legal rights of same-sex couples.

In construing or interpreting a statute the judge will take into account any relevant treaty obligations of the UK and seek for consistency, but no further.[6]

Offence Charged but not Tried Before Repeal

When an offence is abolished by repeal, the repealing statute should make it clear what is to happen to persons arrested, bailed or charged but not tried for the repealed offence when the repealing statute takes effect.[7]

Obsolescence, Desuetude

At the beginning of the Second World War Parliament passed a statute requiring all citizens to have and to produce an identity card on demand by a police officer, non-compliance constituting an offence. After the end of the war, the end of the 'emergency', the necessary order-in-council required to terminate the statute was not made and the police continued to demand the production of the identity card. It was held[8] that despite the end of the war and the emergency, the statute still applied but that an absolute discharge, no penalty, would be appropriate upon conviction. As a result identity cards were torn up and the statute 'died a death'

Obsolescence may be another way of expressing implied incompatibility or inconsistency of an earlier statute with a subsequent statute.[9]

Constitutional, Non-Repealable and Entrenched

The traditional English constitutional principle has long been that Parliament may do what it likes, make and unmake laws, and the constitutional or non-repealable or entrenched statute[10] is not possible, it would be contrary to the sovereignty of

6 See *R v Secretary of State Home Department ex parte Brind* [1991] 1 AC 696. Alec Samuels, 'The effect of a treaty upon English law: Does it confer rights upon individual citizens?' 26 (2005) *Statute Law Review* p. 130. *Fothergill v Monarch Airlines* [1981] AC 251 – French text to prevail over English text in statute giving effect to an international treaty or convention. *James Buchanan v Babco Forwarding and Shipping UK* [1978] AC 141. Woodend (KV Ceylon) *Rubber and Tea v IRC* [1971] AC 321, PC.

7 See *R v West London Stipendiary Magistrate ex parte Simeon* [1983] 1 AC 234.

8 See *Willcock v Muckle* [1951] 2 KB 844, [1951] 2 All ER 367 DC.

9 See *Dobbs v Grand Junction Waterworks Company* [1882] 10 QBD 337, 355, CA.

10 See Entrenchment pp. 123–5 in Sir William Dale, *The Modern Commonwealth* (Butterworths, 1983); also Thoburn [2002] EWHC 195 (Admin), [2003] QB 151.

Parliament, and Parliament cannot bind its successors. Certain statutes may indeed appear to have the appearance of being 'constitutional', for example, Magna Carta 1215, Habeas Corpus 1679, Bill of Rights 1689, Act of Settlement 1700, Act of Union 1707, Reform Act 1832, Human Rights Act 1998, Scotland Act 1998, Government of Wales Act 1998, but some have been repealed or modified by ordinary legislation or by judicial construction and all of them could be repealed in the ordinary way, although naturally there could be real political difficulties involved.

However today a statute may be declared by the English judges to be incompatible with the European Convention on Human Rights, and although they cannot strike it down, the European Court of Human Rights certainly can. An international treaty entered into by the UK (treaty-making is a prerogative power not constitutionally requiring the consent of Parliament) may provide for withdrawal, or may not, and whereas it can always be broken there may well be consequent international sanctions falling upon the UK, whatever UK legislation may say.[11]

As a result of the European Communities Act 1972 membership of the EU has given the UK an overarching fundamental constitution, namely EU law as made by the Directives, and where there is incompatibility the Directives prevail: Thoburn. The Weights and Measures Act 1985 permitted the use of the imperial system by traders. The EU Directive and the consequent UK regulations required the sole use of the metric system by traders. It was held that the Directive and regulations prevailed. The EU constitution permitted and authorised the change of UK statutory law under EU delegated powers. The 1985 UK Act had not expressly nor impliedly repealed any EU law, indeed it was not able to do so. The EU law overruled the UK law, repeal by implication; the UK law did not overrule or repeal the EU law.[12]

The legal reasoning of L.J. Laws is not entirely convincing. He says that implied repeal of a statute is difficult to establish, which is unexceptionable. He says that the 1972 statute is fundamental and constitutional: no doubt it is of the utmost importance, but there is no recognition of a 'constitutional' statute in our law. He says that Parliament remains sovereign and cannot bind its successor: theoretically still true. He says that the 1972 Act could only be expressly repealed and not imputed, constructively or presumptively repealed: a reasonable proposition. He says that the 1972 Act and the EU directives prevail over subsequent inconsistent UK statutes: this conclusion is clearly correct, but may be difficult to reconcile with his preceding arguments. The ultimate justification for the decision has to be that politically, constitutionally and legally Parliament was willing to, and did, modify UK statute law and common law in order to join and to be governed ultimately by the European Union, or at least to the extent of the constitutional powers enjoyed by the European Union.

---

11 See the Factortame litigation. In *A v Secretary of State for the Home Department* [2004] UKHL 56 [2005] 2 AC 68, UK anti-terrorist legislation was found to be disproportionate and irrational, and incompatible with the international human rights convention.

12 See *Thoburn v Sunderland City Council* [2002] EWHC 195 (Admin), [2003] QB 151. Henry VIII clauses are also discussed.

The United Kingdom

The treaty and the statutes bringing about the union of England and Scotland to form Great Britain (the crowns having been united a century before on the accession of James I)[13] seem to imply that the union is to last for ever, though this is not stated explicitly. However the phrases 'in all time' and 'for ever' do appear in specific context, for example, harmonisation of liquor duties. The creation of the Scottish Parliament by the Scotland Act 1998 did not alter the constitutional position of the United Kingdom as a single State and no reference was made to the C18 legislation. As the movement for independence for Scotland appears to gain support there seems to be a general recognition that this could be achieved by an Act of the UK Parliament. Though presumably Scotland might do a unilateral declaration of independence (UDI) (perhaps following a referendum), and establish an independent State by way of political fact.

Extraterritorial Effect of Repeal

When a UK statute is repealed in the UK thought and care must be given to possible extraterritorial effect, if any, in dependent territories and indeed in formerly dependent territories;[14] though with the virtual end of the empire and the emergence of the Commonwealth of independent states the problem, if such it be, has very much diminished.

Post-Legislative Scrutiny

The Law Commission is statutorily charged to keep the statute book under review and to recommend the repeal of obsolete statutes, which it does in the annual reports. Recently the Law Commission considered post-legislative scrutiny and suggested[15] that departments should scrutinise the effectiveness of legislation and there should be a new parliamentary joint committee. Presumably more effective scrutiny should lead to more appropriate and prompt repeal or amendment.

Public Pet Hates

In 2006 the BBC Radio 4 programme ran a competition, results announced on 1 January 2007, among listeners for the piece of legislation that they would most like to be repealed. The reasons given for the six statutes that emerged are interesting.

---

13 See Union with Scotland Act 1706 and Union with Scotland (Amendment) Act 1707 and Succession to the Crown Act 1707.

14 See *Al Sabah v Grupo Torras SA* [2005] UKPC 1, [2005] 2 AC 333.

15 See Law Commission, 'Post-Legislative Scrutiny' October 2006, Law Com No. 302 Cmnd 6945.

1. The Hunting Act 2004. Those opposed to the statute argued principally that they had a moral, social and traditional right to hunt, the expected stance of the hunting fraternity, and hunting controlled the fox pest.

When the statute was challenged in the courts on the basis of an infringement of human rights the Court of Appeal rejected the challenge on the basis that (i) right to privacy and family life article 8 did not apply, (ii) there was no infringement of the right of assembly, (iii) there was no infringement of the right to peaceful enjoyment of property protocol 1 article 1, (iv) there was evidence that hunting was cruel and therefore the statute was proportionate, and (v) there was no interference with the freedom of movement by the citizens of Member States, or if there was it was proportionate and justified.[16]

2. The European Communities Act 1972. The challenge here was the fundamental political challenge to UK membership of the European Union.
3. Serious Organised Crime and Police Act 2005 section 132–8. This prohibits demonstrations within one kilometre of Parliament Square unless not less than six clear days notice has been given and authorisation given by the police, which must be given, but is subject to conditions. The criticism of this statute was on the basis of infringement or interference with the rights of free speech article 10 and of assembly article 12.[17]
4. Human Rights Act 1998. The criticism here was essentially that the human rights conferred on persons such as criminals, prisoners, gypsies or immigrants are excessive and not properly balanced against the rights of victims of crime, non-gypsy citizens and indigenous citizens.
5. The Act of Settlement 1700 section 2 disqualifies from the throne a Roman Catholic or one who marries a Roman Catholic, and requires the sovereign to subscribe and repeat the declaration of faithful protestantism (Accession Declaration Act 1910 schedule). Such a provision is anyway incompatible with the right to freedom of religion in the European Convention of Human Rights.[18]
6. Dangerous Dogs Act 1991. The problem with this statute is that it places restrictions upon the owner of certain 'types' of dog which immediately gives rise to problems of definition and identification; ownership in itself is not prohibited; and the controls over dangerous dogs is limited.

---

16 See *R (Countryside Alliance) v Attorney General* [2006] EWCA Civ 817.

17 For litigation regarding Mr Haw, the anti Iraq war long standing demonstrator, see *R (Haw) v Secretary of State Home Department* [2006] EWCA Civ 532 – the statute covered a demonstration already running and the commencement of the statute.

18 For a comparable issue, see the controversy over the right of a member of the Royal Family, e.g. Prince Charles, to marry or remarry in a registrar office 2003.

Deregulation

The earlier deregulation law proved to be of limited effectiveness. In the course of several years fewer than thirty deregulation orders were made. The orders that were made seem to have taken an inordinate time. The culture of regulation, excessive regulation, and of reluctance to deregulate is still very much with us.

Achieving a remedy is easier said than done. Finding the necessary primary legislative 'slot' may prove difficult or almost impossible. Drafting resources are not available. The political will for deregulation is lacking. The matter is not seen to have a political priority. A parliamentary opportunity and time cannot be found. Therefore, given the almost universally recognised virtue of 'deregulation', the need for reducing regulation to a minimum, ways and means of an alternative procedure, a non-legislative procedure, have been sought. First there was the Deregulation and Contracting Out Act 1994 (now repealed), then the Regulatory Reform Act 2001 (now repealed), and now the Legislative and Regulatory Reform Act 2006 chapter 51.

The best solution to the problem is to improve the quality of the original legislation, so as to avoid unsatisfactory regulation and the consequent need for deregulation. Better pre-legislative procedures are necessary, for example, a more measured political approach, more time, more resources, better consultation, less detail. All legislation should carry a regulatory impact assessment.

Objections

Not surprisingly the non-legislative deregulation approach has aroused very strong criticism, objection and reservation. The making and unmaking of statute law should be the exclusive responsibility of Parliament, not the minister nor the executive. The distinction between primary and secondary legislation is of fundamental significance in a democratic society. Parliament should not be by-passed and the role of MPs, especially Opposition MPs, should not be diminished. Primary legislation should not be altered by way of secondary legislation, by statutory instrument by government. The non-legislative process could involve constitutional issues, common law issues and issues of considerable public and political controversy. Henry VIII clauses[19] have for centuries been recognised and condemned as an abuse or potential abuse of democracy. Parliament, and only Parliament, is the ultimate lawmaker to protect our liberties. The non-legislative process could be given a low profile and 'slipped through' unnoticed. The opportunities for parliamentary, public scrutiny and discussion would be much reduced. There would be no pre-legislative parliamentary scrutiny. A statutory instrument cannot be amended. The safeguards may prove inadequate.

---

19 See N.W. Barber and A.L. Young, 'The rise of prospective Henry VIII clauses and their implications for sovereignty' (2003) *Public Law* pp. 112–27. There may be a reasonable case for them in respect of devolution and of the EU European Communities Act 1972; see 24 (2003) *Statute Law Review* 234 (Wales). A. McHarg, 'What is delegated legislation?' 50 (2006) *Public Law* pp. 539–61, at 553. Report of the Select Committee on the Constitution, HL paper 192 of 2003–04.

The potential for ministerial abuse cannot be ignored. There is no requirement upon government to act reasonably or objectively or by constitutional convention; nor indeed would that be possible to draft in enforceable terms. If government finds an easy way to repeal or to amend legislation it may be tempted to pay less attention to the quality of new primary legislation.

The partial renationalisation of the railways, without compensation, was achieved by the then minister Mr Byers in 2001 under the deregulation procedure by the removal of the rail regulator, and that was clearly a very controversial and indeed constitutional issue.

Government Reassurance

Government sought to reassure opponents. There is a real need to deregulate. Government is constructive and benign. The statute is outcome focussed. The statute contains adequate protections and safeguards by way of principles and conditions which must be observed. Government would expect to accept any rejecting recommendations from the committee considering the statutory instrument. Ministers would keep within their jurisdiction. There has been no abuse of the 2001 statute, and there will be no abuse in the future. The procedure will not be used for constitutional or significant or seriously controversial matters. The procedure will not be used to decriminalise drugs or assisted suicide. One possible advantage of secondary legislation is that it is susceptible to judicial review.

Original Bill

The bill originally introduced into the House of Commons sought to confer very considerable and radical powers upon the executive and contained very limited safeguards, and was severely mauled by members from all sides. The bill was dubbed the Abolition of Parliament Bill. In the event, the bill was much modified and amended and the revised bill introduced into the House of Lords, which was eventually passed, and amounted virtually to a new bill.

The New Statute

The minister may make an order for the purpose of removing or reducing any burden, or the overall burdens, resulting directly or indirectly for any person from any legislation section 1(1), (2). Burden means a financial cost, an administrative inconvenience, an obstacle to efficiency, productivity or profitability, or a sanction, criminal or otherwise, which affects the carrying on of any lawful activity section 1(3). For example, an old statute might be complicated, archaic, difficult to understand and apply. The required forms may be far too complicated. The procedure for obtaining a licence or consent for a regulated activity may be too complicated, too bureaucratic. Exemptions may need clarifying or extending. The deregulation scheme under the order may provide for sub-delegation, and also could involve the creation of a new body, for example, upon the merger and dissolution of existing bodies. In the nature of things the decision of the minister will be political, and politically accountable, and to that extent subjective rather than objective, although he must fulfil his public law duty to act reasonably.

The purpose must be to provide regulatory activities which are transparent, accountable, proportionate and consistent, and targeted only at cases in which action is needed sections 2 and 21. The minister may issue a code of practice section 22.

There are a number of safeguards, 'restrictions'. The pre-conditions are that the policy could not be satisfactorily achieved by non-legislative means, the effect is proportionate to the policy objective, there is a fair balance between the public interest and the private interest, for instance, the interests of any persons adversely affected, there is no removal of any necessary protection, and no prevention from continuing to exercise any right or freedom which a person might reasonably expect to continue to exercise, and the provision is not of constitutional significance section 3. Mere restatement is not permitted unless it would make the law more accessible or more easily understood, for example, the removal of an ambiguity. Consolidating or codifying the law is for primary legislation. The power of a minister to make subordinate legislation requires the approval of both Houses section 4. Taxation may not be imposed section 5. The order may not create new crimes carrying more than two- years imprisonment on indictment or increase the sentence for existing crimes to more than two-years imprisonment, or increase the sentences for summary offences beyond the normal limit, but within that limit may create new crimes or increase existing sentences. Exercise of this power is likely to provoke a critical response, except perhaps where the new crime is a replacement crime and conforms to the statutory principles section 6. Forcible entry and compulsion to answer questions are prohibited section 7. The Human Rights Act 1998 may not be amended or repealed by the order process section 9.

Procedure

There must be appropriate consultation, and a draft order, with reasons and explanatory material, must be laid before Parliament, under the negative resolution procedure 40 days, the affirmative resolution procedure 40 days, or the super-affirmative procedure 60 days section 18. The committee, in either House, may recommend rejection and the draft order then falls, unless the committee rejection is reversed by the House.

The so-called 'veto' was much debated. Government pointed out that the scrutinising parliamentary committee could recommend rejection of the order, and that would be the end of it, showing sufficient parliamentary control. Opponents pointed out that the committee rejection could be reversed by the House if government had a political majority, and thus the minister could ultimately get his way, get his order. Government replied that this is democracy, in the end the ruling party in the House is entitled to prevail.

The European Union

The new statute makes provision for transposing EU law into UK law. Where possible it may be best simply to use the language of the EU instrument, but where UK procedures and laws and traditions make this difficult or impossible then transposition in UK-style may be necessary, and the order procedure may be particularly appropriate for enabling the UK government to fulfil the EU obligations.[20]

The Church of England

The new statute does not apply to the Church of England, which has traditionally governed its own affairs.[21] By convention government legislates on internal Church matters only with consent.

The Law Commission

Originally the bill proposed to include Law Commission proposals under the new order procedure, but the idea was abandoned. Under the Law Commissions Act 1965 section 3 it is the duty of the Law Commission to take and keep under review all the laws with which they are concerned with a view to its systematic development and reform, including in particular the codification of such law, the elimination of anomalies, the repeal of obsolete and unnecessary enactments, the reduction of the number of separate enactments and generally the simplification and modernisation of the law. There are some 30 Law Commission draft bills awaiting implementation, half of which have been accepted in principle by the government, many of which appear to be non-controversial and many of which have been patiently waiting for years and years. However, it was pointed out that some Law Commission proposals are of a substantial nature, they are or may be controversial, they require full parliamentary discussion for they are rarely merely lawyers' law with no policy implications, for example, murder, cohabitation, and would not be suitable for an expedited or truncated parliamentary process, ministerial order, and on a take it or leave it basis with no opportunity for amendment.[22] The Jellicoe special procedure for public bills is much more suitable.

---

20 See 2006 Act Part 3 s 25–9. European Communities Act 1972 s 2(2). *Duke v Reliance Systems* [1988] AC 618. *R v Secretary of State for Foreign and Commonwealth Affairs ex parte Rees-Mogg* [1994] QB 552 CA. A. Samuels, 'Incorporating, translating and implementing European law into the UK' 19 (1998) *Statute Law Review* pp. 80–92.

21 See Church of England Assembly (Powers) Act 1919 s 2. Synodical Government Measure 1969.

22 See the annual reports of The Law Commission; see J. Halliday review of the Law Commission 2003. A. Samuels, 'Consolidation: a plea' 26 (2005) *Statute Law Review* pp. 56–63.

Expected Action

Government gave examples of the kind of things that they were contemplating doing under the new regulation law, amending or repealing primary legislation, such as minor or relatively minor matters involving employment, the construction industry, weights and measures, merging inspectorates, reducing the frequency of inspection regimes, consumer rights, tree preservation orders, game laws Game Act 1831, and fees laid down in primary legislation. In recent times orders have dealt with the fire service and the sugar beet industry and similar matters.

Conclusion

In England, indeed in the UK, the weaknesses of the legislative procedure are embarrassingly obvious as are the remedies. The better the quality of the legislation at enactment the less likely there will be trouble or difficulty in the future. The form of legislation should be such as to lend itself to simple or comparatively simple amendment in the future. There is a lot to be said for limiting the period of operation of a statute, so that it will not become obsolete over time and positive steps will be needed if it is to be continued or renewed. In areas where the statute is in constant daily use by the users, for example, criminal law, family law, landlord and tenant, social welfare, company law, whatever, there should be standing review bodies consisting of appropriate experts charged with producing an annual revised and updated statute. The Law Commission must be adequately resourced so as to play a much more central, enlarged and overseeing role in statute review. Post-legislative scrutiny should be part of the life of a statute, to promote systematic review and systematic keeping up to date, instead of the current *ad hoc* practice, reactive instead proactive. In view of the complicated procedures in Parliament, wherever possible there should be a simplified and expedited parliamentary process, or a proper constitutional means of avoiding the parliamentary process wherever possible.

An English lawyer, brought up in the English legislative system, naturally hesitates to presume to offer advice to a Commonwealth country. This required the experience, commitment and standing of a lawyer like Sir William Dale.

Chapter 9

Pre-legislative Scrutiny

Zione Ntaba

Introduction

Drafting has become an art form in the twentieth century; drafting offices around the world seem to have developed rules and techniques or have adapted existing ones to suit the current system in their country – like concepts and elements of globalisation must now be accommodated in legislation. It has become evident that in all these changes, 'quality' is always emphasised; but what has become even clearer is that there is a need for 'efficiency' and 'effectiveness' in all the legislation that is being passed.

An aspect in the legislative process which has become central is the issue of scrutiny of a bill. This area falls squarely on verifying whether a bill has satisfied the necessary requirements and, furthermore, if all the rules have been followed in the drafting process. This issue cannot be overemphasised in the drafting world but more so because it has a major impact on the legal system. In writing this chapter it has become evident that eminent authors in the field of legislative drafting have ignored this aspect of the legislative process in most of their writings. This is compared to other stages of the drafting process, for example, receiving instructions, which are extensively analysed by available literature, Thornton[1] and Crabbe[2] are perfect examples of this.

This chapter proposes that the statement by G.C. Thornton, that 'the scrutiny and testing of a draft bill is necessary but there is need for a great deal of self-discipline which will require 10–20 drafts to attain a final draft', is not workable in the current system that drafters operate. It is further argued in this chapter that in order to carry out pre-legislative scrutiny drafters have been let down by the academics in this area as there is not enough literature or theories on best practices and standards, on which they can develop uniform standards for checking quality.

In looking at Thornton's proposition, it becomes pertinent to question whether drafting departments need to set up rules and procedures for their drafters to follow so as to ensure that a draft bill has been adequately scrutinised.

1 See G.C. Thornton, *Legislative Drafting*, 4th edn (London: Butterworths, 1996).

2 See V.C.R.A.C. Crabbe, *Legislative Drafting* (London: Routledge Cavendish, 1993).

Methodology

This chapter, noting that the aspect of pre-legislative scrutiny is a practical issue, decided to look at several drafting offices, Botswana, Seychelles, Canada, United Kingdom and Malawi to see what is done in those offices to achieve pre-legislative scrutiny. It should be noted that all these countries are common law-based, have similar legislation styles and incidentally their drafting offices are similarly arranged, for example, they receive their instructions from the various government ministries and departments. Thus, they can be seen as representative case studies of a system of drafting which has based its drafting process mostly in the Executive arm of government.

The chapter intends to look at what eminent authors in legislative drafting have written on the subject of pre-legislative scrutiny of legislation. Moreover, the chapter intends to compare these writings with the techniques and procedures which are used in the above stated case studies. Finally, this chapter hopes to examine whether these rules, used in pre-legislative scrutiny of a draft bill, help achieve quality in legislation and perhaps more importantly whether they improve the efficiency and effectiveness of the legislation when passed.

The Legislative Process: Scrutiny and Testing

Legislation is, among others, a desire to change the social setting of a country; and this desire carries with it a huge burden – that is before it reaches the stage of actually achieving social change. Legislation must significantly be able to pass strict scrutiny tests by all parties concerned before it can become effective. In order to ensure that the legislation passes the scrutiny tests, it cannot be denied that this heavy task is borne by the drafter. Luzius Mader,[3] who has written on the subject of scrutiny, offers major insight on the rationale for ensuring that draft legislation is scrutinised or evaluated.

The drafter in this process according to Thornton,[4] is not a mere policy translator, but a drafter has a lot of bearing on every aspect of legislation from the type, contents,

3 'The analytical model underlying the methodical approach to the preparation of legislation considers the legislative process as a reiterative learning process. It is a process in which the evaluation of the effects of legislation is a fundamental prerequisite, and which ensures that the legislation is responsive to social reality and the social adequacy of legislative action.', in L. Mader, 'Evaluating the Effects: A Contribution to the Quality of Legislation' 22 (2001) 2 *Statute Law Review* pp. 119–31 at 123.

4 'The proper role of a legislative drafter lies somewhere between two extreme views. One extreme view regards drafters as doing little more than selecting words as if from shelf and putting them in the right order. This view holds that policy is for policy makers alone and the drafter should draft as instructed without regard to fundamental principles, practicality or anything else.'

The other view considers it to be the responsibility of drafters to develop a broad idea into a practical scheme. In other words, to take over from the policymakers by developing incomplete policy to a refined and complete state … On the other hand, the proper role is more creative than that of mere wordsmith … The drafter is 'an architect of social structures,

structure of legislation to even deciding whether there should be legislation at all. Therefore, a drafter is vested with an enormous and important discretion and task and must carry it out within the necessary boundaries of standards whether national or international.

Therefore, transforming the legislative idea into a cognitive legal draft is a straight-forward task for a drafter if all proper procedure is followed; but this chapter intends to look at the concept of how a drafter ensures that after following the proper procedure, legislation can have the desired effect of achieving social change. Thus, the contours of a legislative theory[5] are very important for a drafting department, as it makes it possible to achieve all this. It is this aspect that becomes necessary, as illustrated by the latter part of stage 5 of Thornton's theory which is 'testing the draft bill'. This chapter will focus on the issue of scrutiny only. Therefore, it must ask whether in order to achieve pre-legislative scrutiny of a bill (while it is still in the drafting department), is it necessary to develop legislative drafting regulations, standards or a check list. Incidentally, it can still be questioned if this does solve the issue of whether the context is right as well as the concepts because it can ensure that the draft legislation is grammatically and textually correct. In looking at all this, one must remember that drafters in the twentieth century, in most of the above mentioned jurisdictions, are working in 'liberal' democracies with constitutional values where pre-legislative scrutiny is a prerequisite. In other words transparency and accountability in the draft legislation being promulgated must fulfil democratic principles either by promoting or protecting constitutional principles and values.

The term 'scrutiny' in its grammatical meaning denotes the act of examining something (e.g. for mistakes).[6] To enrich this debate, it should be noted that when this chapter discusses pre-legislative scrutiny, the concept is a wide one, as noted from the fact it carries throughout the drafting process and, for instance, in the United Kingdom[7] it is done in Parliament before the bill is introduced before the full house

---

an expert in the design of frameworks of collaboration for all kinds of purposes, a specialist in the high art of speaking to the future, knowing when and how to try and bind it and when not to try at all. The difference between a legal mechanic and a legal craftsman turns largely on awareness of this point'. Although not primarily responsible for policy, drafters do have important advisory responsibilities of a policy kind. Thornton (1996) at 125.

5 See: A. Seidman, R.B. Seidman and N. Abeyesekere, *Legislative Drafting for Democratic Social Change* (The Hague: Kluwer Academic Publishers, 2001) pp. 266–7, where they suggest that there is a need to equip drafters with the skills and knowledge necessary for competent drafting – not only legislative drafting techniques and foreign law and experience but especially an appropriate legislative theory.

6 See (www.wordreference.com), as of 31 May 2007.

7 'There is almost universal agreement that pre-legislative scrutiny is right in principle, subject to the circumstances and nature of the legislation. It provides an opportunity for the House as a whole, for individual backbenchers, and for the Opposition to have a real input into the form of the actual legislation which subsequently emerges, not least because Ministers are likely to be far more receptive to suggestions for change before the Bill is actually published. It opens Parliament up to those outside affected by the legislation. At the same time such pre-legislative scrutiny can be of real benefit to the Government. It could, and indeed should, lead to less time being needed at later stages of the legislative process; the use of the Chair's powers

of Parliament. Scrutiny in its essence and more so in the drafting process becomes synonymous with good practices, adherence to standards, regulations and the rule of law and aims to improve effectiveness and efficiency of legislation. It is on this premise that the chapter is founded.

Analysis of the Current Writings and Drafting Practices

The twentieth century has seen drafters being overworked due to the high volume of legislation that is being produced annually in their various jurisdictions. Due to the evolving world that drafters operate in (a world that is governed by rules, regulations and laws in all aspects of life) it has become of utmost importance that legislation which is being drafted is of quality and not just quantity so as to ensure that the world is just not clogged up with 'useless' legislation. The legal system has realised that the more a draft bill is scrutinised before it gets to Parliament, the most effective and efficient the legislative process will be – as well as the law itself.

It cannot be underemphasised that during the whole drafting process in a civil or common law jurisdiction, work being produced is continuously evaluated by drafters or policymakers.[8] However, the question still remains whether consultations or the various amendments following such consultations are enough. Does there need to be a stage whereby the drafting department using developed internal rules evaluates the draft with a professional eye with the aim of achieving quality?

Keith Patchett[9] advocates that there is a need for a set of standards for drafters especially in transitioning countries. And with regard to scrutiny of draft legislation,

---

of selection would naturally reflect the extent and nature of previous scrutiny and debate. Above all, it should lead to better legislation and less likelihood of subsequent amending legislation.' See Select Committee on Modernisation of the House of Commons, *First Report – The Legislative Process, 1997–98*, HC 190, para. 7.

8 'The process of composition and development includes much revisionary work carried out by both the drafter personally and by the instructing officer. It involves much consultation with the sponsors, and perhaps other interested parties, and involves various amendments to the draft from time to time to meet criticism, changes in instructions and supplementary instructions.

By the time the draft is in final shape it may be perhaps the tenth or even the twentieth version produced by the drafter.' See Thornton (1996) at 173.

9 '13. Common standards and uniform practices for preparing and drafting legislation are set most effectively through the provision of a single set of directives, which have behind them the authority of Government and, as needed, Parliament ... Not only is this the most powerful means by which reforms can be effected, but for the time being it may be the only sure way by which a single set of standards can be set to bind both Government and he Parliament.

14. Ideally, all directives concerned with legislative preparation should be collated into a single source (e.g. a Legislative Handbook) that is thoroughly known and used by everyone in preparing legislation.

15. Three sets of circumstances are typically regulated in legislation specifically concerned with law drafting:

- procedures that are to be followed at different stages in the drafting process;

some good lessons are learnt from the comprehensive manner that Patchett[10] has dealt with the issue, especially looking at a draft that has been finalised and is ready for Cabinet. He states that scrutiny of the legislative text should be a continuous process throughout the drafting process, in order to improve its clarity and to check its practicability. But as a matter of best practice, each version of a draft should be subjected to a specific scrutiny as the last step to check particularly on legal form, clarity and comprehensibility. As the final step in drafting (the final version of a law) this scrutiny should be extended to cover a wider range of matters, including a series of legal verifications. These are necessary as the translation of policy into precise norms may introduce new features into the text.[11]

Furthermore, if a drafter is to eliminate any potential problems, whether legal or otherwise with regard to legislation, especially before it is passed by the legislature, it can be stated that some level of efficiency is being achieved when it comes to verification of the draft bill. It is argued that a drafter might not be able to achieve effectiveness due to the very nature of legislation; however it is a notion that is aspired to by every drafting office that all their laws are effective.

The legislative process has always put in safeguards to ensure that the end product meets with standards used in that particular jurisdiction and that it has taken on board all the instructions given to the drafter as well as views of the people consulted. Therefore, this begs the question as to whether consultation, as it is carried out by drafters in the various jurisdictions, is enough to qualify as pre-legislative scrutiny of a draft bill. This question is being raised noting that a drafter and an instructing officer can decide to ignore suggestions given by subjects of the draft legislation during consultations for all sorts of reasons, ranging from political, social as well as economic ones, without the need to give reasons for doing so.

The issues which must also be addressed when looking at pre-legislative scrutiny are questioning who is tasked to do it, when it should be done, how it should be done and most importantly why it should be done before a bill is taken before Cabinet to transmit to Parliament. First, it is important to concentrate on various aspects of the legislative process with regard to scrutiny. Second, it should be stressed that the concept must concentrate on the final draft because to do otherwise would be inappropriate for the discussion herein.

- uniform rules as to the application and operation of particular kinds of legislative provisions;
- standard requirements as to the form, terminology and style in which legislation is to be drafted.'

K. Patchett, 'Setting and Maintaining Law Drafting Standards: A Background Paper on Legislative Drafting' in C. Stefanou and H. Xanthaki (eds), *Manual in Legislative Drafting* (Cambridge: DFID/University Press, 2005) at 47.

10 '44. Almost all composition needs a series of drafts in order to reach the necessary quality. Such a process has considerable benefits, since it enables each version to be reviewed by the other members of the drafting team, and gaps in policy or problems to be identified and resolved. Drafts can also be sent to other interested Ministries to obtain their reactions to the provisions that concern them.'; ibid. at 56; see also at 57–8.

11 See ibid. at 56, para. 45.

From the various jurisdictions that were asked to evaluate the statement by Thornton[12] as put forward in the hypothesis, it is evident that the general view is that most of the jurisdictions agree with him, in stating that verification as a process is necessary but more so that it does require discipline. However, they mention that Thornton's techniques of achieving verification of producing close to ten drafts before moving to a final draft is impossible in the twentieth century.

In Botswana[13] it is noted that producing up to ten drafts before the final draft is practically unattainable due to various constraints, the major one being time.[14] Thus, they have had to rely heavily on their checklist as well as the good graces of their fellow colleagues[15] to proofread and scrutinise their draft bills ensuring that all requirements have been met before submission to Cabinet. And for them, this is a practice which has worked and has helped in the scrutiny of draft legislation within the time constraints they operate. Similar positions exist in Canada, Seychelles and the United Kingdom[16] and after interviewing drafters from these countries, from their answers it is clear that production of ten draft bills as a minimum is unworkable. However, the gravitas of the bill can to some degree affect the number of drafts that a drafting office will produce as a matter of evaluating that its quality is good.

It is generally agreed that the more drafts that are produced in the legislative process, the better the final product. However, all countries – more so in the developing world – have limited financial and human resources to dedicate to the

12 'Parliamentary Counsel usually prepares a number of drafts before the final draft and that they should study their preliminary drafts, conference after conference and there will be a lot of revision and re-writing'. Crabbe (1993) at 12.

13 Interviews with Botswanan drafters conducted at the Institute of Advanced Legal Studies (12 May 2007).

14 'The work is urgent. It has to be done by at any cost during the limited time available. But when a particular draft is cumbersome with hundreds of provisions requiring careful, patient and minute examination, time is the enemy ... All this involves time and concentration. There is a constant battle between urgency and limited time.' Crabbe (1993) at 12. See also, section 11 of the Malawian Attorney General's Memorandum, 'It may be supposed from my description that the drafting or legislation is a leisurely process, but unfortunately it is not. Rarely is a Bill prepared under ideal conditions; usually the work must be done in a hurry and under pressure. *It must be argued that in the current world due to the numerous legislation that countries are producing in a year, time is not short only for complex pieces of legislation but also for even simple amendments, thus time is a major constraint in the 20th Century.*' [emphasis added].

See also the directive passed by the Canadian Cabinet entitled *The Preparation of Legislation*, Government of Canada (Privy Council, 16 April, 1981) which states:

'(4) ... the Cabinet Committee of Legislation and Housing Planning, assisted by the sponsoring Minister, will scrutinize the Bill as to its drafting and as to its consistency with the earlier policy decision taken by Cabinet ... reports to Cabinet on the outcome of its consideration of a given draft Bill'

15 As Thornton states: '... a drafting colleague who comes fresh to the exercise should be inveigled into scrutinizing the draft and offering comments'. See Thornton (1996) at 174.

16 Interviews with drafters (conducted at the Institute of Advanced Legal Studies (12 May 2007); see also Sir Geoffrey Bowman, 'The Art of Legislative Drafting' 7 (2006) *European Journal of Law Reform*.

process. Therefore, drafters have had to develop means of ensuring cost effectiveness and good time management. One can argue that this may negate the concept of pre-legislative scrutiny. However, this is not the case because since all draft legislation in most countries must still go before the Cabinet for approval before it can be tabled in Parliament. A further concern from this might be that since the Cabinet is a political body and has its own agenda to fulfil (to see its policies realised), their evaluation would not be much on the efficiency or effectiveness of the bill, but rather whether the draft bill translates the policy into law. However, it is argued that if a piece of legislation does not meet the necessary requirements it would not serve the government any purpose as Parliament would throw it out.

In Malawi, the Attorney General's *Memorandum*[17] (referred to as the 'Memo'), provides for what a drafter should do to achieve a level of satisfactory scrutiny. Section 17 offers insight into a very important aspect of scrutiny in Malawi, as it stipulates that before the full Cabinet looks at a draft bill, it must first be referred to the Cabinet Committee on Parliamentary and Legal Affairs who fair the bill and usually note areas of concern. This is an important step as it acts as a further test before the Cabinet checks it and also makes amendments to the draft bill before submission to Parliament.[18] This is a standard rule, as it helps to act as a 'checks and balances' tool for the drafters because if the committee finds the draft bill to be lacking, then the bill is referred back to the Ministry of Justice.

As noted from the above discussion, some jurisdictions have seen it proper to produce techniques or standards so as to achieve a certain level of pre-legislative scrutiny or verification of the bill as pronounced by Thornton. It is evident in the drafting world that a lot of thought and energy goes into the various stages of the drafting process. For instance, rules have been developed for every stage; it is a set principle that a drafter should always start his legislative project only after receiving written instructions[19] from a government department or ministry. The written instructions themselves are a scrutiny tool and not just a planning tool as a drafter can revert back to them to see if the objective has been achieved.

Second, in this democratic dispensation which exists in the various jurisdictions examined, it is necessary to achieve and observe certain standards and, according to Seidman,[20] this can easily be done but it is argued that there is more attention in the process being placed on one aspect while others are ignored thereby affecting in the long run the quality of the legislation produced.

In furthering the argument for the need for a recognised set of standards or regulations in scrutiny of legislation, a classic example can be seen in Malawi, whereby not all draft legislation comes from professional drafters, that is, Private

17 Attorney General's Memorandum, 'Procedure for Obtaining Legal Advice and Procedure for the Preparation, Publication and Passing of Proposed Legislation', Ministry of Justice, 1981.

18 See sections, 8, 14–19 of the Memo for further clarifications into the scrutiny work of the Cabinet plus procedures that must be fulfilled before a draft bill is brought before it.

19 See Crabbe (1993) at 12.

20 See Seidman, Seidman and Abeyesekere (2001) at 29.

Members can promulgate legislation.[21] It has been seen that if not for parliamentary legislation, legislation that is unconstitutional can also easily become part of the law. Although there is not much pre-legislative scrutiny with regard to these types of bills, but as a standard for aiming legislation that achieves social change, then Private Member Bills must also be subject to the same kind of pre-legislative scrutiny.

But in all these, Thornton's set of questions[22] offer a lot of insight as to what aspects must be covered in the checklist if a drafting department decides to develop one. It must be emphasised that once developed the practice or standard must be entrenched in the workings of a drafting department so that is it regimented so as to ensure quality.

Several Commonwealth jurisdictions have announced how much they would like their drafting offices to be more efficient and effective in a world of competing interests which exist in the Executive branch of government, from where the vast majority of legislation emanates. Thus, the idea that rules on how pre-legislative scrutiny should also include the scrutiny conducted by Cabinet is supported by Seidman[23] who further argue that evaluation should feed into the whole process of drafting.

---

21 See Constitution (Amendment Bill, No. 1 of 2002), whereby a Private Member's Bill, commonly referred to as the 'Open Term Bill', and sponsored by Hon. Khwauli Msiska, Member of Parliament (AFORD) (as he was then) was published in the Gazette on 24 May 2002. The bill sought to amend section 83(3) to remove the limitation of the number of terms that President may serve. The bill was defeated in the National Assembly.

22 See Thornton (1996) at 173:

'The scrutiny and testing stage requires a great deal of self-discipline. It is far from easy but the drafter must somehow take a critical and objective gave at the finished product. First, the drafter should read and consider it as a whole. Then following questions should be considered.

- Does the draft achieve all those objectives that the drafter believes to be the intended objectives of the proposal?
- Does the draft fit harmoniously into the general body of the law?
- Does the law comply with basic principles of the legal and constitutional system?
- Does the draft form a coherent well-structured whole and does the material flow in logical sequence?
- Are the content and the language of the draft as clear and comprehensible as the drafter can make them?'

23 'Almost every government has some rules detailing the path a bill must track from Ministry to Cabinet committee to central drafting office to Cabinet. Frequently, drafting offices' internal regulations specify the bills' formal technical features: ... Some departmental handbooks prescribe substantive standards.' Seidman, Seidman and Abeyesekere (2000) at 38. See also Legislation Approval Process, Drafting Direction No. 4.6 (Office of Parliamentary Counsel of Australia, 1 May 2006) at 4, which states:

1. The purpose of the Legislation Approval Process (LAP) is to ensure that draft legislation has received all necessary government clearances before it is introduced into Parliament. All draft legislation must be cleared for introduction by a Parliamentary Secretary or junior Minister designated by the Prime Minister for the purpose (the designated approver). This

The problem, however, in all this is that the focus still seems to be more in Parliament than in the drafting office. For instance, in the United Kingdom[24] in the last decade, focus with regard to pre-legislative scrutiny has been on Parliament which in my opinion has put up rules and regulations which ensure the existence of pre-legislative scrutiny before a draft bill is taken before Parliament.[25] Thus, emphasis has been placed heavily on Parliament for being the organ doing the quality check; however, it is argued here that in order to ensure efficiency of the whole legislative system pre-legislative scrutiny is best served by the actual drafters themselves.

In its first report, the Modernization Committee recommended a more regular and systematic use of draft bills. Moreover, it stated that there is almost universal agreement that pre-legislative scrutiny is right in principle, subject to the circumstances and nature of the legislation. It provides an opportunity for the House as a whole, for individual backbenchers, and for the Opposition to have a real input into the form of the actual legislation which subsequently emerges, not least because ministers are likely to be far more receptive to suggestions for change before the bill is actually published. It opens Parliament up to those outside affected by legislation. At the same time such pre-legislative scrutiny can be of real benefit to the government. It could, and indeed should, lead to less time being needed at later stages of the legislative process; the use of the Chair's powers of selection would naturally reflect the extent and nature of previous scrutiny and debate. Above all, it should lead to better legislation and less likelihood of subsequent amending legislation.[26] This State

---

clearance is given on advice from the Legislation Secretariat in the Department of the Prime Minister and Cabinet (PM&C).

2. OPC's unique role in the process is to provide independent advice that the legislation is covered by appropriate policy authority. The OPC drafter is the only independent player in the approval process who knows enough about the legislation to be able to test it against the policy authority within the usual deadlines. This is not to suggest that other players (e.g. policy officers in PM&C) could not acquire the necessary understanding of legislation, only that they may not be able to do it properly in the brief period between when the legislation is lodged with PM&C and when it is lodged with the designated approver (often less than 2 working days).'

24 See Hansard Society Commission on the Legislative Process, *Making the Law* (London: Hansard Society, 1992); see also G. Power, *Parliamentary Scrutiny of Draft Legislation* (London: The Constitution Unit, 1997–99) at 8, 'Although the Commission acknowledged that publication in draft was not suitable for all bills it recommended that, in general, the Government should encourage departments to follow best practice, stating that "in principle, there should be as full consultations on draft texts, especially in so far as they relate to practical questions of the implementation and enforcement of legislation", and "where there is no great urgency for a Bill, the whole Bill might sometimes be published in draft in a Green Paper, as the basis for further consultation and possibly parliamentary scrutiny".

On procedures for drafting–final stage is validation of law, "If the legislator is a Parliament, the text will need to go through successive stages, at one or more of which it may be amended. It is of crucial importance whether the practice is for MPs themselves to draft amendments to the Bill or whether the original drafter."' See F. Bennion, *Bennion of Statute Law*, 4th edn (London: Longman, 1990) pp.11–12.

25 See ibid. at 10.

26 See Hansard Society Commission, para. 20.

encapsulates why pre-legislative scrutiny is necessary in the legislative process and furthermore why rules or standards – or at the very least good practices – should be adopted by drafting departments to achieve quality in their work.

It is suggested that if pre-legislative scrutiny is done, it is likely that the process as seen from the above discussion, has a direct link with quality as well as efficiency and effectiveness of legislation, as the process aims at ensuring that draft legislation is necessary and more importantly that it meets the intended results.[27] Therefore, once a draft bill has been properly scrutinised or evaluated (within the meaning of this discussion) and shown to have attained all standards, once instructions have been followed and all matters of concerns raised in consultation have been taken into account and incorporated into the bill then it is submitted that quality is an assured result.[28]

Conclusion

It should be noted that on reading most authors in legislative drafting, one comes out thinking that pre-legislative drafting is not a major concern as there seems to be a lot of concern with scrutiny as it relates to Parliament or post-legislatively, but not much pre-legislation. However, as has been noted already in this chapter, that as there are is a lot of laws being promulgated, it should be stressed that as most drafters work in a perceived democratic environment, that they are duty bound to uphold the rule of law and follow constitutional principles, and the process of pre-legislative scrutiny must take centre stage in their work and should be given as much attention as the preparation of the legislative proposal.

Lawmakers or drafters are vested with powers to translate policy into law not just for the sake of it but to try to achieve social change and development. It is from this premise that Seidman argues that they have to ensure that they have available to them tools to help them achieve this and not fail.[29]

Lawmakers that are drafters aim to ensure that the legislation that is produced for the country is of high quality. To achieve this, one needs to adhere to a strict regiment as advocated by John Stuart Mill.[30] Drafters must ensure that they produce standards

27 See Seidman, Seidman and Abeyesekere (2000) at 38.

'Summarized, that methodology consisted of the following steps ...

(4) Introduce the bill in something close to final form without any effort to provide a justification grounded in logic and facts, and let the legislators decide its fate by their vote.'

28 See Mader (2000) at 125–8.

29 'Too often, drafters do not translate policies into effectively implementable legislation. They fail for three principle reasons:

(1) the persistence of the myth that drafters deal not with the law's substance, but only its form;

(2) the weakness of the drafting institutions within which most drafter's function; and

(3) the drafter's innocence of a theory or methodology for making that translation.'

Seidman, Seidman and Abeyesekere (2000) at 29.

30 'There is hardly any kind of intellectual work which so much needs to be done, not only by experienced and exercised minds, but by minds trained to the task through long and laborious study, as the business of making laws.' quoted in E. Freund, 'The Problem of

or checklists as seen in Botswana or Malawi so as to offer them a tool when it comes to scrutinising the draft bill before it is submitted to Parliament.

It can be stated that when it comes to pre-legislative scrutiny, the problem in all the above jurisdictions is one of practicality as well as principles. One can advise that managing the legislative process will sort out the time problems but it does not solve the financial or human resource limitations or the volume of draft legislation. It is suggested that better coordination between the ministries/government departments will ensure that there is more pre-legislative scrutiny at Cabinet level, which is in-depth as it will be following principles and techniques used in the drafting office.

One can recommend that for pre-legislative scrutiny to work, there is a need for an independent body, which is vested in doing this job for all bills – whether emanating from government or the private sector – and is not based in any arm of government so as to ascertain that the draft legislation will be effective and that it will achieve this by using the most efficient means. But despite there being no universal scrutiny checklist or set of rules/standards in the Commonwealth, it is concluded that as a matter of best practice, pre-legislative scrutiny is a very necessary tool for the drafter as it promotes and protects the rule of law because quality legislation ensures the justice system is not delayed with too many legal challenges.

As a final note, it should be emphasised that there is a need for drafting offices to produce standards and regulations to be used by drafters, for instance, checklists to ensure that all necessary procedures have been complied with as a step towards some level of pre-legislative scrutiny. It is advised that all this must be done together with the Cabinet.[31]

Intelligent Legislation,'4 (1907) *Proceedings of the American Political Science Association* pp. 69, 70.

31 'Government needs legislation. The governed need well drafted readable, understandable legislation ... The idea that legislation can be used to achieve great changes in society is very attractive to politicians.' Crabbe (1993) at 19.

Chapter 10

The Role of the Legislative Drafter in Promoting Social Transformation

Richard C. Nzerem

This chapter is in three parts and each part addresses a different aspect of the role of a legislative drafter. Part I is a general part and attempts to define the proper role of a drafter in a modern democratic society. Part II deals with the sometimes troublesome problem of prioritising legislative proposals. Last, Part III deals with drafting with a view to achieving good governance and, in particular, combating a culture of corruption which has a tendency to undermine good governance.

Part I

General Introduction

The general body of the law in force in any civilised society usually exists in a variety of forms. This would include legislation and various forms of 'unwritten' rules such as custom and convention. Again, in most modern societies it is probably true to say that the most important rules that govern human behaviour will be found in written laws that have been passed in the form of legislation by an elected law-making body.

In very simple and practical terms, the first duty of a legislative drafter, the person entrusted with preparing draft written rules before they are passed into laws, is to translate government policies into effective law. The authority of the drafter to carry out this exercise derives from a request that the drafter receives, usually from a government department. This request comes in the form of 'drafting instructions' to draft a specific legislation. However, many notable authors in the field of legislative drafting agree that the function of the drafter is not simply to translate government policy into written laws. It is evident from the writings of these authors that in the law-making process, contrary to popular belief, the drafter plays an important role with respect to both the form and content of a law. The drafter's task is not merely one of communicating the instructions they have received to the general public through the medium of legislation.

In his Preface to the 1st edition of his much acclaimed work on legislative drafting, Thornton was emphatic on the need for the drafter to develop an obsession to draft so as to be readily understood. The drafter's task, Thornton said, 'is not only to "determine" the law but also to "communicate" it'.[1] The form and content of legislation must be linked otherwise the dual task of translating and communicating instructions received cannot be effectively carried out. It should not be thought, however, that it is ever the function of a drafter either to initiate legislative policy or to determine legislative policy as properly understood.

The life of a drafter is not an easy one. The profession of legislative drafting is one discipline of law that requires complete devotion, focused attention and consistent hard work. In drafting any new legislation the drafter has to undertake an in-depth study of the issues involved and has to interact with policymakers, relevant experts, politicians as well as other stakeholders in order to keep abreast of developments past, present and future.[2] The drafter has to deal with many pressures. The reasons for the laws that he or she is called upon to draft do not arise in a vacuum. A drafter has to bear in mind the reasons for the legislation. He or she has to consider the state of the society as it was in the past, as it is in the present and as it is desired that it should be in the future. This means that the drafter has to deal with the problems of the past and present but must also think of the future by laying down rules of conduct for the guidance of society.[3] What this amounts to is that the dividing line between policy and the substance or content of law enacted to implement that policy may be blurred. As a consequence of this, the drafter cannot escape being involved in policy considerations.[4]

In practice, therefore, a drafter often participates in defining the meaning of policy and in translating the broad terms of policy into the law's details. Between policy and legislation, there are open spaces which the drafter may have to fill. This situation arises largely from the fact that instructions to drafters are typically general in much the same way that the instructions an architect receives from a potential house owner to produce the technical drawings for a house are often general. Drafting instructions

1 See G.C. Thornton, *Legislative Drafting*, 3rd edn (London: Butterworths, 1987) at vii. Thornton's choice of emphasis in this regard contrasts sharply with other writers insofar as drafters are not usually ascribed the power to 'determine' laws.

2 See B.R. Atre, *Legislative Drafting–Principles And Techniques*, 'Preface to the 2nd edn' (New Delhi: Universal Law Publishing, 2006), at v, and as to the many problems a drafter has to contend with see V.C.R.A.C. Crabbe, *Legislative Drafting* (London: Routledge Cavendish, 1993) at 1.

3 The position is not made any easier by the need for the drafter to avoid unwittingly giving credence to a popular perception that the drafter is 'undoubtedly the cause of half the litigation' engendered by laws composed by the drafter and to also avoid becoming an even easier target for critics who have little appreciation of the job of a drafter.

4 On the policy aspects of the drafter's role in the legislative process, see A. Seidman, R.B. Seidman and N. Abeyesekere, *Legislative Drafting for Democratic Social Change* (The Hague: Kluwer Academic Publishers, 2000) at 6; Reed Dickerson, *Fundamentals of Legal Drafting*, 2nd edn (Boston: Little, Brown, 1986) at 14 (Dickerson draws a clear distinction between the legal drafting and legislative drafting roles of a drafter, the former covering a wider field than the latter but does not seem to carry this distinction into the role of a 'drafter' in the implementation of legislative policy generally); Elmer A. Driedger, *The Composition of Legislation, Legislative Forms and Precedents*, 2nd edn (Ottawa: Dept. of Justice, 1975) at xv; also see Crabbe (1993) at 11.

to drafters have been known in some cases to be notoriously imprecise. Filling in the details that have not been provided by the instructor therefore inevitably involves the drafter sometimes in substantive 'decision-making'.

If a drafter believes that a proposed bill would result in a particular difficulty or unconstitutionality, they are duty bound to point this out and may, in an extreme case refuse instructions to draft such a bill. Failure to embrace the concept of the unity of form and content has led to the myth that the drafter does not deal with policy but merely translates it into legislation. That would present a timid and unimaginative drafter an opportunity to deny any responsibility for the bills that they draft and also to neglect the probable social impact of the bill. A better approach, perhaps, would be to attempt to work around the obstacle and try to surmount it.[5] One practical and sometimes unfortunate consequence of this myth is demonstrated by the practice in some countries of using legislative precedents without adequate care. The use of precedents, in itself, is not a bad thing. However, if precedents are used indiscriminately, it could result in the adoption of wholly unsuitable legislation originating from and intended to apply only in a foreign jurisdiction.[6]

The Context of Legislation

Law, Development and Good Governance

It is important for the drafter to be always mindful not only of the reasons for a law but also of the context in which that law is to operate. This means, for instance, that there will be such issues as law and development, law and good governance as well as other matters, including form, to consider.

The law must be used as an agent to facilitate development, social change and social transformation, especially in the face of such powerfully overwhelming new forms of potential disempowerment as globalisation. This is more evident in countries going through a period of transition. Typical examples of this are where, as a result of some kind of turmoil, such as emergence from colonial rule, endemic civil disorder or war, society has become dysfunctional and the normal institutions of society can no longer be relied upon to function effectively.

Human Rights and Social Justice

Some jurisdictions now require that laws must be so drafted as to be compliant in certain respects, such as human rights, in line with treaty obligations that have an overriding effect on national legislation.[7] The suggestion is not that the drafter must

5 See Sir Geoffrey Bowman, First Parliamentary Counsel's answers to comments and observations in the Minutes of his evidence to the House of Lords Select Committee on the Constitution, 23 June 2004 (Q. 341–3).

6 [6] See ibid., Sir Geoffrey Bowman's answer to Q. 352 by the Chairman of the Committee.

7 The UK Human Rights Act 1998. Section 19 of the Act requires a minister responsible for a Bill before Parliament to make a statement, *inter alia*, that in his or her view the provisions

attempt to cover every possibility. That would be impossible as it is not possible to foresee every future possibility.

Some modern constitutions have set out deliberately to ensure that the constitution itself is used as a tool for securing social justice. For instance, many newly independent States that wish to demonstrate their democratic credentials give themselves constitutions that contain provisions that are often described generally as the directive principles of State policy, as distinct from those contained in a Bill of Rights which may also form part of the constitution.[8] The difference between the provisions contained in such a statement of principles and provisions contained in a Bill of Rights is that the former are usually non- justiciable while the latter are. An illustration of the relevance of context and the need for the drafter to keep this in view is the way the 1996 South African Constitution is being used to achieve the transformation of apartheid South Africa into a democratic South Africa.

The successive white supremacist governments that held the reigns of power in South Africa from colonial times until 1994, governed in an environment dominated by fear. Fear of the largely dispossessed majority by a relatively affluent minority. By and large, the law drafters of that era generally were not able to rise above the challenges presented by the drafting instructions that they were given. Most were virtual prisoners of, and succumbed to, the prevailing constitutional arrangements. They drafted laws that were intended to maintain the status quo. This is in sharp contrast to their post-apartheid counterparts, at least some of whom, both white and black, had fought apartheid in the courts against daunting odds. Many of these have been able to take advantage of the political and socially pluralistic liberated society that rose from the ashes of apartheid to try to right old wrongs.[9]

After the sun had set on the 1994 provisional Constitution of South Africa, it was not surprising that the dehumanising conditions of the apartheid era, as well as the legitimate expectations of the opponents of apartheid, influenced the calculations of the drafters of the 1996 Constitution. These calculations have continued to loom large in both the form and content of post-apartheid legislation. It was against the background of a widely acknowledged need for change which reflected the aspirations of the new diverse society that the 1996 Constitution was drafted.

No longer shackled by the apartheid constitution and in recognition of the need for change, drafters in the new South Africa now exercise their proper functions without

---

of the Bill are compatible with the European Human Rights Convention.

8 See the constitutions of India, Part IV Articles 36–51: Directive Principles of State Policy; Nigeria, Chapter 2 Articles 14–25: Fundamental Objectives and Directive Principles of State Policy; Papua New Guinea, National Goals and Directive Principles; Sri Lanka, Chapter 6: Directive Principles of State Policy and Fundamental Duties: Articles 27–29; Uganda, National Objectives and Directive Principles of State Policy: General, Parts I–XXIX.

9 Prominent among these was Arthur Chaskalson, SC, founder of the South African Legal Resources Centre, who was the main drafter of the new South African Constitution and who subsequently became President of South Africa's Constitutional Court. It is apparent that Chaskalson shared the views of many other eminent South Africans, who fought against apartheid, that the system of justice in South Africa had been so discredited by its role in upholding apartheid that it might not withstand the transition to democracy. This would have weighed heavily in Chaskalson's mind when he was drafting the new constitution.

fear while at the same time remaining faithful to the individual specific instructions they receive.[10] In this context, it is possible for the drafter, while remaining faithful to the 'instructions', to draft in a way that promotes social justice. However, it would be misleading to suggest that every situation is amenable to the drafter's intervention on policy issues, just as it would be wrong to expect that legislative precedents would work in every situation.[11]

The Legislative Drafter and Ethics

Not unrelated to the importance of the social context of legislation is the need for the drafter to be always conscious of the ethical responsibilities inherent in being a drafter. These responsibilities are based on trust and the professional standing of the drafter as a public official. The scope of the responsibilities of a drafter embraces a duty to the instructing client, often a government department but it is not uncommon for the drafter to have multiple accountabilities.[12] Most importantly, the drafter's responsibilities embrace:

Loyalty Every professional, including a drafter, owes a duty of loyalty to the instructing client and ultimately to the public. The special nature of government as drafter's client calls for some special considerations and poses some problems. By way of analogy, a defence counsel could go to any length, short of fraud on the court, to protect their client whereas the duty of a government lawyer is not to secure a specific result, such as a conviction, at all costs but to ensure that justice is done. In the event of two conflicting government drafting instructions, the matter should be resolved at policy level by a higher authority in order to protect the integrity of the legislative process.

Competence Perhaps, of all the ethical commands, this is probably the most important. Failure in this regard, which is where the client needs the drafter most, would be wholly unsatisfactory. Policy must be effectively communicated in clear unambiguous language and must fit into the existing law. The drafter must therefore be competent enough to be able to draft effective laws.

---

10 For an incisive examination and appreciation of the role of the drafter in constitution drafting, see Jeremy Sarkin, 'The Drafting of South Africa's Final Constitution From a Human-Rights Perspective', 47(1999) *American Journal of Comparative Law* at 67–87. One of the innovative characteristics of the South African Constitution is the inclusion of the concept of the right to administrative justice which is justiciable.

11 For an examination of a less successful attempt, in circumstances similar to the South African experience, to use legislation as an instrument of change, see Theunis Roux, 'Constitutional Property Rights Review in Southern Africa: Record of the Zimbabwe Supreme Court', (1996) *African Journal of International and Comparative Law* p. 755.

12 See the observation of the Chairman of the House of Lords Select Committee on the Constitution at Q. 364 in the Minutes of the evidence of Sir Geoffrey Bowman, First Parliamentary Counsel to the Committee, 23 June 2004.

Confidentiality The position is the same for drafters as for lawyers generally. Unless released or authorised to be released by the client, a drafter should keep the content of instructions and nature of evidence and reports on which the Bill is based confidential until it is submitted to legislature, otherwise officials of the instructing department may be reluctant to work closely with the drafter.

The tradition of independence of the drafter rests on the notion that a drafter can and should be able to refuse to draft bills that contravene the rule of law. Personal convictions could also come into play, for example, a drafter could refuse to draft a bill imposing capital punishment if the drafter profoundly disagrees with capital punishment.

Part II

Prioritisation in the Legislative Drafting Process

The Essence of Prioritisation

Prioritisation is a two-stage exercise. It is carried out at two different levels, in the order in which they occur. First, it is done by the executive authority when it has decided that it is necessary to legislate and second, by the drafting establishment which it instructs to draft the necessary legislation. In the normal course of carrying out its duty to govern, the government, with the finite resources at its disposal has to address a myriad of social problems. It has to respond to the multiple demands made on it. It must provide adequate health facilities, schools, an efficient transportation system, housing and other social and political needs.

In seeking to provide these needs, the government, therefore, must make a conscious decision on where and how to allocate resources. If it decides to legislate to implement its policies and programmes, it will probably end up having a very crowded and busy legislative programme. In determining its legislative priorities the government must, among other things, bear in mind the parliamentary time available.

The Process of Prioritisation

After the government has decided to legislate in order to implement its programme, the drafting establishment which is equally under pressure to produce all the necessary draft legislation requested from it also has to decide in what order to produce the drafts. In many jurisdictions, the resources placed at the disposal of the drafting establishment are often inadequate and time is similarly always short. The drafter, in turn, must therefore also prioritise in order not to waste scarce resources on relatively insignificant bills.

Viewed in this light, prioritisation is largely a political rather than a technical matter. It shapes the government's exercise of State power, in particular its legislative power. If it is accepted that the drafter's role involves making appropriate policy inputs, it would follow almost by definition that the drafter would be involved in helping those primarily responsible for policy to determine priorities in pursuing legislation as a means of addressing problems and bringing about social change.

Generally speaking, in every government some central government agency exercises the function of vetting all legislative proposals to ensure that they are in accordance with government policy. Often this central agency is located in the Cabinet Office and will usually comprise a committee of senior Cabinet ministers who decide which proposals should receive legislative priority. In some jurisdictions, however, there is no such central agency. In such cases, prioritisation is done by the drafting establishment which receives from a variety of government ministries drafting instructions that are sometimes conflicting and incoherent.[13] And yet it is surprising that there is little writing in the field of legislative drafting that gives the subject of prioritisation the serious attention that it deserves. The only attention given to it is merely incidental to the legislative process.[14]

Clearly, there is an advantage in ensuring that legislation is both coherent and relevant to the needs of society. This can best be achieved only if available resources are utilised to maximum advantage. Further, there is a good chance that legislation would be more relevant to the needs of society if two conditions exist. The first condition is if there are clearly identifiable means, such as through a central agency, for prioritising legislation. The second condition is if there are established criteria for doing so.

Whatever the case, it is important that prioritisation should be based upon public interest. It should not be based upon narrow departmental or sectional interests or upon a misconception of the proper role of a drafter. It should also be flexible enough to take into account changing circumstances. If it is not flexible enough, it will not be able to address emerging social problems.[15]

The Institutions for Prioritising Legislation

The agency and location of the agency responsible for determining prioritisation will vary from one jurisdiction to another.[16] Of necessity, this will depend on the constitutional arrangements in the jurisdiction concerned. In some jurisdictions, it

---

13 See Seidman, Seidman and Abeyesekere (2000) 53–4, where they express the view that in the absence of clear cut criteria or procedures, this could lead to haphazard prioritisation. This need not be so, of course, especially if the drafting establishment is well organised and is staffed by experienced drafters who are fully conversant with the government's general policy and legislative programme. Where the government's legislative policy is clearly defined and already prioritised in its legislative programme, the drafter would have no discretion in the matter or, at best, their discretion would be extremely limited. Where the priorities have not been so predetermined, the drafter has discretion which responds to both objective and subjective pressures.

14 See ibid. at 55 *et seq.*

15 See ibid. at 56.

16 In the UK, the Parliamentary Counsel's Office is part of the Cabinet Office and is the central agency for the drafting of all important government Bills. As to how the PCO approaches the subject of prioritising its work, see the answer of Sir Geoffrey Bowman, First Parliamentary Counsel to Q. 317 in the Minutes of his evidence to the House of Lords Select Committee on the Constitution on 23 June 2004.

may be the Cabinet or a committee of the Cabinet, often the Cabinet Committee on Legislation. In others the agency may be located within a government department. There, senior officials will take into account the range of projects that require legislative backing. They will also take into account all relevant background information in the possession of the department that will help to justify inclusion of the legislative proposal in the priority list.[17]

Background information could include whether the project has already received Cabinet approval as part of the overall legislative programme. If not there is a risk that departmental resources may be wasted on projects that cannot be guaranteed to meet Cabinet approval. It could also include an assessment of the chances of the draft bill surviving against other projects competing for legislative backing as well as the rigours of the often crowded parliamentary timetable. This is a further illustration of the proposition that prioritisation takes place at more than one level in the unraveling of the legislative programme and the process of legislation itself.

The essentially political nature of prioritisation requires that those who make the decision must have a good knowledge and appreciation of both the resources available and any technical constraints that may exist.[18] They should also have regard to some criteria on which to proceed in making their decision.

Criteria for Prioritisation[19]

Commonsense would suggest that a prioritising agency should carefully weigh proposed projects and draft legislation for implementing those projects against their relative economic and social costs and benefits. It would help the prioritising agency therefore to have on hand information concerning the resources available, both financial and human.

The power of legislation as an instrument for bringing about social change cannot be doubted or underestimated. In order to understand the proper role of a law and the drafter, it is important to also understand that the law does not operate in a vacuum. There will always be a reason for legislation. The reason for legislating may be to change existing law that is proving inadequate to deal with contemporary problems. It may be to repeal an existing law and to remove it from the statute book. The reason for repealing the law in question may be because the problem has now been resolved. It may be to initiate a completely new law for regulating behaviour in respect of a novel area of activity, for example, commercial space travel.

Prioritisation criteria may be examined under the following general headings:

(a) The gravity of the social problem being addressed, such as improving the quality of life of the majority and alleviating poverty Even in a functioning democracy where

17 See D. Miers and A. Page, *Legislation* (London: Sweet and Maxwell, 1982) pp. 25–36.

18 See the explanations given by Sir Geoffrey Bowman, First Parliamentary Counsel under Q. 349 in the Minutes of his evidence to the House of Lords Select Committee on the Constitution, 23 June 2004.

19 See Seidman, Seidman and Abeyesekere (2000) pp. 57–79.

the institutions of society command the respect of citizens generally, there are still problems that need addressing almost on a daily basis. Law and order will command attention as will education and health. How lawmakers judge the performance of their national institutions will depend on the importance that they attach to the role these institutions should play in shaping the social conditions in their jurisdiction. Their ability to make this judgement meaningfully and authoritatively will require a certain level of economic literacy. The economic life and prosperity of every society is inextricably bound up with the ability of that society to harness its resources and productive energies to the fullest extent possible.

There are compelling reasons why it would make good sense to give a high priority to legislative proposals that seek to enhance the welfare of the general population. Similarly, there would be advantage in giving a high priority to legislative proposals that are intended to improve the efficiency of national institutions that underpin good governance. This is particularly so in poor developing countries in transition from a one party State to multiparty parliamentary government. It is often the same for a country changing from a command economy to an open market economy.

The experience of many such countries, especially those that had been colonised and only recently gained sovereign independence from the colonising power, has not been a particularly happy one. Some discover, immediately after gaining independence, that like any other sovereign State, they now have to find their own way in the world. In one fell swoop, they have to provide hospitals, schools, roads, water and electricity supplies, cultural and leisure programmes, retirement and old age pensions and all the other amenities and attributes of decent life in a modern State. The experience of many of these 'transition' countries is that almost invariably they find themselves in a debt trap. Often, the problems are caused by a combination of poor political leadership and lack of probity in the management of national resources. Sometimes, the problems are exacerbated by manipulative outside 'help' [20] Rather surprisingly, this kind of help will sometimes come from such unsuspected quarters as the more established and respected trading blocs or organisations and international financial institutions including the IMF, the World Bank and WTO. Much has been written about the crippling effect help from these good Samaritan institutions has on the developmental aspirations of hapless developing economies. [21]

Very commonly, the practice of some financial institutions is to impose stringent pre-conditions. These usually come in the form of prescribing the implementation of an across the board structural adjustment programme in the way the economy is

---

20 It is not uncommon for such manipulative practices to be coupled with corruption on a massive scale and to invariably have the effect of compounding the debt burden of a developing country. A common practice is to lend money to the developing country. Somebody in the country diverts the funds to their own private bank account and pays the same funds back to the lender for a cut from the funds and they both leave the poor developing country to repay a debt it never owed. The role of Western developed countries in this respect is said to have been totally disgraceful, see K. Maier, *This House Has Fallen*, (New York: Public Affairs, 2000) at xxii.

21 See Walden Bello, 'Lack of Transparency in the WTO' (2002) 1 *Development Dialogue* 117, accessed at (www.dhf.uu.se/pdffiler/02_1.pdf) where Walden describes the WTO as 'the non-transparent and feudal institution par excellence'

run before any assistance can be provided. Typically, the country will be required to implement some or all of a range of measures including:

- taking fiscal measures that will have the effect of devaluing the national currency which in turn will result in raising the cost of living for most ordinary people;
- reducing the size of public service employees which will usually increase the already high unemployment level;
- cutback in social service spending which will affect such vital services as education and health.[22]

Transforming such developing economies from a state of economic dependency would require the taking of bold root and branch measures. The measures that will effectively address the problems demand that the problems be given high priority in the legislative programme.

(b) The anticipated social impact of the proposed legislation From one point of view, the purpose of a proposed legislation is to ameliorate an underlying social problem. From another point of view, the effect of the same legislation is to benefit some people and not others. A cost–benefit analysis of the proposed legislation may show that the law will impact in different ways on different sections of the society. In this case, it will become apparent that there cannot be one single solution that will fit equally across the board. It would be a situation that more appropriately calls for a positive direct government intervention rather than reliance on a market driven solution or individual good sense.

The choice may, therefore, be to prioritise in favour of laws targeted at improving the living conditions and quality of life of the poor. The government may therefore decide to pursue increased industrialisation with a view to creating jobs for the poorer sections of society.

(c) The practicability of the proposed legislation, having regard to the available resources both financial and human Clearly, there would be no sense in giving high priority to a bill intended to implement a project for which the government does not have the money nor the trained human capacity. It would help to bear in mind that there is lurking in the legislative process a range of forces, some favourable, some unfavourable that the implementation of the project will encounter if there is no guarantee that the project will prevail against all the odds. The realities of modern parliamentary politics is that, even with the best of intentions, some bills do not survive the rigours of the parliamentary timetable. It would therefore be wiser not to embark on drafting legislation that stands little chance of surviving and reaching the statute book. Making the best use of the resources that are available may well be a better course.

(d) An assessment of available drafting resources and the strains that a particular drafting request is likely to impose on them. When all the other criteria have been

22 See Seidman, Seidman and Abeyesekere (2000) at 59.

met, it would be important to take into account that the drafting establishment on whom rests the burden of drafting the legislation have limited endurance capacity. It would be good to remember that the physical strain on the drafting staff could reach a point beyond which they simply cannot operate efficiently or effectively.

By way of a summary, it would probably be true to say that in most jurisdictions the resources, both financial and human, available to the drafting establishment to do its work, lag behind the demand for drafting services. Some jurisdictions are very well endowed in these respects but others are not so lucky.[23] The need to economise and to be selective constitutes a powerful reason to prioritise. The prioritising agency, whether centralised or departmental, would be able to prioritise effectively only if it is in possession of information regarding the current workload of the drafting establishment, the number of drafters available and an estimate of the length of person hours required to complete the drafting of the legislation that is being requested.

Part III

The Drafter and Good Governance[24]

The Meaning of Good Governance

As long as the nation State remains the basic unit within which human beings function, each nation State, whether big or small, must decide for itself how it is to be governed. A nation State may even have important decisions made for it collectively by, for example, a regional grouping of States to which it belongs or by its more powerful neighbours or trading partners.

Whatever the case, the law must be used as an agent for change in order to facilitate development. Development that is appropriate to any given society will usually bring about social change and social transformation, powerful obstacles that stand in the way notwithstanding. Among such obstacles in modern life are globalisation and absence of good governance which tend to disempower rather than empower the most vulnerable in society. In an increasingly globalised international community, good governance therefore assumes a position of special importance.

Good governance may be broadly defined as the use of the resources of the state in a transparent and accountable manner for the benefit of society as a whole. The exercise of executive power in a non-arbitrary manner is one of the main characteristics of good governance. Effective and non-arbitrary decision-making will usually make good governance more likely while their absence will usually result

23 Some of the drafting establishments in the better endowed jurisdictions, like the UK, are able to secure the resources that they require to match the volume of anticipated legislation. Even so, well endowed drafting establishments face other problems, as to which, see Sir Geoffrey Bowman, First Parliamentary Counsel's answers to Q. 317–9 in the Minutes of his evidence to the House of Lords Select Committee on the Constitution, 23 June 2004.

24 See Seidman, Seidman and Abeyesekere (2000) at 343 *et seq.*

in bad governance.[25] Good governance is, therefore, critical especially in countries going through a period of transition where, as a result of a period of turmoil or conflict the institutions of society have become dysfunctional.[26]

The characteristics of effective and non-arbitrary decision-making share the following elements:

- government by rule, in which decisions are grounded in reason and experience and made according to agreed rules rather than according to the whims of the decision-maker[27] In a functioning democracy, good governance also means that the government must act within the law and abide by the rules of administrative law. This means that the actions of the executive arm of the State are subject to judicial review[28]
- accountability – decision-makers are able to justify their decisions publicly and their decisions are subject to challenge or review by a higher authority. Where the decision maker is an elected body the ultimate judge to review the decision is the electorate
- transparency – public officials conduct the business entrusted to them openly so that they can be questioned by interested members of the public. Often the questioning is done by the press which acts in the interest of the public[29]
- participation – by persons likely to be affected by the decision (potential stakeholders) who should be afforded the opportunity to make an input in the decision-making process.

These characteristics complement each other and their combination will help to ensure that good governance and development march together.[30] Applied together, these characteristics would constitute a formidable tool for development.

However, there is as yet an unresolved debate as to whether there is a right to development as such. The proponents of this 'new' right argue that there is such a right under the UN Convention on Social, Economic and Cultural Rights. This has prompted the question as to whether international economic institutions should be subject to and be measured by the same yardstick of accountability and transparency as national institutions?[31]

---

25 See ibid. at 8.

26 See ibid. at 7.

27 Rule here refers to the Rule of Law, a principle widely recognised as the bedrock of a democratic society and which every public official exercising power or authority whether executive, judicial or quasi-judicial must respect and apply.

28 See, generally, *Good Government and Adminstrtive Law, An Introductory Guide* (London: Commonwealth Secretariat publication, 1996).

29 See ibid. for an examination of the implications of accountability and transparency for good governance generally.

30 See ibid. at 8.

31 See Walden Bello (2002) 117 *et seq*; see also Shalmali Guttal, 'Disclosure or Deception – Information Access in the World Bank and the Asian Development Bank' (2002) 1 *Development Dialogue* at 104 *et seq*, (www.dhf.uu.se/pdffiler/02_1.pdf).

Recent developments, it would be fair to observe, suggest that perhaps the international community may be witnessing signs of the beginning of an openness revolution. More and more, social movements around the world are demanding more open, democratic and responsive government. To their credit, whether or not this is sufficient, some governments are responding by enacting legislation guaranteeing to their citizens a right of access to government information that will enable them to 'participate' more meaningfully in the decision making process.[32] Whether or not there is a right to development, it cannot be doubted that it is the responsibility of the government to create an enabling environment in which people can exercise their right to develop in whatever way they choose.

How Can the Drafter Advance Good Governance and Development

Bad governance is as much a cause of underdevelopment as exploitation by say a foreign power or multinational. Reforming institutions as well as behaviour through the instrumentality of the law can promote development because institutions and humans are usually the main instruments and agents of action or inaction. Reforming a country's institutions, if those institutions are clearly not performing, will often clear the way to creating an enabling environment as well as make it more likely to improve the people's standard and quality of life.

Insofar as it is the means through which government policy is handed down, be it in the form of primary legislation, subsidiary legislation, ministerial rules and regulations or military decrees – the law has a pervasive influence on human behaviour. In the final analysis, the government cannot govern without laws. If government decision-makers do not wish it, they will not facilitate development but if they propose to advance development, they usually do so by targeting, through appropriate legislation, behaviour that tends to block the path of development.

Laws will often either proscribe or prescribe certain behaviour patterns and policy expressed in the form of law is seen as endowing that policy with legitimacy. This might explain probably why few people would volunteer to pay any income tax if there were no tax laws. Effectively drafted, the law should enable people to make appropriate choices. As a rule, lawmakers rarely try to redress the situation by enacting unnecessary legislation unless the existing law is ineffective or is inadequate to deal with the problem. This presents every drafter with a principal challenge – how to draft a law that would be likely to induce the desired behaviour. It also raises the important question of why people behave the way they do. The answer lies in the fact that people generally act by making choices within a range of constraints thrown up by their social, political, economic and physical environments. This also, in some way, explains the causal link between law and development and the explanation for the success or failure of a government's attempt to translate proposed policies into effective rules of law.

---

32 See T.S. Blanton, 'The Openness Revolution, The Rise of a Global Movement for Freedom of Information' (2002) 1 *Development Dialogue* pp. 7–21, (www.dhf.uu.se/pdffiler/02_1.pdf).

Thus, to draft laws that the government can implement effectively constitutes the first requirement of good governance. Drafters draft against the background of a range of the social, political, economic and physical constraints. In carrying out the task of drafting legislation, drafters translate these constraints into *legal* and *non-legal* constraints. In doing the translation, the drafter generally addresses two categories of persons namely:

a. those whose behaviour the law proposes to change, and
b. those who work for the agency responsible for implementing the law.

Enforcement measures will often include various conformity-inducing provisions in order to achieve compliance

- direct measures such as criminal sanctions
- indirect measures such as targeted inducements or subsidies.

Good governance requires the exercise of political power through transparent, accountable and participatory decision-making procedures. However, in exercising executive power, and in order to win the consent of the governed, the government must conform to the rules that it has made as the governor. But in every country, one encounters perverse official behaviour. Such behaviour often manifests itself in various forms of corruption. Corruption is the most common form of arbitrary decision-making. Corrupt practices always involve the exercise of public power for private purposes or private gain. Non-arbitrary decision-making must be based on a decision-making process that ensures that:

i. the decision-maker receives relevant inputs and feedback from potential stakeholders and excludes irrelevant and prejudicial matter
ii. the prescribed behaviour is defined in terms of criteria which the decision-maker must take into account
iii. the decision-maker takes into account only the prescribed criteria
iv. the decision-making process meets the requirements of transparency and accountability.

To promote good governance the drafter must therefore draft defensively against corruption.

Identifying the Manifestations of Corruption

The manifestations of corruption commonly are:

i. bribery – receiving value in exchange for exercising discretion in favour of the payer of the bribe
ii. embezzlement (stealing) – taking money from entrusted funds

iii. speculation – using official funds/power to purchase goods or services cheaply for resale at higher price and keeping profits
iv. patronage and nepotism – using official power to favour family and friends such as in employment
v. conflict of interest – exercising legitimate discretion in a way motivated by personal gain.

Corruption flourishes most commonly in certain fertile areas of the business life of any State. Among these areas are government procurement and tendering; customs and excise; tax collection, government enterprise.

Explanations for Corruption

People respond differently to situations and impulses that confront them in the course of their daily life. Their responses may be subjective or objective:

Subjective explanations Although self-interest may be a powerful incentive, it is not the single most important cause of corruption. If it were so the criminal law would probably always be an effective remedy for it. Instead, the criminal law sometimes compounds the situation by providing perverse incentives. Probably the reason for this is that corruption in all its various manifestations nearly always operates in the dark and sometimes results in what is often perceived as 'victimless crime'.

By way of illustration, the parties to a crime, such as drug trafficking and money laundering, benefit from the crime. In many cases, there is no apparent or a specific victim willing to report the crime. Consequently, the police often have to rely on whistle-blowers to report the corrupt practice. Often, this would be in return for immunity from prosecution and some financial rewards as well as protection from retaliation by the culprits. Such practice in the fight against corruption would, in effect, be providing perverse incentives to the repentant whistle-blowers even though they themselves may have participated in and probably benefited from the crime.

An environment of corruption often frustrates the effective implementation of anti-corruption laws, even where conviction for corruption attracts very heavy punishment sometimes including the death penalty. The ineffectiveness of the law could arise from the criminal justice system's institutional limitations. The criminal justice system may be ineffective because the courts do not have the power to initiate investigations themselves and the police may have limited skills and resources. It may therefore be necessary to take subjective causal factors into account in designing measures to overcome institutional causes that foster corruption.

Objective explanations Corruption stems not only from individuals, but also from the weakness of the institutions in which the individuals work. It is therefore necessary to also focus on the objective and institutional factors that contribute to corrupt behaviour. In a different context, the law itself may be a contributory cause. Laws that give officials exclusive or wide discretionary powers to dispense scarce government resources that are in high demand will aid not prevent corruption. Corruption breeds and thrives on the lack of accountability, especial fiscal accountability. The opportunity for corruption will exist when an official has unaccountable power to allocate official favours, such as in procurement, licensing, tendering, privatisation of State enterprises, customs inspection and similar government activities. The view that in normal circumstances market forces would produce a satisfactory result may not always be true. Equally, development and transition which require that government officials be given power to determine the distribution of scarce resources and favours have their disadvantages.

Possessing the capacity to act in any given situation is an important factor. Officials behave corruptly partly because they are able to do so and partly because the opportunity is there. They can do so because there is plenty of loose money lying around. The official knows that the risk of being caught is very small and therefore that they stand a good chance of getting away with it.

Ways of Limiting the Scope of Discretion

Unaccountable broad discretion creates the basis for arbitrary decision-making. A stakeholder cannot participate meaningfully in decision-making unless he or she knows the basis on which the official may make a decision. Therefore, the least scope the official is allowed, the less likely that the official will take an arbitrary decision.

Specifying the range of problems that fall within the official's powers and the kinds of factors the official may admit to address the problem could help to reduce the chances of improper use of discretionary powers. Similarly, specifying the range of solutions the official may choose from and the factors the official must take into account in choosing a solution could help to achieve the same result. Prescribing procedures to be followed, such as precedents or that decisions must be taken by groups of officials rather than by a single individual and a requirement to give written reasons for decisions, are measures that can be taken to ensure that decisions are exercised properly. Corruption becomes more difficult when more than a single official takes the decision. These devices make arbitrary decisions more difficult. Using impact statements, rather than decisions that are capable of being explained on the basis of a wide range of criteria or decisions that cannot prescribe easily applicable criteria, would reduce the chances of the misuse of discretionary powers. If possible, avoid the use of vague criteria such as 'reasonable'

Accountability and Transparency

Accountability and transparency go together and constitute the basis of the rule of law. Accountability requires a decision-maker to answer for and explain an action if explanation is requested and transparency requires openness in the processes of decision-making. This is the only way individuals and civil society can learn about how officials make decisions.

Institutions of Accountability and Transparency

Accountability Institutions of accountability include such offices as the Auditor General and Audit Commissions. Financial/fiscal accountability and regularity could be maintained through such practices as annual audits by an independent auditor and by requiring written decisions; regular evaluations; prescribing a right of appeals by aggrieved persons or review by a superior.

Transparency Institutions of Transparency include such offices as Privacy Commissioner who can enforce individual rights to public information as a counterpoint to supremacy of official secrecy laws. Instead of secrecy laws, inserting in the constitution a section establishing the right to public information that also forbids government secrecy, or introducing a Public Information Act would help to protect the public against excesses perpetrated in the name of State security.[33] A law could impose a requirement on a public authority to advertise its meetings in advance and the right of the public to attend; to publish decisions for notice and comment. It could also permit the intervention in a proceeding not only by those with a material interest but others with an ideological interest who are not immediately or directly affected. Such law could also require the agency to publish its decisions with reasons. The growth in the Ombudsman institution has helped to promote openness and accountability. The name given to the Ombudsman institution varies from jurisdiction to jurisdiction but almost invariably the institution is designed to monitor and police public administration.[34]

Combating a Culture of Corruption

A culture of corruption fosters an attitude of mind that says if everyone does it, why not me. This leads to a belief that nothing can be done and so why bother to try fighting it? It is possible to combat this culture by framing legislative provisions that are likely to overcome the underlying causes of corrupt behaviour. This could be done by:

a. exercising greater care in choosing agents;
b. institutionalising the procedure for checking records;
c. rotating agents periodically;
d. making rules that require leaders to shift emphasis from 'what can I get away with' to 'how can I justify my conduct';
e. condemning rather than seeking to justify self-serving practices or local culture which claim that bribery merely fulfils traditional gift giving.

Therefore, as a matter of principle, the requirement to govern in the public interest should never be negotiable. A culture of corruption will not disappear by ignoring

33 The 'Openness Revolution' has yielded dividends in the form of a Freedom of Information Act in the jurisdictions of a wide range of legal systems. See T.S. Blanton (2001) pp.7–21.

34 In the UK, for instance, there is a variety of bodies that perform the functions of an ombudsman, the main body being the 'Parliamentary Commissioner (for Standards in Public Life)'. Other jurisdictions use other titles such as 'Public Complaints Commission' (Tanzania), 'Investigator General' (Zambia), the 'Public Grievances Chamber' (Sudan).

it. The devices that improve transparency and accountability, considered above, will help to expose corrupt behaviour.[35]

A genuinely democratic society is more likely to have some, at least, of the institutions that promote good governance. It will give meaningful effect to the essential ingredients of democracy, namely regular free elections, freedom of expression and association, judicial independence and the rule of law.[36]

Specific Laws to Combat Corruption

Government Procurement The fostering of development by government offers almost limitless opportunities for corruption in the supply of public sector goods and services. The building of hospitals, schools and roads, and the procurement of equipment would provide such opportunities. There is therefore need for an adequate procurement law and tendering procedures to ensure fairness in the award of contracts. A common practice is to establish an agency to handle tender procedures; open bidding; provisions for ensuring satisfactory performance. A practice that would complement a clear tendering policy is to establish an agency to monitor and provide information on the movement of the prices of goods and services.

'Conflict of interest' situations often arise when public officials are exercising their public duties. Examples of conflict situations involving public officials include engaging in private employment in addition to holding a public office; accepting gifts, hospitality and other personal benefits; employment after leaving a public post; shareholdings, directorships and commercial partnerships; travel perks; and preferential treatment.

Situations, such as the above, often lead to malpractices which enable officials to siphon off public funds and resources for private purposes. The transfer by a public official of official power to a private party to make decisions that would affect the public would fall within this situation. Such situations could lead to erosion of trust in integrity and legitimacy of government action which would defeat the transparency objective.

Conflicts of Interest Legislation could help to combat the above practices and consequences. Criminalising specific activities and practices could help in addressing the potential causes of corruption as would encouraging behaviour that promotes detection. Examples of the latter could include rewarding whistle-blowers and offering informers protection or immunity from prosecution. Other helpful measures that could be taken include eliminating the payment of low salaries, secret and unaccountable decision-making processes; requiring public officials to disclose their outside commercial and property holding interests, requiring the declaration of gifts that exceed a specified value and forbidding the holding of more than one official

35 The flip side of combating a culture of corruption is creating a culture of integrity in which civil society as a whole plays a critical role – the churches, the media, trades unions, professional associations and educational institutions. For an examination of how it might be possible to nurture a sense of social responsibility among citizens, see J. Uhr, *Creating a Culture of Integrity* (London: Commonwealth Secretariat publication, 2003).

36 See ibid. at 3.

position. These measures could be underpinned by establishing an independent implementing agency with adequate powers to enforce the law.

Codes of Conduct Codes of official conduct underpinned by appropriate legislation can play an important role in promoting good governance. Such codes may be called by different names in different jurisdictions and could be used to serve different purposes. For instance, leadership codes are sometimes introduced by legislation to govern the conduct of persons in positions of political authority, sometimes as part of the Civil Service Regulations or scheduled to the constitution. Sometimes, a single code is introduced and is made applicable to all government personnel including ministers, legislators and public servants generally or even political party officials.[37]

---

37 There is, however, some doubt as to the usefulness of Codes of conduct and the extent to which they can help to engender good governance. See, for instance, *Commonwealth Workshop on Accountability, Scrutiny and Oversight* (Canberra: Commonwealth Secretariat and Centre for Democratic Institutions, 2001).

Chapter 11

Improving Democratic Development by Better Regulation

Ulrich Karpen

Introduction

Legislation, good legislation, better legislation is an important instrument to regulate on the relation between individual and State, on society and a vital government in a democratic system. This applies to all democratic States, which may, of course, be in different phases of development. In fully developed nations to curb law inflation may be of prevailing importance. In threshold countries it may be necessary to improve the strength of Parliament and legislation to foster economic development by setting a market economy frame and by improving social state instruments to allow for equal opportunity. And in developing countries the first and essential task for legislation and governance is, finally, to enable the implementation of the law, to assist people in obeying the law. This sometimes requires enforcement. But acceptance of the law is a dominant requirement for public trust in law and State which is in the core of a democratic rule of law system. Legislation is the primary function in a constitutional State, next to executive and judiciary. Better legislation is supporting development.

Development, Democracy and Legislation

Development to the Better

The main goal of all States in the world and of the world community of States – be they organised in the United Nations (UN), the World Trade Organisation (WTO) or the Organisation of Economic Cooperation and Development (OECD) or be they unorganised – is to secure peace, improve living conditions of their people and to enable equal opportunity. These are raisons d'être of any State, irrespective of how its government may be organised. Some tasks of the family of nations are new and global and require the cooperation of all: protecting security against terrorism and coping with the existential challenges of the change of climate. To master these tasks and master them effectively and efficiently development is the key, development to the better.

As mentioned before, all of our countries strive for a model of sustainable development of our societies. Some have made good and steady progress; some need more time and support; some have made significant steps toward reaching this goal, but nevertheless have a long way to go to a secure and prosperous future. In looking at the reasons and the history of these three steps of development, you have to analyse its factors. There is no undisputed, unanimously accepted definition of what development is. Very often it is understood as economic growth. This is too simple. One needs to take a broader perspective. Development has economic, social, cultural, political and legal facets. One may paint a 'magic pentagon' of factors, which enable development. The five edges are: (1) economy; (2) economic growth (GNP, *per capita* income); (3) social cohesiveness (structural changes, education, fair distribution of wealth, effective government and administration); (4) participation; and (5) political and economic independence. This is a useful traditional description of national development. Criterion (5) may no longer be valid in a globalised interconnected world and ecology and climate may be additional factors relevant for development of every nation.

Of course, 'development' is a normative term. It is based on perceptions of the desired direction of social changes; it may be based on theories about reasons of underdevelopment; it relates to patterns of socio-economic transformations and assertions of social groups, which put changes forward (Marx, Keynes, etc.). And definitely 'development' is normative insofar as it includes decisions on the measures to start and uphold social changes (open markets, [holistic] planning, development aid, etc.).

The concept of 'nation building', which was recently introduced by Francis Fukuyama, is based on a model of development on the basis of the factors, as indicated: wealth, coherence and integration, industriousness, responsibility, effective constitution and law. They add to the stability and capacity of a nation: 'nation building' a fully developed State can cope with its responsibilities effectively; a fragile, weak one is more ambitious than effective; a failing State is no more than a fiction of a political entity in geographic borders. Development describes the path of nations in an open field between possible responsibilities and necessary governmental strength to discharge them. The latter in a democratic State is based on and limited by legislation and successful implementation of laws.

Before then proceeding to democratic and legislative factors of development, and not sticking to a perspective of well developed States, one has to raise the question whether and – if so – how far development may be 'exported'. This is the key question of whether developmental aid to threshold and developing countries may be linked with requirements to change the political system. Is there a 'droit d'ingérence' under the assumption that development includes participation and human rights as part of the constitutional State? Is there a right of underdeveloped countries to receive a 'fair share' of global wealth? Is it an obligation of developed nations to discharge developmental aid? And if so, does the latter include claims of protection of individual rights and people's participation in the receiving nation? It seems that the clash between sovereignty of the States and globalisation, namely of ideas and opinions (via the Internet) have to be reconsidered more carefully in our times. Currently, 'democratic imperialism' does not have a good reputation and success seems to be uncertain. The dominance of the democratic rule of law State is not – and never has been – undisputed. On the other hand, the 'state of the art' of political philosophy in our times did not prove to be of temporary strength:

that human rights are indivisible and double standards are not allowed, and that democracy is the surpassing form of government, allowing for creative participation of the individual.

Democracy

One of the edges of the 'development pentagon' is participation. Development needs the support of the people, voluntary cooperation for the common good and qualified interaction of everybody. These prerequisites for development are fully available only in a democracy. Opinion polls show that citizens' approval of democracy as a form of government is growing. Democracy is the form of government, which parallels with liberal market economy, which is based on the market choice of the individual. Democracy, moreover, is the only form of government, which is acceptable to a Human Rights Society with freedom of profession, property and education. Democracy is adapted to a culture based on freedom of speech, press and broadcasting, teaching and learning. Democracy leaves room for creativity and pluralism of belief, creed, ideas and opinions. A democratic State is imprinted by an amalgam of human rights, participation, market economy and free, pluralistic culture. All in all, democracy requires participatory rights, namely elections, civil rights, freedom of speech, assembly, freedom of forming parties and interest groups of society. Finally, democracy requires reliable institutions, namely Parliaments. Participatory and civil rights as well as democratic institutions are essential parts of rule of law, elements of democracy in a free democratic order, a constitutional rule of law state.

Participation as a core of democracy strengthens civil rights and freedom. Participatory rights include more than just elections. They cover direct participation in local government, autonomous bodies, like chambers of commerce, lawyers' representations and universities. Participation takes place in hearings, access to public information and petitions. This is typical for participation in developed countries. In developing countries – and not only there – forms of direct involvement of citizens in public affairs are developed. All forms of bottom-up decisions add to the interest of the individual in public affairs and make them effective. They support creativity and foster integration.

Elections for Parliaments, heads of State, etc., must be free and fair. They must include competitiveness and a secure setting. They must exclude the influence of established pressure groups and of clientelistic networks dominating a distorted decision-making process. A functioning democracy must ensure that (1) political leaders are determined by general, free and fair (namely secret) elections; (2) democratically elected political leaders must have the power to govern without veto powers and political enclaves; (3) independent political and/or civil groups may associate and freely assemble; and (4) citizens and organisations as well as the mass media must express their opinion freely.

These prerequisites of a working democracy are usually vested in the civil rights section of a modern constitution.

The prevailing system of democracy worldwide is the representative democracy, be it the parliamentary or presidential system, sometimes enlarged by referenda.

Parliament has to legislate, to decide on the budget, to vote for government in the parliamentary system, monitor government's actions and has to discuss issues as a 'forum of the nation'. These are the main democratic powers of the legislature in separation of powers systems. There is an old dispute: Does democracy precede the rule of law or is it the other way round? This discussion is academic to a certain extent. Civil rights and separation of powers are essential prerequisites of democratic 'good governance'. On the other hand, democracies as 'electoral democracies', where participatory rights prevail and civil rights – for example, for minorities – are insufficiently protected, may lead towards systems, where checks and balances are defective and rule of law is flawed. So the answer could only be that one needs democracy and rule of law at the same time. The democratic and (liberal) free order of the constitutional State is an amalgam of both basic elements.

It is – unfortunately – true that only a minority of States in the world today are free democracies in that sense. The opinion, however, is gaining ground that development towards participation of the people in public affairs is preferable, necessary and, for the reason of nature of human being, unavoidable – and consequently very useful for development.

Legislation

Both development and democracy need a stable, reliable, sustainable frame, and this is the law: constitutional and statutory law, vested in the rule of law state.

The democratic constitution as an expression of the will of the people is usually an act of legislation and referendum. In a rule of law democracy the constitution regulates on basically four elements:

- democracy and participation;
- political and civil rights;
- rule of law, due process, independent judiciary, separation of powers;
- and in some States: the federal system.

In doing so, constitutional law defines the basic principles of government and the value system of a nation. Constitutional law, mostly a product of the legislator, is the fundamental and paramount law of the nation, the frame of all State activities, the masterplan for a nation. The constitution enjoys special dignity, is an anchor of stability and imprints the 'profile' of a State. The constitution fulfils the following functions:

- It designs institutions, responsibilities and persons who take part in the political decision-making process.
- It should stabilise the governmental system over time.
- It concentrates on essential issues, leaving details to statutory and delegated legislation.
- The constitution is an effective instrument of interpretation of the law.
- It limits and monitors governmental powers.
- It protects individual rights and freedoms.

- Some constitutions mention goals and end of State actions; they are directives for policy; this applies to social State clauses, regulations for ecology, data protection, etc.

Within the framework of the constitution, legislation produces laws for day to day government of the nation, regulations for implementing political programmes and the budget.

- The Law is formal/statutory law, as enacted by Parliament. It covers sub-legal provisions, like delegated law and bye-laws of autonomous institutions, like local government entities, universities, etc.
- The law is a vital factor for implementation of governmental actions, acceptance and effectivity. It is a documentation of the law, overriding contracts and customary law, which may be more violable for unfair treatment or arbitrariness.
- The law is an instrument for building a coherent legal system, unifying terminology and principles of regulation.
- The law protects individual rights, since it prescribes rights and freedoms in detail.
- Finally, the law is a solid basis for law suits and the courts.

In every State, namely in developing democracies, stability of State functions, dependence of government of the law, reliability of implementation and effective decisions in law disputes are vital factors of stability. The law, however, changes when time passes and the field of application of the law itself is changing. The law must provide stability and flexibility at the same time. Stability and flexibility are important facets of qualified legislation. Since social and governmental conditions are subject to dynamic changes, the law needs to be adapted to new situations. This is where questions of interpretation and application of the law occur. It is up to the courts to adapt the law by interpretation. The courts are bound by the law, but at the same time say, what the law is (Oliver W. Holmes). If interpretation comes to an end and may not be overstretched, the amending legislator comes into play. Whether and how often this happens, is at least dependent on the quantity and quality of law. The more detailed, the less flexible in wording and meaning, the more often the legislator must help out.

Legislation – Quantity and Quality of Laws

Quantity of Laws

The impact, which legislation can have on democracy and democratic development of nations, depends on quantity and quality of laws. Of course the evaluation of quantity of laws is dependent of the level of development of a country. In developing countries it may be useful to knit a dense network of law, in order to strengthen the rule of law and redress contractual or customary law. In developing countries, however, the effectiveness of the system suffers from law inflation. To give an example, the body of laws of the Federal Republic of Germany may be chosen. On federal level currently one counts 2,197 laws, covering 46,777 provisions; moreover 3,131 pieces of delegated legislation, with 39,197 provisions, altogether some 86,000 provisions (*FedGaz*. 15/1233 of 25 June 2003).

Since Germany is a federation, on a State level a similar number of legal instruments are in force. Of course one has also to take into consideration a considerable number of local statutes. The European community, the regulations of which are binding on all Member States or European citizens directly, since its foundation in 1957 released 997 guidelines and 2,605 ordinances. The European body of law, the so-called 'acquis communautaire', covers some 91,000 pages of legal provisions.

The paragraphs of modern law gain constantly in length and are more and more detailed. The sentence of Pythagoras covers 24 words, the Ten Commandments 67, the American Declaration of Independence 300 and Article 19a of the German Income Tax Law 1,863. This is too much! The law is neither transparent nor digestible. Security of the law is fading. The assumption, that the citizen can know the law, is a pure fiction.

One definitely has to curb law inflation in developed countries. 'If it is not necessary to make a law, it is necessary to make no law' (Montesquieu). *Plurimae leges – maxima iniuria*! Of course there are reasons for the torrent of laws. The globalised and industrialised technical word requires reliable legislation. The social and welfare state needs equal protection, provided by the law. The active citizen and lobbies are pressing on drafting laws to take care of their interests and finally the courts demand legislation to base their decisions on. No wonder that all modern countries are looking for instruments of reducing the number of laws: consolidation, deregulation and debureaucratisation, agreements and contracts between government and clients instead of legal regulation, more discretion by administrative bodies, etc. Curbing law inflation and regaining flexibility are valued as one the most important tasks of governance.

Quality of Laws

'Bad laws are the worst sort of tyranny' (Edmund Burke). Quality of legislation depends on the legal environment of drafting and implementing the law, in other words: on the level of development of the State. Five criteria may, however, be applied to every piece of legislation, wherever it is drafted:

a. level of legislation;
b. procedural quality of the law;
c. formal quality;
d. substantive quality;
e. costs of the law.

The first question (a) is, whether the legislator regulated at the proper level. In supranational entities, like the European Union, the supranational legislator should not regulate on matters which could be regulated at the lower level of Member States more appropriately and effectively. And national Parliament – in a federation or decentralised system – must not regulate when States or entities of the lower level could better deal with the issue at stake. The same is true for the relation of State and local authorities as well as autonomous bodies. It is a liberal notion, but an important part of constitutional rights and freedoms, that public authorities, on whichever level, should not regulate on matters which are best dealt with by individuals. The idea of choice of the best level may be called 'subsidiarity principle' and even be laid down in constitutions – like in the European Treaties: it is simply a structural instrument of 'better regulation', a most effective one.

The procedure (b) of legislation is prescribed in detail in national constitutions and of the laws. In practice, it is often very hectic. Political pressure pushes drafts through parliamentarian machinery, lacking time to deliberate and work on regulatory details, legal terms, language, transparency, etc. As a result, many laws are inaccessible for citizens and even experts. The legislator hardly finds time and capacity for good legislation and consolidation. As a motorised legislator, he has to amend the law and repair errors. 'Sunset legislation' assists Parliament to monitor its products and delete laws as outdated. The stability of many modern laws is weak: either they are amended shortly or they do not stand the test before constitutional courts.

The formal quality (c) often is lacking. The language may be difficult to understand. The order of sections and articles is misleading. Transparency is shortfalling, cross-referencing is used more often than necessary. Many criteria for substantive quality of a law are efficacy, effectiveness, efficiency and stability. To check the efficacy, first, of a law means to look at the intent of the legislator and whether it is sufficiently achieved by the norm. The target of a law prescribing seat belt fastening in cars is to reduce lethal accidents and severe injury to persons. Experience shows that this goal is achieved to a greater part by the law.

A law is (d) effective, if it is observed and accepted by the addressees. Effectiveness is compliance with the law. Seat belt fastening is obeyed differently in different countries, but as a whole it seems to work. And what is efficiency? The question is, whether the law stands the economic rationality test. It works on a good cost-effectiveness relation, if it produces maximum effects with given costs or produces a given product at minimum costs. The application of this quality criterion requires an evaluation of alternatives. More efficient alternatives deserve precedence before more costly ones. Of course, better roads, building of more protective cars seem to reach the goal to a better extent, but they are more costly if compared with seat belt equipment to reduce severe accidents.

Stability, finally, tries to reduce the probability of amendments after a short period of time. This may be reached by far-reaching regulation on the basis of good prognosis, by flexible regulations, which include general clauses rather then strict and detailed solutions, by entitling administrators to apply flexible discretion, etc.

Costs of the law (e) do not imply primarily charges which are the intent of the law, like tax laws, but burdens which may be reduced in implementing the law. Laws very often cause bureaucratic burdens for enterprises, citizens and administrative bodies themselves: collecting statistical data, applying for a licence or subsidies, etc. New instruments to reduce administrative burdens are e-government, one stop shops, etc.

Regulatory Impact Assessment (RIA)

Quality of legislation is subject to evaluation, Regulatory Impact Assessment (RIA), be it in drafting the law or in monitoring its effects when enacted is the use of social sciences – methods for analysing the impact of legislation, namely the costs of regulation for business, administration and citizens. RIA methods aim at systematically analysing all effects of norms, methodologically inquiring into the worth or merit of laws. RIA could be, in more detail, 'prospective' as evaluation of a draft norm, 'concurrent', during the decision-making process for a norm and 'retrospective', after the law has been implemented ('ex ante-', concurrent or 'ex post-'evaluation). RIA has been widely accepted during the last ten years, since shrinking budgets and a trend towards rationality in legislation supported strict calculation of effects, side effects and costs of regulation. Today there is consent, that goals and measures of rational evaluation are transparency, accountability, enforceability, technical quality, simplicity, clarity, capacity building, necessity, efficacy, effectiveness, efficiency, consistency, subsidiarity, proportionality and continuous learning, etc. Various methods and tools of evaluation are applied: statistics, interviews, workshops, case studies, surveys, document reviews, best practices and focus groups. The standard cost model has proved to be very successful. Good experiences have been collected in evaluating the costs of legislation for business, when applying standard cost methods. One counts in minutes and seconds how much time is needed for filling in forms for application for subventions or licences, collecting data and submitting them to statistic agencies, implementing regulations for limited working time for staff, for health protection etc. In transforming data into manpower hours and payment one can measure exactly the financial burdens of a law for an enterprise. The same applies to an administrative office or the administrative costs of a court. In getting these results a government may, as a yardstick, try to reduce the bureaucratic burden of legislation, let's say, for 25 per cent in five or ten years. It is for the first time that one can evaluate the costs of legislation, at least part of it, in rational, transparent terms, which, by the way, allow for comparative studies, from business to business, administrative office to other ones, from debureaucratisation efforts of one State to another. This is a vital tool for 'competition in better regulation' Currently countries report that evaluations were more cost intensive and resource intensive than expected. The positive long-term effects are, however, not to be overlooked.

RIA becomes institutionalised in more and more States, in procedure and organisations. Procedural measures for implementing RIA are evaluation clauses or submission of periodic reports as well as sunset legislation. Evaluation clauses require that governments initiating a draft, in the arguments, have to produce a detailed RIA, including alternatives. More and more laws, as enacted, require that government after two or three years of implementation has to come back to Parliament to report on the success, advantages or disadvantages of the law. Parliament can then decide whether the law needs to be amended or kept as it is. The same effect, although affecting the Parliament itself, is produced by sunset provisions. Parliament enacts that the law shall expire at a distinct date, unless Parliament decides to prolong it.

Organisational measures for implementing RIA concern the creation of institutions, organs, units, independent or as departments and sub-organs within institutions, which specialise in evaluation of legislation, obeying the separation of principle powers. The legislature is involved in the RIA process as well as the executive. The judiciary is an important factor of retrospective evaluation, since every decision demonstrates how and where a law is successful in dealing with problems and where it is defective. In Parliament as well as in the executive branch one may prefer a centralised solution – one ministry or a Cabinet office as agent for RIA, one committee of the house – or a decentralised one – each ministry writes draft bills and makes RIA, each committee of Parliament makes concurrent RIA in its matters. In some governments RIA is concentrated in the Ministry of Finance and Budget or the Ministry of Justice. In some Parliaments RIA is concentrated in the budget committee or in one legislative committee. Parliamentary auxiliary units may support the substantive as well as the budget or legislative committee.

The exact details of the most appropriate form of RIA depends heavily on the constitutional, legal and administrative framework in which it operates. RIA needs a firm legal anchoring and high-level political support. It must be monitored by a structure dedicated to better regulation and assisted by clear advice, guidelines and training of actors. There are, basically, four options to regulate on RIA. Each has advantages and disadvantages. First, the mandate and details of RIA may be regulated in the constitution. This option offers great visibility and a strong binding force. A detailed regulation is, however, not appropriate for the constitution. In addition, it implies a considerable degree of inflexibility. One would not often amend the constitution. Second, RIA could be regulated on in statutory law. This is visible and binding on the legislature, as well as on the executive, although subject to amendments in a less difficult procedure. Third, RIA could be put into the Rules of Procedure and Standing Orders of Parliament and the executive. This allows for a broad and differentiated regulation, in close contact with working units and provides for flexibility. The regulation is, however, only binding on Parliament or the executive correspondingly. Finally, there is the option of regulating on RIA in detail in circulars and organisational regulations of ministries. This allows for a differentiated and broad regulation of details, but is, however, binding only on the staff of government (if it is a government circular), or binding only on the staff of that particular ministry (if adopted by the minister).

Better Legislation – The Challenge of Legistics

What is Legistics?

Support activities to reduce quantity and improve quality of legislation is a challenge for legistics. Legistics is an interdisciplinary scientific theory for legislative practice. The subject of legistics is legislation in its broadest sense: the legislator, the procedure of legislation, the draft in substance, the law as a product of legislation, evaluation of law. Of course, legistics is closely connected with studies of Parliament and parliamentarianism, which are the focus of political sciences and are also intertwined with theory and practice of law and State.

In more detail, one may delineate six sections of legistics:

1. analysis of the law
2. tactics of legislation
3. methodology of law
4. techniques of legislation
5. management of law
6. evaluation of the law.

Analysis of the law (1) covers theory of law and State, constitutional and statutory law, sub-legal norms, in particular delegated law, bye-laws, the hierarchy of norms, etc. Tactics of legislation (2) looks into organisation and procedure, the work of Parliament and government, hearings, etc. Methodology of law (3) deals with substantive issues and content of the law. How do we get 'good', 'just', effective laws? Efficacy and efficiency are essential elements of material law. Techniques of legislation (4) cover formal issues, the format of the law, the legal style, the system, the dogmatic design, subdivisions and articles, language and linguistics (in countries with more than one official language). Management of legislation (5) is vital in democracies, which require communication with people, with organised interests, the media. Functions of laws have to be looked at as well as best practice of inaugurating projects of legislation.

Legistics takes an explicitly multidisciplinary approach. Legal skills and dogmatics are, of course, indispensable. Since the law is probably the most important tool of politics, political and social sciences are needed. Efficiency of legislation requires cost-benefit analyses of economy, and effectiveness of implementation could be fostered by social psychology. Linguistics play a role in drafting the law, namely in multilingual States.

History and Current State of Legistics

Legistics, as an important element of theory and practice of law and State, have an old tradition. Aristotle and Cicero considered issues of good regulation as an instrument in the hands of the statesman as well as Bentham and Montesquieu. This knowledge, namely its practical side, never got lost in the American hemisphere. On the European continent, the nineteenth century with comprehensive codifications like the Napoleonic Code, the codes of Commerce and Civil Law in France and Germany as well as in Switzerland were the boom time of means and techniques of good legislation. In the twentieth century, however, in Europe, positivism gained ground. Academia concentrated more on good interpretation of the law and writing treatises on that and forgot the skills of legislation. Only in the 1970s some authors 'reinvented' legistics. Since then it is a factor of research and teaching and an instrument of practice.

Legistics are developed, besides universities and governmental centres of legislation, by supranational and national associations. They have as members Parliaments, institutions, universities, scholars and students, lawyers, administrators and other practitioners. In 1991 the European Association of Legislation (EAL) was founded, its 7th Congress took place in The Hague in 2006 under the topic, 'The Learning Legislator', following congresses in Frankfurt (1991), Liège (1993), Rome (1995), Munich (1997), Warsaw (2000), Athens (2002) and Berne (2004). Proceedings centred around methodology of legistics, Parliaments, European legislation, e-government, role of civil society, etc. There is a publication series. Teaching legistics takes place in various European and North as well as South American countries. Only recently, centres for legistics have been established in South Korea. One has to mention, that curricula in Swiss Centres have influenced teaching in many other countries, namely in Murten, Zurich and Lucerne. The same is true for Austria (Salzburg), the Netherlands (The Hague, Amsterdam), Germany (Speyer, Hamburg) and the United Kingdom (London, Edinburgh) and Poland (Poznan). The European Public Law Centre in Athens is also interested in European legislation. The European Association of Legislation is not at least an umbrella organisation for various national associations, like in Switzerland, Austria, Belgium, Portugal, the Netherlands, Sweden, Poland, Greece, Turkey, Cyprus and in the United Kingdom. In the United States there are various Centres which specialise – although not exclusively – in legistics. The same is true for Canada. In Brazil and Bolivia young scholars from European education founded the first centres for legistics. The same is true for South Korea. There are, in the meantime, some eight periodicals in Europe publishing studies on legislation. There are various textbooks and readers which are of great help for teaching courses. Many members of European and national associations are called upon to be experts in Parliaments and governments. Sometimes they have to draft standing orders of Parliaments, organise scientific staff of Parliaments and their committees, or assist – sometimes in multi-national working groups – in drafting laws. The latter has particularly been the case in countries of transition from socialist to liberal rule of law democracies. These working groups very often are gathered by supranational organisations: European Union, Council of Europe, OSCE, OECD, etc. Experts collected detailed information about the social and political systems of Russia, Belarus, Ukraine, Georgia, Albania, Cambodia, Afghanistan, Croatia, etc. Expertise was needed in drafting the constitutions of South Africa, Afghanistan, Bosnia and Herzegovina. Graduates from legistic courses are increasingly working in parliamentary staffs and as assistants to députés. In Germany, since 2006, a price for 'good legislation' is granted.

Perspectives and Frontiers

It may be appropriate to comment on some trends in legistics, namely from the European perspective. There is consent that legistics as a practice-oriented science has to start from political practice. Every deputy, every staff member of a Parliament, every representative of a lobby group has to take into account chances and constraints of legistics. This does not mean that tools of legistics are applied every time. The time pressure and priorities of politics and interests are often obstacles against the implementation of 'good legistics'. However, channels of communication in legislation skills have to be opened, networks have to be knitted. In the ivory towers of academia legistics are of little use.

Effective teaching is necessary. To start with, one should reconsider the real and desirable circle of addressees for courses. Who is interested? Who attends? Here every teaching person collects his own experience. People choose the subject if results are useful for their job or career. One might observe that people who attend are often those who are interested in politics: members of political parties, staff of caucuses or députiés. Contents and methods of courses have to be interdisciplinary. Issues of how to draft a good law should prevail. Language problems and techniques of drafting are important, but not everything. Legistics in general cannot be so much subject to basic training (e.g. undergraduate degree), but more of post-graduate training, often part-time concurrent with a job. Generally speaking, a Master degree will be granted. 'Master of Legistics' would be too narrow; legistics should be an element of a 'Master of Administration'.

As far as research is concerned, some basic issues of legislation go alongside traditional topics, namely procedural, formal and substantive quality. Basic research should concentrate on other instruments of governance and steering, like delegated law, administrative regulation, contracts, instruments of public–private partnership, regulations of labour conditions. To widen the perspective, legistics must be focused as being an element of regulatory theory and governance. It is obvious that the modern social sciences have a major say.

Today societies, States and politics are studied more and more in supranational (European) and international (global) perspective. These facts cannot be overlooked by legistics. The national perspective is too narrow even for national legislation. There is no draft that can be submitted to Parliament without comparative law observations. This applies much more for actions of citizens, economy and political actors in supranational and international context. There is a visible trend towards unification of the law. For EU Member States this is mandatory by guidelines and ordinances, for all European and other States it is an accepted trend for science and practice. This has to be focused by legistics. Comparative law and unified law will increasingly set the agenda of legistics. We do not need 'good law' alone, but 'good supranational (European) and international law'.

Where are the frontiers then of legistics today, the challenges and constraints? Optimism for the future is legitimate. Convergence has made so much of progress, that one can start to work on an EU Code of Best Practice. This is, of course, a code for all nations worldwide, which have constitutional democracies. To promote these common principles of best practice, one has to operationalise criteria. Education and training are certainly a growing business. The scope of legistics has to be widened, including international treatises, compacts and agreements. Legislation, regulation is no longer defined by national or even supranational borders. To build on international legistics one needs to understand that the skill to draft good laws is not – and never has been – a one-way export business. Even if it looks like assisting other countries to make progress, building up international legistics is always an exchange of views and expertise with mutual profit. An International Association of Legislation (IAL) should underline the need for such cooperation.

And which are the constraints? Legistics must not forget that it is not an academic discipline in its strict sense. One cannot set jurisprudence instead of legistics. Legistics, on the other hand, has elements of handicraft. To go one step further, one can say that a good draft is a piece of art.

But legistics is not politics. The adoption of a draft law, be it excellent or not that good, is an act of politics, a political decision. Legistics, academia, legal rationale can add to a good law, but not replace the decisions of politicians. Legists are trespassing if they feel they can take over. And politics, even if supported by good legistic, base their decisions, in addition, on other grounds. As the Founding Fathers of the American Constitution held, 'Let us be guided by experience, because reason might mislead us!'

Conclusion

In the light of development, democracy and legislation there remain three questions. One has to ask, first, whether development, on the one hand, of quantity and quality of the law, on the other, are mutually dependent. Is good law dependent on development and vice versa? The answer clearly is yes. Qualified legislation depends on the level of education and experience of legists and politicians as legislators. And good legislation has to take into account the level of development, education, capacity and willingness of people as the addressees of the law. And to the second question: is success of democracy and legislation dependent on the economic situation of the people as the simple, most important factor of development? Some scholars pretend to know that below a US $600 income of individuals one cannot realistically talk of democracy and legislation. But it seems that one does not need to wait in supporting people's sovereignty and governance by good legislation until a certain level of prosperity has been reached! The other way round: democracy and good governance are mighty factors to develop societies and States. And third: Which is the main field for legistics to prove its strength in? For developing countries one should say: sometimes less is more. Legistics should encourage legislators to make few laws, but to ensure that they are effectively implemented. For developed countries, a bit of good advice could be: Less quantity, but more quality! The legislator should curb law inflation and make it easier for people to understanding the law.

6

Chapter 12

Drafting Principles of Existing European Contract Law

Gerhard Dannemann[1]

Introduction

Sir William Dale asked me to teach on his Government Legal Advisors Course in 1992, shortly after our first encounter at the British Institute of International and Comparative Law. I was to lecture on legislative drafting styles from a comparative angle which went beyond the Commonwealth and looked at Continental legal systems. Sir William, author of a seminal comparative study on legislative drafting techniques,[2] was of course much better qualified for this task than a young scholar who had published hardly anything on this subject, and who had no practical experience in legislative drafting. If he primarily sought to ensure a comparative dimension for his course for the time after he would step down, his strategy was successful, as I continued to teach on the course during the decade which followed.

Sir William, who thus brought me into contact with legislative drafting as a subject of academic study and teaching, at the same time provided me with my first experience in applying his ideas, notably to reconcile English precision with Continental brevity and simplicity. I would regularly set the course participants the task that they should rewrite some UK legislation in Continental-style, for example, the provisions on separation and divorce in the Family Law Act 1996. When returning their marked papers, I would hand out my own attempt at their task and explain how I had managed to reduce the 1,226 words used by the original Act to a mere 540, essentially by removing redundancies and by using a simpler structure, much along the lines formulated by Sir William.[3]

1 The present chapter draws on G. Dannemann, 'Consolidating EC Contract Law: An Introduction to the Work of the Acquis Group' in *Principles of the Existing EC Contract Law (Acquis Principles), Contract I: Pre-Contractual Obligations. Conclusion of Contract. Unfair Terms*, prepared by the Research Group on Existing EC Private Law (Acquis Group) (2007) pp. xxiii–xxxii, and, to a smaller degree, also on G. Dannemann, S. Ferreri and M. Graziadei, 'Consolidating EC Contract Law Terminology: The Contribution of the Terminology Group', ibid. pp. xxxiii-xl.

2 Sir William Dale, *Legislative Drafting: A New Approach. A comparative study of methods in France, Germany, Sweden and the United Kingdom* (London: Butterworths, 1977).

3 See ibid. ch. 14.

Acquis Group and the Joint Network on European Private Law

This experience proved very valuable ten years after my first encounter with Sir William, when I became a founding member of the European Research Group on Existing EC Private Law, or Acquis Group for short. This group was founded in 2002 with the primary aim of formulating principles of existing European Community contract law. It has recently published a first instalment of its work, a compilation of EC law-based rules on, notably, pre-contractual duties, non-discrimination, formation, not individually negotiated terms, withdrawal, and performance.[4] The short name, Acquis Group, confirms that these principles are formulated on the basis of the *acquis communautaire*, in particular Treaties, Regulations and Directives, as applied and interpreted by the courts. The Acquis Group presently comprises nearly 50 scholars from most EU Member States. Before I explain the process, methodology and style of drafting adopted by the Acquis Group, a few words are appropriate about the particular task of this group within the wider European frame.

In May 2005, the Acquis Group became a founding member of the joint network on European Private Law, abbreviated as 'CoPECL' In general, the CoPECL network contributes to setting up a European Research Area for Private Law. The main task is the elaboration of a draft for a so-called 'Common Frame of Reference for European Contract Law'. At the core, this will consist of a structured compilation of legal rules. Most of those rules are drafted by either the Acquis Group or the Study Group for a European Civil Code. The other members of this network include the so-called Insurance Group, the Association Henri Capitant, the Common Core Group, the Economic Impact Group, the Database Group and the European Law Academy. This network allows the Acquis Group to place its work within a common European context, and as the network has secured funding under the 6th Framework Programme of the EC, this has considerably contributed to the funding of the Acquis Group's work.

Within the Common Frame of Reference, it falls on the Acquis Group to formulate those rules which are based on existing EC contract law. So the Acquis Principles serve a dual purpose. On the one hand, they formulate and explain rules based on EC contract law as it presently exists and is applied within Member States. On the other hand, the same rules contain the Acquis Group's draft contribution to a Common Frame of Reference for European Contract law, where its provisions should dovetail with those formulated by other members of the network. This is not an easy task. The Study Group, which primarily contributes to the network rules on those numerous areas of contract law which are little affected by EC law to date, uses (and has to use) a very different methodology. Rather than formulating existing rules based on EC law sources, as the Acquis Group, the Study Group formulates what it sees as

4 See *Principles of the Existing EC Contract Law* (above note 1). A rules only version (without comments) is available from the Acquis Group website at (www.acquis-group.org). The second volume is due for late 2008. Further draft provisions and comments on non-performance and remedies have been published as: Fryderyk Zoll, Non-Performance and Remedies, in: *Common Frame of Reference and Existing EC Contract Law*, ed. by Reiner Schulze (2008).

particularly desirable rules, mainly on the basis of a comparative review of national laws in Europe. Given the obvious differences in methodology, I was pleasantly surprised to note that Acquis Group and Study Group principles had blended rather well in the First Interim Outline Edition of the Draft Common Frame of Reference which was published in December 2007.[5] This feat has been achieved by a so-called Compilation and Redaction Team, of which the present author became a member only in 2008. The fact that a number of scholars are members of both groups will help with this task.

Toolbox, Binding Instrument or Civil Code?

On 18 April 2008, the Council of the European Union endorsed the creation of a Common Frame of Reference on European Contract Law (CFR).[6] The CFR is "a set of definitions, general principles and model rules in the field of contract law" It is primarily intended as "a tool for better lawmaking", which should guide the legislator.[7] It could furthermore form the basis of directly applicable rules on contract law, perhaps in the form of an optional instrument.[8] In the long run, it might even serve as the basis of a future European Civil Code.

Of course it will matter in more than one way whether the Acquis Principles will end up in a dustbin or in a European Civil Code or, perhaps most likely, somewhere in between. That ultimate fate, which can hardly be anticipated, has fortunately rather limited impact on the formulation of the Acquis Principles. If the group manages to consolidate what is already there in terms of EC contract law into one largely coherent and consistent set of rules, it can indeed be used as a 'toolbox' for a revision of EC directives, or for the formulation of new directives, or as a basis for drafting a European Civil Code. The latter is not an ambition of the Acquis Group. The group's own position is reflected in the first provision within Chapter 1 of the Acquis Principles:

> Art. 1 Scope and purpose of these Principles
> (1) The following principles and rules are formulated on the basis of the existing law of the European Community in the field of contract law.
>
> (2) These principles and rules serve as a source for the drafting, the transposition and the interpretation of European Community law.

---

5 *Principles, Definitions and Model Rules of European Private Law – Draft Common Frame of Reference* (DCFR), Interim Outline Edition. Prepared by the Study Group on a European Civil Code and the Research Group on EC Private Law (Acquis Group), ed. by Christian von Bar, Eric Clive and Hans Schulte-Nölke, and Hugh Beale, Johnny Herre, Jerôme Huet, Peter Schlechtriem, Matthias Storme, Stephen Swann, Paul Varul, Anna Veneziano and Fryderyk Zoll.

6 Press Release 8397/08, p. 18.

7 Ibid; similar the European Commission: "toolbox, where appropriate, when presenting proposals to improve the quality and coherence of the existing acquis and future legal instruments in the area of contract law", COM/2004/0651.

8 European Parliament, Resolutions of 12 December 2007, P6_TA(2007)0615, and of 7 September 2006, P6_TA(2006)0352.

(3) They are not formulated to apply in the areas of labour law, company law, family law or inheritance law.

Group Structure and Drafting Process

Sir William's study of legislative drafting examines in great detail the actual process of how legislation is formulated by whom, and how this process influences the resulting legislation.[9] The following is an attempt to provide at least a comprehensive overview of the process in which the Acquis Principles are being elaborated.

Although the Acquis Group has produced numerous rules, none of those serve to explain how it functions. So the following offers no more than simplified observations of how the group has actually worked.

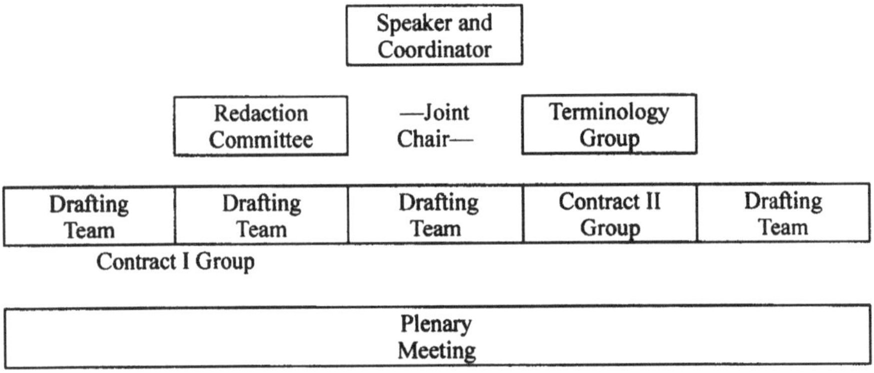

The Speaker of the Acquis Group, Gianmaria Ajani from the University of Torino, represents the group to the outside world, except for day to day dealings with the Commission and within CoPECL. That task falls on the group's Coordinator, Hans Schulte-Nölke from the University of Osnabrück.

The Plenary Meeting is a meeting of all members of the group, presently convened twice a year. Its most important task is to discuss and adopt all Acquis Principles, and it has the final say in this matter. While this democratic nature can make the decision-making process cumbersome and time-consuming, it also offers considerable advantages. It ensures that the group benefits from the combined expertise of its members, and also provides transparency within the group.

The first full meeting of Acquis Group members took place at the European Law Academy at Trier in January 2003, followed by meetings held at the University of Torino (July 2004), the University of Helsinki (March 2005), again at the European Law Academy at Trier (November 2005), at the University of Hull (March 2006), the Autonomous University of Barcelona (November 2006), at the Universities Paris I and II (March 2007), the University of Krakow (October 2007) and the Copenhagen Business School (April 2008). The last six meetings were devoted to the discussion and adoption of rules.

---

9 See Dale (1977).

Drafting occurs in stages which involve individual drafting teams, the Redaction Committee, the Terminology Group and the Plenary Meeting. Drafting teams are set up for particular topics or areas, such as rules on pre-contractual information duties, unfair contract terms or withdrawal from a contract. They produce a first draft of rules with comments for their topic or area.

At the Torino Plenary Meeting in July 2004, a number of drafting teams working on various formation issues were set up and pooled into the so-called 'Contract I Group', headed by Reiner Schulze from the University of Münster. Similarly drafting teams dealing with performance and remedies issues combined to the 'Contract II Group', headed by Ulrich Magnus from the University of Hamburg. This group structure was initially used for joint meetings of drafting teams. The individual drafting teams within the Contract II Group eventually merged into one, whereas the Contract I Group has provided a fairly loose structure for its own drafting teams. The majority of the more recently formed teams do not belong to either group.

Drafting teams will undertake a survey of existing EC law in their area and formulate their proposals for Acquis Principles on that basis. They are assisted by a short written *Drafting Guide* and a glossary of legal terms used by the Acquis Group.[10]

Once a drafting team has completed a first draft, this is passed on to the Redaction Committee. The main task of this committee is to formulate proposals for making the various drafts by different teams dovetail with each other. The Redaction Committee also generally prepares drafts for discussion and decision by the Plenary Meeting, in particular by ensuring that different options are available for discussion where policy issues are involved. If possible, a member of the drafting team concerned is present during the meeting of the Redaction Committee. This drafting team then amends the draft in light of the views expressed by the Redaction Committee.

The Redaction Committee was formed following the Helsinki Plenary Meeting in March 2005, where the present author was appointed Chair of that committee. The committee also includes the Speaker, the Coordinator, the Chair of the Contract I Group and initially other members from Belgium, Finland, France, Poland and the UK. A certain amount of fluctuation among members has since shifted the balance between different legal traditions represented in the committee. Moreover, my initial attempts to achieve a certain gender balance were unsuccessful, as all female colleagues I invited to join were wise enough to turn me down. Any resulting shortcomings in the representativity of the Redaction Committee have fortunately done little to affect the quality of its work. It has increasingly also been used as a general decision-making body between Plenary Meetings. The Redaction Committee has to date held eight meetings, four of which were at the Humboldt University at Berlin (September and December 2005, January and September 2007), and one each at the University Foundation at Brussels (February 2006), the University of Bielefeld (June 2006), the University of Oxford (October 2006) and the University of Torino (February 2007).

The draft is then passed on to the Terminology Group. This group edits the draft with a view towards harmonising the use of terminology and of improving the language and consistency of drafts. Time permitting, it passes on its recommendations to the

10 This glossary is published in vol. I of the Acquis Principles (No. 1), pp. 383–419.

drafting team concerned for further consideration and comment before the draft is finalised for discussion and decision by the Plenary Meeting. A substantial number of drafts went through several cycles of deliberation by the Redaction Committee and/or Terminology Group and the drafting team.

The Terminology Group was formed at the Torino Plenary Meeting in July 2004, with initially two members, Silvia Ferreri from the University Torino and myself as chair. Michele Graziadei from the University of Piemonte Orientale joined soon afterwards. The Terminology Group meets on frequent demand, mostly in cyberspace and occasionally at Plenary Meetings.[11]

Keeping the tasks of the Terminology Group and the Redaction Committee separate has been an efficient way of allocating the human resources of the Acquis Group, which in turn has helped both groups to perform their tasks with focus and consistency. The fact that both are chaired by the same person, acting as chief redactor of the group, has facilitated the necessary coordination between the two bodies. It has also placed me in a good position for making practical use of what I had learned by teaching on Sir William Dale's Government Legal Advisors course.

Several drafts which were adopted by Plenary Meetings (in particular those on pre-contractual information duties, unfair terms and withdrawal) have subsequently been presented and discussed at so-called stakeholder meetings. These are attended by various interest groups and experts. Their comments have been considered within a second cycle of drafting and consolidation of Acquis Principles. Stakeholder meetings were initially required for the entire work produced in the above mentioned Common Frame of Reference. These meetings have produced a number of helpful comments. They were nevertheless discontinued for some time. Recent announcements by Commission officials indicate that stakeholder meetings might be resumed. As these lines are written, their future is still uncertain.

Methodology

The previous section explains the drafting process for Acquis Principles in chronological sequence. A more difficult question in the drafting process relates to methodology. How can one formulate EC contract law rules from a compilation of directives, regulations and case law which is not best known for clarity and consistency? And how can one formulate such rules if most of EC law in the area of contracts is primarily concerned with consumer protection?

In dealing with this difficult task, the Acquis Group has to be wary of two potential pitfalls. The first pitfall would be to insist that EC contract law is confined to some three dozen directives[12] (plus the Brussels I and II Regulations and the Rome

---

11 A more detailed description of the work of the Terminology Group can be found in Dannemann, Ferreri and Graziadei (above note 1) [As e.g. in notes 4, 19].

12 These include Directive 85/577/EEC to protect the consumer in respect of contracts negotiated away from business premises; Directive 86/653/EEC on the coordination of the laws of the Member States relating to self-employed commercial agents; Directive 90/314/EEC on package travel, package holidays and package tours; Directive 1997/7/EC on the protection of consumers in respect of distance contracts; Directive 1999/44/EC on certain

Convention),[13] and that there is nothing in them or in their application by the courts which transcends those statutes and is capable of being formulated at a more general level. This would leave as the only feasible product of the Acquis Group a list of existing EU legislation, to which one could add a digest of cases which apply this legislation. The second pitfall would be to construct a comprehensive EC contract law by generalising consumer protection rules to general rules of contract law. This would clearly overstretch what is there.

The Acquis Group has sought to strike the right balance between those two extremes. It has relied on general methods of interpretation of EC law for formulating rules which transcend the existing piecemeal legislation approach but which at the same time can realistically claim to be based on the acquis. Particular emphasis has been placed on purposive interpretation and the doctrine of *effet utile*.

Purposive interpretation has been helpful for exploring both the possibility and the limits of generalisation of rules. Generally speaking, EU provisions on a particular aspect of contract law can invite two competing arguments: (a) this is an expression of a more general rule, or (b) this is an exception to a more general rule. Frequently, neither one of those two competing arguments wins the day, with the result that (c) the rule stands for itself and cannot be generalised one way or another. Deciding which of these competing arguments should prevail in a given case, or whether the provision in question is not capable of any such generalisation, involves policy decisions. Blank refusal to engage in any such decisions is largely identical with the first pitfall. Instead, the Acquis Group decided to be open about the policy choices which it has thus taken. In a number of situations, the acquis has also been shown to provide insufficient basis for necessary policy decisions by way of purposive interpretation, so that a political decision through the appropriate organs is required in order to solve a particular problem within the acquis. Where this is the case, this is expressly mentioned in the comments (under heading A.3).

The doctrine of *effet utile* can further help to decide which gaps remain open and which can and must be filled. Gaps can and need to be filled to the extent that this is required in order to give an *effet utile* to black letter norms. For example, numerous EC norms require certain information to be given, or a certain form to be observed. These would be deprived of their effect if a violation of these provisions had no consequences whatsoever, or consequences which are so limited that they provide

aspects of the sale of consumer goods and associated guarantees; Directive 2000/31/EC on certain legal aspects of information society services, in particular electronic commerce, in the Internal Market; Directive 2000/35/EC on combating late payment in commercial transactions; Directive 2000/43/EC implementing the principle of equal treatment between persons irrespective of racial or ethnic origin; Directive 2005/29/EC concerning unfair business-to-consumer commercial practices in the internal market.

13 Convention on the law applicable to contractual obligations, opened for signature in Rome on 19 June 1980 (80/934/EEC) soon to be replaced by Council Regulation (EC) No. 593/2008 of 17 June 2008 on the law applicable to contractual obligations (Rome I); Council Regulation (EC) No. 44/2001 of 22 December 2000 on jurisdiction and the recognition and enforcement of judgments in civil and commercial matters; Council Regulation (EC) No. 2201/2003 concerning jurisdiction and the recognition and enforcement of judgments in matrimonial matters and in matters of parental responsibility.

no meaningful incentive. The ECJ said so much more than twenty years ago about the effect of EC anti-discrimination rules on contract law.[14]

The methodology of the Acquis Group can be summarised as follows:

1. Generalisation of rules through search for common denominators. For example, the group has generalised numerous EC provisions relating to duties on pre-contractual information.
2. Generalisation of rules through interpretation of legislation as expression of a more general principle. For example, the group has thus generalised various situations which give rise to a right of withdrawal in consumer contracts.
3. Generalisation of rules through interpretation of legislation as exception to a more general principle. For example, the group has interpreted the limited number of EC form provisions as exceptions to a general principle of freedom of form.
4. Extension of rules under the doctrine of *effet utile*. For example, the group has arrived at the conclusion that violations of information duties or form requirements must have some consequences, and have attempted to formulate those.

It goes without saying that the proper application of this methodology will in numerous instances lead to the result that some EC contract law rules are not capable of generalisation or extension.

Gaps and 'Grey Rules'

The Acquis Principles offer fairly consolidated rules not only in core areas covered by EC legislation, in particular consumer protection law, but also in general contract law areas, such as pre-contractual duties, discrimination, unfair terms and withdrawal. They present rules with considerable gaps in the areas of formation, form, non-performance and remedies. There are some areas where one can find individual rules surrounded by large gaps, for example, in the area of validity. And there are some other areas of law for which the group felt unable to formulate any Acquis Principles.

The Acquis Group makes no attempt to fill such genuine gaps in the *acquis communautaire* with rules of its own choice. Within the Common Frame of Reference, this is largely the task of the Study Group. It has been mentioned above that due to the different methodology, Acquis Principles will not necessarily dovetail with Study Group rules.

Nevertheless, the present set of Acquis Principles contains some bridges which are referred to as 'grey rules', because they are indicated in grey print. These grey rules are other Draft Common Frame of Reference Rules, formulated by the Study Group (usually on the basis of the 'Principles of European Contract Law'),[15] which

14 See ECJ 14/83, 10 April 1984 (von Colson und Kamann).

15 See O. Lando and H. Beale (eds) *Principles of European Contract Law*, prepared by the Commission of European Contract Law (The Hague: Kluwer Law International, 2000).

are reproduced within the Acquis Principles in order to show the reader the context in which particular Acquis Principles can operate. For instance, the acquis contains a number of rules on how a contract is formed, but too little on what amounts to an offer for formulating an acquis principle. The group, therefore, decided to adopt the appropriate Draft Common Frame of Reference Rule as such a grey letter rule. In this way, the reader is presented with a more comprehensive set of rules, but also made aware of which of those rules are not based on the *acquis communautaire*.

Generalisation and Domestic Pre-Understanding

Sir William Dale painstakingly researched French, German and Swedish particularities in drafting legislation and compared those with his own experience in drafting English and British statutes. His views on legislative drafting, and his recommendations, were thus based on comparative experience. Many of the individual members of the Acquis Group had no similar comparative perspective to begin with; comparison was rather a collective experience which took some time to develop and sink in.

Most lawyers have been trained in one particular legal system, and thus tend to see EC law from the perspective of that system. So we approach EC contract law rules through what Hans-Georg Gadamer has called *Vorverständnis* or pre-understanding. We see everything through spectacles tinted in a particular shade, and are normally not even aware of wearing those spectacles. It was inevitable that proposed rules, and often other contributions to the debate within the Acquis Group, would be affected by a particular pre-understanding of those who drafted or contributed in another way. Collectively, such contributions do much to enrich the debate, but they can also make drafting more difficult.

Readers may be familiar with a piece by the Hungarian scholar Gyula Eörsi, entitled, 'Unifying the Law. A Play in One Act, With a Song', which incidentally appeared in the same year as Sir William's *opus magnus*.[16] The delegate from a country with centuries of case law tradition proposes a rule according to which 'The dog shall bark'. A delegate from a country proud of its civil code makes a counter-proposal of 'The cat shall mewl'. A conciliatory and generalising proposal is then put forward, according to which 'An animal shall make a noise'. This is warmly welcomed by functional comparativists (who always look at the output, in this case the sound),[17] but considered incorrect when looking at fish, who make no noise. and also dangerously broad. A compromise whereby 'An animal shall make a non-human noise' is rejected because parrots will do just that. After many more helpful comments, the drafting party comes up with a provision of which it will presently suffice to reproduce the first two paragraphs:

---

16 See G. Eörsi, 'Unifying the Law. A Play in One Act, With a Song' 25 (1977) *American Journal of Comparative Law* pp. 658–62.

17 See R. Michaels, 'The Functional Method of Comparative Law' in M. Reimann and R. Zimmermann (eds) *The Oxford Handbook of Comparative Law* (Oxford: Oxford University Press, 2006) pp. 339–82.

> Article 1
> 1. A noise [sound] shall be made [emitted] by any kind of a non-human [ahuman] being capable of [and fit for] making noise [emitting a sound], including dogs and cats [cats and dogs].
> 2. A noise [sound] under paragraph 1 may be made [emitted] expressly or impliedly. It shall be of such a nature as can in the given circumstances reasonably be expected to be made [emitted] by the non-human [ahuman] beings of a different kind from the one which has actually made the noise [emitted the sound] as well as noises made [sounds emitted] by human beings, provided that such noises [sounds] sound non-human [ahuman] included, and subject to usages widely known to and regularly observed by [any particular branch of] [the branch involved of] the non-human [ahuman] community capable of [and fit for] making noises [emitting sounds]. Such imitation shall, subject to fraud, be deemed proper, if a reasonable non-human [ahuman] being could under the circumstances reasonably be deceived by the said imitation.

In Eörsi's example, attempts to rise above domestic pre-understanding result in a highly complex, yet rubbery rule which is largely void of content.

It will fall on others to judge whether the Acquis Group has been able to escape that fate. It will come as no surprise that some of the first drafts did indeed contain fine examples of 'The cat shall mewl'. A draft rule whereby consumer credit contracts must be authenticated by notaries or similar public authorities could have brought banking business in the UK and in Scandinavia to a grinding halt, because no such public authorities exist in those countries. A mandatory rule whereby all contracts of unspecified duration can be terminated for the future at the free choice of either party was similarly on the questionable side.

Rules like those were ultimately not adopted for reasons which show how the Acquis Group has been coping with the issue of pre-understanding. First, the group has a built-in personalised comparison by having everything discussed by a large group of scholars from different legal traditions. Issues of pre-understanding are often picked up within drafting teams or otherwise get noticed as a draft moves through Redaction Committee, Terminology Group and Plenary Meeting. Thus, a few years of exchange and debate within the Acquis Group have done much to reduce pre-understanding and to turn all active members into comparative lawyers.

Second, closer inspection will usually reveal that there is no basis in the *acquis communautaire* for any particular domestic perspective. One feature which distinguishes the Acquis Group from other international groups aimed at the harmonisation of law is that its primary sources have been drafted with a view towards solving particular problems in a way which can be implemented in very different legal systems. The *acquis communautaire* does not generally attempt to take sides in those issues which continue to divide contract laws in Europe.

Nevertheless, when it comes to arranging contract rules systematically, one sometimes has to take sides on issues on which the acquis is silent. One of those issues was whether there is such a thing as a 'general part' of acquis contract law (as frequently contained in Civil Codes, the German *Allgemeiner Teil* being the most radical example) or whether all rules can be made to fit into particular categories of contract law (comparable to the position of English law). The form rules proved particularly difficult to accommodate in this way. The Acquis Group tried pushing those into formation, splitting them over different areas (pre-contractual information, formation, withdrawal) and relocating most of them to definitions, until finally a rather small 'general part' was adopted which defines the scope of the Acquis Principles, contains key rules on consumers and businesses, and on notice and form.

Terminology and Language

Drafting invariably involves issues relating to terminology and language. A careful balance is required in order to reconcile consistency in use (the same word should always be used in the same meaning and the same meaning expressed with the same word) with clarity (it should be easy for the reader of each provision to understand what is meant) and precision (that as little as possible is left vague). Within the Acquis Group those issues were delegated to its Terminology Group, as has been mentioned above. Its task and approach have been described in more detail elsewhere.[18] It should suffice in the present context to mention a few practical problems and their solutions.

EC terminology is not exactly noted for its consistency. Perhaps the most obvious example can be found in consumer transactions. While 'consumer' has been used consistently and at least with a broadly similar meaning, the same cannot be said for the consumer's contractual partner. Is this party to be called a 'trader', a 'professional', a 'supplier', or even a 'professional supplier'? The Terminology Group, after verifying that no indication could be found in the acquis for different meanings being attached to those different terms, agreed to use 'business' throughout. More difficult are subtle changes in the meaning which occur over time. For example, early Directives use 'written form' or 'in writing' as a form requirement, whereas more recently, mentions of 'on paper' have surfaced. Using 'on paper' has the desired effect that digitally stored texts are clearly excluded, but what this should imply for 'in writing' under earlier or even under recent legislation remains obscure. The Terminology Group eventually decided against 'on paper' and in favour of a consistent use of the older 'in writing' for any text which is generally legible to human beings without resort to technical means. One reason was that written information can be stored not only 'on paper', but also on a variety of print media made from, for example, plastic, metal, or even be proverbially carved in stone.[19] A lesser form requirement, called 'textual form', extends to digital texts and if these are stored permanently they fulfil the form requirement of a 'durable medium'.

The fact that the Acquis Group uses English as sole language for drafting, while avoiding the burdens and difficulties associated with multilingual texts, has also created some other problems.

First, the borderline between law and language is not always easy to draw. Using English expressions can mislead the reader into understanding European provisions through the eyes of English law. English law notions might thus blur the comprehension of European rules. It is for this reason that the Terminology Group attempted, where possible, to avoid English words which are closely associated with particular English

18 See Dannemann, Ferreri and Graziadei (above note 1) [As e.g. in notes 4, 19].

19 See Article 1:306 Acquis Principles (ACQP); see also Articles 1:304 (textual form), 1:305 (durable medium) and 1:307 (signature).

legal institutions, such as 'consideration' However, there are limits to the number of legal terms which are, on the one hand, comprehensible to the reader, without, on the other hand, having a particular meaning in English law which may not be shared by other legal systems. Unsurprisingly, we experienced during the drafting and consolidation process that lawyers who are trained in English law find it more difficult to understand our European law terminology as being separate from English legal terminology than lawyers who have been trained in a different legal system.

Second, drafters can, consciously or unconsciously, fall into English-style drafting simply because they draft in the English language. It turned out during the drafting process that any such fears were unfounded for most characteristic elements of English drafting, such as separating related issues over various parts of a draft, the use of long lists for defining a particular term or the obsession with detail of which Sir William Dale was so critical.[20] Instead, what attracted Acquis Group drafters most to English legislative-style were certain elements of the Victorian language in which many modern Acts continue to be written. Some of these expressions confuse rather than illuminate the reader.

Very popular among the Acquis Group drafters was an expression which is hardly ever used in the twenty-first-century English, but which British legislative drafters (and also their EC counterparts) love to use, perhaps because it appears to add gravitas to any provision. This is the word 'shall' It may well be the most ambiguous word which is commonly used in legislative drafting. A rule providing that 'The dog shall bark'[21] can carry any of the following meanings: (1) a duty or obligation: dogs must bark, (2) a discretion: dogs may bark; (3) a weak or toothless duty: dogs should bark, but there are no consequences if they do not, and (4) a fact or consequence: dogs will bark. The Terminology Group therefore pronounced a complete ban on the use of 'shall'.

Another much beloved English legal term which makes any legal text appear more dignified, but which also has the unwelcome tendency to obscure more than it clarifies, is 'deemed', indicating the use of a legal fiction. Legal fictions have been very popular in English law from the times when contract law cases were dressed up as armed conflicts so that they could qualify for the popular action for trespass,[22] but they should be avoided whenever possible. To date, the Terminology Group has been able to keep 'deemed' out of the Acquis Principles.

It is difficult to speculate what Sir William would have thought of the Acquis Principles if he had lived to read them. I fear that they will not do full justice to his demanding standards on accuracy and precision. On the other hand, I would hope that he might have recognised some of his views, notably those on brevity and simplicity of structure and language as having been put into practice.

---

20 See Sir William Dale (1977), ch. 14; G. Dannemann, 'The Drafting of Consumer Credit Legislation – A Structural Comparison Between the EU Directive and the English, Irish and German Acts' in H. Schulte-Nölke and R. Schulze (eds), *Europäische Rechtsangleichung und nationale Privatrechte*, (Baden-Baden: Nomos Verlagsgesellschaft, 1999) pp. 191–204.

21 See the example, borrowed from Eörsi (note 14).

22 See D. Ibbetson, *A Historical Introduction to the Law of Obigations* (Oxford: Oxford University Press, 1999) at 43.

Chapter 13

Drafting of EU Acts: A View From the European Commission

William Robinson[1]

Introduction

This chapter gives a brief overview of the drafting of EU acts from the perspective of those actually involved in drafting within the European Commission. It focuses on the drafting processes in a standard procedure for the adoption by the European Parliament and the Council of a legislative act under the Treaty establishing the European Community (EC Treaty) and is far from exhaustive. It is divided into three parts:

- the drafting process,
- the concern for quality of EU legislation,
- particular features of EU law which have an impact on the framing of legislation.

Drafting Process

How is EU legislation Adopted?

Almost all EU acts start life in the Commission. Legislative acts are adopted either jointly by the European Parliament and the Council or by the Council alone. As part of the institutional balance, however, the Commission has the monopoly of the legislative initiative: most articles in the EC Treaty[2] conferring power to adopt acts require as a first step 'a proposal from the Commission'

It is the Commission which determines whether it is appropriate to propose legislation and decides on both the form of act to be proposed (unless that is specified in the Treaty) and the content of its proposal. The other institutions can ask the Commission to present a proposal[3] but they cannot oblige it to do so. The independence of the Commission is guaranteed by Article 213(2) of the EC

1 The views expressed are his own and do not necessarily reflect those of the Commission. He would like to thank the colleagues who have given him valuable assistance.

2 Under the Treaty on European Union the Commission does not have a monopoly of legislative initiative since acts may also be adopted at the initiative of the Member States.

3 See Articles 192 and 208 of the EC Treaty.

Treaty, which provides that in the performance of their duties the Members of the Commission 'shall neither seek nor take instructions from any government or from any other body'

Apart from the legislative acts, a large number of essentially implementing and administrative acts are adopted by the Commission itself, generally under one of the procedures involving committees composed of representatives of the Member States.[4]

Drafting in the Commission

The Commission is divided into over 20 technical departments or Directorates General (DG) dealing with the different sectors of the EU's activities. Each DG is responsible for preparing and drafting the legislative acts and implementing acts in its sector.

All major items of planned legislation must be entered in the Commission's work programme for communication to the other institutions. That programme and other aspects of strategic planning are the responsibility of the Secretariat General, which coordinates the work of the various DGs and oversees the Commission's decision-making process. The Secretariat General has also been given special responsibility for administrative simplification and all aspects of governance.

Before drafting legislation, the DG will carry out wide-ranging external consultations and may issue Green Papers to expound problems and invite comment and White Papers to outline the solutions envisaged. On that basis it produces a preliminary draft which will form the basis for all subsequent discussions within the Commission. The first drafts are generally produced not by lawyers but by technical experts who rarely have specific drafting expertise. Few DGs have, within their own legal units, lawyers to help with drafting.

Once a DG has formulated its preliminary draft, it submits it for comment to the other DGs concerned as part of the Inter-Service Consultation (ISC), which is designed to ensure that the Commission works in an effective and coordinated manner. Under Article 23(4) of the Commission's Rules of Procedure[5] the Legal Service must 'be consulted on all drafts or proposals for legal instruments and on all documents which may have legal implications' The Legal Service acts as the Commission's in-house lawyer. It has a staff of almost 400 and reports direct to the Commission President. In the ISC it checks the substantive legal aspects of the act (legal basis, conformity with the law, consistency with other legislation) and the formal presentation and drafting.

The originating DG takes account of the comments it has received from the ISC, which often take the form of textual amendments, and may if necessary carry out further internal and external consultations. The final text will then be translated.

---

4 See Article 202, third indent, and Article 211, fourth indent, of the EC Treaty and Council Decision 1999/468/EC of 28 June 1999 laying down the procedures for the exercise of implementing powers conferred on the Commission (OJ L 184, 17.7.1999 at 23).

5 See OJ L 347, 30.12.2005 at 83.

Official Languages, Working Languages and Drafting Languages

Article 290 of the EC Treaty provides:

> The rules governing the languages of the institutions of the Community shall ... be determined by the Council, acting unanimously.

Those rules were laid down by EEC Council Regulation No. 1, as amended by successive acts of Accession, Article 1 of which provides:

> The official languages and the working languages of the institutions of the Union shall be Bulgarian, Czech, Danish, Dutch, English, Estonian, Finnish, French, German, Greek, Hungarian, Irish, Italian, Latvian, Lithuanian, Maltese, Polish, Portuguese, Romanian, Slovak, Slovenian, Spanish and Swedish.[6]

With effect from 1 January 2007 the EU thus has 23 official languages which, formally, are all working languages of the institutions. To enable the Commission to function efficiently, however, almost all acts are drafted in either French or English. Until the 1990s most were drafted in French but a survey carried out within the Commission in 2000/01 found that 55 per cent of documents had been originally drafted in English, 42 per cent in French and 1–2 per cent in German. The trend towards increasing use of English has continued and now some 80 per cent of documents are written in English.

The drafting language is determined by the DG. There is no requirement for a drafter to be a native speaker of the language concerned and in fact that is rarely the case. A draft act passes through all the internal discussion stages within the Commission in just one language but it must be translated into all the official languages before it can be submitted for adoption by all the Members of the Commission, the College.

All translations are produced by the Translation Directorate General (DGT) which has a large staff of permanent translators and a stable network of freelancers. In addition to translation, DGT offers an editing service to check drafts produced in French or English by non-native speakers. Unfortunately not enough drafters avail themselves of the service, whether because they are not aware that their drafting is deficient or because they have not allowed enough time for editing. DGT also acts as a resource centre for terminology questions and language matters generally.

6 See OJ 17, 6.10.1958 at 385/58. Because of the difficulty of recruiting and training linguists for less widely spoken languages transitional measures may be adopted derogating from the requirement to draft and publish acts in all official languages. A transitional regime for Maltese was adopted by Council Regulation (EC) No. 930/2004 (OJ L 169, 1.5.2004 at 1); it expired in 2007. When Irish was added to the list of official languages by Council Regulation (EC) No. 920/2005 (OJ L 156, 18.6.2005 at 3) a transitional period of five years was laid down.

Legal Revision in the Commission

It is clear that such a drafting process can give rise to particular problems. The Legal Revisers Group in the Legal Service attempts to resolve some of those problems. The Group was set up over 30 years ago and now consists of some 58 revisers with legal qualifications and linguistic skills covering all the official languages. It works to improve the drafting quality of acts across all areas of the Commission's activities and in 2001 was split into three subgroups in order to allow a degree of specialisation.

The first opportunity for legal revision is at the relatively early stage of the ISC. As part of the obligatory consultation of the Legal Service, drafting is checked by the legal revisers while a lawyer specialising in the technical sector concerned examines the substantive legal aspects. The legal revisers check that all the formal rules on drafting have been complied with[7] and suggest how the text can be made clearer and simpler.

The legal revisers' comments on drafting will generally be incorporated in the Legal Service response to the ISC and sent to the DG responsible for the text. In some cases the DG, the reviser and the lawyer may work together to resolve problems. Improving the quality of the preliminary draft reduces the scope for misunderstandings or confusion in all subsequent consultations and negotiations and when the text is translated into the other 22 languages.

While the Legal Service's opinion will in most cases be accepted by the DG, the Legal Service cannot actually block the adoption of a text. A negative Legal Service response to an ISC can be overridden by a DG if justified by pressing political reasons. The Legal Service will generally give a negative response for substantive legal reasons and only exceptionally on grounds of drafting quality alone.

There may be a further opportunity to improve the quality of the text when a proposal is tabled for adoption by the full Commission. Revision at this stage may be requested by the DG concerned (often at the instigation of the Secretariat General or the Legal Service). Such revision is necessarily limited in scope because the text has already passed through extensive external and internal consultations and is often the fruit of difficult compromises. It has also been translated into all the official languages and is to be adopted in a matter of days. As a result any rewriting or restructuring would be risky and revision focuses on correcting formal or terminological errors and ensuring that the legal scope is exactly the same in the different language versions. Because of those limitations and because it is now so time-consuming, requiring the work of 23 revisers, such revision is becoming less common.

---

7 In particular the *Joint Practical Guide of the European Parliament, the Council and the Commission for persons involved in the drafting of legislation within the Community institutions* (www.eur-lex.europa.eu/en/techleg/index.htm), the *Commission's Rules on legislative drafting* (RTL), Annex VI to the Rules of Procedure of the Council (OJ L 285, 16.10.2006 at 47), the *Manual of precedents, drawn up by the Legal/linguistic experts of the Council* (2005 edn), and the *Interinstitutional Style Guide* drawn up by the Office for Official Publications of the EU (www.publications.europa.eu/code/en/en-000100.htm).

In 2006, when some 3,200 Community acts (regulations, directives and decisions) were published in the Official Journal, the legal revisers examined over 1,300 texts. Most of the texts which were not revised were standardised texts or covered routine management of the agricultural markets.

Quality Controls in the Subsequent Legislative Procedure

The proposal from the Commission is passed to the legislative authority, generally the European Parliament and the Council acting together in the codecision procedure, but in certain fields the Council acting alone. Under the EC Treaty, the proposal must generally also be sent to the consultative bodies, in particular the European Economic and Social Committee and the Committee of the Regions, for their opinion.

Council Within the Council, the proposal is examined by a working group composed of representatives from all the Member States and chaired by the representative of the country holding the presidency. The representatives are generally technical experts rather than lawyers and their work focuses on technical issues and on the text of the proposal before them. The proposal then passes to the Permanent Representatives Committee (Coreper), made up of the Member States' ambassadors, which ensures consistency in the work and resolves technical–political questions before submitting the dossier for decision by a vote of ministers from the Member States.

The Council's Rules of Procedure have been amended to include an article on the need for attention to be paid to the quality of drafting and laying down the responsibility of the Legal Service for checking drafting and making drafting suggestions.[8] The Council's team of legal revisers is the longest established in the institutions and now consists of three revisers for each official language. At the very end of the procedure in the Council a meeting is convened of one legal reviser for each language to carry out the final revision of the text, often after its formal adoption. Revision at this stage is subject to the constraint that the text has been the subject of lengthy consultations and negotiations at every level and cannot be changed lightly. The revision meetings are also attended by representatives of the Member States who can reject changes suggested by the revisers.

To tackle those weaknesses the Council's legal revisers are now becoming involved much earlier. As soon as a proposal is received from the Commission a legal reviser will be designated to follow it through all stages of the procedure within the Council and attend all meetings to watch over the formal and drafting quality.

European Parliament (EP) Within the EP, the proposal from the Commission is assigned to the appropriate standing committee and a rapporteur is designated. The committee submits its report to the plenary and generally proposes amendments to the text of the proposal. The text will pass through two readings in the EP and a conciliation procedure between the EP and the Council, unless it is approved at an earlier stage. The EP legal revisers are the newest team but already the most numerous. They are involved at different stages of the EP's procedure and finally in

---

8 See OJ L 285, 16.10.2006 at 47; see Article 22.

the revision meeting in the Council. They focus chiefly on the amendments proposed by MEPs but are increasingly commenting on the drafting of the text as a whole.

The Commission has an important role to play in the negotiations on its proposal at the level of the legislative authority. It may amend its proposal to facilitate agreement or, if it considers that a proposal has been altered by the other institutions to such an extent that it has become 'denatured', it may withdraw the proposal, whereupon the other institutions can no longer adopt an act.[9]

Concern for Quality

Historical Background to Concern for the Quality of EU Drafting

In 1992, the French *Conseil d'état* drew up a report which looked at the growing influence of Community legislation on French law and expressed concern at the volume of Community rules and how difficult they were to understand.[10] It was alarmed by seeing alien traditions of drafting creeping in (such as the use of definitions), evoking French lawyers peering beyond their neatly trimmed box hedges and seeing the gracious disorder of an English garden. That same year the European Council adopted the Birmingham declaration with the pithy demand, 'We want Community legislation to be clearer and simpler.' In 1993, the Council adopted a Resolution setting out what are known as the ten commandments of legislative drafting.[11] They were good as far as they went but they were merely in a resolution and the results were limited.

Conscious of the increasing impact of European legislation on their own statute books, some Member States pursued the matter. In 1995 a report on the quality of Community legislation was produced by a committee of senior Dutch civil servants chaired by a former judge at the European Court of Justice, T. Koopmans.[12] It recommended in particular the introduction of guidelines on legislative quality, like those used in the Netherlands, and the establishment of an independent vetting committee.

In 1997 the Netherlands together with the European institutions organised a Conference on the quality of European and national legislation whose report was

---

9 See Article 250 of the EC Treaty:

1. Where, in pursuance of this Treaty, the Council acts on a proposal from the Commission, unanimity shall be required for an act constituting an amendment to that proposal, subject to Article 251(4) and (5) [provisions on the Conciliation Committee].

2. As long as the Council has not acted, the Commission may alter its proposal at any time during the procedures leading to the adoption of a Community act.

10 Conseil d'état, *Le droit communautaire* (Etudes et documents No. 44, Paris: Rapport public 1992).

11 Council Resolution of 8 June 1993 on the quality of drafting of Community legislation (OJ C 166, 17.6.1993 at 1).

12 See *De kwaliteit van EG-regelgeving – Aandachtspunkten en voorstellen.*

published in book form.[13] Later that year at the initiative of the Netherlands presidency of the Council, supported by the United Kingdom, the Amsterdam Intergovernmental Conference adopted Declaration No. 39 on the quality of the drafting of Community legislation.[14] The Conference noted that 'the quality of the drafting of Community legislation is crucial if it is to be properly implemented by the competent national authorities and better understood by the public and in business circles' and called on the institutions to 'establish by common accord guidelines for improving the quality of the drafting of Community legislation ... and [to take] the internal organisational measures they deem necessary to ensure that these guidelines are properly applied'.

1998 Interinstitutional Agreement In December 1998 the European Parliament, the Council and the Commission accordingly adopted an Interinstitutional Agreement on common guidelines for the quality of drafting of Community legislation.[15] It laid down 22 guidelines on drafting, based partly on suggestions from Member States. Their status is made clear by recital (7) which states, 'these guidelines are to be regarded as instruments for internal use by the institutions. They are not legally binding'.

The first 6 guidelines set out general principles and the remaining 16 cover specific points or parts of acts. The agreement also specified the organisational measures called for by Declaration 39. Those measures are tailored to the fragmented or decentralised drafting system in which many different hands are involved in the drafting process, first within the Commission and then in both the European Parliament and the Council.

The measures included: publication of drafting guidance; reorganisation of internal procedures to involve the legal revisers earlier; establishment of drafting units; ensuring staff receive training in legal drafting; greater use of computers; and increased cooperation both between the Member States and the institutions and between the institutions themselves. The institutions have adopted most of the measures and duly reported on what they have done, albeit rather briefly.[16]

Lisbon strategy In 2000, the European Council in Lisbon 'set itself a new strategic goal for the next decade: to become the most competitive and dynamic knowledge-based economy in the world capable of sustainable economic growth with more and better jobs and greater social cohesion'.[17] To pursue that strategy a high-level group

13 See A.E. Kellermann et al. (eds) *Improving the Quality of Legislation in Europe* (The Hague: Kluwer Law International/The TMC Asser Instituut, 1998).

14 See OJ C 340, 10.11.1997 at 139.

15 See OJ C 73, 17.3.1999 at 1.

16 On 12 March 2001 the Council adopted its report 5882/01 JUR 37. The Commission covers such aspects in its annual reports on 'Better Lawmaking' (2006 report, COM (2007) 286).

17 See Point 5 of the Council Conclusions; see also point 14, 'The competitiveness and dynamism of businesses are directly dependent on a regulatory climate conducive to investment, innovation, and entrepreneurship. Further efforts are required to lower the costs of doing business and remove unnecessary red tape, both of which are particularly burdensome for SMEs. The European institutions, national governments and regional and local authorities

was established by the Member States under the chairmanship of Mr Mandelkern of the French Conseil d'état. Its report stressed the importance of regulation that was adapted to needs and recommended measures to achieve that aim as well as to improve access to EU law and provide sound administrative structures.[18]

In March 2001 the Stockholm European Council welcomed a report drawn up by a Committee of Wise Men on the Regulation of European Securities Markets (the Lamfalussy Report) and concluded, 'The proposed four-level approach (framework principles, implementing measures, co-operation and enforcement) should be implemented to make the regulatory process for European Union securities legislation more effective and transparent, thus improving the quality of the legislative measures proposed.'

Governance The European Commission launched its major governance initiative in July 2001, stating that the EU 'must pay constant attention to improving the quality, effectiveness and simplicity of regulatory acts'.[19] In a paper later that year, it admitted that results so far had been disappointing and called for a new strategy and a new culture of simplification of regulation.[20] In June 2002 it adopted a package of measures as part of the governance initiative designed to lead to better law-making, including an action Plan on simplifying and improving the regulatory environment.[21]

2003 Interinstitutional Agreement Responding to an invitation from the European Council in Seville in June 2002, the European Parliament, the Council and the Commission adopted another Interinstitutional Agreement in December 2003 affirming their common commitment to improving the quality of law-making and to promoting simplicity, clarity and consistency in the drafting of laws.[22] The institutions commit themselves in particular to:

- better preparation of legislation, with detailed programming of initiatives and coordination between the institutions and consultation and impact assessments for individual measures;
- greater transparency, with the provision of more and better explanation of legislative matters;

---

must continue to pay particular attention to the impact and compliance costs of proposed regulations, and should pursue their dialogue with business and citizens with this aim in mind.'

18 Available on (www.ec.europa.eu/governance/better_regulation/documents/mandelkern_report.pdf).

19 See the White Paper on Governance (COM (2001) 428), at point 3.2.

20 See Interim Report on improving and simplifying the regulatory environment (COM (2001) 130) at 3; and the Communication on simplifying and improving the regulatory environment (COM (2001) 726) at 2.

21 See COM (2002) 275, 276, 277 and 278.

22 See the Interinstitutional Agreement on better law-making (OJ C 321, 31.12.2003 at 1).

- improved accessibility of EU legislation, with the acquis being condensed by means of repeals and codification and with better electronic access;
- keeping the regulatory burden as light as possible, by recourse in particular to self-regulation, whereby the business sector is left to adopt codes of conduct for example, and co-regulation, in which the EU adopts an act setting objectives but leaves the practical arrangements for attaining those objectives to the business sector; and
- improved follow-up to legislation adopted, with checks and reports on compliance by the Member States.

Other regulatory reform initiatives At the end of 2003 the United Kingdom Foreign and Commonwealth Office presented a report examining the drafting of EU legislation and identifying problems relating to the application and interpretation of EU legislation in Member States.[23]

In January 2004, the four countries holding the rotating presidency of the European Council in 2004 and 2005 launched a Joint Initiative on Regulatory Reform[24] to maintain the momentum in implementing the Commission's action Plan on simplifying and improving the regulatory environment. That initiative has been taken up by other Member States and Better Regulation is now regularly included among the priorities of each presidency.

Steps Taken to Improve the Quality of EU Legislation

The three institutions involved in the legislative process are committed by the 2003 Interinstitutional Agreement to building on the process initiated by the 1998 Interinstitutional Agreement and to improving the coordination of their work and the information they give on it. They have taken a number of steps to give practical effect to those commitments.

Drafting quality The first step was the publication of a Joint Practical Guide on drafting which was finalised by the three institutions in 2000. That guide is intended to serve as a key tool for all staff in the institutions who draft legislation, for MEPs and for officials from the Member States involved in the EU legislative process. It has been made available in all Community languages in booklet form and on the Internet.[25]

The Commission has adapted its internal procedures to enable its legal revisers to revise early drafts as well as the final texts for adoption. Its legal revisers group has been expanded and structured to cope effectively with its new role. The Commission

---

23 See Robin Bellis, 'Implementation of EU Legislation' (An independent study for the Foreign and Commonwealth Office, London: 24 November 2003) available from (www.fco.gov.uk).

24 Initiative of the Irish, Dutch, Luxembourg and United Kingdom Presidencies of the EU: (www.finance.gov.ie/viewdoc.asp?DocID=1804&CatID=1&StartDate=1+January+2004&m).

25 Available on (www.eur-lex.europa.eu/en/techleg/index.htm).

legal revisers have since 2001 been offering technical staff introductory courses in drafting designed to familiarise them with the Joint Practical Guide and with the basic rules and principles applying to drafting. The training programme has been extended to include practical follow-up courses for the technical staff and courses specifically tailored to the needs of groups, such as translators or secretaries. To raise awareness of legislative issues and share information about different approaches, the Commission legal revisers organise seminars for all those concerned by quality of EU legislation inside and outside the institutions to hear the views of experts from the Member States and beyond.[26]

Accessibility A key role in ensuring access to EU legislation is played by the Office for Official Publications of the European Communities (OPOCE), the publishing house for the institutions and other bodies of the European Union. Since the inception of the Communities it has published the Official Journal on paper, still the only source for the authentic text of EU legislation. Since 1998 it has also published the Official Journal online but the electronic versions are not authentic.

In addition, in response to the calls for improved accessibility of EU law over the years, OPOCE has developed a system of websites and databases covering all aspects of EU law. Between 2003 and 2005 it created a single portal, called EUR-Lex, for accessing all that information which is now available without charge.[27] That portal gives access in particular to:

- the electronic version of the Official Journal;
- collections of the treaties, international agreements, legislation in force, legislation in preparation, case law, parliamentary questions – which can be accessed via hyperlinks;
- search engines for legislation and related measures;
- Pre-Lex, the database on the interinstitutional decision-making process; and
- a site on legislative drafting.

Gathering all information on a single, clearly structured site offers a 'one stop shop', a major improvement on the former situation when users might have to search a number of the institutions' independent sites before finding all the information required.

A key element in making law accessible is the consolidation and publication on EUR-Lex of EU legislation in all the official languages. Consolidation means combining in a single text an initial act and all amendments to it. The consolidated texts are not authentic but offer citizens and professionals rapid and generally reliable information about the current state of the law. They also serve as the basis for the codification and recasting of EU legislation. Some 3,000 acts have been consolidated in this way. The Europa website includes SCADPlus, a collection of fact sheets on

26 Available at (www.ec.europa.eu/dgs/legal_service/legal_reviser_en.htm#3).

27 Available at (www.eur-lex.europa.eu/en/index.htm).

EU legislation which are updated daily. The 2,500 fact sheets are divided into 32 subject areas and cover both existing measures and legislative proposals.[28]

Tidying up the statute book As long ago as 1974, a codification programme began to tackle the problem of legislation that had been amended.[29] In EU law 'codification' consists of merging an original act and all amendments to it in a new act which replaces the original act and the amending acts. The new act must pass through the whole legislative procedure, starting with a proposal from the Commission and ending with adoption by the European Parliament and the Council or by the Council alone. Provided that no substantive changes are made, a fast-track procedure is applied. The drafts are prepared by a group within the Commission Legal Service and a joint working party from the three institutions monitors the process.

Fresh impetus was given to codification in 2001 when an ambitious project was launched to codify the whole of the acquis[30] with a view to reducing the volume of legislation to be translated by new Member States.[31] At the same time, the three institutions recognised that codification was not producing all the desired results and adopted an agreement on a procedure for recasting acts.[32] Recasting consists in the adoption of a new legal act which incorporates in a single text an original act and any amendments already made to it while at the same time making any further changes that are necessary, including restructuring. As in codification, the new act has to pass through the full legislative procedure but the EP and Council commit themselves not to reopen discussions on provisions which remain unchanged.

Both codification and recasting are all too often labours of Sisyphus: even a fast track procedure can take so long that further amendments may come to be needed before the new act can be adopted. The addition of 9 new official languages in 2004 and 3 more in 2007 caused further hold-ups.

As part of the governance initiative the institutions began to look more closely at their statute book. In March 2001 the total volume of the acquis was estimated at 'some 70,000 pages' of the Official Journal. By December that year the estimate was 'over 80,000 pages' In February 2003 a comprehensive survey produced a figure of

28 Available at (www.europa.eu/scadplus/scad_en.htm).

29 See Council Resolution of 26 November 1974 concerning consolidation of its acts (OJ C 20, 28.1.1975 at 1) and the Interinstitutional Agreement of 20 December 1994 on an accelerated working method for official codification of legislative texts (OJ C 102, 4.4.1996 at 2).

30 On a broad interpretation, the acquis includes the whole of EU law, including the case law of the Court of Justice and non-binding acts such as resolutions and recommendations. In Commission documents it is used in this context as covering only binding secondary legislation, that is regulations, directives and decisions as referred to in Article 249 of the EC Treaty (see COM (2003) 71).

31 Communication on the Codification of the *acquis communautaire* (COM (2001) 645).

32 Interinstitutional Agreement of 28 November 2001 on a more structured use of the recasting technique for legal acts (OJ C 77, 28.3.2002 at 1).

97 000 pages. A programme is under way to identify all acts which are obsolete.[33] Wherever possible they will be repealed. If that is not possible, for example, for lack of an appropriate legal basis, the institution concerned will publish a formal notice declaring them obsolete.

Transparency For many years the Commission has published White Papers and Green Papers and consulted bodies such as the European Economic and Social Committee, and its departments have had contacts with external parties in their respective fields. Now a common framework has been established for consultations[34] and the system has been made more transparent by means of a dedicated website.[35]

A standard format and standard content have been laid down for the explanatory memorandum that always accompanies a legislative proposal submitted by the Commission to the legislative authority. It justifies the choice of act, whether regulation, directive or another form, the legal basis chosen and compliance with the principles of proportionality and subsidiarity and gives an account of the scope and results of consultations and impact assessments.

The EP, Council and Commission are to hold joint press conferences to announce the successful outcome of legislative procedures.[36] Following a call from the European Council in June 2006, the Council amended its Rules of Procedure to include provision for its deliberations on legislative acts to be open to the public and broadcast by video-streaming.[37]

New culture A number of steps are being taken as part of the new legislative culture called for by the governance and better law-making initiatives. The shift was clear when the President of the Commission, José Manuel Barroso, said in an interview a year after taking office, 'That Latin idea that all problems can be solved by making a law, it is not true'.[38]

Increased emphasis is being placed on consultation and impact assessment as a tool in structuring policies by defining problems, establishing objectives and then identifying the options for meeting those objectives and analysing the economic, social and environmental impact of those options. The Commission introduced an integrated approach to impact assessments in 2002 and in 2005 adopted new comprehensive guidelines.[39] At the end of 2005 the three institutions adopted a common approach broadly endorsing the line already taken by the Commission,

33 Under the Communication on Updating and simplifying the Community acquis (COM (2003) 71).

34 Communication from the Commission: Towards a reinforced culture of consultation and dialogue – General principles and minimum standards for consultation of interested parties by the Commission (COM (2002) 704).

35 Available at (www.ec.europa.eu/yourvoice/consultations/index_en.htm).

36 See interinstitutional Agreement on Better Lawmaking (OJ C 321, 31.12.2003 at 1), point 11.

37 See OJ L 285, 16.10.2006, at 47; see in particular Article 8.

38 'Cette idée latine qu'on résout tous les problèmes en faisant une loi, ce n'est pas vrai', *Sources say* No 5337, 21.11.2005, DG Press and Communication, European Commission.

39 See COM (2002) 276 and SEC (2005) 791.

agreeing to collaborate closely and undertaking to have further impact assessments carried out before any substantive amendment was made to a Commission proposal. In 2006 the Commission established an independent board to vet the quality of impact assessments carried out by Commission departments and to advise on methodology.

The Commission will keep the regulatory burden to a minimum by proposing legislation only if other alternatives will not do and by ensuring that new legislation is simple and easy to apply. A programme of measuring administrative costs and reducing administrative burdens (that is the extra cost of information obligations that businesses would not have to bear in the absence of the legislation) has been promoted by the Commission.[40] The European Council in March 2007 endorsed the target proposed by the Commission of a 25 per cent reduction in the administrative burden stemming from EU legislation by 2012. The Member States are encouraged to set their own comparable targets.

New legislation will generally include review clauses or other mechanisms to check whether it works and, in appropriate cases, expiry clauses. Existing legislation is to be screened to identify areas for simplification by means of repeals, codifications or recasts or replacement of old acts by new simpler acts.

It is clear that numerous disparate initiatives to improve legislation and the regulatory environment generally have been launched and in some cases relaunched. The Commission is now seeking to bring the various strands together by better coordination and networks. Recognising that in the past results have repeatedly fallen short of expectations, it now produces reports and tables analysing progress made.[41] This is essential if it is to move beyond mere lip service to the aim of quality legislation.

But in order to understand why any progress is slow, it is necessary to look at the broader context of the EU regulatory system.

Particular Features of EU Law with an Impact on the Framing of Legislation

Law Applying to 27 Countries

A unique feature of EU law is that it applies in 27 countries with their own legal systems and in many respects quite different cultures.[42] In 1748, Montesquieu wrote:

---

40 See COM (2006) 691 and COM (2007) 23.

41 Apart from the report each year on Better Lawmaking (2006 report COM (2007) 286) the Commission now produces reports on steps taken under its simplification programme. The first report was produced in October 2003 (COM (2003) 623) and the second in June 2004 (COM (2004) 432). See also the Communication on a strategic review of better regulation in the European Union (COM (2006) 689) and other reports on the Commission's Better Regulation. Available to view online at (www.ec.europa.eu/governance/better_regulation/index_en.htm).

42 See the White Paper on European governance (COM (2001) 428) at 13.

Laws must be so appropriate to the people for whom they are made that it is very fortuitous if those of one nation should suit another.[43]

One of the slogans rather optimistically proposed for the EU is 'United in diversity'. To make laws which are appropriate to the people of all the Member States, it is necessary to take account of their diversity, which itself has different aspects.

Diverse legal systems EU law is far from self-contained. It relies on the national administrations for its application and implementation and on the national judicial authorities for its enforcement. It has to enmesh with the legal systems in the Member States, whose constitutional structures range from strongly centralised systems to federations of regional entities enjoying considerable autonomy. The legal systems vary from common law systems to various families of civil law systems.

Cultural diversity EU legislation has to apply within the widely differing cultures of 27 Member States. Various distinctions can be made: for example, between the Nordic models of society and those of the south, or between the long established democracies and those newly emerging from authoritarian regimes.

Some differences relate to fundamentals like the attitude to the State and to the authority of the law. Some are directly related to legislation, such as views of the respective roles of the administration and of the courts in interpreting the law, on whether law is a matter just for lawyers or for all citizens, or on the use of soft law such as guidelines or codes of practice. Others are more practical. For example, rules were adopted to enable European citizens to travel freely with their pet animals as long as those pets meet basic health standards and have been issued 'pet passports' [44] Those passports are available for cats and dogs, not surprisingly, but also for ferrets, to the bewilderment of the nationals of many Member States where there is no tradition of keeping ferrets as pets.

Economic diversity The economies of the Member States show marked differences, ranging from highly developed to still maturing systems, from production-based to services-based systems, from highly regulated systems to free market systems, and so on. To take examples from some of the larger Member States: Germany has a big industrial sector with numerous small firms, the *Mittelstand*; France attaches considerable importance to its agricultural sector and will go to great lengths to protect the interests of its *paysans*! In the United Kingdom, agriculture is largely in the hands of big farmers and a large proportion of agricultural products are imported,

43 'Elles doivent être tellement propres au peuple pour lequel elles sont faites, que c'est un très grand hasard si celles d'une nation peuvent convenir à une autre', *De l'esprit des lois*, Book I, ch. 3.

44 See Commission Decision 2003/803/EC (OJ L 312, 27.11.2003 at 1).

manufacturing industries are shrinking and the services sector is a major part of the economy.

Geographical diversity EU legislation has to apply from the Arctic Circle in the north of Finland and Sweden to Malta in the southern Mediterranean Sea and from Cyprus and Greece in the east to Ireland and Portugal in the west. Within such an area the climate and the lie of the land vary enormously. For example, agricultural rules have to apply to a small hill farm on a wet mountain in Wales with two hundred sheep, to an estate in southern Spain with cattle roaming an enormous area of semi-desert land, to reindeer herders in the Arctic Circle and to honey producers in the Aegean islands.

Consequences The process of taking account of that diversity inevitably shapes the way in which EU legislation is framed. Drafts become increasingly complex as they progress through the system as qualifications and exceptions have to be added to the general rule. In all systems legislation has to be framed in general terms to enable it to apply to the diverse factual situations existing at one time and also to evolving factual situations. In order to be capable of applying to 27 Member States, EU legislation uses 'fuzzy' or 'general principles' drafting[45] to a much greater extent than common law systems. This leaves the Member States 'wriggle room', the latitude that is necessary for EU rules to mesh with the national rules.

Decentralised Drafting

In the EU legislative process, as we have seen, the draft act is passed like a baton in a relay race from one unit in the Commission to another before being handed over to the legislative authority. In the Council technical work is carried out in the working group whose members may change over time and all decisions are taken by bodies chaired by representatives of the Member State holding the presidency, which changes every six months. In the European Parliament technical work is carried out by the rapporteur and the committee and the political decision is taken by the plenary. The three institutions are autonomous and each jealous of its prerogatives under the treaties. But unlike in a relay race there is often no clean handover from one body to another; for example, the Commission retains an active role even after its proposal has passed to the other institutions. And unlike a baton, the draft act is shaped by all the hands through which it passes.

The only trace of the policy is the draft act itself. Very rarely does there exist separately a clear, comprehensive and up to date statement of the policy. At each stage, persons who wish to have the policy changed will generally do so by suggesting changes to the text of the draft act. Most of those involved in the process will be working in a language which is not their own. Clearly there is great scope for communication breakdown. A change may be suggested on the basis of a misunderstanding of the original text. Or a textual suggestion may be misunderstood

---

45 See G.C. Thornton, *Legislative drafting*, 4th edn (London: Butterworths, 1996) at 50 *et seq.*

by those who have to incorporate it in the draft act. From a very early stage, therefore, nobody will know with certainty what the intention of the draft act is.

Negotiated Law

Most of those through whose hands the drafts pass are concerned more with achieving their own policy goals than with the technical quality of legislation. Few of them are lawyers and fewer still legislative drafting specialists.

Member States often approach EU law in the same way as they approach the negotiation of an international agreement and indeed in French it is sometimes described as *droit diplomatique.* In its 1992 report on the influence of Community law on French law the French *Conseil d'état* noted:

> ... while lawyers strive for precision, diplomats tend to leave things unsaid and do not shun ambiguity. More often than you would think, it happens, therefore, that they agree on a word only because it does not mean the same thing to everyone. And they encourage drafting techniques which will leave room here and there for interesting – and promising – contradictions.[46]

Throughout the EU legislative process efforts will be made to obtain a consensus and to that end compromises will be accepted and techniques used that would in other circumstances be shunned by a legislative drafter.

Languages

EU legislation is authentic in 23 languages. Article 4 of Regulation No. 1[47] provides that all regulations must be 'drafted' in all official languages, which signifies that formally they all have the same status: there is not one original and 22 translated versions. Article 5 requires the *Official Journal of the European Union* (OJ) to be published in all those languages as well.[48] This means that it is not possible to publish first only some language versions and to leave the others for later. A regulation cannot be adopted and enter into force until all language versions are available.[49] EU

46 Conseil d'état, Le droit communautaire (Etudes et documents No. 44, Paris: Rapport public 1992), 'là où les juristes cherchent la précision, les diplomates pratiquent le non-dit et ne fuient pas l'ambiguïté. Il arrive donc, plus souvent qu'on ne croit, qu'ils ne se mettent d'accord sur un mot que parce qu'il n'a pas la même signification pour tout le monde. [...] De même encouragent-ils des techniques de rédaction qui permettront de laisser subsister ici et là d'intéressantes – et prometteuses – contradictions.'

47 See OJ 17, 6.10.1958 at 385/58.

48 As for the Treaties themselves, Article 314 of the EC Treaty, as amended by successive acts of Accession, provides that the texts in all the official languages are 'equally authentic'

49 See Case C-370/96 *Covita AVE v Greek State* [1998] ECR I-7711, paras 26 and 27: 'it should be observed that it is mandatory for Community provisions introducing a countervailing charge to be published in the *Official Journal of the European Communities.* From the date of that publication no person is deemed to be unaware of that charge ...

... it cannot be accepted that a trader such as Covita was aware that Regulation No 1591/92 had been adopted if it proves that the Official Journal of 23 June 1992 was not available on

legislation has to produce the same legal effects in all languages and in its interface with all the national legal systems. It must therefore be drafted particularly clearly and simply, avoiding complexities, nuances or expressions that cannot be rendered in all languages.

Interpretation by the European Court of Justice

The approach of the European Court of Justice (ECJ) to interpretation of EU law differs from that of courts in Member States to interpreting their national law. Particularly striking is the difference from the literalist approach of courts in common law countries, as pointed out by Lord Denning in memorable terms shortly after the accession of the United Kingdom:

> The Treaty is quite unlike any of the enactments to which we have become accustomed. The draftsmen of our statutes have striven to express themselves with the utmost exactness. They have tried to foresee all possible circumstances that may arise and to provide for them. They have sacrificed style and simplicity. They have forgone brevity. They have become long and involved. In consequence, the judges have followed suit. They interpret a statute as applying only to the circumstances covered by the very words. They give them a literal interpretation. If the words of the statute do not cover a new situation – which was not foreseen – the judges hold that they have no power to fill the gap. To do so would be a 'naked usurpation of the legislative function' ... The gap must remain open until Parliament finds time to fill it.
>
> How different is this Treaty! It lays down general principles. It expresses its aims and purposes. All in sentences of moderate length and commendable style. But it lacks precision. It uses words and phrases without defining what they mean ... An English lawyer would look for an interpretation clause, but he would look in vain. There is none. All the way through the Treaty there are gaps and lacunae. These have to be filled in by the judges, or by Regulations or directives. It is the European way.
>
> Likewise the Regulations and directives ... They are quite unlike our statutory instruments. They have to give the reasons on which they are based ... So they start off with pages of preambles ... These show the purpose and intent of the Regulations and directives. Then follow the provisions which are to be obeyed. Here again words and phrases are used without defining their import ... In case of difficulty, recourse is had to the preambles. These are useful to show the purpose and intent behind it all. But much is left to the judges. The enactments give only an outline plan. The details are to be filled in by the judges.
>
> Seeing these differences, what are the English courts to do when they are faced with a problem of interpretation? They must follow the European pattern. No longer must they examine the words in meticulous detail. No longer must they argue about the precise grammatical sense. They must look to the purpose or intent. To quote the words of the

---

that date in its Greek language version at the Office for Official Publications of the European Communities, situated in Luxembourg. If evidence is produced that actual publication of the Official Journal was delayed, regard must be had to the date on which the issue was actually available.'

European Court ... they must deduce 'from the wording and the spirit of the Treaty the meaning of the Community rules'. They must not confine themselves to the English text. They must consider, if need be, all the authentic texts ... They must divine the spirit of the Treaty and gain inspiration from it. If they find a gap, they must fill it as best they can. They must do what the framers of the instrument would have done if they had thought about it. So we must do the same. Those are the principles, as I understand it, on which the European Court acts.[50]

The ECJ itself referred in the *CILFIT* case to 'the characteristic features of Community law and the particular difficulties to which its interpretation gives rise'.[51] It went on:

To begin with, it must be borne in mind that Community legislation is drafted in several languages and that the different language versions are all equally authentic. An interpretation of a provision of Community law thus involves a comparison of the different language versions.

It must also be borne in mind, even where the different language versions are entirely in accord with one another, that Community law uses terminology which is peculiar to it. Furthermore, it must be emphasized that legal concepts do not necessarily have the same meaning in Community law and in the law of the various Member States.

Finally, every provision of Community law must be placed in its context and interpreted in the light of the provisions of Community law as a whole, regard being had to the objectives thereof and to its state of evolution at the date on which the provision in question is to be applied.[52]

The ECJ accordingly takes a broad approach to interpreting a text, relying on core meanings of terms. It may compare the different language versions and attempt to find a 'common interpretation which best reflects the sense in all the languages'.[53]

It looks at a provision in its context, such as the other provisions of the same act and other related acts, and in the light of the aims of the act.[54] It has regard to the reasons on which the provision is based, in particular as stated in the preamble.[55] It also takes account of general principles of EU law such as legal certainty[56] and fundamental rights.[57]

50 See *Bulmer Ltd v Bollinger SA* [1974] 4 ch. 401 at 411.

51 See Case 283/81 *CILFIT and Lanificio di Gavardo v Ministry of Health* [1982] ECR 3415, para. 17.

52 See paras. 18, 19 and 20.

53 See Case 80/76 *North Kerry Milk Products v Minister of Agriculture* [1977] ECR 425.

54 See Case C–136/91 *Findling Walzlager v Hauptzollamt Karlsruhe* [1993] ECR I–1793, para. 11.

55 See Case C–355/95 P *TWD v Commission* [1997] ECR I–2549, para. 21.

56 See Joined cases 42 and 49/59 *S.N.U.P.A.T. v High Authority* [1961] ECR 53; Case T–171/00 *Spruyt v Commission* [2001] ECR FP IA–187, II – 855, paras. 70, 71 and 72.

57 See joined Cases C–465/00, C–138/01 and C–139/01 *Rechnungshof v Österreichischer Rundfunk and Others* [2003] ECR I–4989, para. 68.

Conferred Powers

Under the first paragraph of Article 5 of the EC Treaty, the 'Community shall act within the limits of the powers conferred on it by this Treaty'. The second paragraph of that article goes on to lay down the principle of subsidiarity.[58] Article 7(1) of the EC Treaty provides, 'Each institution shall act within the limits of the powers conferred on it by this Treaty'. Accordingly every act adopted by an EU institution must have a legal basis in a Treaty or in an act which itself has a basis in a Treaty. The legal basis must, under the Council's Rules of Procedure,[59] be specified in the citations at the beginning of the preamble of the act.

In general the Treaty itself confers power on the European Parliament and the Council to adopt basic legislation. That basic legislation will confine itself to the fundamental rules but in turn confer on the Commission powers for the implementation of those rules.[60] It can happen that the legislation in one sector is fragmented because of the need to respect the confines of different legal bases, which may entail different procedures and even different legislative authorities.

Piecemeal Law

EU law did not start with a single coherent plan. One piece of legislation was adopted after another as needs became apparent and as agreement between the Member States could be reached. In the very early days the largest policy area was agriculture where the structure of the legislation was comparatively simple: one basic regulation was adopted for each sector of the agricultural market (such as cereals or wine) with little risk of overlap. All secondary legislation was based on one or other of those basic regulations and so the overall system was transparent and rational.

In more recent years the problem has become more acute and apparent. The network of rules is becoming ever more complex and the rational organisation less discernible. To take just one example, in the increasingly important field of food safety, the basic provisions on trade in animals, meat and meat products may be divided into provisions on intra-Community movements and those on imports from third countries, with different basic acts covering different animals and further divisions being made for live animals and for carcases, for meat and for meat products, for laying hens, chicks or hatching eggs, and for embryos or semen for artificial insemination. But then in order to safeguard food quality from farm to table horizontal rules may be adopted on animal registration and inspection, health certificates, transport conditions, slaughtering, processing and food labelling. And other horizontal rules cover types of animal diseases such as spongiform encephalopathies (mad-cow disease, scrapie in sheep and others) or specific health risks such as salmonella or dioxins. Most of those basic acts will give rise to separate implementing acts and the result may be described as a multilayered patchwork.

---

58 See also Protocol No. 30 annexed to the EC Treaty.

59 See OJ L 285, 16.10.2006, at 47; see Annex VI, Point A.1(c).

60 In accordance with Article 202 of the EC Treaty.

Amendment

It is probably a feature common to most developed legal systems that legislation falls to be amended more and more often. The explanation generally given is that legislation has to cover ever more complex societies with increased interdependence and accelerating changes, technological and other. At EU level many of the features described above serve to aggravate the problem. The rules have to apply to different national systems at different stages of development and evolving at different speeds. The legislative process is a lengthy one, on average some two years for the adoption of an act by the EP and the Council. In that time elections may well have changed the composition of those bodies and their positions may well have shifted. The existing body of legislation has been adopted piecemeal and is often interwoven. A need for change in one act may have a knock-on effect on others.

Closing Remarks

At a Colloquium of the Association of the Councils of State and Supreme administrative jurisdictions of the European Union held in The Hague on 14 and 15 June 2004,[61] it was suggested that EU legislation should be judged by different standards from national legislation. The President of the Association, Mr H. Tjeenk Willink, Vice-President of the Dutch Council of State said:

> The European legal order was devised to serve diversity and pluralism and the EU's legislators must take this into account. Were some law introduced in the name of the free market which made it mandatory for all cafés in Europe to meet the same requirements, it might denote a success for that free market but it would spell failure for the concept of Europe. Of Europe as a cultural and social reality. 'European legislation is not intended to take away the diversity of legal traditions, methods and systems in the Member States, but rather to shape their compatibility'
>
> This means that the EU's legislators do not necessarily play the same role as national ones. While national legislators focus primarily on how to find uniform solutions to what are experienced as common problems, European legislation must define the scope for diverse solutions. National legislators will often indicate what must be done while EU legislators will indicate what must be stopped.

Is it possible then that the lack of clarity and lack of precision resulting from the process by which EU legislation is adopted are not just unfortunate side effects of that process but are actually essential to enable the system to work by giving the Member States the leeway they need to adapt it to their own legal systems? In EU law, is the point of balance between fuzzy and fussy legislation different from that in national systems? Whatever the answer, the acknowledged need for some leeway or 'wriggle room' cannot be treated as licence to leave EU legislation opaque, convoluted and inaccessible.

---

61 See the Association's website accessible from the site of the Belgian Conseil d'état: (www.raadvst-consetat.be/).

The EU has an impressive range of initiatives, strategies, action plans and programmes to improve the quality of its legislation. The institutions and the Member States must now work closely together on the ground to make the EU regulatory framework efficient and effective. This is essential if the EU is indeed to shape standards throughout the world, as envisaged in the Commission's 2007 Communication on a Single Market for Citizens:

> Through the EEA and increasingly through the European neighbourhood policy the rules and standards of the single market stretch beyond the borders of the EU. Frequently the world looks to Europe and adopts the standards that are set here. This works to the advantage of those already geared up to meet these standards, and should contribute to improving the living and working conditions worldwide.[62]

62 See COM (2007) 60.

Chapter 14

Drafting to Implement EU Law: the European Arrest Warrant in the United Kingdom

Valsamis Mitsilegas

Introduction

Perhaps the most far-reaching development in European Union criminal law in recent years has been the adoption of the European Arrest Warrant. The first – and most prominent thus far – example of the application of the mutual recognition principle in criminal matters in the European Union, the European Arrest Warrant has raised a number of issues of legal and constitutional importance, both in the course of its negotiation and adoption at EU level, and in the course of its implementation in Member States. In this context, addressing issues of constitutionality and fundamental rights protection proved to be particularly challenging in the implementation of the European Arrest Warrant for legislators, drafters and judges in most Member States.

The aim of this contribution is to cast light on these challenges as regards the implementation of the European Arrest Warrant in the United Kingdom. In order to do so, the chapter will be divided into three major substantive parts examining: the European Arrest Warrant as a reflection of the application of the mutual recognition principle in EU criminal law and the issues of legality and human rights protection that it raises; the implementation of the European Arrest Warrant in the UK, namely the Extradition Act 2003, both as regards its context and issues related to legislative drafting; and finally the interpretation of the Extradition Act by the House of Lords, focusing in particular on the use of European Union law principles to interpret the domestic Act and resolve drafting ambiguities. In the light of this analysis, the concluding remarks will focus on the limits of legislative drafting when facing the challenging task of accommodating in domestic law highly politicised EU legislation which has raised again the fundamental constitutional issue of the relationship between the Union and Member States and the issue of primacy of Union over national law.

Applying the Principle of Mutual Recognition in EU Criminal Law: the European Arrest Warrant

Calls for the application of the principle of mutual recognition – already tried in the context of the EU internal market – in the field of EU criminal law appeared in the late 1990s – in particular during the UK Presidency of the Union in 1998 – and were reflected in detail in the 1999 European Council Tampere Conclusions which provided an impetus for new legislative action in the field of EU Justice and Home Affairs. Mutual recognition was for some an alternative, for others a complementary mechanism, to harmonisation in criminal matters in the European Union. In an era when the Commission was pushing actively forward harmonisation (if not uniformity) of EU criminal law most notably via the *Corpus Juris* project, more sceptical Member States (such as the United Kingdom) were pushing forward mutual recognition as an alternative – its main advantage being that by accepting to recognise judicial decisions from courts in another Member State they would not have to change their domestic law (something that could happen if they would have to implement a harmonising EU criminal law measure). At the same time, for pro-integration advocates mutual recognition would provide a way out of the prospect of legislative stagnation in EU criminal law (accentuated by the unanimity requirement in voting in the Council on third pillar matters, which could mean in practice that sceptical Member States could block harmonisation initiatives): not only would it lead to the adoption of some EU criminal law (as exemplified by the adoption of the European Arrest Warrant in 2001), but also, if the example of mutual recognition in the internal market were to be followed, mutual recognition would also lead to the adoption of complementary minimum harmonisation standards aiming at creating a level playing field among Member States.[1]

Mutual recognition in criminal matters would involve the recognition and execution by a judge in the receiving (or, according to EU terminology, the 'executing' Member State) of a judicial decision by a court in the sending (or the 'issuing' Member State). The main features of this process are speed, automaticity and a minimum of formality. The executing judge would receive the mutual recognition request in essence via a pro forma form (completed by the issuing judge). The executing judge should in principle not look behind the form and accept the request without asking too many questions. As the EU institutions (and the governments of a number of Member States including the United Kingdom) have repeatedly pointed out in the negotiations of the various EU mutual recognition measures, the basis of mutual recognition is mutual trust in the criminal justice systems of Member States. This perceived mutual trust should thus lead to quasi-automatic enforcement. But in practice the 'no questions asked' mutual recognition effectively consists of a 'journey

1 See V. Mitsilegas, 'Trust-building Measures in the European Judicial Area in Criminal Matters: Issues of Competence, Legitimacy and Inter-institutional Balance' in S. Carrera and T. Balzacq, *Security versus Freedom? A Challenge for Europe's Future* (Aldershot, Hampshire and Burlington, VT: Ashgate, 2006) pp. 279–89; On the Corpus Juris point, see J.R. Spencer, 'The European Arrest Warrant', in 6 (2003–04) *Cambridge Yearbook of European Legal Studies* pp. 203–204.

into the unknown' for the executing judge who is in essence being asked to accept almost blindly a decision which stems from the judicial, legal and constitutional tradition of another EU Member State.[2]

As mentioned above, the first – and most talked about – example of mutual recognition in criminal matters in the European Union has been the Framework Decision on the European Arrest Warrant.[3] Justified primarily as a counter-terrorism measure, it was negotiated swiftly after 9/11 with limited time for detailed scrutiny – agreement on the text reached by the end of the Belgian EU Presidency in December 2001.[4] It was deemed as revolutionising the pre-existing extradition arrangements in the European Union.[5] Notwithstanding its counter-terrorism justification, the European Arrest Warrant applies to a wide range of offences (namely offences punishable by a maximum custodial sentence of at least one year).[6] Pushing the boundaries of extradition law and mutual recognition further, the Framework Decision entailed the abolition of dual criminality for a long list of 32 offences if these are punishable by a minimum/maximum custodial sentence of at least 3 years.[7] The European Arrest Warrant is in fact a form, a pro forma of which is annexed to the text of the Framework Decision. It is this completed form that the executing judge receives – and the Warrant must be executed within tight deadlines.[8] The Warrant requests the arrest and surrender to the issuing State of individuals for the purposes of conducting a criminal prosecution or executing a custodial sentence or detention order.[9] The executing judge is offered very limited grounds for refusal to execute the Warrant. Although it was the subject of heated debate in negotiations, infringement of the requested individual's human rights is not expressly mentioned in the list of grounds for refusal.[10]

The application of the mutual recognition principle in these terms in the European Arrest Warrant raised a number of constitutional concerns across the European Union.[11] A major concern relates to the principle of legality, which is deemed to be threatened by the abolition of dual criminality for a wide range of offences. This could lead to the authorities of a Member State employing their criminal law

---

2 See V. Mitsilegas, 'The Constitutional Implications of Mutual Recognition in Criminal Matters in the European Union' 43 (2006) *Common Market Law Review* pp. 1277–311.

3 See OJ L 190, 18.7.2002, at 1.

4 In the context of UK scrutiny, see House of Lords European Union Committee, *The European Arrest Warrant*, 16th Report, session 2001–02.

5 On the European Arrest Warrant in relation to extradition, see S. Alegre and M. Leaf, 'Mutual Recognition in European Judicial Co-operation: A Step Too Far Too Soon? Case Study – the European Arrest Warrant' 10 (2004) *European Law Journal* pp. 200–217.

6 See Article 2(1).

7 Some harmonised some not – Article 2(2). But there are some safeguards – see Article 4(7).

8 See Articles 17 and 23.

9 See Article 1(1).

10 But Article 1(3) states that, 'this Framework Decision shall not have the effect of modifying the obligation to respect fundamental rights and fundamental legal principles as enshrined in Article 6 of the Treaty on European Union'

11 See Mitsilegas, *op. cit.*, note 2.

enforcement mechanism in order to arrest and surrender an individual for conduct which is not an offence under its domestic law.[12] Legality concerns are inextricably linked in this context with issues of legitimacy and trust, most notably regarding the bond between the State and its citizens.[13] The lack of legitimacy may be an issue in particular in the light of the fact that on the basis of mutual recognition a court in a Member State must accept decisions stemming from standards and laws in the adoption of which the public of the executing State played no part and has limited if not no knowledge of. Further constitutional concerns were raised on the specific issue of the surrender of own nationals which the European Arrest Warrant allows but several national Constitutions expressly prohibited.[14] Last, but not least, a major issue regarding the implementation of the European Arrest Warrant concerned the protection of fundamental rights, in particular the rights of the individual subject to surrender in another Member State before (and crucially) after surrender. It is in this context where the concept of mutual trust has been perhaps most strongly challenged, with a number of concerns voiced regarding the capacity and ability of a number of EU Member States to safeguard effectively the rights of the defendant in their domestic criminal justice systems.[15]

Implementing the European Arrest Warrant in the United Kingdom

The European Arrest Warrant Framework Decision was implemented in the United Kingdom via the Extradition Act 2003.[16] In the parliamentary debates leading to the adoption of the Act, the government stressed the importance of the European Arrest Warrant reflecting mutual recognition in EU criminal law, as an alternative to harmonisation.[17] The government also supported the European Arrest Warrant by highlighting its potential contribution to the fight against organised crime post-EU enlargement.[18] However, this did not stop constitutional concerns – most notably

12 For this argument and counter-arguments see Mitsilegas, ibid.

13 See in this context in particular the judgment of the German Constitutional Court on the German law implementing the European Arrest Warrant. For an analysis, see Mitsilegas, ibid.; see also F.Geyer, 'The European Arrest Warrant in Germany - Constitutional Mistrust towards the Concept of Mutual Trust' in E. Guild (ed.) *Constitutional Challenges to the European Arrest Warrant* (Nijmegen: Wolf Legal Publishers, 2006) pp. 101–125.

14 This has led to the intervention of a number of national supreme courts (in particular in Poland and Cyprus), see Mitsilegas, *op. cit.*

15 To address the issue, the Commission tabled a proposal for a Framework Decision on the rights of the defendant, see Mitsilegas, *op. cit.*, notes 1 and 2; see House of Lords European Union Committee, *Procedural Rights in Criminal Proceedings*, 1st Report, session 2004–05.

16 For an analysis of the Act, see J.B. Knowles, *Blackstone's Guide to the Extradition Act 2003* (Oxford: Oxford University Press, 2004).

17 See the comments of the then Minister for Policing, John Denham, stating that, 'it is precisely, if we want to avoid pressure for a Europe with harmonised laws and a single judicial system that we must be prepared to recognise the judicial decisions taken in other European countries' House of Commons Hansard Debates for 9 December 2002, col. 41.

18 See ibid. col. 43.

related to the abolition of dual criminality and the protection of human rights – being raised by a number of MPs and peers.[19] It has been argued that this attitude demonstrates ideological arguments reflecting a belief in the inherent superiority of the adversarial system.[20] In the Commons debates, the government defended the European Arrest Warrant as an embodiment of the mutual recognition principle in a European Union where all Member States are 'mature democracies'.[21] However, it also took steps to address some of these concerns in the Extradition Act itself.

The Extradition Act did not have as its sole aim the implementation of the European Arrest Warrant Framework Decision. Rather, it was an attempt towards a wholesale amendment of UK extradition law. The government had set out proposals for law reform in March 2001, months before the relevant EU legislation was tabled by the Commission.[22] This may explain why, notwithstanding the attempt by the European Arrest Warrant to introduce a change in terminology (from 'extradition' to 'surrender', which arguably reflects the qualitatively different nature of the new EU procedure from traditional international law extradition), the UK Act continues to refer to 'extradition' throughout the text. The structure of the Act helps towards clarifying the distinction between provisions implementing the European Arrest Warrant and applicable to EU Member States (the so-called 'category 1' territories), and provisions amending extradition arrangements with non-EU countries ('category 2' territories).[23] However, the substance of the Act makes this distinction less clear, by granting the power to designate a country as 'category 1' or 'category 2' territory to the Home Secretary.[24]

A comparison between the texts of the EU Framework Decision and the Extradition Act demonstrates a number of instances where, on the substance of the law, the UK legislator has diverged from the EU requirements. There have been instances of 'gold plating', which could result in both greater enforcement and greater protection for the individual in comparison with the Framework Decision.[25]

19 See inter alia House of Commons Hansard Debates for 9 December 2002, col. 52 *et seq.*; and House of Lords Hansard for 1 May 2003, col. 853 *et seq.*; see also the concerns expressed regarding the abolition of dual criminality by the Commons Home Affairs Committee, *Extradition Bill*, 1st Report, session 2002–03.

20 See Spencer, *op. cit.*, at 211.

21 See Denham, *op. cit.*, col. 49; see also the then Under Secretary of State for the Home Office, Bob Ainsworth at col. 245.

22 See the consultation document *The Law of Extradition: A Review.* For background, see Home Affairs Committee, *op. cit.*; and the Explanatory Notes to the Extradition Act.

23 Part 1 of the Act covers 'extradition' to category 1 territories; Part 2 covers extradition to category 2 territories. Part 3, entitled 'extradition to the United Kingdom', is divided into two sub-parts on 'extradition' from category 1 territories and extradition from category 2 territories.

24 See sections 1(1) and 69(1) respectively.

25 According to the UK Government, 'gold plating' occurs inter alia (in the context of the implementation of first pillar Directives) by extending the scope, adding in some way to the substantive requirement, or substituting wider UK legal terms for those used in the directive; not taking full advantage of any derogations which keep requirements to a minimum; and providing sanctions and enforcement mechanisms which go beyond the minimum needed. See

An enforcement maximisation 'gold plating' instance can be discerned with regard to the abolition of dual criminality: while the Framework Decision dictates that this applies to offences punishable by a minimum/maximum custodial sentence of three years, the Extradition Act lowers this threshold when surrender is related to persons already sentenced for an offence to one year.[26] A 'protective' gold plating instance is the additional element of formality by the Extradition Act stating that the designated authority may issue 'a certificate' if it believes that the requesting authority has the function of issuing arrest Warrants in the category 1 territory.[27] As will be seen below, this has been the subject of uncertainty and high-level litigation.

There are further instances where the Extradition Act is more protective to the Framework Decision. The latter, aiming at speed and maximum efficiency, prescribes specific time limits for execution – unlike the Extradition Act which does not specifically prescribe such time limits.[28] The Act introduces a 12-month penalty threshold in order to treat an 'extraterritorial offence' as an extradition offence.[29] And, perhaps more importantly, the Extradition Act contains additional bars to surrender in comparison with the Framework Decision. The judge may refuse surrender in cases of Warrants executed for convictions in certain trials in absentia[30] and in cases where surrender (or 'extradition' under the Act) would not be compatible with human rights.[31] It is important to note that, while both the above cases can effectively constitute bars to surrender, they are *not* included in the list of the specifically enumerated bars to extradition (sections 12–19).[32] Rather, these are additional steps that the judge has to take once the extradition bars have been examined: if none of these bars stand, the judge has to look at whether there is a conviction in absentia which would preclude surrender; if this is not the case, the next step will be to look at the compatibility of surrender with human rights.[33] The insertion of these sections in the Act represents a clear policy choice reflecting domestic concerns regarding the operation of the European Arrest Warrant where trials in absentia and perceived challenges to human rights protection are involved. Similarly, surrender may be barred and the requested person discharged on grounds

---

HM Government, Department for Business, Enterprise and Regulatory Reform, *Transposition Guide: How to Implement European Directives Effectively*, September 2007.

26 See Section 65(2)(c). The government has justified this change on the debatable grounds of ensuring consistency with the earlier regime; see Ainsworth, col. 245. This move has been criticised by the Home Affairs Committee. *Op. cit.*, para. 52.

27 See Section 2(7).

28 See Spencer, *op. cit.*, at 209.

29 See Section 64(4)(c).

30 See section 20.

31 See section 21.

32 Neither section 20 nor section 21 find an equivalent provision in the European Arrest Warrant Framework Decision, in particular when one looks at the grounds for non-execution. The issue of judgments in absentia is addressed in the Framework Decision within the context of the 'guarantees' to be given by the issuing State; the issue of human rights compliance is addressed by the general provision of Article 1(3) and to some extent in the Preamble of the Framework Decision.

33 See section 11(4) and (5).

of their physical or mental condition or national security – with both provisions scattered in different parts of the Act.[34] Although not explicitly referred to as 'bars to extradition' in the Act (and not being enumerated as grounds for non-execution in the Framework Decision), the sections definitely lead the executing judge in the UK to look closely into these matters taking thus away a degree of automaticity in the execution of a Warrant.

Divergences from the Framework Decision and uncertainty in implementation have not only been caused by concrete policy choices which legislative drafting had to translate into the Extradition Act. Another cause has been the drafting style, which at times is extremely complex. As it has been noted,[35] the provisions on the offences which may give rise to surrender are extremely lengthy and complex.[36] Placed in a rather disjointed way towards the end of 'Part 1' of the Act, under the general heading of 'interpretation',[37] the provisions enumerate a series of 'conditions' for conduct to be an 'extradition offence', again subdivided into cases where a person has been, or has not been, sentenced for an offence. The structure of these provisions, their position in the general framework of the Act and their length are certainly not conductive to clarity. Moreover, the terminology used in these lengthy sections, partly inherited from the 1989 Extradition Act,[38] has proven on occasions to be unclear and has been, as will be seen below, subject to litigation.

The Extradition Act has certainly not copied the European Arrest Warrant Framework Decision. Implementing the UK's EU obligations was part of its aim. Moreover, its drafting and content reflect both domestic constitutional concerns regarding the operation of the European Arrest Warrant, and the existing legal tradition with regard to extradition law. Perhaps in addressing both these elements, the Extradition Act focuses to a considerably greater extent than the Framework Decision on the *process*. The implementation of a number of Framework Decision provisions is structurally subsumed under the 'hearing' headings of Part 1 of the Extradition Act. The emphasis placed on *the hearing* in the implementation of the European Arrest Warrant is indicative of the willingness to give to the domestic authorities as much and as precise guidance possible for the implementation. At the same time, viewing the execution of a Warrant as a process, has enabled the Act to offer a number of safeguards to the requested individual, some not mentioned in the Framework Decision itself. These divergences from the Framework Decision are

34 See section 25 and section 208 respectively. Note that as regards section 208, the Extradition Act retains a role for the Home Secretary in the process (although the European Arrest Warrant would in principle de-politicise and judicialise the process).

35 See N. Padfield, 'The Implementation of the European Arrest Warrant in England and Wales' 3 (2007) *European Constitutional Law Review* at 258.

36 See sections 64–66.

37 For a similar technique see the Proceeds of Crime Act 2002, see V. Mitsilegas, 'Global Standards in Domestic Legal Cultures: the Money Laundering Offences in the UK' in S. Braum (ed.) *Droit Pénal Européen des Affaires*, (Berliner Wissenschaftsverlag, forthcoming).

38 See, for instance, the term 'unlawfully at large' in section 64(1) Knowles, *op. cit.*, at 11.

coupled with instances where the Act reflects specific policy choices not to follow the letter of the European Arrest Warrant in the implementation.[39]

While the aim of the Extradition Act may have been to provide clear, precise guidance to those entrusted with its implementation on the ground, there have been rather paradoxical instances where the detailed wording of the Act has not necessarily contributed to legal clarity. The Commission, in its most recent Report on the implementation of the European Arrest Warrant, has criticised the United Kingdom on a number of occasions. These include the omission by the Extradition Act to include specific time limits for the execution of Warrants, which has led to Framework Decision time-limits being 'far from respected in the UK'.[40] While this legislative choice may be explained by the willingness of Parliament to grant the UK executing authorities as much leeway as possible to examine European Arrest Warrants, the following criticism by the Commission regarding the wording of the Extradition Act on the form and wording of a European Arrest Warrant is noteworthy. According to the Commission:

> the UK has not included in its legislation all the information in Article 8(1) nor indicated whether it uses the correct form ... The UK has, nevertheless, stated that in practice it uses the form in the annex to the Framework Decision. This again does not satisfy the requirement of legal certainty. Moreover, the UK's legislation may give rise to difficulties, as it appears to be somewhat confusing.[41]

This situation may have occurred in spite of the detailed wording of section 2 of the Extradition Act. It may have contributed to what the Commission describes as a practice of UK authorities seemingly sending back forms deemed incomplete and requiring almost systematically that a new European Arrest Warrant is issued.[42] This practice may betray a lack of trust by the UK authorities towards their partners in the requesting EU Member States, and may reflect the emphasis on the domestic legal culture on detail. However, this attitude (aided by the Extradition Act's additional requirement towards issuing a certificate) may lead to a practice which could be contrary to the spirit – if not the letter – of the Framework Decision. The lack of clarity in the wording and structure of the Extradition Act has not helped in this context, resulting in litigation regarding the interpretation of the Act in the light of EU law. The next part will examine such a case, in particular the interpretation of specific provisions of the Extradition Act by the House of Lords.

---

39 For criticism, see the 2007 Commission Report on the implementation of the European Arrest Warrant, in particular the annexed working document SEC (2007) 979, Brussels, 11 July 2007. The UK Government is defiant and accepts that on a number of occasions the UK has not implemented the Framework Decision properly, see Home Office Explanatory Memorandum to the Commons European Scrutiny Committee and the Lords European Union Committee of 13 August 2007.

40 See Commission, *op. cit.*, at 28.

41 See ibid. at 20.

42 See ibid.

Interpreting the Implementing Act: Issues Arising from Legislative Drafting

Unsurprisingly, the implementation of the European Arrest Warrant in the UK has given rise to a number of cases concerning its operation and the interpretation of the provisions of the 2003 Extradition Act. A number of cases involved the accuracy and completeness of the information contained in Arrest Warrants received by British authorities, the admissibility of these Warrants, and dual criminality, while other cases involved substantive human rights issues.[43] Two of these cases have reached the House of Lords, and resulted in important constitutional judgments giving guidance on the interpretation of the Extradition Act more narrowly, and the interpretation of domestic law in the light of European Union law more broadly. The significance of these judgments is accentuated by the fact that the UK Government currently does not allow British Courts to send preliminary references asking for the interpretation of third pillar law to the Court of Justice in Luxembourg – thus, it is interesting to see the extent to which the House of Lords has actually used Union law to interpret the Extradition Act.

Office of the King's Prosecutor, Brussels v Armas (Appelant) and others[44]

The case concerned a request by Belgian authorities to surrender Mr Cando Armas, an Ecuadorean citizen, who was convicted in Brussels in absentia of three charges and was sentenced to five years imprisonment. The European Arrest Warrant sent by the Belgian authority specified that he was a member of an organised gang responsible for the systematic illegal immigration of Ecuadorean citizens towards Europe. The organisation was directed from London by Cando Armas, who also arranged for accommodation and fake passports for illegal immigrants when he was in Belgium.[45] The case thus concerned a European Arrest Warrant issued for the surrender of a *convicted* individual, and for a *transnational offence* which involved conduct in (at least) two jurisdictions – the United Kingdom and Belgium.

In examining the Warrant, UK authorities had to look at whether it would fall within the scope of section 65 of the Extradition Act, which concerned 'extradition offences' for persons sentenced for an offence. There has been a disagreement between the lower courts regarding the answer.[46] In the House of Lords, the appellant argued that section 65 was not applicable, as it concerned an offence included in the list of offences mentioned in the Framework Decision. Reference to this list of offences is made only in section 65(2) – however, this subsection concerns only offences where the conduct has occurred solely in the territory of the requesting Member

---

43 For an overview, see Padfield, *op. cit.*, pp. 257–60; M. Mackarel, 'The European Arrest Warrant – the Early Years: Implementign and Using the Warrant' (2007) *European Journal of Crime, Criminal Law and Criminal Justice* pp. 60–3.

44 See [2005] UKHL 67; for comments, see Padfield and Mackerel, *op. cit.*

45 For the description of the warrant, see para. 12 of the judgment.

46 With the District Judge holding that section 65 did not apply, and the Queen's Bench Divisional Court holding that it did.

State. Given that the offence in question did not occur wholly in the territory of the requesting Member State, section 65 was not applicable.[47]

The House of Lords had thus to look at the labyrinthine structure of section 65 and place it in the context of Part 1 of the Extradition Act as implementing legislation of the European Arrest Warrant Framework Decision. From the outset, Lord Bingham recognised that Part 1 of the Extradition Act 'did not effect a simple or straightforward transposition, and it did not on the whole use the language of the Framework Decision'.[48] Indeed, unlike the Framework Decision, Part 1 of the Extradition Act 'uses the language of extradition' and contains very detailed provisions which exceed the scope of the EU instrument.[49] Looking at the specific issue in question, Lord Bingham found against the applicant noting that there is nothing in section 65 to suggest that subsections 3–6 cannot apply to the framework list of offences when the relevant requirement of dual criminality is met (subsection 2 applied in cases where dual criminality does not apply. He added that:

> No reason of logic or justice was suggested to support such a rule, and it is plain from hypothetical examples suggested in argument that it would lead to results which neither the European Council nor Parliament could ever have intended.[50]

The emphasis here on the intention of the legislator is striking and demonstrates a teleological interpretation of domestic law in the light of the intention of both the domestic and the EU legislator (the Council). As Lord Bingham had already noted, the interpretation of the Extradition Act 'must be approached on the twin assumptions that Parliament did not intend the provisions of Part 1 to be inconsistent with the Framework Decision and that, while Parliament might properly provide for a greater measure of cooperation by the United Kingdom than the Decision required, it did not intend to provide for less'.[51] A similar approach was adopted by Lord Hope, who also pointed out the drafting differences between the Extradition Act and the Framework Decision,[52] and noted that 'the purpose of the statute is to facilitate extradition, not to put obstacles in the way of process which serve no useful purpose but are based on technicalities'.[53] In a similar vein, Baroness Hale noted that 'it would be most unfortunate if the judicial authorities in our European partner states, using the form of Warrant prescribed by the Framework Decision, were to find that the English judicial authorities were unable to implement it'.[54] The House of Lords seems thus to have adopted a teleological interpretation aiming to ensure the effective implementation of the European Arrest Warrant in the light of its purpose and spirit

47 See para. 15.
48 See para. 8.
49 See para. 10.
50 See para. 17.
51 See para. 8.
52 See in particular para. 24.
53 See paras. 40 and 44, where a purposive interpretation of section 65 is advocated.
54 See para. 60.

– and a willingness to remove perceived obstacles that may occur by the complexity and lack of clarity of the drafting of the implementing legislation.[55]

Dabas v High Court of Justice, Madrid[56]

The second case to have reached the House of Lords concerning the implementation of the European Arrest Warrant Framework Decision in the United Kingdom involved a Warrant sent by the Spanish authorities for the surrender of Mr Dabas in order to face trial on terrorism changes, linked with the Madrid bombings of 2004.[57] The appellant challenged the Warrant on a series of grounds concerning both substance – the absence of dual criminality, and formality – gaps in the wording of the Spanish Warrant and (an issue that is particularly linked with the UK implementation of the Framework Decision) the absence of a Certificate accompanying the Warrant.[58] It is on the question of the requirement by the Extradition Act of a Certificate that this analysis will mainly focus upon.

The issue of the relationship between the Extradition Act and the EU Framework Decision was examined in detail by Lord Hope. Quoting the judgment in *Cando Armas,* Lord Hope reiterated the fact that Part 1 of the Extradition Act does not match the requirements of the Framework Decision. However, the wording of the provisions of the Act which are under scrutiny must be construed in the context of achieving the results of the Framework Decision.[59] As regards the Certificate requirement of the Extradition Act, Lord Hope noted that the word 'certificate' was used deliberately by Parliament in section 64(2)(b) and (c) to ensure the accuracy of the statements referred to in these paragraphs (in the light of the fact that these sections contain dual criminality exceptions).[60] According to Lord Hope, the fact that the Framework Decision does not contain any reference to a separate 'certificate' is not determinative of the issue: Parliament has chosen not to follow the same wording as the EU instrument, a choice which is permissible by Article 34 of the EU Treaty which leave Member States with the choice of the method to achieve the purpose of Framework Decisions. Domestic law requirements must be approached on the assumption that, 'where there are differences from what the Framework Decision lays down, they were regarded by Parliament as a necessary protection against an unlawful infringement of the right to liberty'.[61]

However, this attempt to accommodate in principle domestic divergences from the text of the Framework Decision did not lead to a finding in favour of

55 But note that Lord Scott expressed his concern on a separate issue related to the completeness of the arrest warrant sent by the Belgian authorities and the inclusion of the term 'unlawfully at large' given that the case concerned conviction in absentia – para. 58. The scope of the term has now been clarified by the amendment of the Extradition Act by schedule 13 of the Police and Justice Act 2006.

56 See [2007] UKHL 6.

57 For details, see Lord Hope in para. 12 of the judgment.

58 See para. 13.

59 See para. 25.

60 See para. 33.

61 See para. 35.

the appellant. Lord Hope continued by stating that the argument in this case was 'more about form than it was about substance' [62] The purpose of the certificate is not to provide any further information than that which in a Part 1 Warrant is already available – its purpose, rather, is to vouch for, or affirm, its accuracy.[63] It does not follow from section 64(2)(b) that there must be a separate document.[64] The result that the Framework Decision is designed to achieve is to remove the complexity and potential for delay that was inherent in the previous extradition system.[65] There is no doubt that the imposition of additional formalities, not to be found in the Framework Decision itself, by one Member State to suit its own purposes would tend to frustrate this objective.[66] As found in *Cando Armas,* the interpretation of Part 1 of the 2003 Act must be approached on the assumption that Parliament did not intend the provisions of Part 1 to be inconsistent with the Framework Decision or to provide for a lesser degree of cooperation by the United Kingdom than the Framework Decision requires.[67] There is nothing in the wording of section 64(2), 'read as a whole and in the light of the other provisions of Part 1', to indicate that it was the intention of Parliament that a Part 1 Warrant which clearly set out all the relevant information had to be accompanied by a separate certificate.[68] A European Arrest Warrant can *itself* be a certificate referred to in section 64(2)(b) and (c).[69]

The use of such teleological interpretation of the Extradition Act leads to some striking results: effectively, the additional formality requirement of the Act for a *separate* certificate – which is not referred to in the Framework Decision – to be produced in surrender proceedings under the European Arrest Warrant in the UK is eclipsed. This is an important step as domestic law is interpreted to the extent possible in the light of third pillar, European *Union* law. Lord Hope, along with the majority of the other Law Lords,[70] now explicitly refer to and quote *Pupino*, a landmark Luxembourg case which extended the principle of indirect effect from the first to the third pillar requiring national courts to interpret domestic law to the extent possible in order to attain the objective of third pillar Framework Decisions.[71] This is even more significant in the light of the fact that UK Courts are not allowed to send questions for preliminary rulings to Luxembourg, thus having to tackle questions of interpretation of Union law without the interpretative aid of the Court of Justice. The judgment has substantial implications, as – along with the extremely creative interpretation of the certificate requirement in the Extradition Act – it could be argued that it limits the protective provisions of the implementing legislation

62 See para. 36.
63 See ibid.
64 See para. 37.
65 See para. 42.
66 See para. 43.
67 See ibid.
68 See ibid.
69 See para. 44.
70 Lord Hope, paras. 39–40; Lord Bingham para. 5; Lord Brown paras. 75–76.
71 Reference to Pupino; see Mitsilegas.

inserted to alleviate the concerns caused by the application of the principle of mutual recognition in criminal matters via the European Arrest Warrant.[72]

Conclusion

The implementation of the European Arrest Warrant in the United Kingdom has been far from a straightforward task. Both at the level of legislative drafting for implementation, and at the level of judicial interpretation, a number of sensitive issues had to be addressed. From a legislative drafting point of view, it has been pointed out repeatedly that the Extradition Act does not follow the same wording and structure of the EU Framework Decision. This choice may be explained by the effort to ensure continuity with pre-existing extradition law and practice, in particular bearing in mind that the Extradition Act extends beyond the implementation of the European Arrest Warrant to a general reform of the UK extradition system. However, this choice has led to the use of language which is not only different to the terminology of the Framework Decision (with the use of the 'language of extradition' in an era of EU surrender being a striking example), but also far from clear and precise on a number of occasions. Moreover, the emphasis of the Extradition Act has been on the process, in particular the hearing – it is in this context that a number of additional procedural safeguards have been included, which are not mirrored in the Framework Decision. Unsurprisingly, these choices have resulted in substantial litigation aiming to address both instances of lack of clarity and more generally the relationship between domestic implementing legislation and European Union (third pillar) law. In both instances, the House of Lords has proven to be quite ready to accommodate European Union law, in interpreting the Extradition Act to the extent possible in the light of the enforcement aims of the European Arrest Warrant Framework Decision. Given that the legislative drafting of the Extradition Act may have reflected substantive choices of Parliament regarding the protection of individuals in the execution of European Arrest Warrants, such judicial intervention may have substantial constitutional implications for the UK legal order in the emerging system of mutual recognition in criminal matters in the European Union.

72 On this point, see Lord Scott, who dissented in this judgment, paras. 57–71, in particular para.70. According to Lord Scott, 'it is not ... for the judiciary to remove from the Act provision that Parliament thought it right to include for the greater protection of those who are for the time being in this country and therefore entitled to the protection of our laws'.

Chapter 15

Procedures for the Approximation of Albanian Legislation with the *Acquis Communautaire*

Alfred E. Kellermann

Introduction

The approximation of Albanian legislation, according to Article 70 of the Stabilisation and Association Agreement (SAA),[1] with the *acquis communautaire* is a complicated and demanding process. It requires not only that Albania builds its regulatory framework in line with its requirements but also that the administrative structures and other conditions necessary for the implementation of the acquis be assured. According to SAA Article 70 paragraph 2, the approximation of Laws should start on the date of the signing of the SAA Agreement, this was 12 June 2006 and should be finalised by the end of the transitional period in 2016.

Experience has shown that there is not a unified practice in the Albanian Government for the evaluation and reporting on the degree of the draft legislation harmonisation with the acquis from line ministries and other central institutions. Therefore, by a Decision of the Council of Ministers,[2] the Albanian Government introduced a Statement of Compatibility and Table of Concordance, to be completed by the ministries and sent for an opinion to the Ministry of European Integration. Drafts Acts which are not accompanied by this Table of Concordance will be resent to the ministries, before they are approved by the Council of Ministers. The explanatory report of draft legislation is often limited only to a general assessment of its conformity with the acquis, not reflecting the specific provisions and obligations under the Stabilisation and Association Agreement (SAA) and missing a justification of the reasons for non-compliance with the acquis.

This chapter draws on a report prepared in the context of the EU Cards project 'Strengthening the Ministry of European Integration'[3] to raise awareness for a unified practice and to facilitate consistency. The report was drafted with guidelines

1 Council of the European Union, '*Stabilisation and Association Agreement between the European Communities and their Member States, of the one part, and the Republic of Albania, of the other part*', 8164/06, Brussels, 22 May 2006.

2 Decision No. 584 of 28 August 2003 of the Council of Ministers, amended by Decision No. 201 of 29 March 2006.

3 The project's website is (http://www.mie.gov.al/?fq=brenda&m=shfaqart&aid=210&gj=gj2).

and suggestions to support the civil servants and other officials from the Albanian Ministry of European Integration – and the 13 line Ministries in Tirana – who are involved with approximation of Albanian laws to the *acquis communautaire*. This chapter focuses on two issues, which should receive special attention:

1. Approximation with and implementation of EC laws is not a mere technical matter. It implies numerous political choices that will require the involvement of higher levels of government as well as practical and theoretical knowledge and understanding of Community law, to which reference should be made in the Table of Concordance.
2. The implementation process requires a certain capacity and ability of the government to organise and coordinate its work. In this connection we refer especially to the role of the 2006 National Plan on the implementation of the Stabilisation and Association Agreement. This Plan was adopted by the Albanian Government in the framework of the European Partnership as a comprehensive compilation of legislative and implementing measures that Albania aims to complete in order to fulfil its SAA obligations. As regards the Inter-Institutional Coordination particular mention should be made to Order No. 33 of the Prime Minister of 2 April 2007 'on the establishment of the Technical Working Committee, for the implementation of the Stabilisation and Association Agreement.' Inter-ministerial working groups, supported by the European Integration Units, created within the respective institutions, will be engaged in the revision of the Plan.

The EU Cards project is focusing on both aspects. Besides developing these guidelines and a glossary with EU terminology, the project will develop guidelines for internal coordination of decision-making procedures between the Ministry of European Integration and the 13 line ministries. In this chapter we will start by focusing on the actual Albanian procedures for approximation of laws (Part I), in Part II we will discuss the need to understand the primary and secondary EC legislation, in order to be able to draft the Albanian laws that should be approximated and implemented. This knowledge is necessary to complete the Table of Concordance especially to evaluate the degree of compatibility. In Part III we will comment on the general and specific principles of drafting the approximated laws.

Part I. The procedures in Albania for Drafting Proposals for Approximation of Laws

The Role of the Council of Ministers, Ministry of European Integration, the Line Ministries and the Assembly

The instruments for the approximation of Albanian legislation with the acquis (for example, the Table of Concordance) are not a new link in the procedure for the preparation of draft legislation but a consolidation of existing rules and procedures that are prescribed in the Rules of Procedure of the Council of Ministers Decree No. 584.[4] This Decree prescribes in paragraph 2 that:

> The Ministry of Integration evaluates the concordance of draft legislation proposed by line ministries and other central institutions with EU law, which should also reflect the degree of approximation with, and references to, the relevant legislation and jurisprudence in the explanatory reports.

The Council of Ministers Decree No. 317 charges the Ministry of European Integration to submit the proposals within six months to the Council of Ministers.[5]

The role and activity of the Assembly, as the highest legislative body in the Stabilisation and Association Process, aiming at designing a comprehensive legal system, supporting and observing the Albanian integration process towards EU, is regulated in the so-called Zela law. According to Article 3 of the Zela law the Council of Ministers sends regularly information to the Assembly on the work done at the institutions of the EU and its assessments especially regarding draft agreements and draft laws and Acts in the framework of the Albanian EU integration process. The role of the Assembly is further elaborated in the rules of procedure (Article 68) of the Assembly – where the need for formal approval by the Assembly of the explanatory report and the Table of Concordance is formulated – requiring that draft laws must be designed in the format of a formative Act and must have attached a preamble that foresees the objectives that the Act needs to realise, the arguments that the objectives cannot be realised by the actual legal instruments, compliance of draft laws with the Constitution and legislation in force and with the legislation of EU, as well as its social and economic effects.

To fulfil the responsibilities laid down in the Article 4 of the Zela law, the Council of Ministers consults the Assembly regularly. This consultation is obligatory when the powers of the Assembly are in discussion. In every case the European Integration Committee gives its opinion. The other Parliamentary Committees are consulted according to their fields of activities.

According Article 7 of the Zela law, the Assembly will establish an archive with a full and detailed documentation on the Stabilisation and Association Process. The respective documents will then be available for all deputies, especially for the Foreign Politics and International Relations Committee and European Integration Committee. This archive should include the documentation on all stages of the legislative work.

---

4 As prescribed in the Rules of Procedure of the Council of Ministers Decree No. 584 of 28 August 2003, as amended by Decision No. 201 of 29 March 2006 and the Council of Minister's Decree No. 580 of 10 September 2004 'On the Scope of the Ministry of European Integration.'

5 Council of Ministers Decree No. 317 of 13 May 2005 'on the approval of the National Plan for the Approximation of Domestic legislation with EU legislation and implementation of commitments under the SAA.'

Assessment of Compatibility

Every draft law should be accompanied by an 'explanatory memorandum' to explain its provisions in simple, non-technical language. It should also indicate the draft law's compatibility with EU law. The assessment of the compatibility of a proposed measure with the acquis is a two-step process. First, the ministry proposing the legislative measure should analyse and make its own assessment of compatibility with the acquis and indicate this in the explanatory memorandum accompanying the draft. In the second step the MoI certifies compatibility. All legislative proposals are presented to the Ministry of Justice, because it has the primary responsibility for assessing the quality of legislation, including compliance with European law.

The line ministry drafting the Template of the Report and the Table of Concordance of draft legislation should include the following information:

1. Identification of the responsible and cooperating institution(s).
2. The status of the proposed Act in the Legislative Hierarchical Order.
3. The Draft Legislation Report including the objectives of the proposal, a description of the main steps for the preparation, the aimed degree of compatibility, the concordance with the acquis, the reasons why the draft legislation complies in part or does not comply at all, next steps.
4. A description of the Implementation actions. This must include the secondary legislation to be adopted as implementation legislation and the non-legislative actions, including the strengthening of administrative capacities, the establishment of implementation structures, financial and social costs, etc.
5. Review of the quality of legislation by the Ministry of Justice.
6. Confirmation from the Ministry of European Integration.
7. Confirmation by the Prime Minister's Office.
8. Approval by the Assembly.

Part II. Understanding of Community laws is a Must for a Preparatory Analysis

The purpose of this part is to deal in a logical and consistent manner with some of the issues that are known to cause problems in the drafting of approximated texts. A number of problems are connected with the nature and concepts of EC law. Their solution requires a certain level of knowledge in the field of EC law. One problem concerns the analysis of the implementation of the so-called provisions of secondary legislation (EC Directives, regulations, etc.); whereas the second problem concerns the analysis of implementation of the obligations and application of the so-called provisions of primary legislation, such as the EC Treaty/SAA/Interim Agreement/ European Partnership.

Analysis of the Texts of EC Directives and other Categories of Secondary Law

The following text will deal especially with directives. The specific issues regarding regulations will be mentioned where appropriate.

Clarifying the objective of the directive The first step in this process is to identify the legal basis of the directive. The text of a directive can be divided into three parts and elements:

- the legal basis (in other words a reference to one or more provisions of the Treaty)
- the preamble, which states the reasoning, justification and the basic content of the directive
- the articles.

By reading the respective Treaty articles, which are used as a legal basis, a clarification of the general objectives and policy areas of the directive are given. The specific objectives and basis content of the directive are spelled out in the preamble. The preamble will also provide other information, for example, on whether the directive is linked to other directives, as is the case if the directive belongs to a framework directive. Such a structure exists, for example, in the area of foodstuffs.

Identifying the type of harmonisation The preamble will also normally indicate the type of harmonisation that the directive requires. Essentially there are three types of harmonisation:

- *Minimum harmonisation.* In this case the directive does not prevent national rules that are stricter. Directives of this type are often used in policy areas, such as consumer and environmental protection, where the objective is to ensure a certain EU-wide minimum protection.
- *Total harmonisation.* In this case the national law will follow strictly the articles of the text of the directive. This is the case when technical requirements for products are harmonised in order to avoid barriers of trade.
- *Optional harmonisation.* This is more or less a tailor made harmonisation according to, for example, the size, specific work areas and specific norms to be fulfilled by enterprises.

There are directives which lay down two or even three types of harmonisation. Therefore, the nature of a directive can only be sufficiently clarified by analysing and interpreting all the respective articles.

Identifying the operational provisions and other elements of the directive It is also very important that the notions of the directive have been well understood. Even if they look like the ones known in Albanian law, they might have a different meaning.

Clarifying whether the directive presupposes prior implementation of other directives As is often the case, directives within one policy area may presuppose prior implementation of a framework directive or the implementation of a directive from another policy area.

Determining whether the directive or a part of it has direct effect The practical consequence of this legal principle is that, once Albania is a Member State, the national courts are obliged to give priority to EC law and will apply EC law irrespective of national law. A comprehensive description of the principle which was developed through the European Court of Justice (ECJ) case law is beyond the scope of this chapter. It is enough to say that each article of the directive must be examined individually and analysed carefully. If a directive has direct effect one should not deviate from the text on substantial points.

Identifying the national legislation that needs to be reviewed in the light of the directive In many cases there will be Albanian legislation which deals with the same subject matter as the directive. In other cases complete new laws will be needed. However, in such cases, the directive could also be incorporated into existing laws dealing with identical topics.

Consequences for other Acts The implementation of a directive may also call for amendments to other normative Acts. This may require a complete review of related national legislation. Very often a directive will address policy issues which may involve several laws and several ministries. In these cases it is vital from the start to take decisions regarding competence, distribution of tasks and procedures for coordination.

Analysis of the text of provisions and general principles in the Treaties, the Stabilisation and Association Agreement, the Interim Agreement and European Partnership with Albania

For the approximation with and implementation of Community legislation we should look at the texts of secondary legislation (directives, regulations, etc.) and at important general principles which are found in the Treaties and have been refined through the 'case law' of the European Court of Justice. The Treaty itself represents a careful balance between different objectives and policies with the result that no part of the acquis can be separated in practice from the rest. The Treaty expressly underlines this interdependence, for example, in Article 152 EC which provides that a high level of human health protection requirements must be integrated into the definition and implementation of all other Community policies. Article 174, paragraph 2 'environmental damage should as a priority be rectified at source and that the polluter pays'.

The application of the general principles of EC law is more complicated than the implementation of only the text of directives: it requires a greater general and extensive knowledge of European legislation and case law. For the implementation of the SAA and the European Partnership (Council Decision 2006/54/EC on the principles, priorities and conditions) it is also necessary to have knowledge and understanding of the contents of the 1993 Copenhagen criteria for accession, criteria for democracy and the rule of law and human rights and protection of minorities. Assessment of compliance of Albanian legislation with these criteria is not always easy.

For the implementation of the SAA the following questions should also be put forward:

a) Is the interpretation of the objective of SAA provisions identical to the objective of the provision of the EC Treaty? For example, the equivalence with Article 12 (non-discrimination); does the SAA provision have priority?
b) Does the provision have direct effect?
c) Which principles of EU law might by applied in the SAA provisions? (proportionality, loyalty)

Article 12 of the EC Treaty holds that, 'Within the scope of application of this Treaty, and without prejudice to any special provisions contained therein, any *discrimination* on grounds of nationality shall be prohibited.' Article 12 can be applied only if there are no specific provisions on non-discrimination in the Treaty. The case law in the context of Article 12 has been applied to access vocational and educational training, as well as financial aid provided by EU programmes for educational training and intellectual property rights. Specific provisions of non-discrimination are stated in the following separate articles:

Article 29 – elimination of quantitative restrictions on imports;
Article 39 – freedom of movement of workers;
Article 43 – freedom of establishment;
Article 49 – freedom of services;
Article 90 – restrictions on imposing internal taxes in excess of those imposed on similar domestic products;
Article 141 – equal pay for equal work for men and women.

Priority or supremacy means that every national authority and court shall apply EC law when it is applicable. This principle implies an obligation not to apply national law and may require setting aside any provision of national law which conflicts with Community law – irrespective of whether it was passed prior or subsequent to the Community measure. This principle of Community law has not been established by the Treaty itself, but through the case law of the European Court of Justice.

The notion of *direct effect* is also not explicitly mentioned in the EC Treaty. Article 249 EC states, '... A regulation shall have general application. It shall be binding in its entirety and direct applicable in all Member States.' The idea behind this principle was most clearly defined in the case Van Gend en Loos (case 26/62):

> Independently of the legislation of Member States, Community law ... not only imposes obligations on individuals but is also intended to confer upon them rights which become part of their legal heritage. These rights arise not only when they are expressly granted by

> the Treaty but also by reason of obligations which the Treaty imposes in a clearly defined way upon individuals as well as upon the Member States and upon the institutions of the Community.

Though the requirements for finding direct effect might slightly differ depending on the type of legal Act, the following three basic requirements must be in the text:

- sufficiently clear
- unconditional
- not leave any room for exercise of discretion for implementation by Member State institutions.

Proportionality is a principle devised with a view to restraining excessively detailed regulation. It is mainly applied in the context of administrative law, requiring that the means used to achieve a given goal must be no more than that which is appropriate and necessary to achieve that goal or objective.

Loyalty, according to Article 10 of the EC Treaty:

> Member States shall take appropriate measures whether general or particular, to ensure fulfilment of the obligations arising out of this Treaty or resulting from actions taken by institutions of the Community. They shall facilitate achievement of the Community's tasks. They shall abstain from any measure which could jeopardize the attainment of the objectives of the treaty.

According to the case law of the European Court of Justice, the Member States:

- must ensure full effect of Community law in their territory
- provide that national courts are ensuring full and effective protection of rights arising under Community law
- do not impend the due functioning of the Community institutions.

The principle of *subsidiarity* is defined and established by Article 1 EU ('decisions should be taken as closely as possible to the citizen') and the second paragraph of Article 5 of the EC Treaty, where it is stated:

> In areas which do not fall within its exclusive competence, the Community shall take action, in accordance with the principle of subsidiarity, only if and in so far as the objectives of the proposed action cannot be sufficiently achieved by the Member States and can therefore, by reason of the scale or effects of the proposed action, be better achieved by the Community.

The principle essentially seeks to prevent an over-centralisation of power at the level of the Union's institutions. Article 5 EC therefore seems to respect the national identities of the Member States and will not interfere in the distribution of powers between central, regional and local powers in the Member States. The principles of subsidiarity and proportionality are used for an *ex ante* evaluation for new proposals of EC legislation and the respective protocol on the application of these principles offers a set of guidelines for applying the necessity test. Is the EU's intervention justified and does the proposal not go beyond what is necessary to achieve the objectives?

Part III. Guidelines for Drafting of Proposals and the Completion of Table of Concordance

Preparing a draft law is a long process of trial and error. The final draft is often preceded by numerous versions. These versions will themselves document how ideas were developed and what the final decisions were. It is, however, also useful to file the most important accompanying written material, such as notes and memos from experts, opinions from the work groups and other parties consulted, notes regarding the parliamentary procedures, etc. This is the so-called 'legal history' of the law. These files are vital parts of the institutional memory of the administration. This memory is particularly important when staff change frequently. This was the case especially in the Ministry of European Integration in Tirana.

During the first stage of SAA implementation, the adoption and implementation of the acquis will focus on the main internal market elements: competition; intellectual, industrial and commercial property rights; public procurement; standardisation and certification; financial services; land and sea transportation; company law; accounting; consumer protection; data protection; protection of health and safety; justice and internal affairs; agriculture and fisheries and environment.

Which guidelines should be respected for the approximation of Albanian laws? First, we must respect the fundamental and general principles of legislative drafting. One of these principles is that legislation should be consistent, coherent and clear. These requirements are best met by applying uniform drafting techniques that can provide clearly defined, consistent and predictable guidance for the structure and expression of legislation. EURALIUS (The European Assistance Mission to the Albanian Justice System) has developed general guidelines for Albanian legislation. According to the case law of the European Court of Justice,[6] community legislation must be clear and predictable for all who are subjected to it. As a consequence also the implementing texts of community legislation should follow these requirements.[7]

Second, the Table of Concordance should be completed with references to provisions of EC primary and secondary legislation, as far as applicable. Furthermore, an assessment should be made by the line Ministry and Ministry of European Integration afterwards on the compatibility of the Albanian texts with the EC legislation.

Third, the following four questions if applicable, are of interest:

6 See the Court Decision in joint case 212–217/80, Amministrazione delle Finanze dello *Stato v Salumi*.

7 This is not unusual, for example, in the Netherlands these requirements are laid down in the Prime Minister's Instructions for Secondary Legislation of 5 September 1996. Instruction 10, para. 1 holds, 'Every effort shall be made to ensure that regulations are clear, straightforward and durable.'

1. What needs to be changed in national legislation?

    a. It is necessary to determine whether the purpose of the national law corresponds to that of the directive. The purpose of a review of existing national legislation is, in the first place, to identify the provisions that are necessary for serving national objectives and to examine whether they must be amended.
    b. The main operational provisions of the directive should be compared with existing national legislation. If necessary, appropriate amendments should be drafted. This might seem to be an easy task but this is not always the case. Different legal traditions, legislative drafting techniques (more vague and general wording) and different court and administrative practices make comparative assessments very difficult.
    c. The points where the directive offers the national legislator a choice should be identified. Typical examples are the directives that lay down minimum or optional harmonisation. Moreover, in many directives there are possibilities for exemptions. Directives often allow national law to opt for less strict rules in certain situations. In some countries there are general guidelines in order to simplify the legislative process in order to reduce bureaucracy.
    d. The predominantly administrative provisions should be identified. A directive requires an administrative structure capable of taking certain decisions and performing certain control functions. These institutions must, according to the Court of Justice, be able to take speedy and correct decisions so that the *effect utile* of EC law and the rule of law is clearly applied.

2. Can the rules work on the basis of existing institutional arrangements? The institutional issue is of course particularly difficult when it comes to completely new legislation. But even where existing arrangements are concerned, it can be difficult to define new tasks and estimate future needs for additional resources. Resources in the form of training, electronic communication and modern equipment are necessary elements of institution building. In all these cases it is necessary to consider guidelines for mutual consultations and to encourage, in general, a climate of communication. In fact, the concept of a new administrative culture will be an important element in all institution building. This is where public administrative reform will play a particular role.
3. Reasons for deviating from the directive (political, practical). There may be cases where practical reasons may justify a derogation of the acquis to the letter from the start. In such cases it is necessary to identify first of all, the points where deviations would be appropriate either for practical reasons or for reasons of national interest, for example, giving industry a period to adapt to EU norms. In many of these cases it will be possible to plan a gradual approach with legislative development in stages, towards the ultimate full implementation of the acquis. Due consideration can be given to Albanian

interests. Finally, it should be kept in mind that all changes in law imply costs to the industry.
4. Identifying terminology problems. Directives may often introduce a legal/technical concepts which do not have an Albanian equivalent. This could be either because the existing Albanian legal term has a slightly different meaning or because an Albanian term does not exist.

Fourth, special attention should be devoted to the implementation and enforcement of the legislation; this should be explicitly mentioned in the Table of Concordance. According to the SAA, Albania is obliged to harmonise its domestic normative framework with the acquis and ensure its appropriate implementation. Also in The White Paper, adopted by the Essen European Council in December 1994, on the preparation of the associated countries of Central and Eastern Europe, the importance of enforcement is explicitly mentioned, 'a merely formal transposition of legislation will not be enough to achieve the desired economic impact or to ensure that the internal market functions effectively after enlargement'

A good example of the attention that should be given to the enforcement process are the instructions of the Dutch Prime Minister, which give explicit attention to enforcement in their instructions. For example, in instruction No. 11, paragraph 1 it is explicitly mentioned that 'the decision to introduce a regulation shall not be taken before establishing whether it can be adequately enforced' In assessing enforceability, the following are in any event of significance:

- a rule should leave as little scope as possible for disputes over interpretation
- exceptional provisions should be kept to a minimum
- where possible, rules must be directed at situations which are visible or which can be objectively established
- rules should be practicable in the view of both those at whom they are aimed and those who are responsible for their enforcement.

The decision to introduce a regulation should, therefore, be preceded by an investigation to determine whether it is sufficiently enforceable. In instruction No. 11, paragraph 2 it is mentioned that: '... Enforcement by means of administrative, civil or criminal law or by other means shall be looked into, and the most appropriate method selected.' In the explanation it is further clarified that the various methods of enforcement – administrative, civil or criminal law – should be compared.

Impact Assessment

According to impact assessment guidelines, every decision should be based on sound analysis fed by the best data available. This will improve the quality of policy and legislative proposals. Assessing potential impacts of policy options in a systematic manner is always desirable when preparing a proposal. During the impact assessment it is important to consult all interested parties. Collecting reliable data is crucial to ensuring the right policy choices, for example, costs and estimates.

There is a difference in impact assessment for policy proposals and legislation implementing the acquis. No rules should be drafted if there is no guarantee that they can be implemented. For acquis approximation it is, therefore, necessary that provisions are made that the relevant law can be enforced and implemented. In the Explanatory Memorandum accompanying the draft proposal the potential economic, social and environmental impacts will be considered and cost-benefit analysis will be included.

After impact assessment a report with findings should be drafted. In this report should include:

- a short summary of the work undertaken
- an answer to the question 'to regulate or not to regulate, that is the question' on the basis of a costs and benefit analysis
- identification of potential obstacles and incentives to compliance with the legislative proposals, for example – not easy to understand and high compliance costs including administrative burdens
- technical details or supporting documents, in an annex
- any assumptions or uncertainties
- simple and non-technical language should be used.

Preliminary Concluding Remarks

The instruments of legislation approximation have been adopted by all new Member States and other countries in the SAA process. The above mentioned procedures, reports, template and Table of Concordance were developed by the Albanian Ministry of European Integration with support of EU technical assistance taking into account the Slovenian, Polish, Croatian and Macedonian models. Albania has received already a lot of technical assistance in this field; however, due to the change of staff, memory has to be refreshed. In our preliminary concluding remarks we will limit ourselves only to those recommendations which can lead to an improvement and acceleration of the approximation process, without changing the capacity of the ministries. It is clear as a bell that enlargement of the capacities of the ministries by training and raising the number of employees will improve and accelerate the approximation process. Our recommendations only concern those aspects which should be added as suggestions for an improvement of the actual procedures of approximation. They have recently been supplemented with Hungarian experiences due to a study trip to Budapest on 25–27 June 2007.

1. Explicit mention of the respective provisions of the EC directive or if applicable, primary provisions of SAA should be inserted not only in the Table of Concordance but also in the preamble of the legislative proposal, as is the practice in EU Member States. This requirement is important for the legal protection of citizens, since tables of Concordance might easily disappear, whereas mentioning the EC directive in the preamble guarantees a better and more durable transparency of national law with EC law. If this practice is

followed, Table 2 of the Table of Concordance is no longer necessary and can be removed and derogated.

This recommendation is in line with the Hungarian practice in the pre-accession period which we found in Article 40(3) of the Act on Legislation which holds that if the Bill concerns topics falling under the scope of the Europe Agreement information must be given on the reasons to the extent the proposed legislation fulfils the obligation of approximation and whether it is compatible with EC law. The Bill should refer to obligatory sources, for instance, directives, but should avoid referring to non-mandatory Community norms and unclear formulations, such as 'euro-conform', that EU accession requires. In the reasons or preamble it must be set forth in detail and in merit whether the proposed legislation complies with the respective obligation of approximation. According to the Hungarian practice in the pre-accession period the primary legal obligations as well as the interpretation by the European Court of Justice of the relevant legislation must be indicated. The aim of the references to law harmonisation and Community law integrated in the final provisions, according to the Decree No. 12/1987 of the Hungarian Minister of Justice, is basically to make the activity of the approximation of laws transparent and traceable and not to make the Hungarian laws legally binding, without being integrated into Hungarian law. Moreover, it should be mentioned that from the beginning of the 1990s, the texts of the Community Directives held an obligation for the Member States that when promulgating national legislation adopted for the implementation of the directive, they should refer to the directive. In Point 95 of the Communication of the Hungarian Minister of Justice 8002/1999 (IK. 10.) IM on the management of matters relating to law harmonisation, three model texts for Hungarian laws of references to EC legislation are presented as examples.

2. The existing Glossaries of EU Terminology have to be integrated and enlarged in order to have guidelines to be used in the implementing legislation concerning the uniform reference to the Community Institutions and legal terms. They could be developed by EU sector-compliance studies. These glossaries will facilitate the legal approximation process and will contribute to the monitoring of outsourced translations.

3. It will be impossible to draft detailed uniform compatibility tests for approximation and implementation of Community law. Compatibility tests will have to be tailor-made and appropriate for implementation of every specific law. The general principles of Community law will have to be interpreted case by case.

4. The main challenge for Albania in taking over internal market legislation lies not in the approximation of its legal texts but in adapting its administrative machinery and its society to make the legislation work. This is a complex process requiring the creation or adaptation of the necessary institutions and structures, involving fundamental changes in the responsibilities of both the

national administrative and judicial systems, and the emerging private sector. The presence of the necessary enforcing authorities is crucial to provide certainty to other Member States that legislation is properly implemented. Therefore, a special section should be devoted in the Table of Concordance to this aspect of implementation in order to be able to improve the monitoring of the implementation.

5. The 2006 National Plan for the implementation of the SAA was developed as a basic instrument for the planning, prioritising and monitoring of the Albanian EU integration process. Improving the structure of the National Plan as a tool of management to monitor the implementation and approximation of the acquis is still a priority. The National plan offers an extensive documentation of all the following items.

    1. non-legislative tasks like increasing the number of staff, establishment of institutions, organisation of tenders, creation of systems of registration and surveillance, equipment IT.
    2. legislative tasks
        a. initiatives (titles of laws to be drafted)
        b. draft laws, and
        c. adopted and implemented laws.

    Consulting the National Plan and its extensive documentation needs a lot of time for those who are not involved in the drafting of it. In order to facilitate consultation and monitoring of the adopted and implemented Albanian laws related to the SAA, etc., the National Plan should include a specific chapter with adopted and implemented laws with reference to the timetable, European Partnership priorities, SAA and Interim Agreement obligations. This will facilitate the consultation also for the European Commission as only adopted and implemented legislation will count to measure progress.

6. The Hungarian experiences with law approximation in the pre-accession period should be taken into account by the Albanian administration.

    a) In the pre-accession period no impact analysis (cost and benefit analysis) of draft legislation and no cost estimates are necessary as approximation of laws is in any case obligatory, even if the costs are high and implementing laws have to be drafted anyhow! Impact analysis costs a lot of time! That time could be better used for approximation of laws!
    b) The quantity of tasks for approximation of laws justifies a thorough and careful examination and planning of the execution, according to an exact programming of law approximation in a comprehensive and uniform way, as defined by the government. It aims not only at the fulfilment of obligations deriving from the European Agreement and the alignment with the internal market

system, but is also designated to become the basic document of legal preparation – primarily in legislation – for the accession to the EU.

The law approximation programme is divided into parts according to the topics of the permanent working groups of the Inter-Ministerial Committee for European Integration (ICEI), unlike Albania where only *ad hoc* working groups are established! The screening of the acquis made the transformation of the structure of the ICEI working groups necessary, their adaptation to the chapters of the screening. The table is divided into the following parts: Community legislation (in case of cooperation in the field of justice and home affairs, the programme should also contain other sources of law adopted within the third pillar of the EU), national Hungarian legislation, responsible authority (the ministry indicated first among those responsible, is the so-called main responsible agent) and other remarks. The purpose of the programme of law harmonisation is to contribute, by pointing out the tasks of alignment with European Community law, to the formulation of governmental working and legislation plans, ensuring that the provisions of law approximation are fulfilled in full by the date of accession at the latest.

A database indicating the compatibility of Hungarian legislation with that of the Community in the form of a table is regularly updated by the Ministry of Justice. Reference is made to the title of the chapter in the official list that the Act belongs to, (must be referred to the English name of the Community Act) and then the number of that chapter and identification number in the CELEX-legal database must be indicated. The updated version of the database must be submitted to the European Commission every two months. In addition like in Albania, so-called tables of Concordance are prepared and collected by the Ministries of Foreign Affairs and Justice. For already adopted laws concordance tables are no longer necessary, due to lack of time.

7. Other suggestions for improvement of the consultation of the National Plan could be to make a clear reference and distinction between the legal bases of the Short (ST) and Medium Term (MT) priorities. A clear distinction of ST and MT priorities must be made according to the implementation period in order to facilitate the assessment of the progress of Albania. All information mentioned in the National Plan should be accompanied by EU references and references to the Short and Medium Term priorities; all information should use the same formulation, wording and time schedules as mentioned in the EU documents; all ST and MT priorities should explicitly be formulated and no details should be left out.

8. The most important and difficult exercise, however, is to organise and implement sector compliance studies of the acquis, in which for every chapter of the National Plan an evaluation of the progress can be made in the respective policy sector. For this sector – policy studies' STE experts will

assist the SMEI project team. These impact assessment studies will facilitate for MoI procedures of reviewing the National Plan as well as the assessment and screening by the European Commission and will measure where Albania stands in the area concerned. Experiences up till today have shown that we should limit these studies only to some sectors, as these studies require more STE man days, than are included in the budget of the SMEI project.

9. Finally, The Ministry of European Integration of Albania has requested the SMEI project[8] to conduct an in-depth gap analysis in the current legal framework for all sectors of the acquis.

   The aim of this gap analysis is to identify the problems and most urgent measures that are feasible for adoption by the Albanian government. In order to establish this overview we have established for every field of community policy, a table reviewing the obligations which must be fulfilled according to the respective time schedule as laid down in the provisions of the Stabilisation and Association Agreement (SAA), Interim Agreement (IA), EU Treaty and secondary EC legislation and the Short and Medium Term priorities mentioned in the European Partnership (EP) of 2005 and 2007.

We have focused on two kinds of Gap analysis. Firstly. There is the legislative gap analysis, which should give an answer to the question, which laws have to be drafted and which laws are still not yet adopted and missing? Secondly we will comment on the administrative gap analysis. Do the administrative structures and administrative capacity required for implementation, comply with the needs?

For the Administrative Gap-analysis we should also investigate if the institutional structure and administrative capacity of Albania in the respective area are complying with the EU requirements for an effective management of a national government. Albania as a potential candidate country must bring its institutions, its management capacity and administrative and judicial systems up to Union standards, with a view to implementing the acquis effectively or, as the case may be, being able to implement it effectively in good time before accession.

The systematic assessment of the candidate countries' administrative capacities and institutions takes places in the framework of the Commission's Regular Reports. Such an assessment presupposes a clear view of the main administrative structures that are required to implement the various chapters of the acquis, of the main functions that each of these structures must fulfill and of the characteristics that these structures must have to duly fulfill their functions.

The European Commission had developed, in an informal working document, for each area of the acquis prepared a list of:

- administrative structures explicitly required by the acquis
- administrative structures not explicitly required by the acquis, but necessary for an effective implementation of the acquis.

8 SMEI Cards Project "Strengthening the Ministry of European Integration".

In order to facilitate an effective Gap Analysis per sector, it is necessary to have:

1. A Table with provisions of SAA, EU, IA, European Partnership Priorities, Secondary legislation holding obligations including a specific time schedule for implementation;
2. A good understanding of Community law and its principles direct effect, loyalty, discrimination etc, which is a must to clarify the objectives of the Community provisions;
3. An overview of adopted Albanian laws with references to the respective provisions of EU, SAA/IA, EP and Directive;
4. The new Albanian laws should meet the criteria from the guidelines for approximation for example they should be clear, understandable; consistent, coherent and include EU references;
5. Permanent Inter-ministerial Working groups per sector of the acquis to manage the assessment of the Gaps analysis per sector; The existing inter ministerial coordination structures could develop, regularly or at least yearly, a governmental legislative programme, based on the respective legislative gap assessments per sector of the acquis.

Chapter 16

Compromise and Clarity in International Drafting

Eileen Denza

Introduction

In 1997, the Security Council adopted Resolution 1132 whose ultimate objective was the restoration of the constitutional order in Sierra Leone through the restoration of the democratically elected government of President Kabbah, which had been overthrown in a military coup. The Council expressed strong support for the efforts of the Economic Community of West African States (ECOWAS), which had adopted a three-pronged approach of diplomatic negotiation, economic sanctions and the use of force. In the operative part of the Resolution, the Security Council decided that all Members of the United Nations must impose an arms embargo blocking the supply of arms to 'Sierra Leone'. The British Government implemented the Security Council Resolution through Orders in Council under the United Nations Act 1946[1] which made it an offence punishable by up to seven years imprisonment to supply arms or military equipment to any person connected with Sierra Leone. Sierra Leone was defined in the Order in Council in very wide terms which included 'the Government of Sierra Leone' – a term which for the British Government denoted the lawful government of President Kabbah. This wide interpretation was consistent with the policy of the British Government to support the restoration of President Kabbah's Government only through peaceful means, and so to restrict supply to the region of any further arms.

In 1998, Sandline, a private UK company providing military training and arms, and its officers were charged by UK Customs and Excise with the export of arms to the government in exile of President Kabbah. It emerged that there had been widespread confusion even among the British Diplomatic Service as to whether the Security Council arms embargo applied to supporters of the democratically elected government or only to the usurping Junta. The United Nations Assistant Secretary General (Legal Affairs) made clear that in his view the Resolution was to be construed in the light of its ultimate objective of restoring the government in exile of President Kabbah so that it did not apply to his supporters. Sandline before going ahead with the arms supply had checked the position with the British High Commissioner to Sierra Leone, Peter Penfold, and in the light of his assurances had assumed that their conduct would be lawful. The prosecution was discontinued, with considerable

1 See S.I. 1997 Nos. 2592, 2599 and 2600.

embarrassment to the Foreign and Commonwealth Office, recrimination and public enquiry.

The Foreign Affairs Committee of the House of Commons carried out an enquiry into the Sandline affair. Noting evidence from the FCO Permanent Undersecretary that it was not unprecedented for there to be debate about the precise meaning of language in a Security Council resolution, the Committee recommended that the United Kingdom should not normally agree to any Security Council resolution which relates to an arms embargo, and which therefore needs to be translated into United Kingdom law, unless the resolution is clear and unambiguous.[2]

Drafting of International Instruments

The recommendation of the Foreign Affairs Committee – while justified in the context of the sorry saga of Sandline – is a counsel of perfection. There are a number of inevitable constraints on the international draftsman which do not apply to his counterpart in a purely national context. In particular:

1. Compromise may sometimes be even more important than clarity. If negotiation of a multilateral instrument had to await a decision by all delegations that the wording was from their own individual perspective clear and unambiguous, the number of Treaties and other legally binding international instruments adopted would be very small indeed. Even where there is uncertainty as to the underlying purpose and effect of a compromise text it may be better to settle for the best available wording. Perhaps the best known example of ambiguity knowingly accepted by opposing negotiators was Security Council Resolution 242 of 22 November 1967, in which the Council affirmed that the establishment of a just and lasting peace in the Middle East should include the establishment of both the following principles:
   (i) Withdrawal of Israel armed forces from territories occupied in the recent conflict;
   (ii) Termination of all claims or states of belligerency and respect for and acknowledgment of the sovereignty, territorial integrity and political independence of every State in the area and their right to live in peace within secure and recognised boundaries free from threats or acts of force;

   Subsequently, Egypt and Jordan maintained that this Resolution meant that withdrawal by Israel from *all* territories occupied in the 1967 war was a precondition for negotiations, while Israel argued that the question of withdrawal could only be settled through direct negotiations with the Arab States and conclusion of a treaty – which would not necessarily require withdrawal from *all* occupied territories;
2. The role and function of the draftsman is generally more restricted in international conferences and councils than his role in the preparation of

2 See Foreign Affairs Committee Second Report, 1998–99, HC 116 vol. 1, at para. 15.

national legislation. Lawyers – if present at all during high-level diplomatic negotiations – are usually treated as subordinate to ministers and diplomats and not invited or encouraged to raise 'legalistic' doubts as to the meaning or acceptability of a compromise brokered by politicians;[3]

3. A treaty or other international instrument will have to take effect in several national legal orders, so that terms which are clearly understood in only one or a few of these must so far as possible be avoided. In the diplomatic context, for example, English Courts have had great difficulty in construing 'real action' and 'disturbance of the peace of the mission' both of which have a sense in English common law quite different from the meaning intended in the context of the Vienna Convention on Diplomatic Relations.[4] When ambiguities in international instruments become a matter of public controversy, nationally qualified lawyers are tempted to join in the fray with enthusiasm – but as pointed out by Professor Philip Allott and Professor Alan Dashwood in the context of the legality of the use of force against Iraq in 2003, 'The UN Charter system for controlling the use of force by States is not a set of rules to be construed and applied like a road traffic Act';[5]
4. Most Treaties or other international legislative instruments are drawn up in several languages and may provide that all language versions are equally authoritative. While an 'authentic' text is merely a true version in the relevant language, an 'authoritative' text carries equal legal weight – even though it may have been translated, or approved by 'jurist-linguists' from the text in the language used by those who negotiated the crucial compromise;
5. For a treaty, the governing rules of interpretation will be those set out in Articles 31 to 33 of the Vienna Convention on the Law of Treaties,[6] as well as definitions in the treaty itself. These rules permit, under limited circumstances, recourse to preparatory work 'travaux préparatoires', and to subsequent statements and practice of the parties to the treaty as supplementary means of interpretation. They are likely to differ from the rules applicable in the national law of any one party, and national judges are likely to have difficulty in applying them because of their unfamiliarity.[7]

While these constraints cannot in the nature of international legislation be avoided, they do not mean that the search for clarity should be abandoned by international draftsmen, but rather that the process of preparation must be handled with as wide as

3 On the general responsibilities of UK Foreign and Commonwealth Office Legal Advisers in the drafting of Treaties, see D.H. Anderson 'The Role of the International Lawyer in the Negotiation of Treaties' in C. Wickremasinghe (ed.) *The International Lawyer as Practitioner* (London: BIICL, 2000) pp. 26–7.

4 UK Treaty Series 1965 No. 19. See, for example, the cases of Intpro *v* Sauvel [1983] 1 QB 1019 on 'real action' and R *v* Roques, Judgment of 1 August 1984, unreported.

5 Joint letter to *The Times*, 18 March 2003.

6 See UK Treaty Series 1980 No. 58. On the principles of interpretation, see R. Gardiner *International Law* (Longman Law, 2003) pp. 47–51 and 78–92.

7 On the interpretation of Treaties in UK and other national courts, see Gardiner: at 144–162.

possible an awareness of the challenges they pose. There are also a number of ways in which the risk of divergent or damaging interpretations of international instruments may be minimised during their negotiation or reduced after their adoption and application. Since an ever increasing proportion of national legislation is drawn up in order to apply or to implement international Treaties, European Union instruments or resolutions or standards adopted by other international organisations, there are powerful reasons for governments and others to try to ensure both the clarity of international legislation and uniformity in its application.

Methods of Ensuring Clear Drafting of International Instruments

There are a number of ways in which the quality of drafting of a treaty or other international instrument may be improved, even if in the last resort the need for compromise prevails on some crucial points. Some of these are more readily available to States with extensive legal and diplomatic resources.

1. Advance preparation by legal and technical experts is the most reliable guarantee of a clear and acceptable final result. The preparation of a proposal or draft convention may be entrusted to an independent body such as the International Law Commission for United Nations conventions[8] or the Commission of the European Union for a very high proportion of European Community legislation. While such bodies ensure both an objective approach and a high standard of expertise, governments must also play an active role throughout the process of preparation which may take many years. The 2004 United Nations Convention on Jurisdictional Immunities of States and Their Property, for example, represented the outcome of 22 years of work – 12 years of deliberations in the International Law Commission (assisted by many opportunities for comment from the governments of Members of the United Nations) and a further 10 years of deliberations in the Sixth (Legal) Committee of the General Assembly and its working parties.[9] In the case of European Community regulations and directives, where the Commission of the European Union almost always has a monopoly right to make a proposal, there will often be a long period of gestation during which expert bodies and the governments of Member States may make informal representations or take part in formal working groups with Commission staff and legal advisers.[10]

2. Where there is no independent body formally entrusted with the preparation of international legislation, governments who are aware of and sympathetic

8 See I. Sinclair: *The International Law Commission* (Cambridge: Grotius, 1987); ch. 3 'The International Lawyer and the Codification of International Law' in Wickremasinghe (2000).

9 See Fox, 'In Defence of State Immunity: Why the UN Convention on State Immunity is Important' 55 (2006) *ICLQ* at 399.

10 For an account of the contrasting law-making procedures under International and European Community law, see E. Denza *The Intergovernmental Pillars of the European*

to arguments for a treaty or other instrument should bear in mind the tactical advantage of preparing a negotiating draft themselves. For the draftsman of a treaty or non-binding memorandum of understanding there is excellent practical guidance along with precedents and entertaining examples of bad drafting offered by A. Aust.[11] In the European Union context, the advantage enjoyed by the European Commission in consequence of its near monopoly right of proposal is well known, and is particularly strong because of the rule in the Community Treaties that the Council of Ministers may amend a Commission proposal only by a unanimous vote. But even outside this formal framework the State which has devoted the energy and effort to preparing and circulating a draft enjoys a substantial advantage over another State which merely offers criticism. The burden falls on the State seeking to change the draft, and many points (which may be assumed to be clear and satisfactory to the drafting State at least) will by default remain unchallenged. By the same token, where a State regards a provision in a draft as unclear or unsatisfactory it should itself draft an amendment (allowing time for it to be translated where relevant). Other States are much more likely to endorse its criticism where it is supported by a clearly drafted amendment which can be carefully considered as an alternative to the original draft provision. It will also be useful to show any draft instrument or amendment to likely allies in the negotiation before it is formally tabled or circulated. This will ensure that initial criticism of the drafting is sympathetic and constructive rather than hostile and destructive. It may also pave the way to those allies cooperating in the presentation of a joint amendment, or at the least expressing public support and voting for it in the formal conference or council proceedings. The Council Secretariat (in the case of the European Union) or other secretariat of a conference or international organisation will also be able to provide helpful advice on the drafting of a proposal or amendment as well as on negotiating tactics in the light of their wide experience of the particular legal and political background.

3. Governments should ensure that draft Treaties or other proposals for international law-making instruments are considered in advance by national experts in the relevant area (whether within or outside the government), by lawyers competent to assess compatibility of the proposals with existing national laws and prior international commitments and, in the case of Federal States or States with devolved powers, by the authorities of the individual regions, provinces or States. Full consideration of draft Treaties by all those who would be affected by its adoption and implementation by the government can often open the way to minor drafting amendments during negotiation and

---

Union (Oxford, Oxford University Press, 2002) pp. 9–11.

11 See A. Aust, *Modern Treaty Law and Practice*, 2nd edn. (Cambridge: Cambridge University Press, 2007) ch. 23 Drafting and final clauses; see Lord Gore-Booth and D. Pakenham (eds) *Satow's Guide to Diplomatic Practice* (London: Longman, 1979) in ch. 29–33 also provides extensive guidance on the drafting of treaties – soon to be updated in a 6th edn.

thus to easier implementation. The United Kingdom experienced particular difficulties with the application to its dependent territories of Treaties requiring specific changes to domestic laws and during the 60s and 70s sought to negotiate 'territorial application' clauses under which it could initially confine acceptance of a treaty to the metropolitan territory of the United Kingdom and extend to colonies and protectorates only after review by each territory had made appropriate changes to domestic legislation or determined that they were not required. Such clauses however became for political reasons unnegotiable, so that, for example, the UK had to accompany its ratification of the United Nations Covenants on Human Rights with a lengthy list of reservations needed to preserve the laws and customs of individual dependencies. (The rule that marriage should be entered into only with the 'free and full consent of the intending spouses' was not, for example, to be applied 'in regard to a small number of customary marriages in the Solomon Islands'.) Wider consultations at an earlier stage with dependent territories might well have led to adoption of provisions which took more account of the conditions in very small or remote islands and could have made some of these reservations unnecessary.

4. Where resources permit, delegations to conferences or Council Working Parties in the case of Council legislation should contain lawyers and expert representatives of regions, bodies or areas directly affected. This may raise problems of accreditation of individuals from outside the central government, but these can often be overcome. Even where Heads of State or government are in conclave alone or accompanied only by their Foreign Minister in the interests of more easily securing compromise agreement, a lawyer or expert in an anteroom may avert an unhappy or unclear outcome more easily than one in a home capital. In 1980, for example, the then UK Secretary of State for Foreign and Commonwealth Affairs, Lord Carrington, attended a meeting of European Community Foreign Ministers convened to agree on sanctions against Iran without any lawyer or government official having direct knowledge of the previous week's debates in the House of Commons on the enabling legislation. He agreed in Naples that collective sanctions should be imposed retroactively from the date of Iranian seizure of the US Embassy and hostages – an outcome which those who had been directly involved knew would not be acceptable to the House of Commons and which in the event he was unable to deliver.[12] Lawyers may also act as heads of delegation where thetreaty or other instrument under negotiation has a high legal content – for example, Foreign and Commonwealth Office Legal Advisers were heads of UK delegations to the 1969 Vienna Conference on Diplomatic Relations, the 1963 Vienna Conference on Consular Relations, the 1979 Vienna Conference on Succession of States in respect of Treaties, the 1998 Rome Conference which drew up the Statute of the International Criminal Court and the bilateral negotiations with the Soviet Union on the Settlement of Financial and Property

12 On lawyers as negotiators, see Anderson, ch. 2 in Wickremasinghe (2000) at 36–8; A. Aust *Modern Treaty Law and Practice* (2nd edn, 2007) ch. 23 'Drafting and final clauses'.

Claims arising before 1939. Lawyers are heavily involved in the drafting of Security Council resolutions, particularly in the case of France, the United Kingdom and the United States among the permanent Members.[13]

Mitigating the Damage: Devices to Clarify an Ambiguous Provision

There are numerous possibilities whereby a State may seek to secure acceptance of its own preferred interpretation of an ambiguous or imperfect provision which its minister or Head of Delegation has accepted in the interests of achieving compromise or overall agreement, or on which he has been outvoted. These include, in the chronological order in which they are available:

1. Statements in the Conference Records or the Minutes of the Council or other negotiating body are used to record the understanding of a government as to the true meaning of an ambiguous expression. Practice differs between international bodies as to the interpretative weight given to such statements, but as a general rule they carry more weight if they are made on a collective basis or are widely endorsed by other delegations and if there is an official record of the proceedings of the conference or Council. Many international organisations circulate conference records or minutes in draft to all participating delegations, and it is important to check that such statements have been accurately recorded as a precaution in case of subsequent dispute.

2. Statements to the press or to national parliaments. It is increasingly common after agreement is reached at political level for the different ministers emerging from the conclave each to put his own gloss on a compromise formula. To take perhaps the most notorious ambiguity in a recent international instrument, following the adoption by the Security Council on 8 November 2002 of Resolution 1441 on Iraq, there emerged a spectrum of public statements from the participating governments. As the UK Attorney General stated in paragraph 25 of his opinion of 7 March 2003 to the Prime Minister on the legality of military action against Iraq without a further resolution.

   Where the meaning of a resolution is unclear from the text, the statements made by Members of the Council at the time of its adoption may be taken into account in order to ascertain the Council's intention. The statements made during the debate on 8 November 2002 are not, however, conclusive.

   The same was true of the public statements made at the time by the United States, the United Kingdom, by Syria, and the Joint Statement issued by China, France and Russia – all of which made it clear that a further meeting of the Security Council would take place in the event of further material breach by Iraq, but each of which suggested a different version of what should happen if

---

13 See Wood, 'The Role of Legal Advisers at Permanent Missions to the United Nations' in Wickremasinghe (2000) 81–4.

the Council then failed to agree.[14]

3. Interpretative declarations on signature or ratification of a treaty are very widely used by States. They may, but need not, follow the terms used in the statements in the negotiating record or for the press (described above). Interpretative declarations have certain advantages over reservations, in which Parties to a Treaty indicate that they do not intend to be bound by one or several of its provisions. Reservations are often excluded in modern Treaties – particularly where the object of the treaty is to establish a uniform regime and where a balance of advantage and disadvantage has been carefully negotiated – and even where they are not expressly excluded they may be challenged as being incompatible with the object and purpose of the treaty.[15] Interpretative declarations have become more and more extensive with successive revisions of the European Community Treaties, as the growth in the number of Member States has made it increasingly difficult to negotiate a text which all Members regard as being on its own clear and satisfactory. On 21 April 1970, when there were only the six original Member States of the European Communities, the Council adopted a Decision on the Replacement of Financial Contributions from Member States by the Communities' Own Resources (which formed the foundation of the system whereby the Communities and later the European Union derive their revenue). This Decision was accompanied by four Declarations of which three were interpretative in character. By 1986, when the Single European Act was adopted by twelve Member States, there were twenty Declarations attached. The general declarations adopted mostly by 'the Conference' were in the main political, although an important General Declaration directed at the internal market, defined as 'an area without internal frontiers in which the free movement of goods, persons, services and capital is ensured …', protected the right of Member States 'to take such measures as they consider necessary for the purpose of controlling immigration from third countries, and to combat terrorism, crime, the traffic in drugs and illicit trading in works of art and antiques'. Unilateral Declarations by single Member States, Greece, Portugal, Ireland and Denmark to the Single European Act, were all interpretative and intended to protect individual national interests from encroachment by possible wide construction of the new treaty powers. The United Kingdom on its accession to the European Communities in 1972 made a unilateral Declaration to the Communities in which it defined the categories of its own citizens that it wished to be regarded as its 'nationals' for the purposes of Community law and in particular free movement. This Declaration was replaced in 1982 following the changes made in the British

---

14 See D. McGoldrick, *From '9/11' to the Iraq War 2003* (Oxford and Portland, OR: Hart, 2004) pp.58–67.

15 See Vienna Convention on the Law of Treaties, UK Treaty Series No. 58 (1980), Articles 19–23; A. Aust: *Modern Treaty Law and Practice* (2nd edn, 2007), ch. 8, especially pp. 126–8 on interpretative declarations; Anderson in Wickremasinghe (2000) ch. 2, p. 23 and 24.

Nationality Act 1981. Both Declarations were shown to other Member States in advance of their being formally lodged. The European Court of Justice in the case of *R. v. Secretary of State for the Home Department, ex parte Kaur*[16] held that 'the 1972 Declaration must be taken into account as an instrument relating to the Treaty for the purposes of its interpretation and, more particularly, for determining the scope of the Treaty *ratione personae*. The Reform Treaty – expected to be signed in Lisbon in December 2007 – is (in November) already accompanied by 53 flanking Declarations, and this is unlikely to be the final score.

4. A State which expressly incorporates or transforms an international obligation into its own national law may clarify ambiguities in the international instrument or reflect them in terms which are more precise or which are more readily understood within its national legal system.[17] Thus, for example, section 134 of the Criminal Justice Act 1988[18] gives effect in the United Kingdom to Article 1 of the UN Convention against Torture and Other Cruel, Inhuman or Degrading Treatment or Punishment. A careful comparison of the two shows that the UK Statute is in several ways drafted with greater precision. It is made clear that a 'public official' or other person acting in an official capacity may be of any nationality and that the act of intentionally inflicting severe pain or suffering may be carried out 'in the United Kingdom or elsewhere' It is spelt out that the pain or suffering may be physical or mental and may be caused by an act or omission. Another example is shown in section 2 of the Consular Relations Act 1968[19] which gives the force of law in the United Kingdom to scheduled provisions of the Vienna Convention on Consular Relations of 1963[20] and requires their construction for that purpose in accordance with a number of interpretative subsections. Some of these give precision for UK Courts to terms such as 'authorities of the receiving State' and 'national of the receiving State' which were by necessity generally formulated in the Vienna Convention so as to be capable of application in over one hundred separate sovereign States. Others give precision to compromise formulae in the Convention such as 'grave crime' (for which consular officers may exceptionally be arrested or detained) – which is defined in the Act with greater clarity as meaning 'any offence punishable (on a first conviction) with imprisonment for a term that may extend to five years or with a more severe sentence'.[21] There are however

16 See Case C–192/99, 2001 ECR I–1237, at para. 24.

17 On techniques of legislative implementation of Treaties, see F. Vallat, *International Law and the Practitioner* (Manchester: Manchester University Press, 1996) pp. 10–17.

18 See ch. 33.

19 See ch. 18.

20 See 596 UN Treaty Series 261.

21 For a detailed account of the efforts made at the Vienna Conference in 1963 to negotiate a more precise formula in regard to the exception to the personal inviolability of consular officers set out in Article 41, see L.T. Lee, *Consular Law and Practice* 2nd edn (Oxford: Oxford University Press, 1991) pp. 477–81. All the amendments proposed to the text prepared by the International Law Commission were defeated, leaving the compromise

constraints on the extent to which this may be done – in the United Kingdom enabling statutes, such as the International Organisations Act 1968 and the United Nations Act 1946, permit national implementation only so far as is necessary or expedient for the effective implementation of the international obligation.[22] So the possibility must not be relied on as a reason for failing to seek maximum precision in an international instrument.

5. A State may give publicity in other ways to its preferred interpretation of an ambiguous or compromise formula in an international instrument. The rules of interpretation of Treaties in Article 31.3 of the Vienna Convention on the Law of Treaties require the taking into account together with the context of:

> '(b) any subsequent practice in the application of the treaty which establishes the agreement of the parties regarding its interpretation';

A State may set out its view of the interpretation of a provision in ministerial speeches or statements to its national Parliament or in a digest of practice in international law such as now appears in law journals, such as the Revue Générale de Droit International Public, the American Journal of International Law and the British Yearbook of International Law. On matters of diplomatic or consular law it may send a circular to heads of mission in its capital.[23] It should make its position plain to writers on international law drafting commentaries on the relevant treaty or general area of international or European law. The statements of practice may be followed by other Parties interpreting the same ambiguous provision and over time a consistent practice will crystallise into international custom. The teachings of 'the most highly qualified publicists of the various nations' are included in Article 38 of the Statute of the International Court of Justice as 'subsidiary means for the determination of rules of law'. In the case of *Trendtex Trading Corporation v. Central Bank of Nigeria*[24] in the English Court of Appeal, both Lord Denning and L.J. Stephenson used the writings of the authorities Professor Sir Hersch Lauterpacht and Dr Francis Mann as evidence of a change in customary international law. A body with special

---

formula to be interpreted by each Party in the context of its National Criminal law. The 'more severe sentence' in the UK referred to the death penalty which had not been completely abolished in 1968. See S. Fatima, *Using International Law in Domestic Courts* (Oxford and Portland, Oregon: Hart, 2005) ch. 3 on Incorporating Statutes which sets out the various ways in which domestic legislation makes Treaties part of UK law.

22 This point was taken by the UK House of Commons Foreign Affairs Committee Report into the Sandline affair (see note 2 above) at para. 22.

23 The construction of the term 'permanent resident of the receiving State' in the 1961 Vienna Convention on Diplomatic Relations, for example, was clarified by the UK in a circular Note sent to all diplomatic missions in London in 1969, and this guidance has not only been accepted and applied in numerous legal contexts in London but has also been broadly followed by guidance given to diplomatic missions in other States, in particular Canada, Australia, and since 1991 the United States. See E. Denza, *Diplomatic Law*, 2nd edn (Oxford: Oxford University Press, 1998) pp. 343–9.

24 See [1977] QB 529 at 555 and 563.

responsibility for the application of a particular treaty may also issue a subsequent commentary or guidance, such as for the 1951 Geneva Convention relating to the Status of Refugees,[25] the *Handbook for Procedures and Criteria for Determining Refugee Status* issued originally in 1979 by the High Commissioner for Refugees. The Handbook has been extensively relied on for the purpose of giving precision to the terms of the Convention by the governments of States Parties and by their national courts.

European Initiatives to Improve Legislative Drafting

The Treaty on European Union as originally drawn up at Maastricht was rejected by the Danish people in a referendum late in 1992. The European Council convened by the United Kingdom Presidency in Edinburgh in December 1992 was therefore greatly concerned to devise measures which might pave the way to a favourable view of the Treaty by Denmark but without amending the actual text so as to require reopening the ratification process which had already been completed in many of the other Member States.[26] One initiative launched against this background had the objective of improving the quality of drafting of European Community legislation. This initiative was followed up by Declaration 39 adopted by the Conference at Amsterdam in 1997 which amended the Treaty on European Union and the Treaties Establishing the European Communities. In this Declaration:

> The Conference notes that the quality of the drafting of Community legislation is crucial if it is to be properly implemented by the competent national authorities and better understood by the public and in business circles.

The Conference called on the three institutions involved in the procedure for adopting Community legislation, the European Parliament, the Council and the Commission to lay down guidelines on improving the quality of the drafting of this legislation, to follow these guidelines and ensure that they are properly applied. On 22 December 1998, the three institutions adopted an Interinstitutional Agreement on Common Guidelines for the Quality of Drafting of Community Legislation.[27] The recitals to this Agreement recall the need for 'Clear, simple and precise drafting of Community legislation' for the reasons identified in the 1997 Declaration quoted above, and recall that

According to the case law of the Court of Justice, the principle of legal certainty, which is part of the Community legal order, requires that Community legislation must be clear and precise and its application foreseeable by individuals.

The general principles adopted are for the most part of universal applicability to the drafting of any instrument, but they also take account of features special to

---

25 See UK Treaty Series 1954 No. 39.

26 On the role of lawyers in this subtle exercise, see Anderson in Wickremasinghe (2000) at 27.

27 See Council Doc. 13284/1/98 JUR, later published in OJ C 73/11 at 17 March 1999.

international drafting, such as the need for drafts to be framed in terms and structures, which respect the multilingual nature of Community legislation and for concepts or terminology specific to any one national legal system to be used with care.[28] They specify that the purpose of the initial recitals to Community Acts is to set out the legal basis of the Act and the main steps in the procedure leading to its adoption.[29] They recommend that where terms to be used are ambiguous they should be defined together in a single article at the beginning of the act, and that this definitions article should not contain normative provisions. The enacting terms should have a standard structure: subject matter and scope, rights and obligations, implementing powers, procedural provisions, implementing measures, transitional and final provisions.

Under the Interinstitutional Agreement the Legal Services to the three institutions were instructed to draw up within one year a joint practical guide for persons involved in the drafting of legislation within the institutions. The Joint Practical Guide is available on the europa website[30] and is constantly updated in the light of comments from all those involved in the drafting of Community acts. It follows the broad structure of the guidelines in the Agreement and develops them with detailed comments and with individual examples, including examples of bad drafting and suggestions as to how it could have been improved. It is to be used in conjunction with more specific instruments, such as the Council's Manual of Precedents and the Commission's Manual of Legislative Drafting.

The comments on the principle requiring respect for the multilingual nature of Community legislation are of particular general interest in the context of this chapter. The draftsman is reminded that the original must be particularly simple, clear and direct, since over complexity or ambiguity however slight could result in inaccuracies, approximation or mistranslations in one or more of the other Community languages. Jargon, 'vogue words' and Latin expressions used in a sense other than their generally accepted legal meaning are to be avoided. Examples in English given include 'proactive', 'integrated resource management system' and 'quasi-abolition of central *ex-ante* visa controls' Words with no exact equivalent in other languages and terms too closely linked to one national legal system should also be avoided – and the example given is the French term '*faute*' which has no direct equivalent in German or English law. Links to a particular text used as a precedent must be made clear to the translators so that the language from the precedent in the language of translation is followed precisely.[31]

A more specific guide to legislative drafting in the field of contract law is now under preparation. This initiative, known as the Common Frame of Reference (CFR), originated in the European Commission's 2001 Communication on European Contract Law and was formally proposed in the Commission's Action Plan on Contract Law. The objective was to draw up principles, definitions of legal terms (such as 'damage') and model rules to assist in improving the *acquis communautaire* in this field and the CFR might be accepted as the basis for an optional instrument. It would go beyond

28 See General Principle (5).

29 See General Principle (9).

30 See online at (www.eur-lex.europa.eu/en/techleg/index.htm).

31 See Practical Guide: comments on Principle 5.

drafting into substance, but is not intended to form a single European law to replace national laws. Some aspects, in particular common definitions of legal concepts, would if accepted assist in the clear and uniform drafting of Community instruments in the field of contract law.[32]

Initiatives of this kind can be developed only within the context of a body which already has a long tradition of legislation and of approximation of laws. It is a feature of European Community law which contrasts with public international law that in many areas it intrudes more deeply into national legal orders.[33] There is also within the European Union a lengthening tradition of cross-fertilisation of national legal systems which have had the effect of greater understanding of legal differences as well as of common features and principles. It would not, therefore, be practicable to envisage the formulation of guidelines for the drafting of international agreements and other instruments creating legal obligations under international law which were as detailed and general in their cover as the forms of guidance, described above. Many of the principles and detailed rules which have been agreed and are followed to a large extent within the European Union are however of general application and could with advantage be studied and applied by European Union draftsmen and by negotiators in the international context.

32 See Beale, 'A legislator's guide', *European Advocate*, Autumn 2007 at 4. For detailed analysis and criticism of the CFR, see House of Lords Select Committee on the European Union 12th Report, 2004–05, HL 95, *European Contract Law – the way forward?* ch. 3, The Common Frame of Reference.

33 On this contrast in approaches, see E. Denza, 'The Relationship between International and National Law' in M.D. Evans (ed.) *International Law*, 2nd edn (Oxford: Oxford University Press, 2006) pp. 427–8.

Chapter 17

Can Legislation Rank as Literature?

Helen Caldwell

Shelley once said that poets were 'unacknowledged legislators of the world'.[1] Does the reverse apply? Can drafters be, if not poets, at least writers of great prose?

Most of us are aware of this passage from the American Declaration of Independence:

> We hold these truths to be self-evident, that all men are created equal, that they are endowed by their Creator with certain unalienable Rights, that among these are Life, Liberty, and the pursuit of Happiness ...

G.K. Chesterton alluded to the Declaration of Independence as being 'great literature'.[2] A website I found called 'Great Literature Online'[3] includes not only the Declaration of Independence but also the US Constitution among its 'Great Literature Classics'.

If the Declaration of Independence, and the US Constitution, are 'great literature', won't it also be true that some UK legislation can rank as literature? In a parliamentary debate on a recent bill, it was said:

> Clause 1 contains a statement about a vision of humanity and how humanity is to be regarded. I hope children in generations to come will study that as one of the clearest and most eloquent expressions of what we think a human being is and how a human being is to be treated.[4]

This is strong stuff. Does it imply that UK legislation is capable of being 'literature'? I could tell you what I think the answer to this is straightaway, and then say what I can in support of it. But I think that would be rather dull. I would rather give you some facts and leave you to consider, as I lay them before you, what conclusions you think emerge from them. So I would like to start by taking a look at vocabulary, and, in particular, at vocabulary size.

The paradigmatic example of 'great literature' is the works of Shakespeare. In a BBC news online poll to mark the millennium, Shakespeare was overwhelmingly

---

1 *A Defence of Poetry* (1819) in H.F.B. Brett-Smith *The Four Ages of Poetry; A Defence of Poetry; Browning's Essay on Shelley* (Oxford: Blackwell, 1921) at 59.

2 *What I Saw in America* (New York: Dodd, Mead and Company, 1922) at 7 ('perhaps the only piece of practical politics that is also theoretical politics and also great literature').

3 Accessed at (www.greatliterature.org).

4 See HL deb., 10 January 2005 col. 54 (the Lord Bishop of Worcester, regarding the Mental Capacity Bill).

voted the greatest writer in the last 1,000 years, gaining six times as many votes as the runner-up (Jane Austen).[5]

One of the facts that 'everyone knows' about Shakespeare is that he had a very large vocabulary. David Crystal has estimated that, in his *Complete Works*, Shakespeare used something like 20,000 different words.[6]

At this point one has to acknowledge that the process of counting Shakespeare's words, or anyone else's, is problematic. If one counts how many different words there are using a simple automated method, 'goes', 'going' and 'gone' will be treated as three separate words. Using this method, Shakespeare could be treated as having a vocabulary of about 30,000 words.[7] But most ordinary people would treat 'goes, 'going' and 'gone' as being merely variants, or forms, of the same basic word 'go' I think linguists would call the essential unit to which these three words belong a 'lemma' When estimating that Shakespeare had a vocabulary of about 20,000 words, the second counting method is the one that is being used – it is based on counting 'lemmas' rather than word forms. Even this estimate of 20,000 is not wholly unproblematic.[8] Nonetheless, let us assume that for present purposes it gives us a rough indication of the size of Shakespeare's vocabulary.

A related piece of information that I would like to throw in here is that David Crystal seems to be regarded as having deflated the myth that Shakespeare's vocabulary was unparalleled in size. He has suggested that nowadays a typical educated person has a vocabulary much larger than Shakespeare's. He gives an example of a secretary in her mid-fifties who had a 'passive' vocabulary of getting on for 40,000 words and an 'active' vocabulary of about 30,000 words.[9] (The 'passive' vocabulary consists of words that the person knows, and the 'active' vocabulary of words that the person uses.) In this test, the counting method was based on the person's responses to entries

---

5 Accessed at (www.news.bbc.co.uk/1/hi/world/286082.htm).

6 See David Crystal, *The Cambridge Encyclopaedia of the English Language*, 2nd edn (Cambridge: Cambridge University Press, 2003) at 123. H. Joachim Neuhaus at the Shakespeare Database project, Westfälische Wilhelms-Universität, Münster, Germany, has given a similar estimate, accessed at (www.shkspr.uni-muenster.de/start.php).

7 See M. Spevack, *Complete and Systematic Concordance to the Works of Shakespeare* (Hildesheim: Georg Olms, 1968–80), in 9 vols., listed 29,066 words in the complete works in the Riverside Shakespeare (ed. Gwynne Blakemore Evans).

8 There is unlikely to be a consensus when counting 'lemmas' because questions will arise over whether a word which is (or ought to be) hyphenated is one word or two; how one counts idiomatic uses of ordinary words (e.g., 'get at' and 'get it'); whether a word which has two meanings for a single form is two words or one, etc. Crystal in 'The Language of Shakespeare' in Stanley Wells and Gary Taylor (eds), *The Complete Works* (Oxford: Oxford University Press, 2005), at lxi estimates the size of Shakespeare's vocabulary as being between 17,000 and 20,000 words. The lower figure excludes proper names, foreign words and malapropisms. See (www.crystalreference.com+articles.htm).

9 *The English Language* (2nd edn, 2002) at 49. The exact figures he gives are 38,300 words for the passive vocabulary (consisting of 30,050 words known 'well' and 8,250 known 'vaguely') and 31,500 for the active vocabulary (consisting of 16,300 words used 'often' and 15,200 used 'occasionally').

in a dictionary – the count was based on 'dictionary headwords' The notion of a 'dictionary headword' is much the same as that of a 'lemma'.

As in the case of counting up Shakespeare's vocabulary, it is fairly obvious that the whole exercise of estimating the vocabulary size of a 'typical educated person' is fraught with difficulty.[10] Others have offered a more conservative estimate, suggesting that educated, native speakers of English probably know around 20,000 'word families' [11] The concept of a word family is similar to, but slightly wider than, that of a lemma: whereas a lemma consists of permutations within the same part of speech, such as a verb ('goes', 'going' and 'gone'), a word family can include permutations within different parts of speech (for example, 'stimulate': verb, and 'stimulation': noun). This estimate of 20,000 is based on excluding proper names, compound words, abbreviations and foreign words.

So let's hold on to these ideas, that Shakespeare had a vocabulary of something like 20,000 words (in the sense of lemmas) and that the vocabulary of a supposedly typical educated person today is probably no smaller than that; and now let us turn to look at the size of the legislative vocabulary.

I am not aware of anyone having obtained any hard facts about this. Indeed, it was not obvious to me at first how I could arrive at any estimate. The commercial databases to which I have access do not, I think, provide the ordinary user with a way of discovering the number of words used in Acts passed during any particular period. But then it struck me that I might be able to get a very rough estimate of the number of words used in recent Acts of Parliament based on the database we have at the Parliamentary Counsel Office (PCO).

Before I go on, perhaps I should tell you a bit about the quality of the data in this database. We created it at a time when we did not have desktop access to any other databases of legislation. The PCO database contains the text of most[12] Acts passed since 1980. They are stored in 'pdf' format – so the pages look like the printed pages of Acts, including running headers. The texts are of the Acts as enacted. Some of the texts are based on text used when we were helping the Lords Public Bill Office to prepare the Royal Assent proofs. Others – those for the early 1980s – were keyed in by secretaries at PCO. I mention this because our versions of the texts of Acts cannot be treated as infallible; but they are not bad and probably good enough to give us a reasonable idea of the size of vocabulary used in Acts since 1980.

Our database system indexes words in these Acts so that we can do word searches. What I am about to tell you is based on information extracted from the index.

Again, before I go on, I think I should tell you a couple of basic things about how this index works. First, it does not count occurrences of 'stop' words. 'Stop' words are those in most frequent use, such as 'as', 'at' and 'because' – there were 120 of these. Secondly, it treats words with different endings as being different words – it treats 'goes', 'going', and 'gone' as three different words rather than as variants of a single word.

---

10 For a start, who is a 'typical educated person'?

11 This is based on I.S.P. Nation *Learning Vocabulary in another Language* (Cambridge: Cambridge University Press, 2001) at 9.

12 There are some omissions, e.g., Appropriation and Consolidated Fund Acts.

So, getting back to the main point, it was possible to obtain from the PCO database a list of different word forms used in our electronic versions of Acts passed between 1980 and 2005. How many words do you expect there to be in this list? Bear in mind that we are looking at a collection of texts that represent the output of various different Parliaments, and governments, over quite a long period.

The answer is that there were about sixteen and a half thousand words on the list.

The actual number of words on the list was 16,483, including 120 stop words. The list included abbreviations, proper names and acronyms. Hyphenated words were recorded as separate words. The words listed covered a wide range of subjects, reflecting the many varied elements of modern life. Thus they included, to take a random selection: amortisation, buy-back, reinsurance and VAT; isotope and radioactivity and a whole variety of named chemicals and gases such as fluoride, ethane or arsine; biomass; gamete and zygote; immunodeficiency, pathogens and neoplasm; aerospace; therms; video and holograph; kilovolts; dioptres; sewage and sewerage; freight and haulier; parrot, mandrill and nepenthes.

You may remember that I asked you to hold on to the idea that Shakespeare is supposed to have had a vocabulary of about 20,000 words, and that a supposedly typical educated person has a vocabulary that is no smaller and if anything is rather larger. And I have just told you that the number of words used in Acts from 1980 to 2005 was probably about sixteen and a half thousand. There is an obvious discrepancy. The UK legislative vocabulary is smaller. Perhaps the discrepancy does not seem very significant? WhaT'Ss three or four thousand words between friends? I would make two points.

The first is that the list includes quite a lot of 'specialist' words of the kind I mentioned a moment ago, for example, kilovolts, and so on. (More than I expected.) The existence of specialist vocabularies in modern times is a factor which I believe is thought to increase the size of the average vocabulary nowadays compared with Shakespeare's.

The second point is more important. You may remember that I said that when people were counting how many words Shakespeare, or the typical educated person, used, they were not counting each thing that was spelt differently as a different word. In the case of Shakespeare, the estimate of about 20,000 was based on 'lemmas'; in the case of the educated person a similar estimate was based on counting 'word families'. But this list of words used in modern Acts was not a list of 'lemmas'. It was a list of different 'word forms' The significance of this is that counting lemmas rather than word forms significantly reduces the total. You may remember that Shakespeare's vocabulary was thought to contain about 30,000 word forms but only about 20,000 lemmas. So it seems likely that the sixteen and a half thousand or so word forms in my list of words used in recent Acts would be significantly reduced if one counted 'lemmas' rather than 'word forms'. If the reduction was similar to the difference between the estimated number of lemmas and word forms in Shakespeare, the reduction would be about a third. Or, to put it another way, 'lemmatising' the list of words used in Acts could perhaps reduce the total to about half the total for Shakespeare.

At this point, I have to admit that I have not made any effort to 'lemmatise' my list. If one were going to go to the trouble of doing that, I think one would need to go the whole hog and set up a corpus according to the stringent standards recommended for these purposes,[13] rather than taking advantage of a dataset that happens to have been accumulated, not entirely systematically, for other purposes.

So, what I am saying is rather speculative. I would not want to go any further than that there are grounds for believing that evidence could probably be found, by anyone who has the time to do the necessary work, to support the hypothesis that the UK legislative vocabulary is fairly impoverished compared with Shakespeare's.

If this hypothesis were to be put on a firm empirical footing, I doubt whether it would come as a surprise to most of my colleagues. When I first joined PCO (in 1987) one of the things that senior members of the office used to remark upon then was how limited the legislative vocabulary was. It was just one of those things that they all 'knew'

I would now like to turn and take a look at word frequencies.

I shall make only the briefest of remarks about word frequencies in Shakespeare. Here is a short selection of some of his favourite words: one of them was 'love': he used it 2,271 times; others were 'heart', 'death', 'man', 'life', 'hand', 'blood' and 'honour'; 'good' was his commonest adjective.[14]

Now let's look at what words appear most frequently in Acts. The layman might perhaps think that there would be a high frequency of words which could be described as 'legal jargon': for example, 'thereto', 'thereby', 'thereunder', 'henceforth' and 'heretofore'. In fact, this is not in fact the most striking thing. None of these were particularly common in Acts since 1980.[15]

Possibly the most striking thing is that some of the most frequent words are those for identifying other bits of legislation – 'section' (first on the list) followed soon after by 'subsection', 'paragraph', 'order', 'Schedule' and 'regulations' [16] Also very high up are words about what is required to or is permitted to happen: 'shall' and 'may' appear at 3rd and 5th places.[17] 'Above' is 9th on the list. But 'below' does not appear until much later – at 56th place, or about a third of the way down page 2.

---

13 See L. Burnard 'Metadata for corpus work' in M. Wynne (ed.) *Developing Linguistic Corpora: a Guide to Good Practice* (Oxford: Oxbow Books, 2005) pp. 30–46. Available online from (www.ahds.ac.uk/linguistic-corpora/) accessed 10 July 2007.

14 *Op. cit.* vol. vi, *Severity to Zwagger, Appendices*, Appendix A: A Word-Frequency Index, pp. 4177–237. The frequency count for 'love' includes hyphenated words. The words mentioned in the text all appear in the first two pages of Spevack's 60-page index.

15 This list (unlike Spevack's) was not in columns and was 367 pages long. The first three words mentioned appear at pages 39, 53 and 66 respectively; the last two at page 335. But 'prejudice' and 'notwithstanding' (at pages 7 and 11) are too high up for my liking.

16 At places 4, 6, 10, 12 and 37 on the list. 'Act' came second, but I am ignoring that, because 'Act', unlike other words, would have appeared in every header for every page of every Act stored in our database, giving it an unfair advantage. It also, of course, has a dual meaning – the index is not case sensitive. 'Part', at place 8, is similar – it appears on each page of an Act divided into Parts, and also has a dual meaning.

17 Going with this is the fact that 'effect', 'apply' and 'applies', at places 25, 41 and 42, are also fairly common.

I would like to leave these points with you for the moment, to mull over in the back of your mind, while I tell you about some other frequent occurrences.

Another extremely common word – 7th on the list – is 'person' 'State' and 'secretary' are also common – 13th and 16th places, or about half way down page 1 of my list. Still roughly at the middle of page 1 are 'purposes', 'relation' and 'respect' (14th, 15th and 18th places). Other common words relate to time: 'period', 'time', 'notice', all on page 1, with 'year' and 'day' on pages 2 and 3. Another feature that you may find interesting is that the singular is more common than the plural. 'Person' is much commoner than 'persons', and very much more common than the 'natural' plural of 'persons', 'people'.[18] 'Payment' appears before 'payments' and 'tax' before 'taxes'. This pattern is repeated many times over in the list. You may also be interested to know that, among the adjectives, 'appropriate' and 'reasonable' are high up (pages 3 and 5 of the list). What could loosely be described as money-related words are also common. Here are some of them, in descending order of frequency: amount; tax; interest; payment; income; account; payable; chargeable; and charge. The last of these is on page 4. The list is 367 pages long – so all these are still common words.

I would now like to move to the other end of the spectrum, to words which are not used in Acts or are seldom used. It may not surprise you to discover that Shakespeare's high frequency word, 'love', does not appear in my word list. Similarly for 'heart' – it does not appear. 'Death' does cast its shadow over Acts (it is on page 13).[19] It comes before another Shakespearean favourite, 'life' (on page 14). 'Man' appears at page 25, 'hand' at page 50, and 'good' at page 23. None of the selected Shakespearean favourites appears anywhere near the words I have listed as favourites in Acts.

I can give you some other examples of words that are infrequently used in Acts. This time my investigations were based on using one of the commercial databases which contains all the Acts enacted in the UK.[20]

Horrible: this word appears to have been used only twice. It occurred in section 1(c) of the Children and Young Persons (Harmful Publications) Act 1955, which referred to 'stories portraying ... (c) incidents of a repulsive or horrible nature ...'; and, before that, in the Attainder of Guy Fawkes and others Act 1605, in the phrase 'heinous, horrible and damnable Treasons'. *Beautiful*: to find this word in an Act, you have to go back to the Lincoln's Inn Fields Rate Act 1734 which at one point referred to buildings having to be built 'in a more firm or beautiful Manner'. *Handsome*: this does not appear except in an Act of 1859 which was talking about a handsome bridge. *Lovely*: this does not appear at all; *nice* does not appear except as *Nice* (the place); *gentle* appears only in the phrase 'gentle lemurs' (inserted by amendment in the Endangered Species (Import and Export) Act 1976). *Happy* has not appeared except in old legislation (nineteenth century and earlier) where it appears only in

18 112072, 27903 and 1025 occurrences respectively.

19 Shortly after a rather more prosaic word: 'inspection'.

20 This commercial database can be used for finding how often a particular word is used but I could not see a way of printing out a complete list of words used in frequency order, or of confining that list to a particular (modern) period.

the phrase 'Happy Reign' or 'Happy accession' *Kindly* has not appeared except in Scottish legislation, in the context of abolishing 'Kindly Tenancies' (whatever they are). *Elegant* has not appeared except in the phrase 'elegant parakeet' (also in the Act I just mentioned about endangered species). *Villainous* seems to have occurred once only, in the Maiming Act 1670. Bearing this last point in mind, it is perhaps curious to note that – to revisit my list of words used in modern Acts – 'virtue' occurs as high as page 1 (44th place).

I have bombarded you with what may seem to be an entirely random collection of remarks about the peculiarities of the legislative vocabulary compared with Shakespeare's. The time has come to consider the significance (if any) of all this in the context of the question whether legislation can rank as literature. At this point I turn to two questions that it would have been more logical to use as my starting point. One: What is literature? Two: What is legislation?

The Shorter Oxford English Dictionary gives various meanings to 'literature' But there is a broad contrast between two main meanings which is brought out at entry 3a. The first is 'Literary productions as a whole; the body of writings produced in a particular country or period, or in the world in general.' And the second is 'Now also specially that kind of written composition valued on account of its *qualities of form or emotional effect*' [21] When people describe the works of Shakespeare as literature, they are undoubtedly thinking of literature in this second sense.

Legislation, or legislation of a particular jurisdiction in a particular era, could perhaps be 'literature' in the first, less restricted sense. But I think it is normally quite a long way off being 'literature' in the second, more restricted sense.

After all, what is legislation *for*?

The function of an Act is to state legal rules. It is this fact that leads to its distinctive features. This is a point that has been made, and made more authoritatively, before: see, for example, *Jackson v Attorney General*.[22] This was the case in which the House of Lords was considering the validity of the Hunting Act 2004. Lord Steyn quoted a passage from a note from the then First Parliamentary Counsel (Sir Christopher Jenkins) to the Select Committee on the Modernisation of the House of Commons[23] which made this point very clearly.[24]

---

21 See 5th edn (2002), entry 3a (my emphasis). A 6th edn is due out in September 2007.

22 See [2005] UK HL 56.

23 Second Report, HC 389 (3 December 1997), Appendix, at 2, Annex A.

24 The passage runs 'a Bill is not there to inform, to explain, to entertain or to perform any of the other usual functions of literature. A Bill's sole reason for existence is to change the law. The resulting Act is the law. A consequence of this unique function is that a Bill cannot set about communicating with the reader in the same way that other forms of writing do. It cannot use the same range of tools. In particular, it cannot repeat important points simply to emphasise their importance or safely explain itself by restating a proposition in different words. To do so would risk creating doubts and ambiguities that would fuel litigation. As a result, legislation speaks in a monotone and its language is compressed.' (Occasionally, of course, enactments are not designed to change the law, but merely to restate it.) A similar point is made in Sir Ernest Gowers, *The Complete Plain Words* 3rd edn, S. Greenbaum and J. Whitcut (eds) 1986, at 6, to which I return later.

Although this is a point that has been made before, it is a point that is worth making again and again. So, to repeat: the function of an Act is to state legal rules. It is *not* primarily designed to appeal to the reader primarily on the ground of 'the beauty of its form or its emotional effect'. So it ought not to be surprising that Acts, unlike the works of Shakespeare, hardly ever use the word 'love': Acts are not about regulating love; Acts are not about matters of the heart. Words like 'handsome' and 'beautiful' do not abound. Unlike a work of Shakespeare, it is not the function of an Act to produce an emotional effect. To the extent that Acts are meant to appeal to any human faculty, the faculty that they are meant to appeal to is the faculty of reason. So it is perhaps not surprising that in Acts 'appropriate' and 'reasonable' are more common than the Shakespearean favourite, 'good'.

If one bears in mind that the essence of legislation is to state rules, the peculiarities of its vocabulary become more readily comprehensible. Let's look again at some of the features that I touched on earlier.

So: question: Why is the legislative vocabulary relatively small? Answer: because, if you want to state a rule, you should not express the same idea in a multiplicity of different ways. This is different from literature, where it is common for the text to contain many variations on a theme. When drafting you should try to express a point once only and if for some reason you need to repeat it, you should express it in the same way – unless you want to produce a different effect. One might usefully compare the language range of legislation not so much to literature, but to a high-level programming language. No one expects a high-level programming language to have a large vocabulary, or to indulge in elegant variation just for the sake of it.

Again: question: Why does legislation seem to spend so much time talking about itself? Why do words like 'section' and 'subsection' occur so frequently? Answer: because it needs to deal with the relationship between one rule and another.[25] Why are 'shall' and 'may' common? Because this is how obligations and powers are traditionally imposed or conferred.[26] The curiously high placing of 'virtue' is not so curious after all. This is not virtue in a Shakespearean sense (virtue as opposed to villainy). It is virtue in the sense of 'by virtue of section x', a phrase often used where a legal result is obtained because of the interaction of more than one provision, but the cross reference is fastening on one provision only.[27] Why does legislation use 'above' and 'below' so much? This too is a symptom of the need for rules to deal with their relationship with each other. 'Above' and 'below' have of course typically been used in phrases such as 'section 1 above' and 'section 3 below'.

But why has 'above' been used more frequently than 'below'? Well, I think that this brings out another interesting contrast between legislation and literature. In

25 It might be said that using the texts of Acts as enacted as the basis for making generalisations about word frequencies unfairly exaggerates the frequency of words like 'section' and 'subsection', because texts of Acts as enacted (as opposed to texts of Acts as amended) will include provisions making textual amendments: I do not think so. In real life Acts make textual amendments. Changing existing rules is what legislation is often about.

26 'Shall' is of course now giving way to 'must' and other alternatives; but this is relatively recent.

27 Nowadays 'by virtue of' is also (rightly) often giving way to 'plain English' alternatives.

literature, the author may want there to be an element of drama, to keep alive the reader's interest. So a story may not be told in its natural or logical sequence. There may be flashbacks; or the action may suddenly fast forward. The author may want to keep the reader in suspense, to retain an element of surprise. To a certain extent, I was, in a feeble way, trying to play this sort of literary trick on you by posing my initial question and then, instead of answering it straightaway, meandering slowly through some detailed points about vocabulary. I wondered if I could keep you guessing.

Contrast this approach with that of legislation. Generating a sensation of delicious suspense in the reader is not the main objective. The prime objective is to communicate rules in their natural order. That is usually a 'need to know' order. So one is more likely to need to refer back to an earlier proposition than to refer forwards to a later one. This is why 'above' has occurred more frequently than 'below'.

Another question: Why does 'person' occur so frequently? Because although it looks like an ordinary word, it is a term of art. Legislation often needs to regulate activity regardless of whether it is carried out directly by individuals or through corporations or unincorporated associations. In this jurisdiction, all of these are normally embraced by the simple word 'person' (see Schedule 1 to the Interpretation Act 1978). 'People' is used relatively infrequently because that would not bring in corporations and unincorporated associations in this way. An example of the use of 'people' is in the definition of a 'civil partnership' in the Civil Partnership Act 2004 – but here it is safe, because a civil partnership is about a relationship between two human beings.[28] Why does legislation use the words 'state' and 'secretary' so often? This is an easy one: because it needs to deal with the powers of government, which, in this jurisdiction, are normally exercisable by 'the Secretary of State'. This stands for any of the named Secretaries of State (see Schedule 1 to the Interpretation Act).

More questions: Why are the words 'purposes', 'relation' and 'respect' so common? Answer: because legislation needs to identify the *precise* situation in which the rules will operate. A rule operates for the purposes of such and such, a definition is supplied in relation to something, or with respect to something. Why are 'period', 'time', 'notice', 'day' so common? Because if someone has to, or is to be able to, do something, there often needs to be a time frame during which it is to be done. Why is the singular more common than the plural? Because legislation usually needs to achieve a result in a particular type of case. A rule can usually target a situation more precisely if it is expressed in the singular rather than the plural. These facets of the vocabulary can all be seen as reflecting the need for precision in well-formulated rules.

So my theme so far is that a lot of the peculiarities of the legislative vocabulary are directly related to the fact that the function of legislation is to state rules. They are symptomatic of the difference between legislation and literature, because the purpose of the latter (at least in the sense I am choosing to take it) is to appeal to the reader on the ground of its beauty of form or emotional effect.

---

28 Cf. section 1(1) of the Partnership Act 1890 'Partnership is the relation which subsists between *persons* carrying on a business in common with a view of profit.'

I said earlier that, by meandering through points about vocabulary, I was trying to play a literary trick on you. I shall now confess it was a rather unfair trick. Vocabulary is, I suspect, not necessarily the acid test. There are poems which I am sure rank as literature but which do not call on a large vocabulary. And, although I think that the peculiarities of the legislative vocabulary are related to its non-literary character, I would say that legislation has other peculiarities which betray its non-literary character even more. For now I shall just mention two.

The first is layout. Authors of great literary works do not chop their prose up into clauses, machete the clauses into subsections or axe the subsections into paragraphs. But we do this routinely when drafting legislation, because doing so can help to make the meaning of the rules much clearer. This becomes very obvious if one is ever involved in consolidating[29] old legislation containing very long, unparagraphed text. Sometimes, as part of the consolidation process, the text can be paragraphed, or divided up in some other way, without difficulty and this may make the legislation more accessible to the reader. But sometimes this cannot be done without resolving an ambiguity in the text, and so may[30] be outside the scope of the consolidation process.

The second non-literary feature of legislation to which I wish to draw your attention is the fact that it is the product of many hands on many different occasions.

In our system, a bill is usually drafted by at least two drafters – a senior and a junior – who are in turn working with a departmental team instructing on the bill. But the collective authorship of legislation does not stop when the bill is introduced into Parliament. After it is introduced, it may have amendments made to it during its passage which were never envisaged at the outset. And after it is enacted it is likely to be the subject of amendment by subsequent Acts probably drafted by different drafters. This amendment process can distort it beyond all recognition. I daresay we can all think of legal textbooks which in their first edition were written in an exemplary style but which gradually lost their shape and lucidity as a result of accretions in subsequent editions, particularly after a change of editor. The same happens to legislation, only more so. How different is literature – 'great literature'. It is typically the product of the creative genius of a single mind. It is not a team product. Once accomplished, it is usually left mercifully alone. The sequel or the prequel written by a different author has not yet risen to being a generally admired art-form.

But, you may say, you have overstated your case: the matter might take on a different complexion if Acts drafted in the latest style were used as the touchstone; one might take a different view if one would only trouble to look at the 'right' Acts.

Of course, times do change. Nowadays a lot of effort is put into making legislation accessible to the ordinary reader. This process of making legislation more accessible could, on one view, be characterised as making it look less like an exercise in rule-

29 Consolidation involves bringing together different enactments on the same subject matter to form a rational structure and making more intelligible the cumulative effect of different layers of amendment. The aim is to make the legislation more comprehensible.

30 Sometimes small changes can be made during the consolidation process, for example, by means of amendments to give effect to recommendations of the Law Commission.

making and more like literature. This is not the occasion to launch into a survey of the whole array of modern drafting techniques. Instead I shall just pick two aspects to talk about briefly: handling cross-references; and purpose clauses.

One of the features of legislation which betrays its primary function of stating legal rules, and which at the same time is one of the things the ordinary reader is likely to find most off-putting, is the fact that it is often larded with cross-references. Cross-references are off-putting for two main reasons. First, they use numbers and most of us find numbers harder to remember than words. Secondly, they expect the reader to remember too much: for instance, to remember the provision referred to while reading the referring provision. Both these points amount to the same thing – both are about imposing an undue burden on the reader's memory.

There are various ways of lessening this burden. One has been to make the cross-references less cumbersome, so that they are easier to digest. I mentioned earlier the use of 'above' and 'below'. These words occurred frequently in my list of words in Acts from 1980 to 2005. But by the mid-1980s, 'progressive' members of PCO had already dropped them as part of a general drive to simplify the language of legislation. This gradually caught on so that nowadays they are not used except by a few in special cases (for example, for consistency when amending an old Act).

Another approach is to use words in brackets to describe the provision to which reference is being made. An early example of this approach can be seen in the Copyright and Designs Act 1988. Parenthetical words can be a useful memory jogger for the reader who otherwise would be unable to remember what the provision referred to is about. But the advantages are not all one way. The parenthetical words will make the text containing the cross-reference longer, thus creating a different obstacle to easy communication: short sentences are generally easier to follow than long ones. So one could take a pragmatic view, and add parenthetical words only when one thinks they are really needed as a memory jogger – not, for instance, if the section referred to is the immediately preceding section. But this in turn may create its own distraction: the reader may waste time wondering why parenthetical words are sometimes used and sometimes not used.

Another device is to use a label instead of a cross-reference. I used this device in the Trustee Act 2000 – instead of referring to 'the power under section 1', I labelled the power under section 1 as 'the general power of investment' and then used this phrase whenever I would otherwise have needed to refer to section 1. But this is not a magic bullet. It can misfire. There is a risk that a label will be treated (inappropriately) as being more than a mere label – as having some independent life of its own. And then it would have defeated its object.

Sometimes the solution may be simply to avoid making the cross-reference, on the basis that it will be implicit anyway. For example, it may be possible to leave out 'Subject to section x', or 'Without prejudice to the generality of section y' on the basis that it should be self-evident that the current provision is subject to section x, or is not meant to prejudice section y. This is part of the 'less is more' school of drafting for which there is much to be said.

These various techniques for handling cross-references – and this description is not meant to be exhaustive – may help to make legislation seem less rebarbative and therefore, perhaps, more literary in tone.

But I suspect that the effect is more cosmetic than real. Such techniques may help the reader over some initial hurdles on a first reading; but there is usually no escape from the underlying fact that in a system of rules there are likely to be various, often complex, interrelationships between the rules, and that getting to grips with them is one of the major challenges involved in understanding any legislative text.

Another device that has been advocated as an aid to understanding legislation is the so-called 'purpose clause' The Renton Report was in favour of them.[31] But in PCO we have tended to be more wary. There may be a conflict between the generalities in the purpose clause and the more detailed provisions that follow. This may create ambiguity rather than aiding understanding. If the purpose clause is meant to prevail, what is the need for more specific provisions? If the more specific provisions are meant to prevail, what is the point of the purpose clause? It is this sort of consideration which led the House of Lords Select Committee on the Constitution to conclude, in October 2004, that a purpose clause should not form part of a bill.[32]

But nevertheless one can sympathise with the reader who may welcome being given an idea to hold on to before entering the deep dark legislative maze. Sometimes it is possible to square the circle by starting a bill with a general statement about principles to be applied or factors to be taken into account when applying other more specific rules – most obviously, when making a decision as to whether to exercise a power. These are not purpose clauses in the full sense. But they give some scope for the expression of aspirations.

It is in this context – the context of these quasi-purpose clauses – that I suspect legislation inches closest towards literature. The example I mentioned at the beginning, section 1 of the Mental Capacity Act 2005, is perhaps a case in point. An earlier example of a somewhat similar nature is to be found in section 1 of the Children Act 1989.[33] However, although provisions of this sort inch closer to literature, they move further away from 'hard' law.

Section 1 of the Mental Capacity Act is about important values – a person must be assumed to have capacity unless shown to lack capacity, any act done or decision made for a person who lacks capacity must be done, or made, in the person's best interests, and so on. So is section 1 of the Children Act 1989 – when a court determines any question with respect to the upbringing of a child (etc.), the child's welfare must be the court's paramount consideration. The protection of children and those who lack mental capacity are among the worthiest of mankind's aims. These statements are not so dissimilar from the sort of statements that one finds in conventions about human rights.

But the statute book cannot consist just of high-minded objectives. Most of the time, the working, everyday, law has to grapple with more mundane matters. For

---

31 Report on the Preparation of Legislation Cmnd. 6053 (ch. 11).

32 House of Lords Select Committee on the Constitution 14th Report Session 2003–04, Ordered to be printed 13 October 2004 and published 29 October 2004 HL Paper 173–I, paras 82 to 87.

33 Whether to have a purposive statement of any kind is of course not just a drafting question. Factors other than purely drafting ones affected whether such a statement would have been appropriate in the Civil Partnership Act 2004.

every clause 1 of a bill that contains laudable aims of this sort, there usually needs to follow a raft of rules that can be used to decide specific issues. Legislation about an individual's mental capacity cannot consist just of presumptions against lack of capacity; it needs to include other rules as well – for instance, rules defining mental capacity and what being unable to make decisions means, or regulating how persons suspecting that their mental capacity is declining may address that possibility by granting another a lasting power of attorney. Legislation about children cannot consist just of a proposition about the welfare of the child being the paramount consideration; it needs to include other rules – for instance, rules regulating the circumstances in which a child is to be looked after by a local authority, or is to reside with one parent rather than another following the breakdown of a marriage. Unsurprisingly, basic propositions about human rights are usually the stuff of international conventions or fundamental laws. They are not ordinary bread and butter legislation.

There is an excellent discussion of 'purposive drafting' in the Tax Law Rewrite Project's Second Technical Discussion Document.[34] At the end of that document, they concluded 'Since this summary of the discussion opened with the 1975 Renton Report it is perhaps fitting that it should give Lord Renton the final word on the need for detailed rules. In a House of Lords debate held on 21 January 1998 Hansard[35] Lord Renton said, "I have never taken the view that the aim of purpose clauses was to dispense with detail. It was to lead to better understanding of detail that such clauses have, within my knowledge, always been recommended."'

This, I think, is the major difficulty for anyone who wishes to contend that legislation can rank as literature: it cannot consist just of grand statements. The bulk of it is likely to be fairly mundane. That is its nature.

Although I have asserted that ordinary legislation would not rank as literature, this does not necessarily mean that there is no room for creativity in drafting. But how much room is there?

An exercise conducted for the purposes of a conference at Boulogne-sur-Mer in July 2005[36] put this to the test. Three drafters from different jurisdictions were asked to produce a draft in response to the same set of instructions without conferring with one another or anybody else. The result of this exercise was three very different drafts. But I am not sure how much one can properly infer from this. The drafters involved came from different jurisdictions and one might perhaps expect their drafts to look a bit different.

What I find more interesting is whether, if were to give the same instructions to different drafters from the *same* jurisdiction, they would produce radically different drafts. I do not think this has been empirically tested. But there is no harm in speculating about the answer. I suspect that the room for creativity in drafting is significantly affected by the subject matter. At one extreme, some changes in the law – for example, a change in a rate of tax – will leave no room for creativity. At the other extreme, a bill which involves legislating on a green field site is likely to leave much more room for creativity. The more significant the changes in the law, the more

34 See (www.hmrc.gov.uk/rewrite/tdd/tdd2/p3.htm).

35 See col. 1598.

36 See *Clarity* issue No. 54 (November 2005).

likely it is that those instructing on the bill will have been unable to think through the details to the *n*th degree. In these circumstances, the drafter is likely to explain that the first draft is merely designed to set the ball rolling, to raise questions rather than provide answers, and will discuss issues and options with those instructing on the bill. But however carefully this is done, the chances are that the draft which is merely designed to set the ball rolling will in fact set it rolling in a particular way. So some drafting assignments may involve a significant element of creativity. The resulting legislation may be different depending on who is assigned to draft it.

So, to return to my original question.

I do not think legislation is much like literature in the sense of writing claiming attention on account of its qualities of form or emotional effect. The closer it gets to being literature in that sense, the further it moves away from the primary function of legislation, which is to provide a system of rules. But legislation can be literature in another sense, the sense of a body of writing produced in a particular context. And, among all the many other skills that are required to produce that body of writing, there is plenty of room for creativity and, indeed, for good writing.

Please do not feel disappointed by the conclusion I have offered you. There is a view still prevalent in some quarters that is harsher than this. According to *The Complete Plain Words*:

> Acts of Parliament ... have a special purpose, to which their language has to be specially adapted ... The legal draftsmen ... have to ensure to the best of their ability that what they say will mean precisely what they intended ... If [legal drafting] is readily intelligible, so much the better; but it is far more important that it should yield its meaning accurately than that it should yield it on first reading, and legal draftsmen cannot afford to give much attention, if any, to euphony or literary elegance ... All this means that legal drafting is not to be judged by normal standards of good writing ... By normal standards of good writing legal drafting is usually both cumbrous and uncouth ...[37]

This, to my mind, is too harsh. I believe that modern legislation can be judged by normal standards of good writing and need not usually be cumbrous or uncouth. And if it passes this test despite needing to mean precisely what it was intended to mean: that is no small achievement and one which, in a democratic society, is more important than being ranked as literature.

---

37 See Sir Ernest Gowers *at* 6.

Chapter 18

Open Management of Legislative Documents[1]

Giovanni Sartor

ICT and Legislation in the Knowledge Society

Predicaments of Legislation

It has been affirmed that the primacy of legislation is coming to an end: we are moving from the age of legislation to the age of administration (by specialised technical bodies) or jurisdiction (creation of law by judges, supported by jurists) or custom (as emerging especially from economic relations, contracts and decisions by private arbiters) or even computer code (enabling or constraining actions in virtual environments). This would be required by a variety of factors:

- legislative authorities are national, economic and social networks are global;
- legislation is slow, current problems require quick solutions;
- elective assemblies are political bodies, complex problems require technical, economic and legal competence;
- legislation is static, accelerated economic and technical progress requires continuous adjustments.

This picture has undoubtedly some elements of truth and indeed nowadays parliamentary legislation is just one among other sources of legal regulation.

However, the fact that legislation needs to coexist with other sources of the law does not make legislation less important and less central nor does it diminish the unique contribution that parliamentary legislation can provide to societal governance. Let us shortly consider what we may identify as the values that are inherent in parliamentary legislation, the values which a good legislation should implement:

- Means–end rationality. Legislation should provide regulations that are likely to solve effectively the problems they address, according to the best available knowledge.

1 This chapter was prepared for The Global Centre for ICT in Parliament, an initiative of the United Nations Department of Economic and Social Affairs (UNDESA) with the Inter-Parliamentary Union (IPU).

- Discoursive rationality. Legislation should emerge out of a debate as open as possible, where all interests at stake are considered, the relevant pros and cons are evaluated and the possible alternative are taken into account.
- Responsiveness to citizens' needs and preferences. Legislation should reflect the reasoned views of citizens, though representatives should be able to focus on the common good and filter emotional and unreasoned reactions.
- Progress (ability to change). Legislation should be able to adapt to social change, adapting the legal framework to new needs and in particular to introduce comprehensive reforms as other sources of law (such as custom or case law) are structurally unable to do.
- Legal certainty. Legislation should contribute to the certainty of the law, providing normative information which gives effective guidance to citizens and legal decision makers. By providing a common focus it should keep in line their expectations and prevent the exercise of arbitrary power.
- Citizen's rights. Legislation should enable the citizens to have a clear idea of what their rights are, so that they may be able to make justified complaints when these rights are violated.

Preserving the dignity of legislation[2] in the information age requires that the values listed above are approximated, at least to a certain degree, by legislative reality: it is not sufficient to imagine an ideal legislator, it is necessary to show how ideal legislation can become, to a reasonable extent, a concrete reality. The need to improve the quality of legislation is indeed the focus of a number of national and international initiatives.[3]

The Role of ICTs

ICT can contribute to all of the purposes we have listed at the end of the previous section:

- Means–ends rationality. ICT can contribute to align legislation to its intended purposes by providing legislators with tools for anticipating the impact of new laws on the legal system, on administration and on society or for monitoring and evaluating the impact of an existing law.
- Discoursive rationality. ICT can promote critical debate around legislation: by providing communication tools for promoting the informed debate within Parliaments and outside of them, by facilitating the preparation of legislative

---

2 For this idea, see J. Waldron, *The Dignity of Legislation* (Cambridge: Cambridge University Press, 1999).

3 Among the latter, see : OECD (1994) 'Improving the Quality of Laws and Regulations: Economic, Legal and Managerial Techniques' OECD/GD(94)59. Technical Report; OECD, 1997. Regulatory Impact Analysis: Best Practice in OECD countries (Paris: OECDs, 1997); Commission of the European Communities, 'Better Lawmaking 2002 A shared Responsibility' Brussels, 2002; Commission of the European Communities, 'A strategic review of Better Regulation in the European Union'. COM(2006)689 (14 November 2006).

proposals and by offering citizens and their associations new ways to participate in the legislative process.

- Responsiveness to citizens' needs and preferences. ICT can facilitate the contact between citizens and their representatives, providing the citizen with new ways to express their views and with feedback about the choices of their representatives.
- Legal certainty. ICT can enable citizens to anticipate the impact of legislation on them by providing access to laws and cases, by facilitating the drafting of more understandable regulations and the maintenance of the legal system's comprehensibility as much as possible.
- Citizens' rights. ICT can contribute in ensuring that laws may protect citizens' rights by making knowledge about rules and remedies more accessible and by ensuring that information about the officers' behaviour becomes public.

We should indeed consider that ICT is both a part of the problem that legislators currently have to solve and a part of the solution to the problem. On the one hand, ICT is a source of problems for legislation because:

- it is the infrastructure of globalisation: it enables economic and social networks transcending borders;
- it is the engine of economical and social development: it increases the speed of change;
- it is the enzyme of complexity: by increasing knowledge and possibilities available to individual actors it increases the complexity of their interaction.

On the other hand, ICT is a part of the solution since in particular:

- it can provide an infrastructure for legislative networks: by enabling a network of legislative bodies it can favour shared (or coordinated) replies to global issues;
- it can support dynamic drafting: it enables us to control the mass of legislative material and to intervene upon it making the required changes;
- it can provide the information system of legislation: it can help legislators in modelling social complexity and responding to it. ICT is going to play a fundamental role in the working of Parliaments. As in many other domains of social life, Parliaments too are moving into relying upon a ICT-based information systems (as opposed to the use of paper, as the exclusive medium for storing and communicating data, which can only be processed by humans). The various agents – internal and external to Parliaments – that are involved in legislation increasingly access information and communicate much of it through such a system, which becomes the pivot of their interaction (see Figure 18.1).

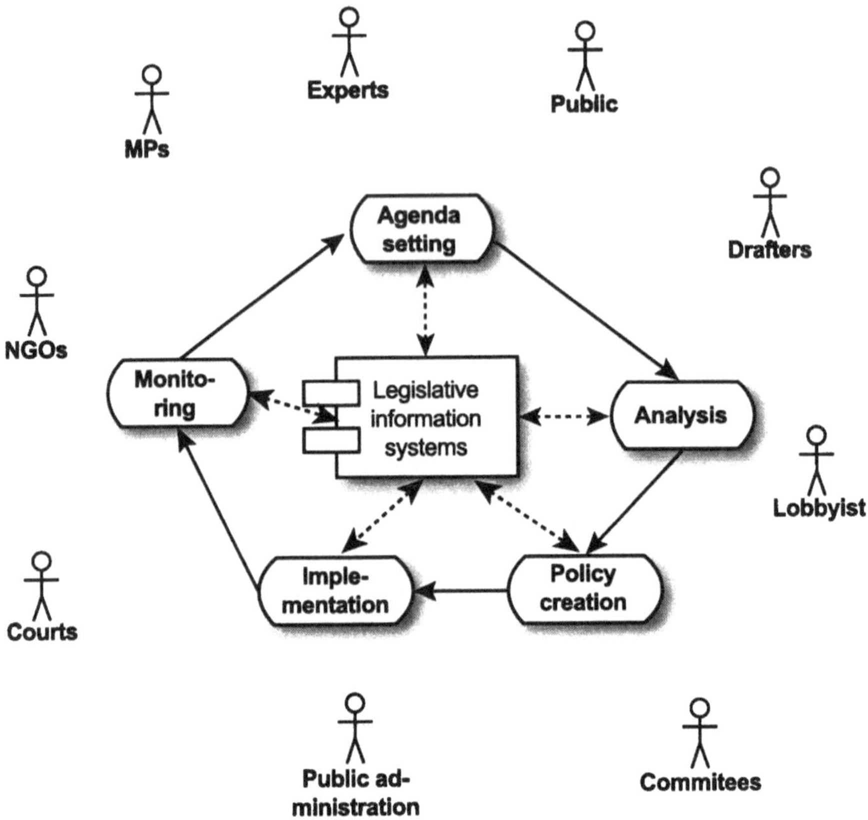

Figure 18.1 Legislative information system

Many Parliaments are already using advanced information system to support all main internal activities, as well as the connections with the political and social environment (see Figure 18.2).

Legislative Information Systems

The importance of legislative information systems has vastly increased in recent years, especially since the advent of the Internet, which has dramatically changed the ways in which all information is produced and communicated.[4] Nowadays the Internet already has become the principal source of legal cognition for citizens, and it is rapidly becoming the main source of information also for lawyers, as the previously existing legal sources are moving into the Internet and new sources of legal information are emerging.

4 See M. Castells, *The Internet Galaxy* (Oxford: Oxford University Press, 2001).

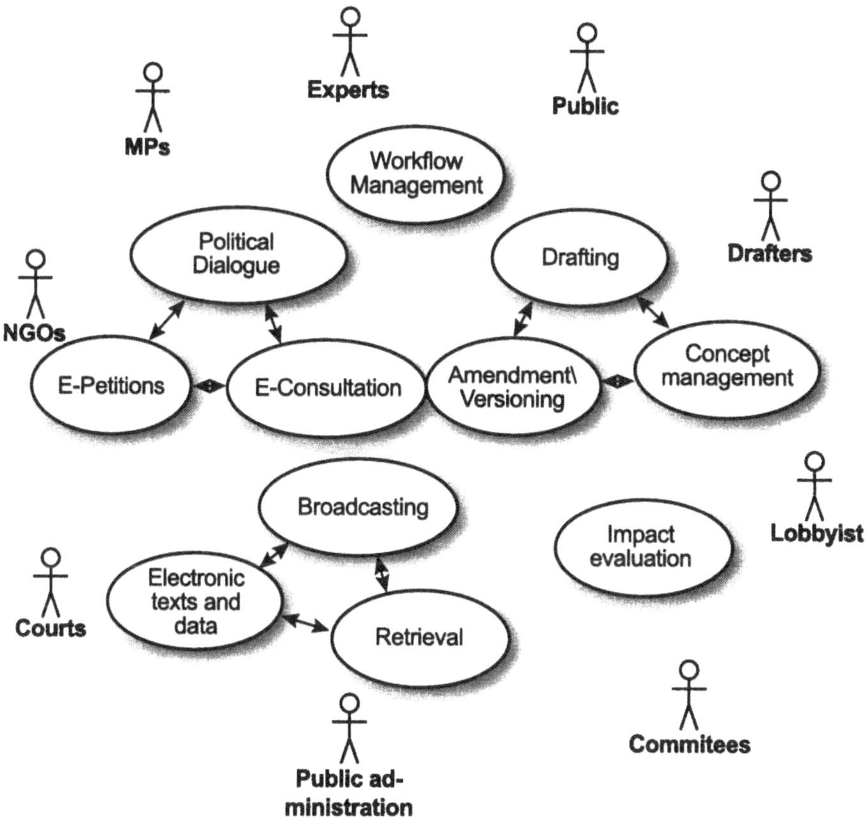

Figure 18.2 A legislative information system: the supported activities

The law has massively entered into the so-called knowledge soup, namely, in the mass of information which is nowadays available on the Web: the law constitutes an important set of the information provided in the Web and a set of information that is distinguished not only by its particular (legal) content but also for the fact of being densely interconnected (since legal documents so often refer to each other, while having relatively few links to non-legal materials). Consequently, it is possible to say that a *legal Web* is emerging, as a distinct subset of the broader World Wide Web.

Besides being the source of legal information the Web is increasingly becoming the place of political and legal interactions.[5] It is the place where political debate occurs (consider, for instance, the many websites and forums currently devoted to US elections), citizens interact with institutions and with their representatives (through the many institutional sites now provided by public administrations and in particular by Parliaments and other elective assemblies), legal transactions are performed (through online e-government applications), legal decisions are commented and

5 For various interesting observations, see, among the others, Castells (2001) and A. Gore, *The Assault on Reason* (New York: Penguin, 2007) ch. 9.

criticised (through the many legal fora, blogs, web pages devoted to controversial legal issues, such as the patentability of software).

In the Internet era a parliamentary information system needs to have a Janus-like face: one face must look at the internal side of the Parliament and support all parliamentary activities; the other face must look outside and provide citizens with information on Parliament's activities and outputs, as well as opportunities to participate in parliamentary activities.

These two faces need not be sharply divided as far as technologies are concerned: in the Internet era increasingly the same protocols, models, languages and tools can be used both inside an organisation and for its relations with the external world. Following the trend already existing in many domains, each Parliament can exploit Internet technologies for building its Intranet, namely, its own private version of the Internet, whose access is limited to MPs and staff and which offers them the various computer applications available within Parliament as well as new ways of communicating and cooperating. The same technologies and protocols used in the parliamentary Intranet can be employed in the Parliament Extranet, which gives citizens (as well as their associations and economic and social organisations) access to information and applications existing within the Parliament, and ways of participating in the parliamentary activity.

A moving and flexible border separates between the information remaining accessible only through the parliamentary Intranet and the information externally distributed through the parliamentary Extranet, a border depending on changing political and organisational choices, as well as on the passage of time (what is internal now, i.e. a proposal discussed in a committee, may and should become public tomorrow, when the proposal is approved and subject to public debate). Thus, such information must, from the start, be encoded in such a form as to enable all ways of its future use and distribution (while adopting all technological and organisational measures to maintain its confidentiality, when this is needed and is consistent with transparency requirements).

Moreover, Parliaments need not be the only providers of parliamentary information. In pluralistic and democratic societies such information may indeed be distributed – organised and presented in different ways and possibly enriched with additional information – by other actors, private or public, profit or non-profit. Such further activities, though they are not directly controlled by Parliament and performed by the parliamentary information system can indeed contribute to the achievement of the main purposes of such a system, namely, to support the best use of parliamentary information and to facilitate citizens' involvement and participation. Of course, such purposes can be achieved not only through direct provision of information services to the internal or external actors but also by making available to third parties, in appropriate electronic formats, the parliamentary data needed for providing such services.

The link between Parliamentarian democracy and ICT is further enhanced by considering that emergence of a global society (constituted by a network of networks of global, national and local social systems, based upon ICT-based communication) can be matched by a network of networks of democratic legislative authorities, using a distributed shared set of documents and information. Sharing information not only enables each one to learn from the experience of others so that best practices can spread, it may also induce national legislators to take into account the needs of other countries, so that they move beyond a narrow view of national interests and frame legal provisions in the light of all concerned interests, also outside national borders.[6]

Legal and Legislative Informatics

The issue of the management of legislative documents involves both aspects of parliamentary information systems considered above: the 'Intranet' aspect, concerning computerisation within Parliaments and the 'Extranet' aspect, concerning the provision of legal information (and of various services) to external actors, since most documents produced during the legislative process will both be used internally and provided externally (as required by democracy and transparency).

Moreover, the discussion of the management of legislative documents cannot be limited to parliamentary information systems. As we shall see later, legislative documents are (and should be) stored and processed also by other actors. Legislative informatics is not limited to the study and development of computer applications for Parliaments. It also includes orchestrating, for the benefit of legislation, activities, applications and systems existing within Parliaments and outside of them (in other branches of public administration or in the private sector, both profit and non-profit).

This is even more relevant today, in the age of web services (software systems designed to support interoperable machine to machine interaction over a network, according to the definition in W3C[7] where complex functions – rather than being executed by an integrated separate system, covering all aspects of them – will be provided by combining the performances of separate heterogeneous systems (agents) interacting according to shared protocols. In particular, as we shall emphasise later in this chapter, the issue of the management of legislative documents is not reduced to the issue of their storage and processing within Parliaments; it also includes the discussion of how such documents, after being produced by Parliaments, can become shared resources, whose decentralised and autonomous reuse can contribute to the ideal of an open Parliamentarian democracy.

The following pages will be devoted to the analysis of the evolution of legal information systems. First, we shall describe the achievements of the past and then we shall consider the current emerging trends.

A Short History of Legal Information Systems

In the present section we shall shortly describe the evolution of legal information systems in the past century, from its beginnings in the 50s until the emergence of

6 On the ability of democratic process to include the perspective of others, see R. Goodin, *Reflective Democracy* (Oxford: Oxford University Press, 2003).

7 For W3C, *Web Services Glossary: W3C Working Group Note*, 11 February 2004.

the Internet in the 90s, focusing on the issue of documents management.[8] Then we will consider the approaches currently debated, trying to discern an emergent evolutionary trend.

The beginnings The history of systems for dealing with legal information starts in the second half the 50s when the first application of computers in the legal domain was realised.[9] This was a systems developed at the Health Law Centre of the University of Pittsburgh, following a request by the legislator of Pennsylvania, dealing with a typical problem for legislative informatics, namely, textual amendments. The problem that this legislator had to solve was that of substituting in all State legislation the phrase 'retarded child' (which was seen as disrespectful) with the phrase 'exceptional child' Given that it appeared that performing this task manually (by having a team read all legislation and mark all occurrences of the words to be changed) would be not only costly but also unreliable, it was decided to transfer the legislation onto a magnetic tape (the only storage device available at that time) and then search for all occurrences of the string to be substituted. This was successfully done, but once the data were available on an electronic support, it appeared that searching for that particular string was not the only possibility: the tape could be searched for any textual string, to identify and retrieve the piece of legislation containing that textual string. In this way the first instance of electronic text retrieval in the legal domain was accomplished.

This example was soon followed by some entrepreneurial initiatives, aimed at providing computerised information services. At that time, obviously, what could be asked was just a printout of the texts containing the search terms, which were collected by a long search of the tape where the data were collected. No real time answer (and adjustment of the query) was possible.

The thesis: The remotely accessible centralised systems of the 60s and the 70s During the 60s a number of information retrieval systems for legal sources where created, both in Europe and in North America. In the United States such initiatives were mainly developed by private firms, while in Europe the initiative was mainly taken by public bodies, in particular inside public administration. The motivation behind such initiatives was the idea that legal sources had grown so much in quantity (in particular since the welfare state started to regulate minutely social benefits as well as economic activities) and were changing so quickly that only computers could effectively provide knowledge of the law.[10] Significant technological developments, taking place between the 60s and the 70s would provide the basis

8 Our account mainly relays on J. Bing, *Handbook of Legal Information Retrieval* (Amsterdam: North Holland, 1984) and J. Bing, 'The Policies of Legal Information Services: A Perspective of Three Decades.' in L.A. Bygrave (ed.) *Yulex 2003* (Oslo: Norwegian Research Centre for Computers and Law, 2003) pp. 37–55. For a comprehensive account of legal informatics, see P. Leith and A. Hoey, *The Computerised Lawyer* (London: Springer, 1998).

9 For a description of the beginning of legal informatics, see Bing (1984) ch. 6.

10 This idea was popularised in particular by S. Simitis, *Crisi dell'informazione giuridica ed elaborazione elettronica dei dati* (Milano: Giuffre, 1977).

for the successful development of legal information services: the availability of big disk memories, allowing much quicker access than tapes (and consequently enabling real time responses from automated information systems), and the integration of telecommunications with computing, which enabled remote access to information system (through telephone lines).

In those years in Europe various legal information systems were constructed. For example, in Italy in 1963–64 the Court of Cassation (Corte di Cassazione), the highest judge in matters dealing with civil and criminal cases, started a database of abstracts ('massime') of its own decisions, which grew progressively expanding to the State laws, administrative regulation, etc. (and still is the most extensive information systems available in Italy). Similar initiatives where taken in France by the Conseil d'Etat (the Supreme Judge in administrative cases), in Germany by the Ministry of Justice, in Sweden by the Directorate of Court administration, in Finland by the Supreme administrative court, in the EU by the legal service of the European Commission. In general the initiative for building such systems would not come from the legislature, but rather from the bodies interested in the application of the law, namely from the judiciary and from public administrations.

Though such systems started with the limited coverage (usually the decisions of particular courts), they tended to expand with further contents, and in particular with legislation and regulations. The emerging vision was indeed that of a single national legal information system, where all legal sources (legislation, precedents, regulations, treaties, etc.) would be electronically stored and made available for retrieval. This is the vision that seems to underlie the efforts of the 70s, a vision which, as we shall see in the following pages, a *thesis* that would soon change under the influence of technological development (we will describe the evolution of legal information systems as a sequence of theses, antitheses and synthesis, following the triadic pattern which characterises Hegel's philosophy, but this is just a presentation form, without any philosophical commitment).

At that time, computers were not yet used during the phase of document drafting (word-processing was not commonly available, so that the original documents were written on paper). Consequently, there was a complete separation between the preparation of legal documents and their subsequent storage in an information computer system (documents would have to be typed again in order to be made electronically available). Thus, Parliaments would be mere users of such systems (alongside other users). Parliament staff would make use of electronic information systems during the drafting phase, in order to access the relevant pieces of existing legislation. This would typically take place through a telephone line, which enabled the remote user to query the electronic legal database (residing in a big and costly computer, a so-called mainframe), to scroll the retrieved documents and possibly to print them. The users of such systems would not be able to reuse the retrieved electronic documents: the printouts would be delivered from a terminal linked to the remote database. As Bing observes, the only users of such systems were professional (judges, civil servants, lawyers and their assistants), while citizens could access them only in very limited, exceptional cases.[11]

11 See Bing (2003).

The systems described above had a mixed history of success or failure and only a few of them have survived today. In the USA, the publicly owned systems FLITE and JURIS died out, while the private providers Westlaw and Lexis have prospered and even expanded to other countries. In particular, Westlaw has become part of Thompson, a huge media company, which has also acquired Lawtel, the legal information system available on Prestel (pre-Internet British system for delivering online legal information). Similarly the independent systems existing in Britain or Australia did not survive. However, certain systems, such as the Italian service Italgiure-Find (provided by the Court of Cassation, in the early days of Italgiure)[12] or the Norwegian System Noris (managed by Lovdata, a private foundation established by the Ministry of Justice and the University of Oslo) are still continuing, progressively increasing their contents and their services.

The antithesis: The multiple isolated systems of the 1980s The personal computer (PC) was the invention that characterised the 80s, leading all of us into the information society. The PC enabled computing to enter all economical and social activities, and also all legal activities, from public administration, to the judiciary, to legislation and to private law practices. In the legal domain personal computers started being used mainly for word-processing, but this was soon followed by further applications, like accounting, filing and information retrieval. Though PCs could access remote databanks through a telephone line, the emphasis moved to applications directly available on the PC, whose facility of use and advanced interfaces users had learned to appreciate and which were not subjected to the costs and the delays of remote telephone services.

Consequently, legal documentation moved to the PC, where it could be independently used by individual users, thanks to the storage of legal databases on a new high capacity storage medium, the compact disk, which would be accessed through retrieval software residing on the PC. This technological change determined the entrance of new actors in the domain of electronic legal information, namely, private publishers who could sell legal databases through the existing channels available for the sale of books and journals (since legal databases were embodied in an easily tradable physical object, namely, the CD). In comparison to remote databanks, CDs were inferior with regard to the breadth of their coverage and the frequency of update (which required purchasing a new edition of the CD); however, they were highly superior with regard to ease of use and the integration with further legal materials. In fact, many publishers provided CDs merging the various materials at their disposal, namely, official texts and copyrighted doctrinal contributions illustrating the content of the latter. This anticipated the merge of different sources of legal knowledge which is now taking place in the new framework of the Internet.

One important implication of the office automation revolution of the 80s was the computerisation of the production of legal texts. At the most modest level this just involved using computers merely as advanced typewriters, but this had the effect that an electronic version of the legal text was available at the very time when the text was produced, without additional costs. Moreover, both the final document

12 See R. Borruso, *Civilta del computer* (Milano: IPSOA, 1978).

and all preliminary documents that had been produced during the procedure aimed at the creation and adoption of the final, legally binding, document were available in electronic form (the *travaux préparatoires* in a broad sense). This was the case for the various studies, drafts and opinions produced during the legislative process (and similarly for the various documents produced by the parties of a case and by the judge during a judicial procedure).

As a result using computers in the production of legal documents, an integration of the production of legal documents and their distribution in electronic form, became possible. This had different effects:

- it enlarged the range of documents which could be made available to the public: not only the final, legally binding acts, but also the documents produced at earlier stages;
- it enabled a strict connection between the procedures aimed at producing new law and the legal information systems: the procedure itself could deliver the electronic document and this document could be used within the same procedure (for its further steps) but also could be made available outside of it;
- it strengthened the role of legal authorities – the producers of the original legal texts – who could start distributing their own outputs electronically without the need for professional publishers.

Since legal authorities could themselves, with little additional cost, make the legal texts they produced accessible to the public, professional providers of electronic legal information (in particular private publishers) had to change their mission. They could no longer limit themselves to the provision of the bare legal sources but they needed to provide added value to their legal documents (comments, notes, doctrine, etc.) if they wanted to continue to play a significant (and economically rewarding) role in legal documentation.

The synthesis: the universally accessible but plural systems of the 1990s The synthesis between the thesis of the 70s (the construction of unitary national legal information systems including all legal sources and remotely accessibly by all) and the antithesis of the 80s (the distribution of multiple instances of multiple databanks to be used on individually accessible personal computers) was achieved in the 90s through the Internet revolution and in particular through the World Wide Web. The Internet resulted from (and contributed to) the integration of computing and telecommunications: by making distances irrelevant it enabled the virtual integration of resources resident on different computers; by supporting the seamless interaction of systems and application it enabled merging the services of different applications, interacting with different resources, into complex functionalities; and by making systems communicate it enabled communication between their users.

We can say that the Internet provided a synthesis between the unifying approach of the 70s and the separating approach of the 80s, since it allowed each one to access from a single point (namely the Internet itself) all legal information, while preserving (and even increasing) the diversity of such information.

One of the major effects of the Internet has indeed been the empowerment of individuals and groups. By drastically reducing the costs related to the production and public distribution of information the Internet has enabled individuals and groups to contribute actively to the production and the delivery of information, rather than being mere passive users of it.[13]

With regard to legal information we have recently seen an impressive and diverse richness of initiatives. As Bing observes,[14] we have 'a profusion of initiatives ... each court, each agency, each institution presented their own site to the public'. This increased supply of legal information presents the user which a tendency toward fragmentation: legal information is provided by different agencies and split in different sites but 'these sites often do not have standards for updating response, document design, retrieval strategies, etc.'

This puzzling diversity has increased by the fact that not only have institutions been providing legal information but private law firms too have started to upload legal information into the Web as a way to lure possible clients to their websites and inform them of the competence of the firm. Similarly, non-profit organisations have started to provide online legal information related to their activities.[15] So, multiple copies are now available online of many legislative Acts (especially the more frequently used Acts, such as regulations on privacy, contracts, intellectual property, rents, product liability, etc.) in a plurality of sites and in different formats.

Nor has the provision of legal information been limited to the reproduction of legal sources or, anyway, of documents produced by public authorities; it has been extended to comments on legal sources (news reports, political evaluations and academic analyses) and, more generally, legal doctrine. One of the richest sources of doctrinal information is the Social Science Research Network (www.ssrn.com), whose e-Library consists of two parts: an 'Abstract Database' containing abstracts on over 162,600 scholarly working papers and forthcoming papers, and an 'Electronic Paper Collection' currently containing about 130,000 downloadable full text documents in Adobe Acrobat (PDF) format, a large section of which is constituted by papers in legal doctrine.

In addition, we must consider the domain of legal blogs, which has rapidly become one of the richest sources of doctrinal information.[16] There are also many discussion groups devoted to legal issues and even websites devoted to the presentation–discussion–promotion of important legal topics.[17]

The Internet's synthesis has lead to an enormous growth of the body of legal information available to all – the shared *Jurisphere* – an expansion that has benefitted all legal researchers and many practitioners. However, finding the information we need in the Jurisphere is not an easy task: such information is to be extracted from

---

13 On this, see Y. Benkler, *The Wealth of Networks: How Social Production transforms Markets and Freems* (New Haven, CT: Yale University Press, 2006).

14 See J. Bling (2003).

15 See the various legal sources on human rights, available at (www.amnesty.org).

16 See (www.becker-posner-blog.com) where two leading legal academics address current legal and political issues.

17 See (www.nosoftwarepatents.com/en/m/intro/index.html) on software patents.

a huge and diverse collection of materials, dispersed in multiple sites which have different standards of document design, kinds of material, level of accuracy, retrieval and update strategy. Typically we use one of the generally available search engines and find all texts containing certain words or combinations of words, ordered according to their relevance (on the basis of the relevance algorithm used by the search engine). Usually the output would be a very large list of documents, but such a result would just represent the beginning of our inquiry: we would have to browse through the retrieved documents, checking for their relevance with regard to our objective and for the reliability of their source.

Even after solving the problem of *noise* (false positives, namely the retrieval of irrelevant documents), we would still have to solve the problem of *silence* (false negatives, namely, failure to retrieve relevant documents), which is only partially addressed by the richness of the documentation available. In fact the documents that can be automatically retrieved remain limited to those containing the words in the user query. For addressing this problem we would need an advanced search, able to map the user query to the documents that, using whatever linguistic form, express information relevant to the user. Moreover, some further documents are relevant by their relation to documents pertaining to the users' query (consider, for instance, laws modifying, abrogating or suspending the documents which deal with the users' interests).

Finally, even when the users retrieve the document most relevant to their interests, unless they are assisted by advanced legal information systems, they still have the task of combining the different bits of information (possibly contained in different documents) pertinent to their problem (i.e. they would have to construct the law in force by mentally performing all the required textual modifications).

Legal information institutes The Internet, besides enabling anyone to add his or her bit of information to the available 'legal–knowledge soup' – by republishing existing sources (possibly in new combinations), producing new versions of existing sources (for instance, consolidated texts) or adding original comments or doctrinal contributions – has also enabled new actors to engage in the construction of broadly scoped legal information systems. This is the case in particular for Legal Information Institutes (LII), namely, independent bodies aimed at providing free access on a non-profit basis to multiple sources of legal information, originating from multiple public bodies (see www.worldlii.org/).

The activity of such institutes is based upon the idea that all legal limitations to the duplication of legal information (as deriving in particular from the so-called Crown Copyright which State entities traditionally have in Commonwealth countries over official documents), should be overcome, as it is affirmed in their joint 'Declaration on Free Access to Law', which states the following principles:[18]

- Public legal information from all countries and international institutions is part of the common heritage of humanity. Maximising access to this information promotes justice and the rule of law.

18 See, Free Access to Law Movement, 'Declaration on Free Access to Law', 2004.

- Public legal information is digital common property and should be accessible to all on a non-profit basis and free of charge.
- Independent non-profit organisations have the right to publish public legal information and the government bodies that create or control that information should provide access to it so that it can be published.

According to the same declaration, public legal information is defined as follows:

> Public legal information means legal information produced by public bodies that have a duty to produce law and make it public. It includes primary sources of law, such as legislation, case law and treaties, as well as various secondary (interpretative) public sources, such as reports on preparatory work and law reform, and resulting from boards of inquiry. It also includes legal documents created as a result of public funding.

The experience of the Legal Information Institutes started in 1992, when the Legal Information Institute of Cornell Law School (www.law.cornell.edu) was launched by Peter Martin and Tom Bruce. One aspect of the vision of legal research institutes, which strongly distinguished it from all previous initiative in legal documentation, consists in the purpose of extending electronic access to the law for outside professional users. As Peter Martin puts it:[19]

> One of our powerful early discoveries was how much demand outside those professional sectors there was, ordinary citizens trying to make sense of laws that impinge on their lives.

Cornell's initiative (which covers now codes, federal laws, decisions by the Supreme Court and by the New York Court of Appeal and many further collections of legal materials) was followed by the creation of other similar institutes in many countries. In particular, the Australasian legal information institute (www.austlii.edu.au) has been particularly successful[20] and has represented the model for further initiatives in various countries, like Canada, the UK and South Africa. A World Legal Information Institute has also been established, which provides an access point to the collections of various Legal Information Institutes, containing 865 databases from 123 countries and territories.

Bing (2003) observes that legal information institutes provide a useful service in contributing to make original legal sources available to both legal professionals and lay citizens, as required by the idea of *publicatio legis* (the idea that the law should become binding only after being made available to all) an idea which is related to fundamental principles such as those of legal certainty and democracy. However, according to Bing, such institutes must now face two problems. First, it may be contested that knowledge of the law can be ensured effectively by providing citizens with the original texts. Lay citizens would rather need '... a problem-

19 Cited from J. Bing (2003).

20 See G. Greenleaf, G. Mowbray, King, and P. van Dijk, *Public access to law via internet* (The Australasian Legal Information Institute, 2002).

oriented gateway to the material, where the authentic instruments are commented and explained'. Second, as we have observed above, the function of providing the original texts tends to be assumed directly by public bodies. Such bodies can build their electronic repositories as a (almost) costless by-product of using ICT for the purposes of drafting and workflow management, which enables them to provide free generalised access to their sources without the mediation of a third party.

The Dialectics of Current Approaches

Different trends and different models can be anticipated for legal information systems in the framework of the Internet synthesis later in this chapter. We will distinguish two main approaches, again a thesis and an antithesis:

- the thesis (presented in the next section) consist of a newly conceived centralised and comprehensive public legal information system, integrated with the management of legislative (and judicial) procedures, and using the Internet for dissemination;
- the antithesis consists of the decentralised non-governmental development of legal information systems and services on the basis of the public availability of electronic legal documents.

We shall then argue that a synthesis of these two models is currently emerging, where independently prepared and managed legislative information is unified through the use of shared standards.

A new thesis A centralised legal information system for the Internet age This thesis is clearly presented by Jon Bing,[21] who argues that the way ahead in legal documentation is represented by the move from retrieval into regulatory management. This requires adopting a different view of the services to be provided by legal information systems, a view that is not restricted to their being used for conducting legal research (for retrieving stored documents) but which also includes their use in the preparation of new regulations (drafting, reviewing, amending, etc.) and in the application of such regulations (by judges and administration).

This approach, he argues, is mostly appropriate for developing countries, which are not – like the North American or European jurisdictions – 'seeped in traditions and established arrangements, where the new computerised service has to find its place among legal publishers of primary and secondary sources, legal gazettes, and other well established practises'. Such an integrated system should cater for the need of different users: the legislator, the administration, the judiciary and private lawyers, as well as the common citizen (to the extent in which the latter may be content with the legal sources).

According to Bing's vision the core of such a system should consist of a mother database, containing all documents, marked according to the same markup

21 See J. Bing and M.G. Schoenberg, *Improving Regulatory Management: The Use of Information Systems* (NORIS (96) II, Fourth version, 1994); also see Bing (2003).

language.[22] Such a database should be prepared and updated through a centralised editorial process which controls the input documents, normalises them, and gives them the appropriate format (see Figure 18.3).

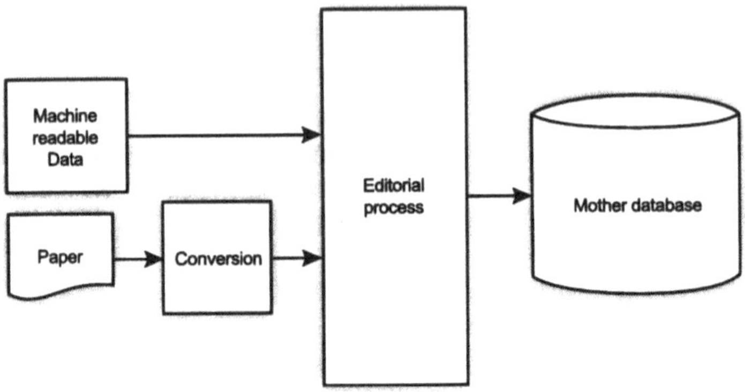

Figure 18.3 Jon Bing: the production of a mother database

From the mother database different outputs in different format should be produced (see Figure 18.4).

In particular, the mother database should deliver the following outputs: a *status* database (a database that provides the law in force, and offers high performance to professional users), a legal gazette with the new legislation, compilations of the law in force and freely accessible text for Internet browsing.

Note that in many jurisdictions, a gazette in electronic form is already published together with the gazette in paper form. Given that electronic text can be delivered immediately and without cost, the electronic gazette is gradually substituting the paper version as the main reference for professional lawyers and for ordinary citizens. This fact has been officially recognised in some countries, for example Norway or Austria, where the electronic publication already represents the original legal text. In Austria, in particular, the federal Constitution has been changed in order that the official gazette be constituted by the text published online in Austrian legal information systems[23] a text which has been digitally signed by the Federal Chancellery.

A new antithesis: Access to distributed legal resources The antithesis to Bing's centralised solution (universal access to a central official legal database) is the

22 Bing considers a markup based on SGML (Standard Generalized Markup Language), a metalanguage for defining markup languages for documents. Now SGML has been almost completely substituted by XML, a simplified rework of it.

23 See: (www.ris1.bka.gv.at/authentic/index.aspx).

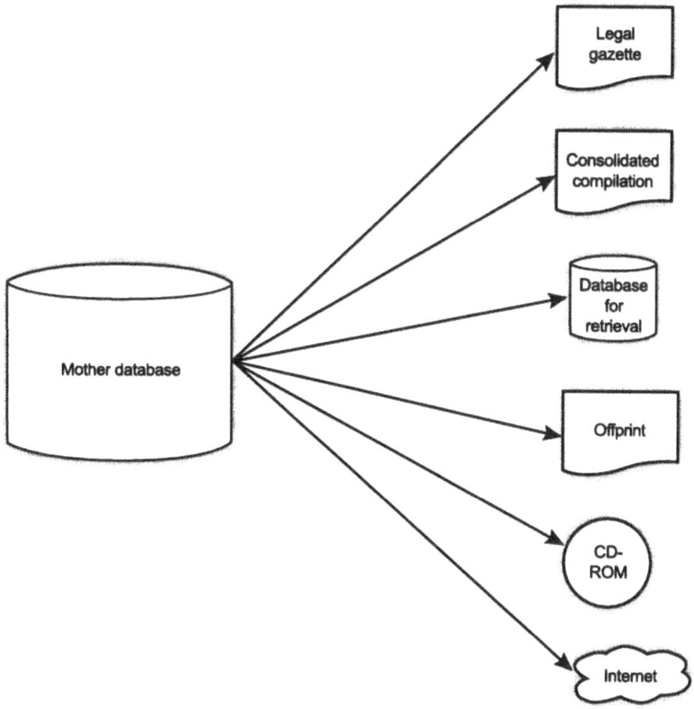

Figure 18.4 Jon Bing: the outputs of the mother database

provision of one or more universal access points to distributed legal resources. Such resources will reside in the information systems of the authorities creating the stored legal texts, but different content providers (public or private, profit or non-profit) will provide access to them, either by building an index to such resources or by also copying them to a central repository. In this model the Internet provides both the channels through which information is extracted from the distributed original databases and the channel through which the user accesses such information, as you can see in Figure 18.5.

The latter view is advocated by Graham Greenleaf, one of the leaders of the Legal Information Institutes movements, according to whom the centralised solution proposed by Bing may be adequate to a certain context (small countries having an efficient, homogeneous and integrated public systems, e.g. the Scandinavian ones) but it is not appropriate for coping with large, heterogeneous and diversified contexts. For legal systems fitting within the latter profile (and for integrating different legal systems), only a decentralised architecture can work.

Greenleaf argues that for achieving adequate provision of legal information it is not necessary that public authorities provide directly a service covering all possible needs: such needs can also be covered in different ways, by different providers, among which an important role can be vested to the Legal Information Institutes.

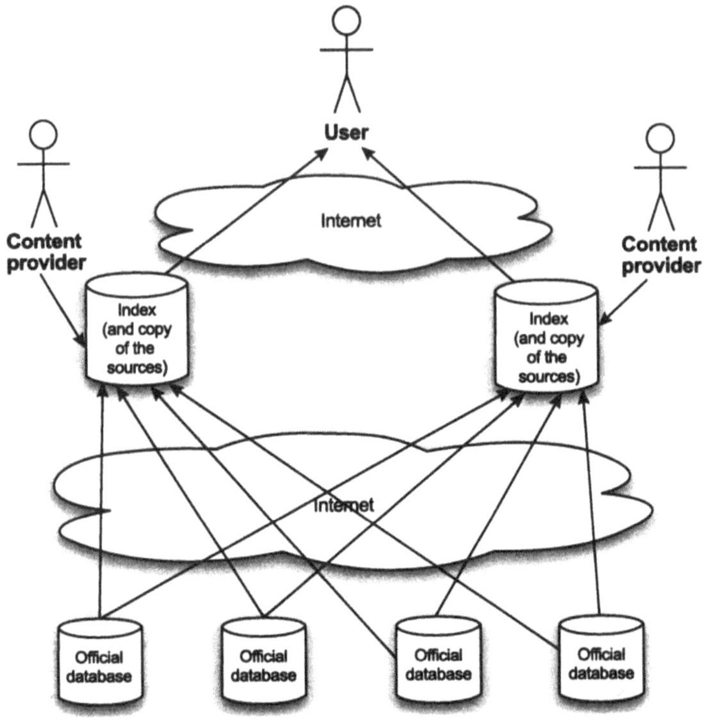

Figure 18.5 Providing information from distributed legal databases

Public authorities are rather required to comply with the obligation to provide 'free full access to the law' by which he means the obligation of the legislator (as on any other producer of legally binding documents) to provide 'free access to the computerised sources of legal data to those who wish to publish it'.[24] More specifically, according to the philosophy of the Legal Information Institutes, legal authorities have the obligation to make available legal information in such a way that the provision satisfies the following requirements:[25]

- Provision in a completed form, including additional information best provided at source, such as the consolidation of legislation, and the addition of catch words (index terms) or even summaries to cases.
- Provision in an authoritative form, such as use or court-designated citations for cases and (eventually) use of digital signature to authenticate the versions distributed.
- Provision in the form best facilitating dissemination, which should always now mean in electronic form, should in most cases be possible by e-mail or

24 See G. Greenleaf, 'Jon Bing and the History of Computerised Legal Research: Some Missing Links' in O. Torvund and L.A. Bygrave (eds) *Et tilbakeblikk pa Fremtiden* (Institutt for rettsinformatikk, 2004) pp. 61–75.

25 See ibid. at 69.

more sophisticated form of data delivery, and should be possible in a form facilitating conversion.

- Provision on a marginal cost recovery basis to anyone, so that governments do not attempt to profit from the sale of public legal information, thereby creating artificial barriers to access to law.
- Provision with no reuse restrictions or licence fees, subject only to such minimal restrictions as are necessary to preserve the integrity of published data.
- Preservation of a copy in the care of the public authority, so that an archive of the data is preserved to enable greater competition whenever a new entrant wishes to publish the date and whether or not the public authority publishes the data itself.
- Non-discriminatory recognition of citations, so that court-designated citations are not removed from 'reported' cases, ending the privileged status of citations of 'official' reports.

Once public authorities have made legal texts accessible in this way, they can rely on non-governmental actors for distributing and enriching the legal information (or can intervene by supporting the operation of such actors, rather than directly).

Greenleaf also observes that nowadays the task of collecting different sources into a distributed unique database does not necessary require an editorial process, but can be performed automatically by spiders or web-robots (also called crawlers) which can peruse the Web indexing all relevant sites, and that the 'noise' in information retrieval can be reduced by using relevance ranking as performed in leading search engines, such as Google.

A new synthesis: Standard-based legal information in the jurisphere Both approaches just described present significant advantages. The model of the unique official mother database is based upon the idea that all legal sources should be stored in a uniform format, according to a consistent editing procedure and that such sources should include all machine processable information needed to support subsequent multiple uses. Consequently, it seems capable of providing significant advantages:

- Reliability of (and consequently trust on) legal information would be ensured, since such information would always be extracted from the official database.
- Formal coherence of the different legal sources and of their formats would be achieved (for instance, in the way of expressing references) since all of them would result from the same repository.
- Noise in information retrieval would be reduced, since only the official database could be searched (rather than the multiple overlapping repositories now available over the Internet).
- No strong technological requirement would be put on the drafters of legal sources, who could just use ordinary word-processing tools, since the texts would to be structured and enriched with metadata only at the moment of their transfer into the mother database.

Also the idea of extracting information from distributed legal databases – and more generally, from distributed repositories of legal sources, possibly managed by the same authorities who have adopted the stored normative Acts – has distinctive advantages:

- It would enable a diversified and competitive provision of legal documents.
- It would facilitate the integration between legal procedures and the provision of legal information (each producer of normative Act would deliver to the public the documents in the same electronic form they had when resulting from the procedure leading to their adoption).
- It would provide decentralisation and autonomy, since each (kind of) authority would be able to organise its document management system according to its needs, possibly enriching it with additional services (e.g. a point in time legislative database), and tailoring it to the needs of its users.

Fortunately we are not facing here a tragic choice between the two approaches just presented, namely, a choice where the adoption of one approach would entail loosing the advantages of the other: recently a synthesis has emerged that is able to preserve the advantages of both approaches. This synthesis is based on the decentralised production of electronic legal (and in particular, legislative) documents according to shared standards. Thus, the unifying aspect no longer relates to the creation of a unique database, or a uniform editorial activity, but rather in the adoption of a common standard specifying how legislative and other legal documents are to be given unique names and how they can be enriched with machine processable data specifying their structure, indicating their links and describing their content. The standard should provide ways of expressing the structural elements of the text (articles/sections, subsection, chapters, titles, etc.) as well as references and modifications (so that, in particular, the text of the law in force can be automatically constructed).[26] Moreover, the standard should be expandable so that further components can be accommodated in it, if required by further applications (e.g. for checking the logical consistency of the norms expressed by the text, for analysing the ontology of the concepts it uses, and so on).

According to this vision, standard compliant legal documents, produced by different entities, but primarily by the bodies adopting such documents, can be stored in distributed or centralised databases, can be drafted and processed using the same standard compliant software, can be reused by any person or system (knowledgeable of the same standard) and can be enriched by adding further information and ways of processing it. In this way the users interested could be

26 See M. Palmirani and R. Brigh, 'Time Model for Managing the Dynamic of Normative System' in M. Wimmer, H.J. Scholl, E. Grunlund and K.V. Andersen (eds), *Electronic Government*, 5th International Conference, EGOV 2006, Krakow, Poland, 4–8 September, (London: Springer, 2006) pp. 207–18; also see G. Governatori, A. Rotolo, R. Riveret, M. Palmirani and G. Sarto, 'Variants of temporal defeasible logics for modelling norm modifications' in *Proceedings of Eleventh International Conference on Artificial Intelligence and Law* (New York: ACM, 2007) pp. 155–9.

provided with new derived legislative works, which could be constructed by the parliamentary offices or by third parties using the legislative materials. For instance, texts could be expanded with doctrinal comments or semantic metadata or even with a machine processable representation of concepts and norms.[27] However, the official instances of such documents will remain distinguishable and their content (both the text and the originally added machine processable information) will be controllable and reliable.

Standard-based management of legislative documents The Norme in rete *example* One significant (though still at an early stage) example of what can be achieved by a standard-based approach to the management of legislative documents is constituted by the Italian project *Norme in Rete.* On the basis of the definition, a common standard for legislative documents, a federated system has been developed based on a distributed model involving all bodies which adopt normative Acts: Parliament, government and ministries, authorities, local autonomies.

In this model each public administration is supposed to store its document in a separate database, but to structure such documents according to the shared standard and to make them accessible to centralised retrieval facilities. The central indexes are built automatically, by web spiders visiting the sites of the federated authorities (Figure 18.6 represents the architecture of the system).

Note that in a first phase of the project the involvement of the Italian Parliament has been limited: Italian laws, when approved by both chambers, are promulgated by the President of the Republic, and then published under the responsibility of the Minister of Justice. The final text is provided by the database of the Court of Cassation (managed by the Ministry of Justice), as well as by the official journal. In the future, however, a stronger parliamentary involvement is being considered:

- the text of the Acts approved by the Parliament (and transmitted to the President of the Republic for promulgation) must already contain all structural information and the metadata that are available at that stage (obviously data about subsequent activities, such as the promulgation of the document can only be provided after such activities have take place);
- the Parliament should make available to the public all documents produced during the procedure leading to the approval of legislative Acts.

Note that in such a model no editorial intervention is considered, since it is assumed that new documents will be provided by the normative institutions in a standard compliant format and that all software dealing with such documents (for

27 Which could then be applied with the support of a knowledge-based system, see, for instance, S. Dayal and P. Johnson, 'A Web-based Revolution in Australian Public Administration, in Proceedings Law via the Internet '99' *2nd AustLII Conference on Computerisation of Law via the Internet* (Sydney: University of Technology, 1999); for a general discussion on the formal representation of legal contents, see G. Sartor 'Legal Reasoning: A Cognitive Approach to the Law' *Treatise on Legal Philosophy and General Jurisprudence*, vol. 5, (Berlin: Springer, 2005).

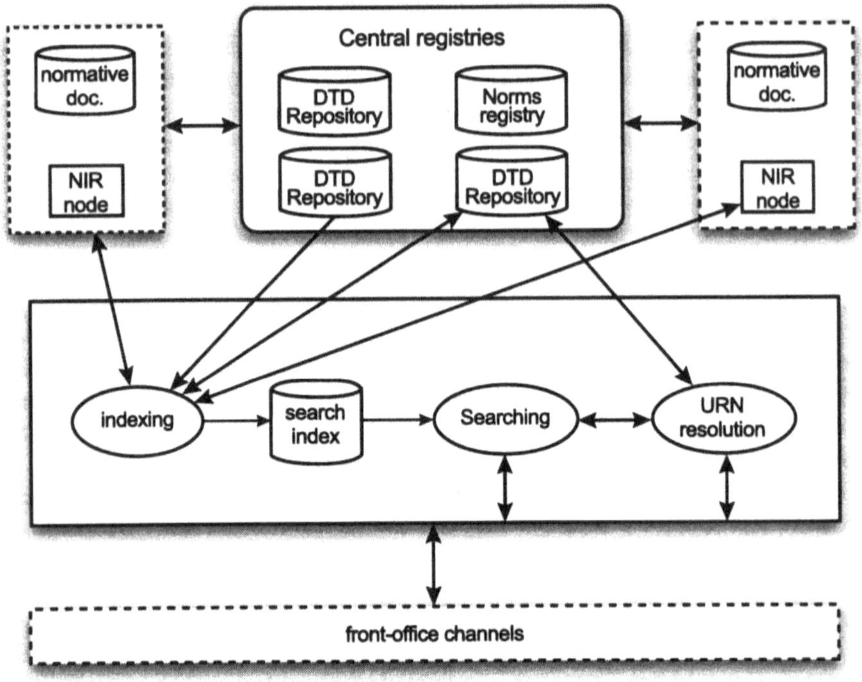

Figure 18.6 The cooperative architecture of '*Norme in Rete*' (adapted from slides by Caterina Lupo)

drafting, for managing their workflow, for their storage, for their retrieval, for their further processing) will take the standard into account. It is assumed, on the contrary, that the very availability of a common standard will be a decisive factor favouring the development of software tools enabling the preparation of documents from the start in a standard compliant form. Figure 18.7 shows the expected final outcome of the *Norme in Rete* project.

Currently besides setting up this new framework for new legislation (a framework which is partially at work, see www.normeinrete.it) existing legal documents are edited, with the support of automated tools, in order to set them in the appropriate format and make them available in standard compliant databases.

Interestingly, the project is committed to providing information to the public and to making normative documents, in the required format, available to publishers and other third parties so that such documents can be reused and further distributed. According to this idea there is no State monopoly on legal information; on the contrary the provision of legal information to the public is open to the contribution of non-governmental profit and non-profit institutions (such institution while aiming at their legitimate commercial or non-commercial purposes also contribute to the common objective of increasing the knowledge of the law). This is indeed what is required by the European discipline on reuse of public information of Directive 2003/98/EC, which requires (article 5) that:

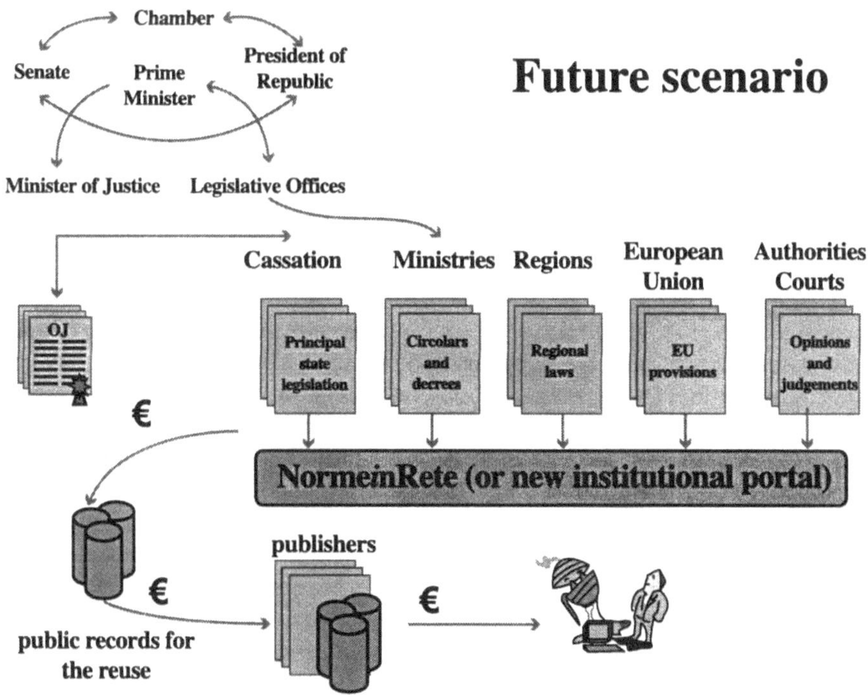

Figure 18.7 The '*Norme in Rete*' distributed model

> Public sector bodies shall make their documents available in any pre-existing format or language, through electronic means where possible and appropriate ... Where charges are made, the total income from supplying and allowing re-use of documents shall not exceed the cost of collection, production, reproduction and dissemination. [28]

As a matter of fact, a double channel to distribute publicly legal documents is emerging in Italy:

- on the one hand, the *Norme in Rete* portal offers central access to the distributed databases of the different authorities;
- on the other hand, all such document are reproduced in the central database held at the Italian Corte di Cassazione.

The latter database has in fact evolved into accepting the *Norme in Rete* standard. This is respected by the new documents being inputted into the Cassazione-database, and old documents are being reformatted (and supplemented with the required meta information) so that they comply with *Norme in Rete*. In fact, in the Internet framework (where the physical location of digital objects is irrelevant, all

28 See Directive 2003/98/EC of the European Parliament and of the Council of 17 November 2003 on the re-use of public sector information, OJ L 345, 31 December 2003 at 94.

of them being instantaneously accessible) it does not really matter whether legal documents are (only) retrieved from distributed databases or whether they are retrieved (alternatively or additionally) from a central databank. What matters is that the official version of such documents (including the required machine processable information complementing the raw text) is provided by the competent authority, according to an agreed upon standard, and that such texts are made available for retrieval from a central facility, as well as for further processing by any entities that may be interested in doing so.

Standard-based management of legislative documents The AKOMA-NTOSO example The *Norme in Rete* project is just one instance of the many projects centred upon standards for legislative documents. Here we just need to observe that besides national projects some international projects aimed at standardising the format of legal documents (while respecting national traditions concerning the drafting and the presentation of such documents) have been undertaken. By providing an internationally agreed standard such projects contribute to results that would not be obtainable on the basis of merely national standards, namely, supporting the exchange of legal information at a transnational level, and creating competitive transnational markets for standard-based software products.

Among the international projects we can mention the AKOMA-NTOSO project,[29] which building on the basis of the most advanced experiences existing worldwide has been developing a standard for legislative documents for Africa, and is supporting the use of such a standard with a legal drafting methodology and with the provisions of a system for supporting legislative activities (Bungeni). AKOMA-NTOSO does not only only provide an XML standard for legislative Acts, it also provides for documentation, legislative reports and debate reports (Hansard). Moreover a standard for judicial precedents is also being defined. Here is how the AKOMA-NTOSO model is described:[30]

- The AKOMA-NTOSO model has been informed by the following strategic goals:
- To create a 'lingua franca' for the interchange of parliamentary, legislative and judiciary documents between institutions in Africa. For example, Parliament/court *X* should be able to easily import a piece of legislation made available in AKOMA-NTOSO format by Parliament/court *Y*. The goal here is to speed up the process of drafting new legislation/writing sentences/etc. by reducing the amount of rekeying, reformatting, etc. required.
- To provide a long-term storage and access format to parliamentary, legislative and judiciary documents that allow search, interpretation and visualisation of such documents several years from now, even in the absence of the specific applications and technologies that were used to generate them.

29 See F. Vitali and F. Zeni, 'Towards a Country-Independent Data Format: The Akoma Ntoso Experience' Proceedings of the *V Legislative XML Workshop* (European Press Academic Publishing, 2007) pp. 67–86.

30 See (www.akomantoso.org).

- To provide an implementable baseline for parliamentary, legislative and judiciary systems in African institutions. It is envisaged that this will lead to one or more systems that provide a base layer of software 'out of the box' that can then be customised to local needs. The goals here are two-fold. First, to facilitate the process of introducing IT into African institutions. Second, to reduce the amount of reinvention of the wheel that would result if all institutions pursued separate IT initiatives in the area of parliamentary, legislative and judiciary document production and management.
- To create common data and metadata models so that information retrieval tools and techniques used in Parliament/court *X* can be also be used in Parliament/court *Y*. To take a simple example, it should be possible to search across the document repositories of multiple Parliaments/courts in a consistent and effective way.
- To create common resource naming and resource linking models so that documents produced by Parliaments/courts can be easily cited and cross-referenced either by other Parliaments/courts or by other users.
- To be 'self-explanatory', that is to be able to provide all information for their use and meaning through a simple examination, even without the aid of specialised software.
- To be 'extensible', that is it must be possible to allow local customisations to the models within the AKOMA-NTOSO framework so that local customisation can be achieved without sacrificing interoperability with other systems.

Another international project deserving particular attention is lex[31] which, unlike AKOMA-NTOSO, does not aim at directly providing a standard for legislative documents, but aims instead to provide a way of mapping different standards, so as to support the interchange of legislative materials. Lex has been integrated, in the framework of the Estrella project, with LKIF, a proposed set of standards for dealing with legal contents, namely norms and ontologies.[32]

Conclusions

In the information society, Parliaments need ICT to be able to properly discharge their function. Legislative information systems must meet the challenges of our time, such as the necessity to cope with the increase in quantity and complexity of legislative texts and with their accelerated change, but also the needs to enhance the quantity and quality of information available to legislators, to make legislative processes more transparent and open to citizens' participation, and to enable experts

31 See A. Boer, R. Hoekstra and R. Winkels, 'MetaLex: Legislation in XML' in Proceedings of JURIX 2002 (Legal Knowledge and Information System, 2002) pp. 1–10.

32 See T.F. Gordon 'Constructing Arguments with a Computational Model of an Argumentation Scheme for Legal Rules' Proceedings of the Eleventh International Conference on Artificial Intelligence and Law (ICAIL–2007) pp. 117–21; A. Boer, R. Winkels and F. Vitali 'XML Standards for Law: MetaLex and LKIF' in *Proceedings of JURIX 2007* (Amsterdam: IOS, 2007).

and interested parties to contribute their knowledge and their perspectives to the discussion of regulatory problems. Finally, as international interdependence grows, problems become more complex, but also common to different countries: on the one hand, the same problems (e.g. regulation of ICTs or biotechnologies) appear in different countries, and on the other hand, there are problems transcending the borders of a single country (e.g. environmental protection). This requires sharing legislative information, for comparing legislative solutions and identifying best practices but also to coordinate efforts for addressing global issues.

Though the functions of legislative information systems cannot be limited to the production and management of documents, a central feature of a parliamentary information systems consists indeed in its ability to manage legislative documents. These documents are not limited to the legally binding normative Acts adopted by Parliaments, but also include all preliminary materials produced during the legislative process.

The evolution of legislative information systems shows some emerging trends:

- a comprehensive digital management of legislative documents, which concerns all documents produced during the legislative process;
- the integration of digital documents into the legislative process, where such digital documents result from, and contribute to, the management of the legislative workflow;
- the opening of the legislative information system to society, where documents produced in the legislative process are made available to public access, and documents resulting from public debate and interventions are inputted into the legislative process;
- a diversified provision of legal information, where legislative documents are seen as a common societal resource to be distributed and reused in diversified ways, by public and private, profit and non-profit actors;
- the move toward the semantic Web, namely, the enrichment of documents with machine processable information, which can facilitate access to and use of legislative document in unprecedented ways.

We have argued that the way forward is in standard-based open access to legislative documents, namely, in establishing a shared, open standard for legislative documents, so that these documents can be enriched with machine processable information usable by any computer system and any standard compliant software. We have also argued that this information – covering the structure of the document and its identification, its description, its links, its lifecycle and aspects of its content – should be represented using the resources provided by the semantic Web (such as, in particular, the metalanguage XML) and it should concern all documents produced during the legislative process.

Once such a standard is defined, a set of compliant tools needs to be developed, for assisting the preparation and the revision of standard compliant documents but also the management of their workflow, as well as their subsequent distribution and reuse. Some of these tools need to be used inside the Parliament, but their development need not be performed in-house, since the use of a shared standard (common to multiple legislative assemblies, possibly of different countries) will support the creation of a wide enough competitive market. Moreover, the openness of the standard enables other actors to reuse and redistribute (possibly with added information) standard compliant documents, subsequently contributing to the knowledge of the law and to participation in the legislative process.

Chapter 19

Between Policy and Implementation: Legislative Drafting for Development[1]

Ann Seidman and Robert B. Seidman

A moth flutters up to the Wise Old Owl. 'Owl,' she says, plaintively. 'The Fall nights are already cold, and getting colder. Winter comes apace. I know I shall not live through that cold, dark winter – unless you help me. Oh, tell me, Wise Old Owl, what shall I do? Help me!'

WOO answers in a wise, old voice: 'Child, that is not a problem. Turn yourself into a bee, and hibernate through the long winter months.'

The moth stops sobbing, sighs with relief, and turns away. Suddenly she flutters back, and speaks again. 'Wise Old Owl, *how* do I turn myself into a bee?'

WOO looks down at her for a moment, wisely, then shrugs, and answers: 'Ask the implementation guys. *I* do Policy.'

Introduction

Everywhere one goes, and nowhere more often than in the developing world, one hears a common complaint, 'We have good laws, but they are poorly implemented.' Relating to Law and Development, scholars study two roles: those who specify the objectives of legislation, and those who carry out the commands of the law – the 'implementing guys'.[2] Only rarely do they study the role of those who translate the law's generalised objectives into detailed legislative prescriptions – that is, broadly conceived, that of the legislative drafter.

This chapter discusses three themes relating to the drafter's role: (1) the design of the detailed substantive rules that 'bridge the gap' between policymakers and with 'boots-in-the-mud' tasks of implementing policy; (2) a legislative theory and methodology to guide drafters in designing rules likely to prove effectively

1 Many thanks to Professor Wendy Gordon for a perceptive and very useful critique of this chapter; and to Matthew Decker, for thoughtful and expert research assistance, and useful substantive comments.

2 See Epigraph.

implemented with the desired social impact;[3] and, (3) theoretical problems that require further scholarship.

An early effort to use law for development exemplifies the policy–implementation gap:

> In the early years of Soviet rule in Central Asia, the ruling Party – which viewed women in Central Asia as a potential 'surrogate proletariat' -- attempted to use legislation to 'liberate' them from gender-related religious exploitation. They enacted swingeing legislation abolishing the marks and signs of male oppression, including the Koran's requirement that women wear a veil. To symbolize feminine liberation, the Party orchestrated mass unveilings in Central Asian cities. In Central Asia in those days, many men believed that, by unveiling, a woman dishonors the family and demonstrates her own loose morals. Husbands, fathers and brothers cast wives, daughters and sisters out of the family. Some, having no other means to survive, became prostitutes.[4]

Those early Soviet efforts typify many attempts to use law to transform underdeveloped societies.[5] 'Policy' usually specifies a proposed law's broad objectives. Various officials and ordinary citizens – the 'implementing guys' – together perform the detailed tasks required to achieve those objectives. To the extent that the law's detailed provisions in practice grant them discretion, the 'implementing guys' decide how to implement them. Too frequently, they do no better than did those early Central Asian Soviet lawmakers.

Most current Law and Development literature focuses on aiding our understanding of the relationship between 'Law' and 'Development'[6] – a valid and worthwhile scholarly effort. This chapter, however, urges scholars to study the practice of the

3 In this chapter, a bill *works* if (a) it actually induces its prescribed behaviours, and (b) those behaviours actually ameliorate the targeted social problem.

4 See G.J. Masell 'Law as an Instrument of Revolutionary Change in a Traditional Milieu' 2 (1968) *Law and Society Review* at 179.

5 The Soviet Central Asian experiment serves as a metaphor for many analogous legal disasters. Two examples: After some 55 years of operations, the Guyanan Forestry Commission had paid no money into the Guyanese treasury, and was $300.000.000 in debt (See A. and R.B. Seidman 'Report of a Two Week Workshop in Guyana' (2004) accessed at (www.iclad-law.org). After nationalising its copper mines, and massive losses, Zambia reprivatised the mines (See L. Ng'andwe 'Justifying a Bill to Establish a Law and Integrated Commission in Zambia: A Research Report' in A. Seidman, R.B. Seidman, P. Mbana and H. Li (eds) *Africa's Challenge: Using Law for Good Governance and Development* (Africa: World Press Books, 2006). In these (and many other) cases, a principal explanation for the relevant law's failure to bring about the desired change consisted of the failure of the drafter to design the bill's substantive details adequately – that is, to 'fill the gap'.

6 See D.M. Trubek and A. Sanchez (eds) *The New Law and Economic Development: A Critical Appraisal* (Cambridge: Cambridge University Press, 2006); (J. Hatchard and A. Perry-Kessaris (eds) *Law and Development: Facing Complexity in the 21st Century* (London: Cavendish, 2003); L. Nader 'Promise or Plunder? A Past and Future Look at Law and Development X' 7 *Global Jurist* Article 1, available at (www.bepress.com/gj/iss2/art1).

legislative *drafters,* who design and write proposed laws, and thus purport to fill the policy–implementation gap.[7]

Everywhere, the legal academy focuses primarily on the *judicial* function.[8] *Per contra,* the newly discovered philosophy of 'Legisprudence' focuses attention on issues in the processes of making and implementing *legislation.*[9] In this 'legisprudential' vein, this chapter centres attention on the design and drafting of detailed rules to translate policymakers' large ideas into effective legislation that *works.*[10] Those rules must effectively bridge the gap between policy and implementation. Without a theory to guide the *design* of transformatory legislation, drafters impose limits on the development project – too often, unknowingly.

Preliminarily, this chapter's Part I explains the importance of law in the development process. It briefly reviews the naysayers' objections. These scholars contest the proposition that law can and should serve as an instrument to achieve the deliberate social, political or economic change required for people-oriented 'development'. Part II describes the key role that drafters must play in *designing* the substantive details of a bill to bridge the gap between a policy's broad objectives and the detailed behaviours of those who seek to implement that policy. Part III describes how institutionalist legislative theory and its problem-solving methodology can serve to guide the design and drafting of legislation. Especially in conditions of development, such a guide makes it more probable that a bill will *work.* Part IV raises six theoretical problems that call for a solution.

This chapter concludes by proposing a conception of Law and Development and an agenda for further 'legisprudential' scholarship. That conception focuses on the instrumental use of law to create productive employment opportunities, reduce vulnerability, and improve governance and the quality of life of the 80 per cent of the world's population who still struggle for bare survival on a fifth of the world's global income. In Law and Development scholarship, study of the processes of designing and drafting legislation, and strengthening legislative theory to guide that practice, should hold pride of place.

Preliminarily, this chapter considers the use of legislation as an instrument of social change.

---

7 See *Accord:* P. Westerman 'Governing by Goals: Governance as a Legal Style' (2007) 1 *Legisprudence* pp. 51, 53 ('If we want to understand the products – the rules and principles that form the material of both the practising lawyer and the legal scholar – and if we want to understand the various ways – formal and informal – in which they can affect our lives and decisions, we should also understand the process that has helped to form those products.')

8 See L.J. Wintgens (ed.) *The Theory and Practice of Legislation: Essays in Legisprudence* (Aldershot: Ashgate, 2005).

9 See Westerman (2007) at 52 ('The prevailing attitude of most legal scholars or students of legal theory is to regard policy-making … and governing … as activities that should be kept separate from law. Lawyers deal with the product, not the process that precedes it.')

10 See note 3.

Part I: Using Legislation to Solve Social Problems

Why governments everywhere seek to use law for social change

Everywhere, to help resolve social problems, governments seek to exercise State power through law.[11] In the developing world, they do so primarily to change the way inherited institutions perpetuate external dependence and poverty.

The word 'institution' has many different definitions.[12] All include repetitive patterns of social behaviours. Its institutions define a society: its schools, banks, families, hospitals, sports clubs, courts, legislatures, prisons, and on and on. To describe a society, describe its *patterns of repetitive social behaviours.*

When the patterns of behaviour that comprise an institution appear to conflict with the public interest, they create a social problem. To describe Newstate's poverty, describe the *institutions* of the economic system that shape its production and distribution of resources. To describe Newstate's problematic health delivery services, describe the *institutions* that comprise those services. To describe a social problem, describe the *patterns of repetitive social behaviours that comprise the problematic institutions.*[13] 'Development' requires changing the problematic

---

11 In the United States, think of the Agricultural Extension Law, 7 U.S.C. pp. 341–9 (2008) (originally enacted as Act of 8 May 1914, ch. 79, 38 stat. 372). That Law created an institution to teach farmers better agricultural technologies, and in general to help farmers improve their productivity and incomes; the National Labor Relations Act, 29 USC. pp. 151–69, that transformed labour-management relations; the Homestead Act, Act of 20 May 1862, Public Law 34–64 (repealed 1876), that ensured that the new Western lands brought into the federal union would become part of a market system, not a subsistence economy system.

12 See S-E. Sjostrand 'On Institutional Thought in the Social and Economic Sciences' in S-E. Sjostrand (ed.) *Institutional Change* (The Netherlands: Springer, 1993) pp. 9–12; D.C. North 'Institutional Change: A Framework for Analysis' in S-E. Sjostrand (1993) pp. 36 and 37; Harry M. Johnson, *Sociology: A Systematic Introduction* (New York: Harcourt, Brace & Co, 1960) at 22.

13 Many social problems display a superficial appearance that does not seem to involve problematic *behaviours* – for example, a great hospital that has no medicines or a community suffering severe drought and the resulting famine. Faced by a problem defined in terms or resource allocation, the law stands helpless. It cannot command medicines to appear on the hospitals shelves, nor the rain to fall on the hapless community. A lawmaker looking to use legislation instrumentally to solve such a problem can use law to change *behaviours*. A hospital has no medicine on its shelves because the institutions that supply the medicines – the *behaviours* that do that – function in problematic ways. A community suffers drought and famine because the institutions that normally function to supply water fail to do so. The challenge for the drafter, of course, consists in finding the *institutional* solution that, considering the available resources, will best ameliorate the consequences in human suffering of a hospital without medicine, or a community without water. The problem-solving methodology, described *infra*, text following note 72, specifically addresses the problem. Addressing a social problem that seemingly does not involve *behaviours*, the drafter ought to restate the problem in terms of the institutions and hence the behaviours that result in the problematic situation.

behaviours – the institutions – that induce the majority's poverty and vulnerability to natural and man-made disasters.

Many community organisations seek to resolve social problems: churches, schools, advocacy organisations, professional groups, trade organisations, all the organisations that collectively comprise 'civil society' In an increasingly complex global society, however, everywhere people call on *government* to help resolve their social problems. To do so, government must change the problematic behaviours – the institutions – that foster those problems. For that purpose, they have little choice but to use law.

How else might a handful of senior government policymakers change the behaviours of gaggles of government servants and hordes of citizens? As Koen van Aeken points out, 'the lawmaker operates as a special kind of policymaker, with a smaller toolbox, but one that contains tools of remarkable potential'.[14] To induce changed behaviours, government necessarily employs *rules*. A norm promulgated by the State and implemented by government agency officials: That constitutes a 'law'

In short, to address a social problem, government promulgates *rules* – that is, *law* – to define desired new behaviours and communicates those rules to the relevant actors.[15] It uses law and the legal order instrumentally to change problematic behaviours, and thus to transform dysfunctional institutions.

Some Scholars Deny That Government Can or Should Use Law as an Instrument of Social Change; They Err.

An entire stable of scholars deny that government should or can use law instrumentally to change behaviours to resolve social problems and bring about social change. Those who deny that government *should* use law to trigger social change frequently argue that the 'market' serves better than government to regulate social affairs. Others assert that the instrumental use of law violates basic humanitarian notions.

---

14 See K. Van Aeken 'Legal Instrumentalism Revisited' in Wintgens (2005) pp. 66 and 67.

15 Occasionally, specific historical circumstances make it possible for government to use a different tool than 'law'. For example, China's famous 'one-child policy', invoked to reduce the Chinese birth rate, began with a letter from Deng Xiaoping, (the then Secretary of the ruling Communist Party). Because that letter specified no implementing agency, it did not meet our definition of a 'law'. Various forms of implementation of the one-child policy did spring up. In some communities, voluntary local committees without explicit government authorisation visited families to discuss the one-child policy. In other communities, government expressly imposed sanction – for example, not paying child welfare benefits for more than one child, or, in the case of a government official who had more than one child, delaying promotion of that official. See 'China's One-Child Policy' visited 7 January 2008, accessable online at (www.faculty.harker.org/adm/population/studentpages/china1/). Note that even in that case, government, acting through the Party's General Secretary, sought to change behaviours by use of a *rule* – even though that rule did not qualify as 'law'

(As proof, some cite the Nazi and Soviet experience.)[16] Yet no inbuilt motive, either vicious or benevolent, need drive the instrumental use of legislation. Just as one State used law instrumentally to carry out the Holocaust, another State may use the law instrumentally to protect minorities, ensure minimum wages, protect consumers, make workplaces safe and defend women's welfare.

Other authors argue that the state *cannot* use law instrumentally. William Graham Sumner taught that a society's mores define its laws, 'Stateways cannot change folkways'.[17] Some writers, misinterpreting historical materialism, hold that the 'superstructure' – roughly, the ideas, values, and non-economic institutional arrangements – cannot change the 'base', that is, the system of production of goods and services.[18] Others insist that human behaviours result from causes so complex that they defy analysis; unless we can disentangle law's effects from other factors affecting behaviour, we cannot use law to facilitate *deliberate* social change.[19] Still others maintain that politics, not a law's words, decide policy. The law, they say, remains 'unimportant'; study the policy that underpins it.[20] Still others, adopting deconstructionist literary theory, hold that as a 'text', a law has no determinate meaning. Since readers rely on their own construction of a law's words, they will not likely all construe a law as the author intended. That law, therefore, will not likely, in every case, induce the behaviour that its author intended.[21] Some naysayers argue that 'static' inevitably infects the communication channel between the legislature that enacts the law and the law's addressees. The prescription that the addressee receives therefore differs from that intended by its author.[22]

Many writers view law as always playing 'catch-up' with society. Society changes; law changes to express the new social relationships.[23] Some suggest that deliberately

---

16 See Von Aeken (2005); B.Z. Tamanaha, *Law as Means to an End: Threat to the Rule of Law* (Cambridge: Cambridge University Press, 2006) at 101.

17 By 'mores' Sumner meant 'the popular usages and traditions, when they include a judgment that they are conducive to societal welfare, and when they exert a coercion on the individual to conform to them, although they are not coordinated by any authority' (See W.G. Sumner, *A Study of the Sociological Importance of Usages, Manners, Customs, Mores and Morals* (Boston: Ginn and Co, 1906) at 30.

18 See D.V. Williams, 'The Authoritarianism of African Legal Orders: A Review and Critique of Robert B. Seidman's The State, Law and Development', 5 (1980) *Contemporary Crises* at 255.

19 See R.L. Kidder *Connecting Law and Society: An Introduction to Research and Theory* (Englewood Cliffs: Prentice-Hall, 1986).

20 See J. Griffiths 'Is Law Important?' 54 (1979) *N.Y.U. L. Rev.*at 339.

21 See J. Singer 'The Player and the Cards: Nihilism and Legal Theory' 94 (1984) *Yale Law Journal* at 1.

22 By 'static' we mean that, in the process of communicating a law, inevitably the law passes through a variety of officials, each of whom puts their own gloss upon the text. The text as received by the addressee, thus only accidentally resembles the law as originally promulgated. Van Aeken (2005) pp. 71and 72, 74–6.

23 See G. Sawer, *Law in Society* (Oxford: Oxford University Press, 1963) at 147; J.P. Reid *A Law of Blood: The Primitive Law of the Cherokee People* (New York: New York University Press, 1970) at 3 ('Law is the signet of a people and a people are the product of a land. The primitive law of the eighteenth-century Cherokee nation reflects the mores,

designed law never proves as beneficent as law that 'has grown up and established itself unconsciously over a period of time'.[24] Yet others, following Coase,[25] argue that in an ideal 'free market' economy – that is, a market free of 'transaction costs'[26] – if law remains stable for a sufficient time, parties will bargain their way around the law to reach the same social allocations of goods and services, whatever the law in force.[27] Finally, some philosophers hold that the State inherently lacks capacity to accomplish the large-scale social engineering[28] required for development. Some would restrict law's function to dispute settlement.[29]

The naysayers err. To defeat their assertion of the *impossibility* of changing social relationships through law, one need point to only *one* case where law indubitably changed the relevant institutions. Out of many, we submit two examples: But for the law, nobody would pay a tax. But for the law, nobody would cast a vote in a national, State or municipal election. At least in these two cases, but for the law, the prescribed behaviours would not take place. Nevertheless, for every case where the law does trigger behavioural change, one can cite at least as many (and likely many more) cases where a law failed to bring about the anticipated social change. Consider the early Soviet case summarised earlier. Or consider laws criminalising various sorts of sexual conduct (e.g., adultery), all famously ineffective.

Some laws *work*.[30] Other laws, like those aimed at eliminating adultery, do not *work*. As their primary task, lawmakers must discover what factors lead to a law that *works*, and what factors make that outcome unlikely. In this chapter, we assert that, in *designing* a bill's *substance*, as well its *form*, legislative drafters play a critical

---

the integrality, and the rapport of the Cherokee people just as the characteristic traits of the Cherokees themselves reflect the physical environment of their existence: the mountains upon which they lived, the harvest reaped from forest, field and stream, and the enemies – both in nature and mankind – that their geographical position required them to fight.')

24 See M. Oakeshott *Rationalism in Politics and Other Essays* (London: Methuen, 1962) at 26.

25 See R.H. Coase 'The Problem of Social Cost' 3 (1960) *Journal of Law & Economics* at 1.

26 Coase used 'transaction costs' as a marker for the opposite of a freely competitive market. Ibid.

27 See, J.M. Buchanan 'Politics, Property and Law: An Alternative Interpretation of Miller v. Schoene' 15 (1972) *Journal of Law & Economics* at 439; *contra*: J. Ahrens *Governance and Economic Development: A Comparative Institutional Approach* (Cheltenham and Northampton: Edward Elgar, 2002) pp. 28 and 29: 'Today, even the World Bank ... concedes "that development requires an effective state, one that plays a catalytic, facilitating role, encouraging and complimenting the activities of private businesses and individuals." The Bank concludes that "state dominated development has failed. But so has stateless development ... History has repeatedly shown that good government is not a luxury but a vital necessity."' quoting World Bank, *World Development Report 1997: The State in a Changing World* iii (World Bank, 1997).

28 See K. Popper *The Poverty of Historicism* (London: Routledge and Kegan Paul, 1961).

29 See E.A. Driedger *The Construction of Statutes* 2nd edn (Ontario: Butterworths, 1983).

30 See *supra*, note 3.

role in determining the 'limits of law'.[31] In the next part, we seek to demonstrate that role's significance.

Part II: Laws That do not *Work*: the Importance of the Drafter's Role

This part addresses the first of this chapter's three themes: The crucial importance of the legislative drafter's role in filling the gap between policymaking and implementation. The public and most legal academics too frequently regard the legislative drafter as a mere technician, responsible only for the *form* of legislation. The drafter, they assert, chains words together in an acceptable 'legal' format, but have no responsibility for the law's probable social impact.

The Soviet failure to design a law that actually liberated women in Central Asia[32] illustrates the danger of ignoring the drafters' role in designing a law's substantive provisions. In this Part, we identify the drafter as a critical actor in the widespread failures of efforts to use law instrumentally. We describe and briefly explain the drafting behaviours that led to those failures.

The Drafter's Central Role in Designing Effectively Implemented Law

As noted above, most people recognise only two roles in the process of making law to foster development: the policymakers, who determine the law's objectives; and the law implementers, responsible for attaining those objectives. In that view, the two principal roles in the Soviet Central Asia drama consisted of (1) the policymakers who identified Central Asia women to lead the modernising revolution; and (2) the local party officials who, without regard to Central Asian realities, sought to use law to impose the policymakers' 'vision.' Those officials' failure to consider the country-specific realities limited the likelihood that the proposed law would *work*.

That case teaches that, to understand and to improve the practice of Law and Development, scholars of the legislative process must study an additional, third role: that of the legislative drafter who designs and drafts the proposed law's detailed provisions. Half a century ago, E.A. Driedger emphasised that, properly to 'design' a bill, a *drafter must determine its substantive detailed provisions*:

> Legislative policy is not the same thing as the legislative plan; the former is the objective to be achieved, and the latter an outline of the method by which it is to be achieved. For example, it may be laid down as a policy that certain grants are to be paid to a class of persons under specified conditions. In order to effect such a policy, the draftsman needs to know that his statute must, among other things, prescribe the persons who are to benefit, specify the amount of the grant, and the condition under which it may be paid, and provide authority for payment out of the Consolidated Revenue Fund, for suspension for breach

31 Government does not become omnipotent merely because it uses law as an instrument of social change. Government has limited resources. The task of changing behaviours through law requires specific resources, human and physical – for example, competent legislative drafters. By 'the limits of law' we mean the limits that scarce resources in the particular circumstances impose on government's abilities to effectuate social change through law.

32 See *supra*, text at note 4.

> of conditions and for recovery of unauthorized payment, for applications, decisions and awards, for penalties for misrepresentation or other wrongful conduct. In the case of an amending statute the draftsman must decide what statutes are to be amended, what sections, and in what manner ...[33]

Typically, policymakers simply call for a law to achieve their vision of conditions they believe necessary to replace those characteristic of the targeted social problem.[34] (For example, policymakers usually do *not* instruct the drafter by identifying the social problem that the policymaker wants legislation to address; for example, they seldom say, 'Draft a law addressing the social problem of discrimination against women.' Instead, they identify the goal or objective of the proposed law, 'Draft a law ensuring women's rights to equality'.) The former requires the drafter to begin by studying what *is* the case. The latter invites the drafter to begin by drafting the rules to achieve the policy 'vision' – too often with negative results.

The founders of 'legisprudence'[35] correctly argue that, to draft an effective law to resolve a social problem like that of gender discrimination, drafters require a theory. They need a guide in gathering and using the relevant available evidence to produce laws that *work.* A law's detailed provisions consist almost entirely of commands, prohibitions and permissions.[36] A drafter designs a law by writing prescriptions logically likely to change the relevant social actors' behaviours, thus to ameliorate the social problem identified by the policymakers. *That legislative 'design' – the substantive details of a bill – largely determines whether the bill induces the behaviours prescribed, and whether those behaviours will likely ameliorate the targeted social problem.* The drafter's design determines whether the bill *works.*

For a metaphor for the drafter's role in the law-making process, consider the architect's role designing a family's new house:

> A family identifies a poor dwelling as a problem that requires a solution. It decides on its 'policy': to build a new house. At that point, the family members can define the word 'house' only in general terms. They retain an architect. They discuss budget, the rooms needed, the preferred style of architecture, the location of the house on the land, a myriad of issues. The architect produces plans and specifications that define their new home in detail. Now, if one asks the family what they mean by the word 'house' (that is, of what their family 'policy' consists) they point to the plans and specifications.

Who determined the family's 'policy': The family or the architect?

In an ideal world, specialised ministerial officials, experts in a proposed bill's subject matter, would work with legally trained drafters to design a bill's detailed substantive provisions. Rarely, however, does the drafter/scrivener and the drafter/

33 See E.A. Driedger 'The Preparation of Legislation' 31 *Can. Bar. Rev.* pp. 33, 39 (1953). Note that Driedger uses the word 'plan' to mean what we express by the word 'design'

34 See J. Dewey *Essays in Experimental Logic* (Chicago: University of Chicago, 1916).

35 See *supra,* note 8.

36 See R.J. Martineau *Legislation and Rules in Plain English* (St. Paul: West Publishing Company, 1991); J. Stark, *The Art of the Statute* (Colorado: Rothman and Co, 1996).

researcher/expert/ministerial official even work in the same department. Much more often, in practice, the official who actually writes out the bill perforce also designs it.

In China, for example, a bill concerning underground water supplies nominally came under the jurisdiction of the Ministry that dealt with underground water. An American consultant on underground water told us that he became convinced that the experts in that Ministry knew the location and pollutant content of ever cubic meter of underground water in China – but nothing about the uses of law to reduce its pollution. The drafter who actually decided what words to chain together into the bill, and how to accomplish that task, worked for the central drafting office of the State Council.[37] He knew very little about the problems of underground water. The drafters – that is, the drafter/experts and the drafter/scriveners – worked together to design the water pollution bill.[38] Relying on the research conducted by the Ministry officials, the drafters, both expert and scrivener, worked together to produce an excellent bill. Collectively they assumed a position analogous to that of the architect, concerned with designing a house for a client.[39]

How well a drafter designs a bill's detailed provisions determines whether the bill, enacted into law, *works*. A drafter in effect warrants to the client that the bill will actually induce the behaviours it prescribes, and that those behaviours will likely effectuate the client's 'policy'. To do that, the drafter must predict the behaviours a bill will likely induce. How well the drafters design a bill, and how well they predict the behaviours it induces, depend in main part upon the *theory* and the *methodology* they use to guide the research and design of that bill, and the *techniques* they actually use to draft it.[40] Most drafters use inappropriate methodologies and theories to draft laws. Their laws frequently fail to *work*.

Lacking a Theory, How Does the Drafter Design a Bill?

In the real world, for two reasons, more frequently than not, neither expert officials nor those who put pen to paper employ a methodology to design a bill that stands up to close analysis. First, at least in former British colonies, a long tradition teaches that those conventionally called 'drafters' have nothing to do with a bill's substance,

---

37 In China, the State Council occupied a position in the Chinese government roughly equivalent to Cabinet in other countries.

38 In the 1992–97 UNDP Project to draft 22 priority laws called for in China's 1989 National plan, the drafter/scriveners and the drafter/experts joined together in teams to draft the detailed bills required to resolve the specified social problems.

39 See K. Van Aeken (2005) at 68 ('Opening up a discussion to a revisiting of law in the world of policy-makers, synonyms such as lawgiver, lawmaker or norm constructor will be supplemented by terms such as the policy constructor, *always bearing in mind that policy embraces law*.') Emphasis added.

40 We do not here discuss the importance of drafting techniques; see A. Seidman, R.B. Seidman and N. Abeysekere *Legislative Drafting for Democratic Social Change* (The Hague: Kluwer Law International, 2001) Part III. Because words comprise the substance as well as the form of a bill, a choice of a bill's *words* constitutes a choice as to the bill's *content*. (Form and content constitute but two sides of the same coin.)

but only its form.[41] Second, in part a result of that tradition, few drafters have a methodology or theory to guide them either in conducting research or designing a bill's substantive details. Instead, the world around, most drafters usually design laws by one of four 'entropic' methods:[42]

- Frequently *sub nom.* 'international best practice', drafters copy law from other jurisdictions, with precious little concern as to whether the environment in their country seems similar to that of the law's original 'home'.[43]
- Drafters adopt the substance of the bill seemingly agreed to by relevant interest groups' bargain.
- Drafters criminalise unwanted behaviour, without regard to the dangers of over-criminalisation which seldom resolves the targeted social problem.
- Drafters draft a bill's prescriptions in vague general terms, leaving substantive detail to subordinate legislation or administrative regulation – often without any effective legislative oversight.

None of these entropic methods require the drafter to examine the constraints and resources of the specific circumstances likely to influence the social actors' behaviours in the face of the new law. Too often, except serendipitously, the new laws fail to induce the relevant actors to behave in the new ways prescribed, or, if they do induce their prescribed behaviours, they fail to implement the policymakers' anticipated social change.

Some lawmakers justify copying laws from an acceptable exemplar or 'international best practice' as the most practical way to design a bill. Others believe that, where different interest groups support different legal provisions, bargaining constitutes an *inevitable* methodology for designing a bill. The seemingly harsh strictures imposed by reality, however, do not implacably confine a drafter to the entropic methodologies. Other drafting methodologies *do* exist.

---

41 See A. Seidman, R.B. Seidman and N. Abeysekere (2001) pp. 30–34. Also see R.B. Seidman 'Law, Development and Legislative Drafting in English-Speaking Independent Africa' 19 (1981) *Journal Modern African Studies* at 133.

42 See A.Seidman, R.B. Seidman and N. Abeysekere (2001) at 40; for a sociological explanation; Johnson, *supra* note 12, at 22.

43 With Thomas Waelde, we edited a collection of articles about how foreign consultants developed the laws they recommended to their developing or transitional world clients. In one way or another, at the end of the day all advised the drafter to copy foreign law. A. Seidman, R.B. Seidman and T. Waelde (eds) *Making Development Work: Legislative Reform for Institutional Transformation and Good Governance* (The Hague: Kluwer Law International, 1999).

Part III: Using Law as an Instrument for Social Change: Designing and Justifying a Bill in Terms of Facts and Logic[44]

Why do People Behave as They do in the Face of a Law: a Brief Review of the Literature

Many academics have investigated the influence of law on human behaviour. Economists frequently argue that 'incentives' constitute the most important explanation for all human behaviour, including social actors' behaviour in the face of a rule of law.[45] Others explain behaviour in the face of a rule of the law, not only in terms of immediate incentives, but also the influence of 'embedded' social norms.[46] Still others consider behaviour so complex that they dismiss as inherently impossible efforts to analyse law's effect on it.[47]

William Evan argues that only if law becomes 'institutionalised' does it become truly effective. For that to happen, he suggests, the agency responsible for implementing the law must 'convert *forced* compliance into *voluntary* compliance' [48] Like Evan, writing in the sociological tradition, Arnold Rose emphasises that drafters should conduct research and design implementation measures, not to punish violations of the law, but to encourage conforming behaviours.[49]

Psychologists offers an alternative theory called 'cognitive dissonance.[50] Will Maslow asserts, 'We are beginning to understand that law tends to make certain conduct unrespectable and thus discourages it. We also realise that changing one's

44 This paper summarises a legislative theory and methodology that we have elsewhere set forth at length. A. Seidman, R.B. Seidman and N. Abeysekere (2001); also see A. Seidman and R.B. Seidman *State and Law in the Development Process: Problem-solving and Institutional Change in the Third World* (New York: St. Martin's Press, 1994).

45 See R. Posner *The Economic Analysis of Law* 7th edn (The Hague: Wolters Kluwer Law & Business, 2007).

46 See N. Mecuro and S.G. Medema *From Posner to Post-Modernism and Beyond* 2nd edn (Princeton: Princeton University Press, 2006) ch. 7: R. Ellickson, *Order Without Law: How neighbors settle disputes* (Cambridge, Mass: Harvard University Press, 1991).

47 See Kidder (1986).

48 That is, people obey a law because they think they *ought* to obey it, not merely out of fear of sanctions, but because circumstances *educate* them to accept it. Evans offers seven variables, but offers no empirical warrant for the proposition that these constitute necessary and sufficient conditions for the law to perform an 'educative' function. See W.F. Evan, *The Sociology of Law* (New York: Free Press, 1980).

49 See A. Rose 'Sociological Factors in the Effectiveness of Projected Legal Remedies' 11 (1958) *Journal of Legal Education* at 470.

50 See L. Festinger *A Theory of Cognitive Dissonance* (Stanford University Press, 1957); L. Festinger and J.M. Carlsmith 'Cognitive Consequences of Forced Compliance' 58 (1959) *Journal of Abnormal and Social Psychology* at 203, available at (www.psychclassics.yorku.ca/Festinger/); 'Two studies reported by Janis and King (1954; 1956) clearly showed that, at least under some conditions, the private opinion changes so as to bring it into closer correspondence with the overt behavior the person was forced to perform.'

patterns of behaviour will in time modify attitudes, and do so more effectively than a frontal assault on the attitudes themselves' [51]

Legislative drafters, however, confront a somewhat different problem from that sociologists and psychologists address. Drafters need a theory to guide the research and design of a law likely, in the context of their countries' unique realities, to induce conforming behaviours to ameliorate[52] pressing social problems *now*.[53] Such a theory must begin with explaining why people behave as they do in the face of a rule of law.

A Legislative Theory and Methodology to Guide a Drafter in Designing an Institution-changing Bill

To design a bill, in addition to specific skills denoted by a legislative drafter's job title (for example, drafting techniques, research skills relevant to the drafting task,[54] knowledge of the relevant legal system) a drafter needs a two-track guide: (1) a *legislative theory* to guide the search for relevant evidence in response to the question, 'Why, in the face of a rule of the law, do people behave as they do?' and (2) a *legislative methodology* to organise the available evidence logically as a basis for deciding on and justifying a bill's prescriptions for changing those problematic behaviours.

Why do people behave as they do in the face of a rule of the law? A Legislative Theory[55] People and collectivities act by choosing among the constraints and resources of their environment[56] in response to multiple causal factors in their environment. Incentives, chosen by many economists as the sole cause of human behaviour,[57] may constitute an important, but seldom the sole, cause of behaviour. Many sociologists

---

51 See W. Maslow 'The Uses of Law in the Struggle for Equality' 22 (1955) *Social Research*, pp. 297 and 298.

52 In an ideal world, one would hope that drafters could always devise a law that would *resolve* an identified existing social problem. In the real world, most of us would settle for a law that reliably *ameliorated* the problem.

53 Drafters undoubtedly should consider the potential effect of cognitive dissonance and the means Evan and Rose suggest for persuading their law's addressees to internalise the law's norms. In addition, however, they need a theory to guide them in designing legislative measures likely to alter or eliminate the objective factors, embedded in their country's unique circumstances, likely to cause their proposed law's addressees' existing problematic behaviours.

54 See text following note 103.

55 See Seidman, Seidman and Abeysekere (2001) at 17; see also A. Seidman, R.B. Seidman and N. Abeysekere *Assessing Legislation: A Manual for Legislators* (2003), available online for download at (www.iclad-law.org/).

56 See F. Barth *Models of Social Organization* (Royal Anthropological Institute Occasional Paper 23, 1966).

57 See Posner (2007).

view the actor's 'values and attitudes' as the primary causal factor.[58] Other causes, however, also exist, sometimes in conjunction with these, sometimes sufficient in themselves. (No matter the market price for a crop, without sufficient water, a Tanzanian peasant cannot increase its output.)

As illustrated by Figure 19.1, a law always addresses at least two sets of social actors: A primary addressee ('role occupant'),[59] and the agency responsible for implementing the law's detailed provisions. In the face of a law, what constraints and resources seem likely to explain a primary role occupant's behaviours? Figure 19.1 suggests three major categories:

(i) the words of the rule of the law, whether the role occupant knows those words, and whether they understand what that law's authors intend them to say;
(ii) the expected behaviour of the agency responsible for implementing the conformity-inducing measures the law prescribes; and
(iii) the 'non-legal' constraints and resources of the role-occupants' circumstances.

Figure 19.1 underscores the futility of copying (transplanting) law from another country. The circumstances prevailing in the country in which the copied law will function rarely match the circumstances in the country of its origin; surely no drafter should assume that they do. Figure 19.1 also explains why so many efforts to use law instrumentally fail – not simply because the drafters uncritically copied other countries' laws, but because they failed to examine their own country's specific circumstances likely to influence the relevant social actors' behaviours in the face of the law.[60] That requires a detailed analysis of Figure 19.1's residual category, vaguely labelled 'non-legal constraints and resources' of the country circumstances likely to influence the role occupants' behaviours. To generate 'middle-level' hypotheses about those influences on a specific role occupant's behaviour requires a research agenda to unpack that broad residual category.

---

58 Some sociologists assert that one's values determines how one behaves in the face of a law. That leads to what some have called 'the sociologist's paradox': If one's values align themselves with the behaviours prescribed by a law, one will obey. If they do not, one will not obey. So why have a law?

59 The sociological term, 'role occupant' refers to role of the social actor targeted by a norm *e.g.*, a law: As a parent, a professor, a truck driver – whatever role that actor plays in the social context defined by the law. *Strictu senso,* a policeman or another actor in an implementing agency also counts as a role occupant. Placing the implementing agency as role occupant raises the question, 'Who serves as implementing agency for the implementing agency?' As one proceeds up the bureaucratic ladder, the implementing agency becomes more and more wraith-like. That merely indicates the obvious: The higher in the bureaucratic ladder, the greater the official's discretionary power.

60 See Van Aeken (2005) at 78 (Increasingly complex societies call for ever more instrumental law. At the same time, the speed with which society becomes ever more complex makes it that much more unlikely that a new law will 'work' That calls for an 'evolutionary' approach. 'It is trivial that the naïve form of instrumentalism is untenable: … The instrumental vision thus adapts itself to a changing societal context …')

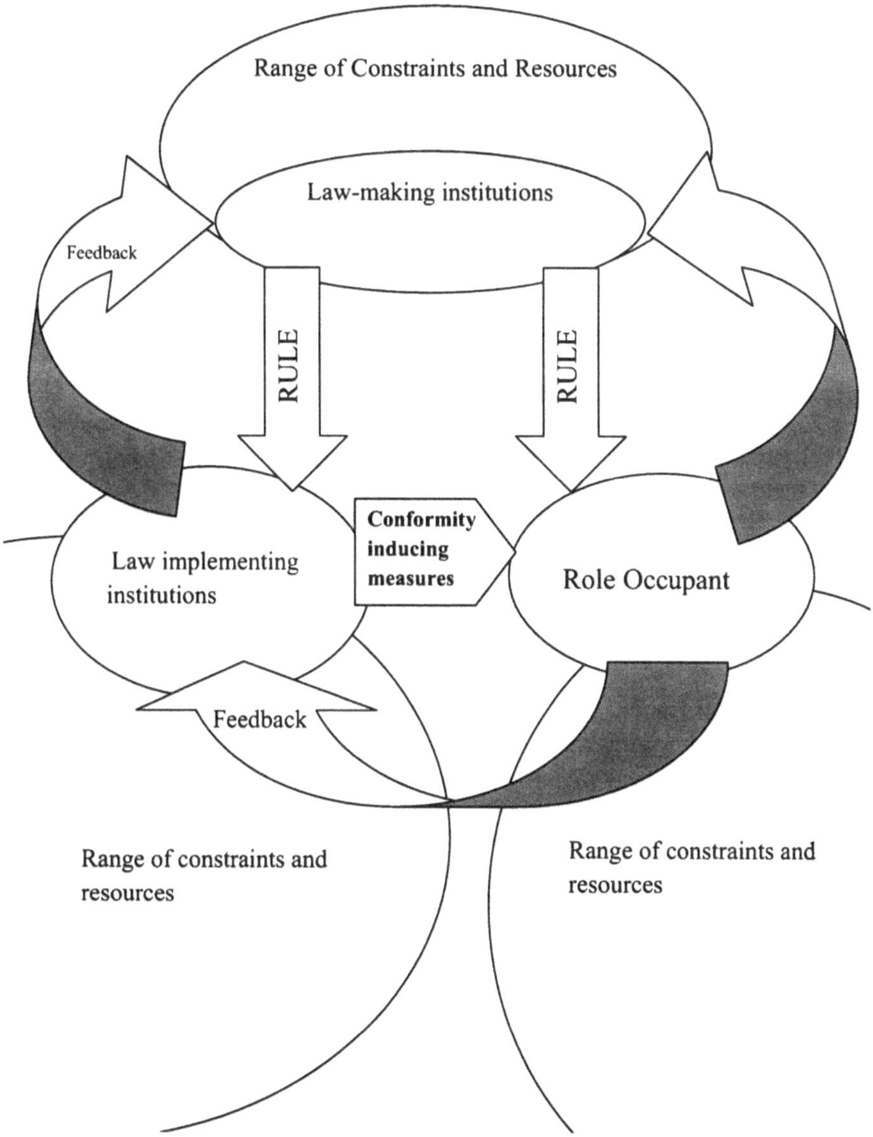

Figure 19.1 A model of the legal system

We suggest seven categories towards which, in the search for explanatory hypotheses, a drafter should turn attention. Consider, first, two 'subjective' categories:

- whether the role occupant has the Incentive (or Interest) to obey or disobey (favored by neo-liberal economists); and
- whether the Role Occupant's Ideology (i.e., values, beliefs, attitude) causes the role occupant to obey or disobey (many sociologist's favourite explanation).[61]

To explain behaviour in the face of a law in order to *predict* the behaviours the new law may induce, however, also requires consideration of five additional 'objective' categories:

(i) the words of the Rule of the law;
(ii) whether the authorities have Communicated the rule of the law to the role occupant;
(iii) whether the specific circumstances give the role occupant Opportunity to obey;
(iv) whether the role occupant has Capacity to obey (i.e., the skills and resources to decide whether or not to obey); and
(v) by what Process does the role occupant (especially in a complex decision-making organisation like an implementing agency) decide to obey or disobey the Rule.[62]

In any particular case, one or more of these categories may prove an empty box.[63]

The model in Figure 19.1 does not qualify as a 'theory' (How might one falsify it?) The ROCCIPI mnemonic does prove helpful to assist the drafter in considering hypotheses as a guide for discovering relevant factual data. To develop a law likely to induce the behaviour prescribed, a drafter should consider all the possible 'middle-level' explanatory hypotheses – 'educated guesses' – suggested by the ROCCIPI categories, and search for evidence likely to falsify each of them. Thus do the ROCCIPI categories guide a drafter in ploughing fields of evidence.[64] (Later

61 See *supra*, note 58.

62 The first letters of these categories' names make a useful mnemonic, 'ROCCIPI'

63 For example, almost always, analysing 'Process' identifies significant causes of an implementing agency's problematic behaviours. Process seems less useful in explaining an *individual's* behaviour. (Current research in individual decision-making, however, suggests that 'Process' may in the near future become a significant source of useful hypotheses, not only for complex organisational decision-making, but also for individual decision-making; see W.G. Huitt 'Problem Solving and Decision Making: Consideration of Individual Differences Using the Myers-Briggs Type Indicator' (1992) *J. Psychol. Type 24*, pp. 33–44, available at (www.chiron.valdosta.edu/whuitt/papers/prbsmbti.html) visited 28 December 2007).

64 See G. Homans 'Social Behaviour as Exchange' 63 (1964) *American J. Sociology* at 597. For example: To develop a remedial law, a drafter had explain why, despite its charter's plain commands, South Africa's Development Bank authorised no loans to very small farmers. It proves insufficient to state that the officer had no 'incentive' to do so, or lacked 'capacity' to service the loan. The drafter must formulate more precise hypotheses: that small loans do not generate sufficient interest income to warrant the expenditure of time in making or servicing

in the investigation, the ROCCIPI categories may guide the drafter in predicting the new law's probable impact in changing the causal factors that seem to influence a role occupant's behaviours.)

In addition to ROCCIPI categories, a drafter needs an appropriate methodology as a guide for organising the information gathered.

A Methodology to Guide Drafters in Organising the Available Evidence Logically[65]

Institutionalist legislative theory offers a methodology to guide drafters in structuring their propositions about matters of fact ('the available evidence') logically. That constitutes a basis both for prescribing the relevant role occupants' appropriate behaviours, and, as we discuss below, structuring those 'facts' into a *justification* for the proposed bill's detailed provisions.

Aristotle taught that, in deciding what one *ought* to do, one should employ 'practical reason'. One first conceives of the objective to be achieved, and then determines the most efficient means of achieving it.[66] Among concerned legal academics, that remains probably the most popular methodology for determining a law's detailed content.[67] 'Practical reason' (at least in that 'ends–means' version) does not serve the turn, however, for at least two reasons. First, most adherents of practical reason follow positivist notions that 'values' and 'facts' remain incommensurate.

---

the loan; and the Bank's loan officers lack experience in making micro loans to small farmers. See A. Seidman, R.B. Seidman and M. McCord 'A Theory and Methodology for Investigating the Function of Law in Relation to Government Institutions: The Case of the Development Bank of South Africa' in H. Corder (ed.) *Administrative Law Reform* (1994).

65 See Seidman, Seidman and Abeysekere (2001) ch. 4.

66 'Practical reason' ... has as many definitions as it has proponents: 'the reasoning of ends to means' V. Wellman 'Practical Reasoning and Judicial Justification: Toward an Adequate Theory' 57 (1985) *University of Colorado Law Review* pp. 45 and 46; 'the methods by which people who are not credulous form beliefs about matters that cannot be verified by logic or exact observation' Richard A. Posner *The Problems of Jurisprudence* (Cambridge Mass: Harvard University Press, 1990) pp. 71 and 72; 'the methods that people use to make a practical or ethical choice' Richard A. Posner 'The Jurisprudence of Skepticism' 86 (1988) *Mich. L. Rev.* pp. 827 and 837; 'the ability to take a complex set of facts, identify the key relevant attributes, and understand their societal significance' Daniel A. Farber, 'The Inevitability of Practical Reason, Statutes, Formalism and the Rule' 45 (1992) *Vand. L. Rev.* pp. 533, 536 (summarising K. Llewellyn *The Common Law Tradition: Deciding Appeals* pp. 39–41, 62–72 (1960); 'the capacity to act intentionally in various circumstances on reasons for action, notably norms' Steven J. Burton 'Law as Practical Reason' 62 (1989) *So. Cal. L. Rev.* at 747; *but see* R. Audi 'A Theory of Practical Reasoning' 19 (1982) *Am. Phil. Q.*25('practical reasoning is a term of art with little life in ordinary parlance and a multiple personality in philosophical literature'). See A. Seidman, R.B. Seidman and T. Uate 'Assessing Legislation to Serve the Public Interest: Experiences from Mozambique' 20 (1999) *Statute Law Review* at 1.

67 See M. Atienza 'Reasoning and Legislation' in Wintgens (ed.) *supra*, note. 8, pp. 297 and 303; Edward L. Rubin 'Legislative Methodology: Some Lessons from the Truth-in-Lending Act' 80 (1991) *Georgetown Law Review* at 233.

Warranting a statute thus remains impossible[68] Either one agrees with the 'policy' or one does not.

The methodology that a drafter uses to design a statute also necessarily serves as the methodology that the drafter uses to *justify* the statute, that is, to persuade others that the statute deserves support not only by those of its originator's political persuasion, but also by those 'on the other side of the aisle'.[69] Where a statute ultimately rests on its originator's *ipse dixit*, agreement, if any, with its broad objective does not rest on warrantable argument, but on one's gut reaction.[70]

John Dewey and the American pragmatic school of philosophy suggest an alternative methodology[71] Applied to the drafter's task, that pragmatic methodology suggests the following four steps:

1. State the *social problem* that requires attention.
    a. Describe the *superficial appearance* of the social problem.
    b. Because law can only resolve social problems by changing behaviours, describe the *repetitive social behaviours* (i.e., the *institutions*) that constitute the identified social problem (including those of the primary role occupants and the relevant implementing agencies).[72]

---

68 The positivist argument holds that a statute constitutes a set of 'ought' statements. It expresses the 'values' of the policymaker. In the extreme positivist view, a drafter therefore cannot warrant a statute by factual evidence (nor can its opponents employ 'facts' to diswarrant that statute). See *infra*, text following note 105.

69 See H. Pitkin *The Concept of Representation* (University of California Press, 1967); J. Habermas *Between Facts and Norms: Contributions to a Discourse Theory of Law and Democracy* (W. Rehg, trans., 1995); J. Rawls *A Theory of Justice* (Oxford: Oxford University Press, 1971).

70 See H. Putnam *Reason, Truth and History* (Cambridge: Cambridge University Press, 1981) (espousing the view that 'there is an extremely close connection between the notions of *truth* and *rationality*; to put it even more crudely, the only criterion for a fact is what is *rational* to accept ... There can be *value facts* on this conception', at x); but also see A.D. Oliver-Lalana 'Through Rationality: Parliamentary Argumentation as Rational Justification of Laws' in Wintgens (ed.) *supra* note 8, pp. 239–41. Where a statute rests on its originator's *ipse dixit*, agreement rests not on 'facts and logic', but one's gut reaction. Inevitably, in such a case, the mode of political persuasion ultimately finds its foundation in power, whether parading as 'interest group bargaining' or as power undisguised. E.E. Schattschneider *The Semisovereign People: A Realist's view of Democracy in America* (New York: Holt, Rinehart and Winston, 1960) pp. 34 and 35 ('The flaw in the pluralist heaven is that the heavenly chorus sings with a strong upper-class accent.') That ultimately seduces the drafter back to the 'entropic' methods. See above, text at note 42.

71 See Dewey (1916); J. Rawls *Theory of Justice* (Belknap Press, 1971) argues that only 'public reasons' serve to justify a public policy. By public reasons he means what we have elsewhere denoted variously as 'facts and logic' or 'reason informed by experience' or 'an argument that should satisfy a rational skeptic'.; see also E.J. Meehan *Value Judgment and Social Science* (Hommerwood: Dorsey Press, 1969); A. Sesonske *Value and Obligation: The Foundation of an Empiricist Ethical Theory* (Berkeley: University of California Press, 1964).

72 See *supra*, note 13.

2. State the *explanations* for those behaviours. (Here, use the 'ROCCIPI' categories to generate tenable explanatory hypotheses.)
3. Draft a *proposed bill* (i) that addresses the explanations for the constituent behaviours; and (ii) that is the most socially cost-effective among the various potential alternatives.
4. Include in the bill provisions for systematic *monitoring and evaluation* of the statute as implemented.[73]

The four step problem-solving methodology meets the demands of both *instrumental* and *discursive* rationality.

> Intentional actions acquire [instrumental] rational status in so far as they ... [are] planned and performed on the basis of knowledge in such a way that they would be able to explain why it was possible to achieve a given set goal. In other words, actions which produce a certain effect only accidentally and whose effectiveness we are unable to explain, are not instrumentally rational.[74]

Discursive rationality has two levels:

> The first level involves the assumption that every communicative use ... [of language aims to lead to] an understanding with the addressee. The second level involves the assumption that the content of the message should be such that the addressee could not only understand, but also accept it.[75]

To meet those requirements with respect to legislation requires a justification that ought to satisfy a 'rational skeptic'. That kind of justification also satisfies the requirements of instrumental rationality.[76] With respect of legislation, therefore, the requirements of discursive and of instrumental rationality seem identical: they both require justifying a bill by using elementary rules of logic and better facts. The problem-solving methodology outlines the structure of such a justification. A theory to guide the search for relevant evidence, and a problem-solving methodology to guide both designing and justifying a bill: these constitute the drafter's essential tools.

---

73 'Evaluation ... like explanations, generates expectations as to real-world consequences. These real-world consequences are as much the arbiter of the human usefulness of a set of values as any set of facts that test a scientific explanation. Values, like explanations, are human instruments and derive what validity they possess from their practical operation ... The evaluatory enterprise, like that of science, can have a humanly significant, self-corrective character.' N.E. Long in 'Meehan' (1969) at vii.

74 See W. Cyrul 'How Rational is Rational Lawmaking' in Wintgens (ed.) *supra* note 7, at 93 and 95.

75 See ibid. at 95, citing J. Habermas *Theory of Communicative Action: Reason and Rationalization of Society* (Boston: Beacon Press, 1981).

76 See text at notes 74 and 75.

In recent years, 'soft law' has become the object of scholarly interest.[77] We all assume that the drafter's quiver contains laws that more or less fit the form to which long experience has accustomed us, that is, laws that command, permit or prohibit. Soft law arguably does none of those. To what extent can a drafter use 'soft law' to accomplish the institutional transformations that development requires?

Soft Law and Development

Soft law, or 'the communicative style' of legislation,

> ... relies on persuasion rather than punishment. It takes law as an invitation to dialogue between more or less equal parties: state officials (including the executive, public prosecutors, judges, etc.) intermediary organizations, and citizens. [footnote omitted]. The legislator knowingly and willingly waives the opportunity to intervene directly in social reality, and lays down in the law a fundamental value – for example, equality – in order to promote a gradual change in attitude and behaviour within the legal community.[78]

Grainne de Burca and Joanne Scott speak of 'new governance':

> ... a construct which has been developed to explain a range of processes and practices that have a normative dimension but do not operate primarily or at all through the formal mechanism of tradition command-and-control institutions. [New government processes] generally encourage or involve the participation of affected actors (stakeholders) rather than merely representative actors, and emphasize transparency (openness as a means of sharing and learning), as well as ongoing evaluation and review ... A further characteristic ... is the voluntary or non-binding nature of the norms ... This feature is often described in terms of 'soft law' ...[79]

Some authors draw a sharp line between 'instrumental law' (by which they mean conventional law, usually with a punitive sanction attached),[80] and 'soft law,' defined as 'rules of conduct which in principle have no legally binding force but which nevertheless may have practical effects'.[81] Long social experience with drafting in

77 In legislating for its several Member States, the European Union has freely used 'general and open ended guidelines rather than rules, [which provide] no formal sanctions for Member States that do not follow the guidelines, and is not justiciable ...' D.M. Trubek and L.G. Trubek 'Hard and Soft Law in the Construction of Social Europe: The Open Method of Coordination' 11 (2005) *European Law Journal* at 343.

78 See W. Witteveen and B. van Klink 'Why is Soft Law Really Law? A Communicative Approach to Legislation' at 1, accessed at (www.rechten.uvt.nl/bartvanklink/softlaw.pdf) visited 27 March 2008.

79 See G. de Burca and J. Scott 'New Governance, Law and Constitutionalism' pp. 3–5, online at (www.ucl.ac.uk/laws/clge/docs/govlawconst.pdf) visited 27 March 2008.

80 See Witteveen and van Klink, *supra* note 81.

81 See F. Snyder 'The Effectiveness of EC Law' in T. Daintith (ed.) *Implementing EC Law in the UK* (Chichester: Wiley, 1995). 'These new governance methods may bear some similarity to hard law. But because they lack features such as obligation, uniformity, justiciability, sanctions, and/or an enforcement staff, they are classified as "soft law" and contrasted, sometimes positively, sometimes negatively, with hard law as instruments for

terms of misty 'visions' or 'objectives' – one of the four 'entropic' drafting strategies – ought to make a drafter wary of a scheme, like 'soft law', that seemingly treads close to those kinds of visions or objectives. On the other hand, 'successful' instances of laws drafted in a 'soft law' mode can teach 'hard law' practitioners the importance of, and new ways to facilitate participation in the drafting process.[82]

'Soft law' offers some lessons about how to tease out appropriate new forms of those inputs. Rapidly changing global history has put learning those lessons high on development practitioners' agenda.

Using Law to Foster Development: A Summary

This part examined how law influences behaviours. Without a theory of how law does that, a drafter cannot predict the behavioural consequences of a proposed law. Without accurate predictions, the instrumental use of law whistles with the wind. After examining the relatively sparse literature on the subject, this part has put forward an 'institutionalist' legislative theory and a problem-solving methodology to guide drafters in designing legislation likely to prove effectively implemented to achieve its stated objectives.

Everywhere, efforts to foster 'development' encounter a whole series of problems that thrust themselves forward, demanding legislative solutions. Today, Law and Development studies principally two roles. It studies the policymaker, usually a political leader, who defines the 'ends' or 'objectives' of a proposed law. It studies the role of the 'implementing guys', by which we mean the personnel, both official and non-official, that seek to realise the policy, and those who supervise or oversee the performance of tasks that a law prescribes.[83] Law and Development scholars study the substantive policies that various international development agencies (the World Bank, UNDP, USAID, etc.) today espouse. To study how the countries involved actually *do* Development, those scholars today examine policymakers, and how relevant implementing agencies and others carry out their policies.

That omits a significant step. Role occupants and implementing agencies together carry out the policies prescribed by policymakers. They behave as they do, however, in the face of rules designed and drafted by legislative drafters. An academic or law teacher concerned with Law and Development should study the processes by which the law-makers, including drafters, formulate the substantive details of the laws that

---

European integration.' See also D.M. Trubek, P. Cottrell and M. Nance '"Soft Law", "Hard Law", and European Integration: Toward a Theory of Hybridity' accessed online at (www.law.wisc.edu/facstaff/trubek/HybridityPaperApril2005.pdf) visited 29 March 2008.

82 See Seidman, Seidman and Uate (1999) The defenders of 'soft law' frequently assert that 'hard law' by its very nature implies coercion and other aspects of bureaucracy. On the other hand, Westerman reminds us that 'hard law' frequently serves 'as mechanisms which enable people to live together despite the fact that they have different, even conflicting interests and goals.... By prescribing concrete behaviour, rules facilitate coordination and mutual adjustment of acts despite the fact that intentions, interests and goals do not run parallel.' Westerman (2007) at 59.

83 See Seidman, Seidman and Abeysekere (2001) ch. 5.

'span the gap' between the broad dictates of 'policy' and the behaviours of those who purport to carry out that policy. Especially, they should study legislative theory and methodology. Drafters need guides in the process of designing, drafting, enacting and implementing problem-solving laws, whether 'soft' or 'hard', to improve governance and people-oriented development. Law and Development itches for scholarly reflection on drafting processes and methods. On what issues might Law and Development scholars most fruitfully focus that study?

Part IV: Law and Development: Persistent Problems

The third theme of this chapter concerns ongoing problems in the field of Law and Development, especially, those attendant upon drafting law for Development. Drafting legislation to make the swingeing social changes demanded for development requires overcoming at least six significant theoretical and practical problems which the legislative theory and methodology outlined above have left largely unresolved:[84]

- First, does the instrumental use of law square with the ideologies loosely gathered under the rubric of the Rule of Law?
- Second, elected legislatures seem inherently ill-equipped to assess and enact laws that look to the broad, radical transformations that developing countries so desperately need. Given that legislative disability, how to draft relatively short bills, focused on resolving specific narrow problems, to accomplish broad, far-reaching institutional change?
- Third, 'good governance' requires effective civil society (i.e., NGO) participation in governmental decision-making. Yet, even in developed country democracies, public participation in government frequently means little more than a fifteen-minute exercise in voting for a representative or a President at stated intervals. How can government stimulate more meaningful participation?
- Fourth, what sort of social science research methodology should legislative drafters employ to ground development law on facts, logically organised as required by institutionalist legislative theory?
- Fifth, how ought drafters, using legislative theory's problem-solving methodology to structure the available evidence, deal with the question of 'value choice'?
- Sixth, can drafters use the research report as a *quality control* for their legislation?

We describe these issues and suggest some lines of attack.

---

84 Developing theory always remains a project in progress. As the world shrinks and changes, those of us concerned with the use of law to facilitate peaceful, democratic change will always confront new challenges. The six problems mentioned here includes those problems attendant on the attempted use of legislative theory and methodology that, at the time of writing, strike us as requiring further work. No doubt our readers will – and should – think of additional issues related to theory that require further exploration.

Does the Instrumental Use of Law Offend the Rule of Law?

To what extent, if at all, do – or should – the values clustered around the ideology of the Rule of Law constrain *legislative* discretion? Although every scholar writing on 'The Rule of Law' seems to define the term differently,[85] the literature repeatedly refers to two propositions: the Rule of Law means at least (1) 'A government of laws, not of men',[86] and (2) 'no person is above the law'.[87] On their face, these rules purport to apply not only to the executive and the judiciary, but also, at least insofar as positive law so states, to the legislature.[88]

How to tease out of these two dicta prescriptions to make it less likely that the legislature will legislate arbitrarily, without hobbling its necessary discretion to devise legislative solutions for pressing social problems? We – tentatively – identify four criteria of legislative decision making required to conform to the Rule of Law.

- The legislature must conform to positive law.[89]
- As for the judiciary and executive, the Rule of Law demands non-arbitrary legislative decision making. That in turn requires transparency, accountability[90] and maximum feasible participation.[91]

---

85 See J. Shklar 'AA Political Theory and the Rule of Law' in C. Allan, Hutchinson and P. Monaghan (eds) *The Rule of Law: Ideal or Ideology* (1987) at 1.

86 See *Constitution*, Massachusetts, Art. XXX (1780) ('In the government of this commonwealth, the legislative department shall never exercise the executive and judicial powers or either of them: the executive shall never exercise the legislative and judicial powers, or either of them: the judicial shall never exercise the legislative and executive powers, or either of them: to the end it may be a government of laws and not of men.')

87 See A.V. Dicey *Lectures on Law and Public Opinion in England* (1882) pp. 114–15. ('[N]ot only that ... no man is above the law, but (what is a different thing) that ... every man, whatever be his rank or condition, is subject to the ordinary law of the realm and amenable to the jurisdiction of the ordinary tribunals ...).

88 Authors have not always assumed that the Rule of Law constrained the legislature. See J.D. Goldsworthy *The Sovereignty of Parliament: History and Philosophy* (Oxford: Clarendon press, 1999); S. Sherry 'Independent Judges and Independent Justice' *61 (1998) Law & Contemporary Problems*. (The classic description of legislative omnipotence was that 'an act of parliament can do no wrong, although it may do several things that look pretty odd' City of London v. Wood, 12 Mod. Rep. 669, 678 (KB 1701).)

89 For example, the US Constitution forbids Congress from enacting a law impairing freedom of press or speech, forbids bills of attainder prohibits a law that violates the *nulla poena sine lege* maxim. These tend to make arbitrary law-making less likely. See, generally, Jeremy Waldron 'Legislation and the Rule of Law' 1 (2007) *Legisprudence* pp. 91 and 106.

90 See *infra*, text following note 120.

91 A well-organised legislature's procedural rules tend to produce non-arbitrary legislative outputs. Waldron (2007), following Dicey, *supra*, note 93 points out that:

Legislation is not the same as passing a resolution or the issuing of a decree; it is a formally defined act consisting of a laborious process; in a well-structured legislature that process involves successive stages of deliberation and voting in each of three institutions, in two of which the legislation in subject to scrutiny at the hands of myriad representatives of various social interests.

- Non-arbitrary decision making requires that lawmakers *justify* a law by demonstrating that it constitutes the product of a *reasoned choice.*[92]
- The *remedy* – the substantive content of the legislation – must itself conform to the Rule of Law.[93]

'Drafting Small' to Make Large Institutional Change[94]

Institutions consist of interacting patterns of repetitive behaviours. The larger the institution, the more sets of behaviours comprise it. To change a large institution therefore requires drafting a host of detailed rules. A single bill containing all the detailed rules to change a large institution runs to many, many pages.[95] In every legislature, legislative time constitutes a scarce resource. The longer the bill, the more time it requires – and hence the less chance of the bill receiving a full hearing on the merits. Presented with a huge bill, the legislature too readily throws up its hands in frustration. More frequently than not, it tables the bill indefinitely, adjourns without acting on the bill, or defeats or enacts the bill without genuine legislative scrutiny.[96]

How might a drafter draft 'small' bills, each hacking away at a relatively small sector of a larger institution, and yet ensure that the legislative programme has coherence, so that, at the end of the day, the law accomplishes major transformations? We suggest five potential strategies that invite further investigation:

92 As described in Part III above, institutionalist legislative theory and its problem-solving methodology offer a guide for preparing a research report that, based on the relevant facts logically organised, will likely persuade a rational skeptic that the proposed law results from a reasoned choice.

93 For example, a law that creates an agency with broad, unreviewable, secret, unlimited decision-making discretion to hold 'enemy combatants' prisoners without charge, without trial, for an unlimited time, runs afoul of the Rule of Law – and never mind the quality of the deliberations that preceded that law's enactment...

94 Large portions of this section derive without further attribution from A. Seidman and R.B. Seidman 'Introduction' (in Ukrainian) to the Ukrainian edition of Seidman, Seidman and Abeysekere (2001, 2007).

95 For example, in 1992, the Democratic Party held a majority in both houses of the Congress, and also the presidency. The Clinton administration presented the Congress with a Health Care Bill containing slightly more than 1,300 pages of text. The bill failed of passage.

96 A large bill enhances the probabilities of well placed actors secreting in the bill provisions that operate against the public interest. (For example, in the US, the Patriot Act (P.L. 107–56, 26 October 2001, enacted in the frenzy that followed the terrorist attacks of 11 September 2001, contained *1,016* separate provisions. Many complained about provisions of that Act that surfaced after enactment – but evaded discussion during enactment. Hidden in the fine print, these provisions too easily escape open discussion, let alone intelligent, informed voting. Another example: consider the custom of the United States Congress to obtain funding for 'earmarks' Individual representatives and senators add these to spending bills. They consist of specific funding provisions for specific projects, of interest to the earmark's sponsor. These rarely become the subject of debate. Congress enacts them *sub silentio,* and (save for the item's sponsor), in ignorance.

- Prepare a legislative programme, probably for adoption by the legislature. That programme would specify *who* will do *what* to draft the many successive 'small' bills required to change the larger institution. Draft an 'intransitive' bill, in which the law creates an agency, and delegates to that agency the power to write the detailed rules for the entire sector.[97] (Note that an intransitive law grants legislative power to appointed, not elected officials.)
- In the tradition of the Law Reform Commissions, popular in many common law jurisdictions in the middle of the last century, create a Law and Development Commission to draft *for enactment by the legislature* the many 'small' bills required to transform a large institution.
- Draft a 'framework' law, for instance, a law creating the new implementing institutions required to instate the new, larger institution (which would then require further detailed legislation).
- Use 'soft law' to state the general objectives that the lawmakers desire the new, transformed larger institution to achieve.[98]

Each of these several responses may, in appropriate circumstances, solve the problem of 'drafting small' to achieve large results. Further research seems essential to evaluate these and other possible strategies as a basis for resolving the paradox implicit in 'drafting small' to transform large institutions. We suggest that the law will more likely induce conforming behaviour if the stakeholders in prospective legislation participate in the law-making process.

Ensuring Participation

As we have earlier argued, to meet the standards of the Rule of Law and good governance alike, government generally must, so far as practicable, engage stakeholders in the decision making process. Democratic imperatives suggest that that requirement applies with peculiar importance to the law-making processes. How might stakeholders participate in the law-making process? More narrowly, how might they participate early in the drafting process?

We pointed out earlier that, too often, even scholars think of drafting as a more or less mechanical, 'technical' process. Not so; just as an architect holds a central position in the house building exercise, so a drafter holds a central position in the bill drafting exercise. Both 'fill the gap' between policy and doing, and thus inevitably take part in policy making.

Like other governmental decision making institutions, the drafting process must meet the standards of good governance. That includes participation by stakeholders, either in person or through the elements of civil society (i.e. NGOs). Here we ask how might stakeholders participate in the drafting process? That question becomes, *where* in that process might stakeholders meaningfully participate, and how? By

97 See Seidman, Seidman and Abeysekere (2001) pp. 155–65.

98 See *supra*, text at note 82.

what *means* might they do so?[99] That constitutes a problem that, for Law and Development, merits a place on the agenda.

Social Science for Drafting

Legislation will only *work* if based on accurate estimates of the behavioural consequences of proposed legislative interventions. As Figure 19.1 suggests, that depends upon accurate information about the social circumstances within which the new law will function.

That poses an additional problem for a practitioner of Law and Development. The information required plainly falls within the general purview of the social sciences. Social science, however, comes in a variety of forms and styles. What kinds of social science does a drafter concerned with Development require? We discuss three ways in which the instrumental use of law demands a different sort of social science practice than that used by many, probably most social scientists.

The objective of the research Most of the social science that one learns in university consists of efforts to develop a theory that accounts for the maximum quantity of evidence: the more the evidence that a theory orders, the more robust the theory.[100] Academic social scientists look for such 'covering' laws.[101]

Covering laws help in understanding the world.[102] A covering law presumes that a mono-causal explanation suffices. In order to design a law that *works*, a drafter must look for multi-causal explanations. Looking for a 'covering law,' academic social scientists tend to look for covariant factors, evidenced by as wide a sample as practicable. They use the familiar 'tools of social science', for example, survey or polling data. In cases where a drafter must do their own research, they usually do not use the 'tools of social science'.They have little choice but to rely on 'qualitative' evidence – anecdotes, case studies, focus groups, and the like.[103]

99 For a first attempt at that problem, see Seidman, Seidman and Uate, *supra*, note 82.

100 See L. Mjøset 'Understanding of Theory in the Social Sciences' *ARENA Working Papers* WP 99/33 (www.arena.uio.no/publications/wp99_33.htm) visited 22 January 2008. Dominant theory in social sciences is the 'deductive–nomological notion of theory.' 'This is also called the covering law model of explanation: The law [in the sense of a "scientific" law] is the black box which transforms causes into effects. Theory is a set of such laws. Theory is compact knowledge: Many regularities can be subsumed under the same general law, making research systematic and cumulative ...Theory is thus an ever more complete system of universal laws.' at 1.

101 Mjøset, *supra*, note 110.

102 For example, from classical economics, 'one can explain all human behaviour by incentives'; from the New Institutional Economics, 'One can explain all market-oriented behaviours by transaction costs'; or from Marxism, 'All history is the history of class struggle.'

103 At any rate, drafters seldom have an interest in the *frequency* of specific behaviours. Whether the murder rate in Newstate is 100 per 100,000 population per year, or 1,000 per 100,000 population, Newstate likely still needs a murder statute.

Controlling 'values' in the drafting process

A law consists of a set of commands, prohibitions and permissions – that is, of *normative* propositions. The choice of *this* normative proposition instead of *that* one constitutes, people say, a *normative* choice. That choice imbricates a choice between alternative 'values' 'Values' and 'facts' are incommensurate.[104] Because of that incommensurability, they say, a 'value' proposition – a proposition stating what a person *ought* to do – defies control in terms of facts and logic.[105] If that argument holds, surely we blow with the wind when we urge that one can justify a proposed law in terms of facts and logic.

The pragmatic philosphers come to a different result. A drafter following the problem-solving methodology[106] arrives at the final form of the proposed bill as a result of a series of *discretionary choices*.[107] To what extent can one obtain intellectual control over these discretionary choices?

We suggest that one might discover an answer in a suggestion made by Sesonske.[108] As applied to law, the statement that 'such and such is a good thing to do' constitutes either a statement of the *suitability* of the prescribed behaviour to help ameliorate a specified social problem, or a statement of *preferences* made by the lawmakers.

Many discretionary choices do not involve preference choices. Norton Long points out that the many different kinds of hammers exist. Using a hammer in action, workers in one trade discover ways that they might change and improve the hammer to make the hammer better adapted to the specific task at hand. Not 'values and attitudes', not subjective preferences, but actual practice, in each case warrants the changed design of the hammer.[109]

---

104 Some denote that as 'the fact/value dichotomy' in H. Putnam *Reason, Truth and History* (Cambridge: Cambridge University Press, 1981) at 127.

105 See G.E. Moore *Principia Ethica* (Cambridge: Cambridge University Press, 1903); A.J. Ayer *Language, Truth and Logic* (New York: Dover Publications, 1936).

106 See *supra*, text following footnote 75.

107 For example, What social problem should the law address – and is the state of affairs that one person calls 'problematic' also seem problematic to another? What behaviours constitute the specified social problem? What range of explanations ought the drafter put to empirical test? What range of potential alternative solutions ought the drafter consider?

108 See A. Sesonske *Value and Obligation: the Foundations of an Empiricist Ethical Theory* (Berkeley, University of California Press, 1957) at 11 ('Statements containing either 'right', 'good', or 'ought', whether ethical or non-ethical, serve either one or both of two functions. They express judgments of worth or judgments about the existence or satisfaction of requirements.')

109 See Norton Long 'Introduction' in E.J. Meehan (1969). Some argue that no difference ultimately exists between suitability and preference choices: both depend on a preference choice. (The upholsterer must first state that they *wants* to upholster the chair.) The worth of the suitability judgment, however, does not depend on the prior existence of a preference choice to do upholstery. One might restate the proposition thus, 'If one wants to upholster a chair, an upholsterer's magnetic hammer works better than another sort of hammer.' The accuracy of that proposition does not depend upon a prior 'value' choice. Independently of 'values', one can assess the suitability judgment in terms of factual evidence generated in *doing* upholstery.

So also with law. Actual practice resolves issues of suitability. Can actual practice also resolve issues of *preference*, of desirability? A preliminary response: most of the daily grist of the legislative mill consists of matters of relatively non-controversial character. For example,[110] The defined social problem consists of loan officers in the South African National Development Bank who give loans not to small peasant farmers, but only to large commercial farmers. You assert that the only actor with whom a bill need concern itself consists of those loan officers. I assert that the new law should also address the behaviours of the bureaucratic superiors of those loan officers, who either willfully or negligently permit the loan officers to mis-prioritise the Bank's loan funds. The issue between us does not depend upon our subjective preferences, but on the quality of the propositions about matters of fact that each of us submit to justify the relevant claim.

Another example, A bill addressed the problem of widespread post-partum depression ('PPD') among post-natal mothers.[111] The proposed bill required: (a) that on discharge from the hospital, the hospital should provide the post-natal mother with a pamphlet warning her of the possibilities of PPD, how to recognise its symptoms, and elementary steps to take if she finds herself suffering from it; (b) that a practising gynaecologist attend a one-day post-qualification course in the problems of PPD; and (c) that a gynaecologist examine a patient for PPD in the six-week post-natal examination of the patient. The drafter demonstrated convincingly by facts and logic (a) that a surprisingly large proportion of post-natal mothers suffer from a degree of PPD, (b) that a strong explanation for the effects of PPD lies in the ignorance of post-natal mothers about PPD; (c) the two contact points between the medical care system and the post-natal mother occurred at the two points mentioned in the proposed bill; (d) that very few gynaecologists have had training in dealing with mental illnesses generally or PPD in particular, and (e) that the additional cash and social costs resulting from the proposed solution seem negligible, and the benefits manifest.[112] People may differ in the priority that they might assign to enacting a law addressing the social problem of wide-spread PPD. Considering the low cost factors, and the relatively high benefit factors, surely experience teaches that, either immediately or very soon thereafter, an appropriate agency ought to design, draft and implement such a bill.

For those bills, it would seem that the requirements of justification in terms of facts and logic satisfy the conditions both of rational and of discursive discourse.[113]

---

110 See A. Seidman, R.B. Seidman and M. McCord 'A Theory and Methodology for Investigating the Function of Law in Relation to Government Institutions: The Case of the Development Bank of South Africa' in Hugh Corder (1994).

111 A student at Boston University, Addie Strombolo, prepared such a bill and a supporting research report (2007), on file with the authors.

112 The cost of producing the required pamphlet seems very small; the gynaecologist today customarily performs both a pre-discharge and a six-week post-partum examination of the client; and, for a stated number of days per year, under existing law a physician must attend post-qualification medical education yearly. (The proposed one-day instruction in diagnosing and treating post-partum depression would count towards satisfying that requirement.)

113 Try putting the argument over same-sex marriage into the problem-solving methodology mentioned above. Can one state exactly what constitutes the social problem that

A few bills in every legislative session concern matters that seemingly do not lend themselves to rational argument. These frequently concern matters more symbolic than substantive – in our era, for example, the debates over same-sex marriage, or concerning bigamy. For these hot-button, usually 'social' issues, many doubt that either side can formulate an argument that can catch the approbation of the other side.[114]

Quality Control for Legislation: Effectiveness, the Rule of Law and the Public Interest

By what criteria might one assess the relative *quality* of a proposed law? That has three legs. First, will a proposed bill likely *work*? Second, does the bill conform to the imperatives of 'the Rule of Law'? Third, will the bill advance the 'public interest'? (How might one determine the public interest? How to determine whether the bill will advance it?)

The first two of these we have already discussed.[115] How to determine before its implementation whether a proposed law will advance the public interest?[116] As already mentioned,[117] Hannah Pitkin, Habermas and Rawls have an underlying agreement. A proponent of a bill must justify it in terms that should win acceptance both by its proponents, and *by a rational skeptic* 'across the aisle'. The parties can reach that consensus by either of Habermas's two forms of argument: by arguments based on 'power' (that is, by bargaining), or by 'rational' argument.[118]

---

same-sex marriage poses? Or ask similar questions about a bigamous marriage?

114 Hannah Pitkin holds that a representative who votes in a way that most of their constituents oppose must justify their vote in terms that should persuade them – a position close to that of Habermas, *supra* note 69 and Rawls. That does not apply to these highly contentious matters. So contentious, she asserts, are these hot-button issues, that a representative seemingly must abandon trying to justify their vote in terms of facts and logic (Better: on many, probably most 'hot-button' issues, one or the other party takes a position impervious to rational argument).

115 Whether the bill *works*, see *supra*, Figure 19.1 and accompanying text; whether the process and the bill meet the requirements of the Rule of Law, see *supra*, text following note 71.

116 Obviously, after a bill comes into force, only by post-enactment evaluation can one determine whether it furthers the public interest.

117 *Supra*, text following note 69.

118 See R. Bolton 'Habermas's Theory of Communicative Action and the Theory of Social Capital' accessed at (www.williams.edu/Economics/papers/Habermas.pdf). 'One of his best-known ideas is communicative action, in which actors in society seek to reach common understanding and to coordinate actions by reasoned argument, consensus, and cooperation rather than strategic action strictly in pursuit of their own goals.' (Habermas, 1984 at 86); Wikipedia (www.en.wikipedia.org/wiki/Discourse_ethics) 'Kant extracted moral principles from the necessities forced upon a rational subject reflecting on the world. Habermas extracts moral principles from the necessities forced upon individuals engaged in the discursive justification of validity claims, from the inescapable presuppositions of communication and argumentation.'

As we have argued, if a bill wins support 'across the aisle' the bill comes as close as may be to serving the *public* interest. Only an argument grounded in facts and logic has the potential of attracting support across the political spectrum.[119]

The extent to which a bill furthers the public interest – the metric of its quality – depends upon the arguments made in its favour and against. That implies that every substantial bill ought to come to the legislature accompanied by a research report stating the justification for the proposed new law. Such a research report acts as quality control over legislation. It simultaneously satisfies the requirement of accountability, by requiring legislators to literally give an account of their votes. To institutionalise that requirement, existing law-making institutions likely require significant change, and therefore a new or amended constitutive law.[120]

Summary

This part focused on six topics that seemingly require additional scholarly attention. All relate to the drafter's task of designing the substantive details of a law, and thus filling the gap between policy and the practical tasks of Development: new attention to the Rule of Law as it affects legislation; solving problems of 'drafting small' to make large institutional changes; ensuring stakeholder participation in the law-making process; designing social science enquiry to suit the problems of drafting; solving the problem of 'value choice'; and institutionalisation of a research report requirement as a quality control over legislation. In addition, as urged in earlier parts, rationality in the drafting process requires the adoption of institutional legislative theory and methodology; in legislative design and its justification, the consistent use not of 'preferences' to justify choice but facts and logic; above all, close attention to the role and function of drafters and drafting in the law-making process and therefore in Development: These all require a new 'legal culture'. That constitutes the challenge to Law and Development scholars: How to develop the tools to 'bridge the gap' between those who 'do Policy' and 'the implementing guys,'[121] and, so doing, to create that new legal culture.

Conclusion: Whither Law and Development?

Poverty, vulnerability, poor governance and ineffective administration of the Development project plague the world's poor countries. Development frequently fails because of the poor quality of the laws that purport to 'fill the gap'. A developing

119 See Pitkin *supra,* note 69.

120 It does not suffice merely to require a research report. The new laws on law-making institutions must also specify the minimum content of a research report. A research report so structured can serve as quality control with respect of legislation susceptible of rational justification, and where the parties to the discussion both fit the paradigm of 'rational skeptic'

121 See the Epigraph to this chapter.

country more than most requires laws that translate the broad 'visions' of policymakers into *detailed* rules to guide those who must achieve policy's objectives.

Today, everybody, it seems, has an opinion about the future of Law and Development. Most of the current literature on Law and Development tends to further our understanding of the ever-problematic relationship between 'law' and 'development'.[122] That literature advances our larger *understanding* of the law and development enterprise, frequently in searching fashion.[123]

For academics, the law has an important *theoretical* aspect. Scholars can (and some do) supply an important critique of the current strategies for development. That critique has great interest to one engaged in determining the *priorities* that, with respect to legislation, at least, constitutes the essence of 'policy'.

Law, however, does not serve only academic interests. Lawyers in the trenches of development do little to determine the *priorities* of the problems that they engage. They have as well other, *practical* interests. A practising 'development' lawyer needs to know how to use existing law to benefit their clients, whether third world governments or transnational corporations: The substantive and procedural laws dealing with patent and copyright, lease-back agreements, land reform, foreign direct investment, fifteen feet and more of volumes of codes and regulations to understand and to use in the trenches.

That does not exhaust the practical work of practical 'development' lawyers. This paper focuses on the little studied but enormously important task of legislative drafting, broadly conceived. To further the development enterprise, the law must transform the institutions which condemn the poor countries of the world to poverty, vulnerability and poor governance. That requires the drafters to 'bridge the gap' that too often separates the broad generalities of 'policy' from the boots-in-the mud work of Development: building roads, staffing legislatures, operating land reform programmes, inspecting for compliance with environmental protection measures, a infinity of tasks.

The parties doing that boots-in-the-mud work need instruction about how to carry out their tasks. Drafters uniquely play a role that positions them to write those rules and thus to 'fill the gap.' By plans and specifications, an architect gives detailed instructions to the builder – and thus determines the operative face of a family's new house 'policy'. By designing the substantive details of the laws, a drafter gives detailed instructions to those who will implement the law – and thus determines the operative face of development policy. Whether the law's addressees conform their

---

122 See Nader, *supra*, footnote 6 (the relationship between indigenous dispute settlement systems and those put forward by the 'legal missionaries' who carry forward the work of Law and Development); D. Kennedy 'Three Globalizations of Law and Legal thought: 1850–2000' in Trubek and Santos (eds) *supra*, note 6 (study of Law and Development should, *inter alia*, concern itself with the 'repositioning' of 'law' with respect to 'development'); David Kennedy 'Laws and Developments' in Hatchard and Perry-Kessaris, (eds) *supra*, note 6 (the uses of law or the market to achieve distributional equity); Philippe Cullet 'Patents and Heath in Developing Countries' in Hatchard and Petrry-Kessaqris (eds) *supra*, note 6, at 78 (specific laws with a more or less direct relationship to the development project).

123 See K. Rittich 'The Future of the Law and Development Enterprise' in Trubek and Alvaro (eds) *supra*, note 6, Kennedy *supra*, note 123.

behaviour to the law's prescriptions, and whether those prescriptions appropriately address the social problem to remedy which the law aims – whether the law *works* – depends upon the *detailed* content of the rules. The drafter must address those rules to two broad sets of actors: the primary role occupants, and the agencies charged with overseeing the behaviours of those primary role occupants.[124] Whether a law *works* depends upon the skill of its drafter.

Nevertheless, most contemporary law and development syllabi and scholarships treat the question of the design of a bill with silence. Their silence shouts that they view the problem of designing legislation as unproblematic, hardly worthy of intense intellectual effort.

Law, however, is not a free good in unlimited supply. It comes in very short supply, crafted only with difficulty. *Effective* policy finds expression not in the statements of a policymaker, but in the product of the legislative drafter. How to design a bill's detailed content in a way likely to induce behaviour both conforming to the law, and effective in ameliorating the targeted social problem, should constitute a central concern of scholars. It should hold an important place in syllabi of courses *sub nom.* 'Law and Development.[125]

This article suggests radical changes in the conception of the proper subject-matter for the sub-discipline of Law and Development, and equally radical institutional changes in the law-making process. The argument rests on four propositions.

1. The legion of social, economic and political problems of the world's poor countries consist of problematic *institutions*, that is, problematic patterns of repetitive *behaviours*.
2. State power inevitably plays a central function in changing those problematic behaviours.
3. The law – broadly conceived – constitutes governments' primary means of exercising State power.
4. Those who design and draft the law's *detailed* commands, permissions and prohibitions play a crucial role in determining whether the law effectively implements a policy purporting to require changed social behaviours.

Only if carefully designed can legislation accomplish its behaviour changing tasks. This chapter presents a legislative theory and methodology to accomplish that purpose. It then discusses six areas that require scholarly attention: issues relating to the Rule of Law, drafting 'small' to achieve large institutional change, ensuring stakeholder participation in law drafting, social science for drafters, 'values' in the bill creating process and developing a mechanism to provide quality control for bills.

To focus on the role of the legislative drafter requires a radical change in today's legal culture. Academics concerned with law and development ought to focus not only on large questions of law and development *policy*, but also on the *practice* of law and development, especially, on the role of the legislative drafter.

124 See Figure 19.1 and accompanying text.

125 See *Accord*: Cyrul *supra*, notes 74 at 101.

That thesis conforms to the principal premises of legisprudence. That new variety of law-centred philosophy holds that legislation deserves the same sort of academic attention that the judicial process and litigation lawyering have traditionally received. Legislation consists of rules and standards for the exercise of State power, the organised force of the organised community. At least in the early years following a change in the law, in order to *work*, those rules demand exposition *in detail. Development depends on how those rules work.* How to formulate and to assess those rules to ensure that they do *work* is worthy of sustained and concentrated attention.

Some years back, with words that we repeat here, we concluded a book that we wrote:

> The last decade of [the Twentieth Century] began with hopes of third world independence as littered shards across a seemingly desolate moonscape. Dante inscribed one alternative over the gates of Hell: 'Abandon all hope, ye who enter here.'
>
> Another alternative exists. Human beings constructed that despair; human beings can change it. They can do so, however, only by invoking their specifically human characteristics: their capacities to solve common problems through democratic participation and cooperation grounded on reason informed by experience.[126]

No place does that injunction sound more loudly and more clearly than with respect of the uses of law to bring about the kinds of social change we denote as 'Development'

126 See Seidman and Seidman *supra*, note 112.

Chapter 20

Drafters, Drafting and the Policy Process

Constantin Stefanou

Introduction

Henry Thring's initial approach that the drafting office does not consider policy or substance just form has been quite prevalent amongst drafters – especially in common law jurisdictions – for most of the twentieth century. Experts, of course, have noted that it is inevitable for drafters to involve themselves with substance as well as form:

> At first glance the purists' belief that a drafter should leave policy decisions entirely to others is attractive. Certainly a drafter has not been elected or appointed to make policy. However, if drafters deferred to elected and appointed officials on every policy issue, those persons would spend an inordinate amount of time making picayune decisions and drafters would do very little drafting.[1]

Indeed some experts have explicitly exposed Henry Thring's approach as a 'myth' which had adverse consequences for policymaking, especially in the developing world.[2] The link between drafters, drafting and the policy process is made in practically every textbook on legislative drafting. Yet, with few exceptions, discussion tends to be reserved to the 'legislative process' (which is a part of the wider policy process) and not the policy process as a whole[3] (see Figure 20.1).

This chapter will attempt to examine the drafter's input on the wider policy process. Strictly speaking, according to Henry Thring's approach, the role of the drafter should be confined to just one stage of the policy process: Formulation. However, in practice, the role of the drafter spills over into other stages. In this chapter, I will examine the role of drafters in each of the stages of the policy process in an attempt to show that drafters' input and involvement spans across most – if not all – of these stages. Moreover, I argue that what determines the extent of the drafter's role are: (a) the size of the jurisdiction and (b) the nature of the drafter's

---

1 See J. Stark *The Art of the Statute* (Colorado: Rothman and Co, 1996) at 17.

2 See A. Seidman, R.B. Seidman and N. Abeyesekere, *Legislative Drafting for Democratic Social Change* (The Hague: Kluwer Law International, 2001) pp. 30–41.

3 See V.C.R.A.C. Crabbe, *Legislative Drafting*, (London: Cavendish, 1993) ch. 2, pp. 19–36; see also G.C. Thornton, *Legislative Drafting*, 4th edn (London: Butterworths, 1996) ch. 7; see D. Greenberg (ed.) *Craies on Legislation* (London: Sweet and Maxwell, 2004) pp. 201–302, section on the Legislative Process.

appointment, for example, does the drafter work for a central drafting office, a ministry or local government.

I should point out here that I am not taking a prescriptive approach. In other words, I do not imply that the drafter should usurp the opportunity and make policy behind the backs of legislators (not that a drafter would encounter much opposition since 'going along is easy, for the legislator generally lacks information to support a dissent').[4] I am simply documenting an ongoing involvement between drafters and the wider policy process that most drafters take for granted but experts tend to bypass.

The Policy Process

'A policy is a broader notion than a decision ... a policy covers a bundle of decisions ... it reflects an intention to decide in a particular way in the future' [5] The policy process refers to the series of stages/steps that policy must go through in order to be completed. Graph 1 shows the stages of the policy process as well as the stages of the legislative process.[6] The reason for including the stages of the legislative process is very straight forward. As already mentioned most experts refer to the input of drafters in policy-making with reference to the 'legislative process'. As can be seen in Graph 1, the legislative process is a part of policymaking in the sense that it is part of the policy process located between the formulation stage and the implementation stage. It is, though, by no means the only part of policymaking where drafters are involved.

Large and Small Jurisdictions

Spare a thought for the Attorney General's office of Lesotho in the late 1990s. With a total staff of three (including the Attorney General himself) the same three public servants liaised with government, provided legal advice and opinions, drafted legislation and then proceeded to prosecute offenders on the basis of their own drafts. Was it possible – or indeed even prudent under the circumstances – for the drafting office of Lesotho to avoid considering policy or substance just concentrating on form?

Clearly there is a difference in the way drafting offices operate in large and small jurisdictions. Large jurisdictions usually have dedicated units or individuals who specialise in drafting. It is, therefore, possible for drafters to 'insulate' themselves from the different stages of the policy process. In contrast, in small jurisdictions the drafters' position is more '*sui generis*' – depending on the idiosyncrasies of the jurisdiction and, of course, the volume of work.

---

4 See J. Davies, *Legislative Law and Process*, 2nd edn (St Paul: West Publishing, 1986) at 7.

5 See R. Hague and M. Harrop, *Comparative Government and Politics*, 6th edn (Basingstoke: Palgrave 2004) at 309.

6 The stages of the legislative process do vary in different jurisdictions, The Graph indicates basic stages of the legislative process that exist in all jurisdictions.

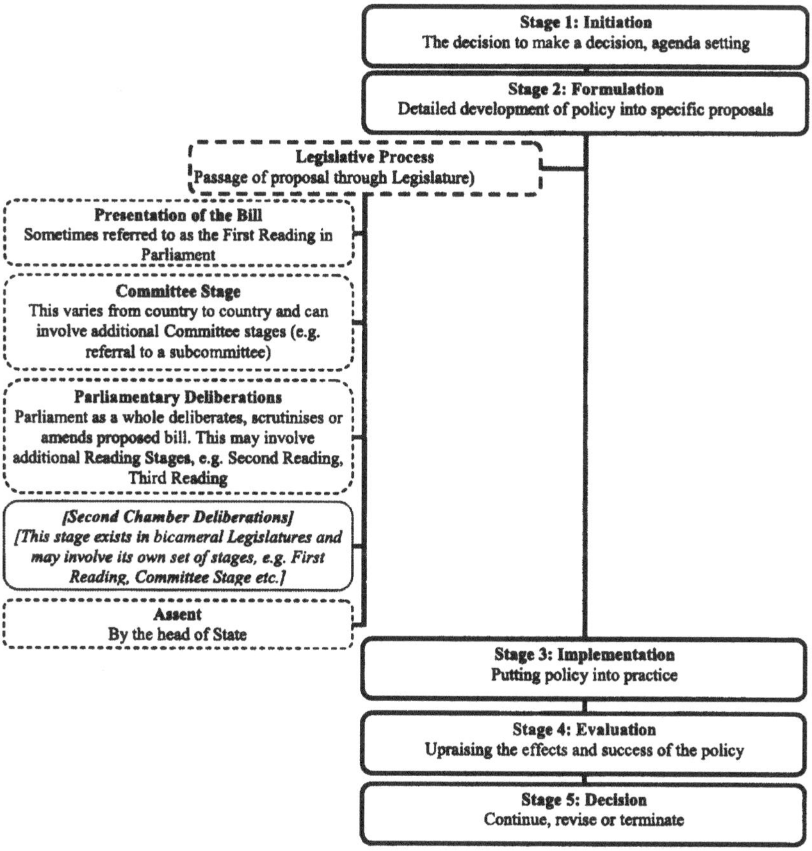

Figure 20.1 The stages of the policy process and the legislative process[7]

From a practical point of view, in small jurisdictions, the involvement of drafters with the different stages of the policy process is almost self-evident. Professional drafters who have worked in small jurisdictions tend to take it for granted that their involvement will go beyond pure drafting and do not perceive this involvement as a conflict of interest. No doubt necessity dictates slightly different roles between drafters in small and large jurisdictions.

7 Adapted from Hague and Harrop (2004) at 256 and 309; also see G. Mahler, *Comparative Politics an Institutional and Cross Cultural Approach* (New Jersey: Pearson, 2003) Table 4.9.

Drafting and the Policy Process

Policy Initiation and the Drafter

Strictly speaking in most liberal democracies policy initiation is usually the domain of the executive (government). The origins of legislation vary from country to country according to its constitution; however, there are some broad similarities which exist across liberal democracies:

- Government legislation can often be traced to the political manifesto of the party which won the general elections.
- Obligations arising from International treaties or agreements.
- Legislation introduced by other bodies specifically allowed to do so in that country (e.g. in some countries the Central Bank has the right to propose legislation).
- Routine legislation, which is passed every year whichever government is in power (e.g. finance bills).
- Recommendations from Commissions established for a particular purpose.
- Individual Members of Parliament can propose bills concerning local/ constituency issues (e.g. bills concerning local or regional hospitals).
- Science (new scientific developments).
- Technology (the application of scientific developments).
- Emergencies (e.g. earthquakes, floods etc).
- Media pressures.

Depending on the jurisdiction the role of the drafter might range from no involvement to major involvement. As Tommy Neal put it, 'Ultimately, decisions are made by elected officials, but those decisions may be heavily influenced by the input of staff'.[8]

In some large jurisdictions the drafter will have no role in policy initiation. Having said this, often in the US the help of a drafter is sought at an early stage as parliamentarians tend to be 'ideas persons' and Legislative Counsel offices in both the Senate and the Congress have teams of trained drafters who provide parliamentarians with impartial advice.[9] In small jurisdictions, however, the drafter might even be the one who commences the process for new legislation or revision of existing legislation, for example, in small jurisdictions drafters are often solely responsible for the introduction of some types of routine legislation.

We must make a distinction here between brand new legislation and reform of existing legislation. Most drafters in most jurisdictions revise existing legislation.

8 See T. Neal, *Lawmaking and the Legislative Process* (Phoenix: Oryx Press, 1996) at 24.

9 See A.E. Black, *From Inspiration to Legislation How an Idea Becomes a Bill* (New Jersey: Pearson Prentice Hall, 2007) at 65 and 66. However, as Strokoff points out, Legislative Counsel is bound by statute not to try to influence policy; see S. Strokoff, 'How our Laws are made: A Ghost Writer's View' US House of Representatives, Office of the Legislative Counsel, August 2003, accessed at (www.legcoun.house.gov/drafting_public.htm).

Opportunities to draft brand new legislation are relatively rare and tend to come in batches. For example, decolonisation of Africa offered drafters the opportunity to create brand new legislation in African jurisdictions. Similarly, the collapse of the Eastern Bloc and the USSR offered drafters the opportunity to create brand new legislation in Eastern Europe and the former Soviet Republics. In established large jurisdictions it is quite rare for drafters to be asked to produce brand new legislation. For example, in the UK the last time this happened was the drafting of the 1998 Human Rights Act and, as Sir Edward Caldwell noted, it required consultations which cut across existing structures and involved numerous government departments over a prolonged period of time.[10] In other words, a key feature of the 'political decision' to proceed with a Human Rights Act was the *feasibility* of the proposal not merely in terms of a draft text but with reference to whether or not such an Act can become an organic part of the existing system. The view of the drafter on the feasibility of such policy proposals plays an important role in the final decision to proceed with a particular policy or with the timing of the introduction of a new policy. As Thornton put it:

> Involvement and input by an experienced drafter before the policy has been fully developed and accepted are likely to avoid delays during the drafting process.[11]

In smaller jurisdictions discussions with drafters concerning the ability of the drafting office itself to deal with brand new and complex policies are quite regular and not regarded as a breach of democratic processes. In fact, in smaller jurisdictions the *feasibility* question often becomes a decisive element in the introduction of a policy. For example, in the 1990s many small jurisdictions were urged to introduce legislation to combat money laundering. Despite urges by the US and the EU to do so quickly for many of these jurisdictions the problem was an objective one, that is, the ability of their drafting offices to produce such draft legislation quickly. Eventually, some simply copied legislation from other jurisdictions while others had to employ the services of professional drafters who had experience in drafting anti-money laundering legislation.

What becomes obvious is that drafters do have a role in policy initiation. It is not an 'institutionalised' role nor is it present for every single policy initiation decision. Obviously drafters in small jurisdictions are more – and more often – involved. But what is certain is that once again it appears that the notion that drafters consider neither policy nor substance is a myth.

Policy Formulation and the Drafter

Irrespective of jurisdiction this stage is dominated by drafters in the sense that they are the ones who will translate instructions or broad ideas into actual drafts. In fact, this stage of the Policy Process is often referred to as *Drafting of Legislation*.

---

10 Sir Edward Caldwell, 'Who did the Act? And How?' Lecture at the Institute of Advanced Legal Studies, 16 October 2006.

11 See Thornton (1996) at 26.

Depending on the jurisdiction the drafter might have detailed instructions or very broad instructions. This means that sometimes it is the drafter's responsibility to 'devise' appropriate legislation. In fact in some jurisdictions drafting instructions are so vague that:

> The policy objectives of the vast majority of draft proposals are poorly, ex post or even not formulated at all, and as such are not clear or are inadequate for the drafting of quality regulations and policies … the fact that many of the basic choices end up in the hands of the drafters alone means that the drafting can develop in a political vacuum …[12]

Another example, often repeated as an anecdote by professional drafters of that era, come in the aftermath of African decolonisation when it was not uncommon for politicians to give drafters instructions such as 'I want clean water in every household of every village in the land'

As is well understood by now, there are different styles of drafting depending on the jurisdiction. In the past distinctions were made between the common law and civil law styles of drafting. Indeed Sir William Dale himself noted the two different styles and although clearly preferring the common law style he, nevertheless, saw some of the merits of the civil law style.[13] Broadly speaking the main distinction between common law and civil law jurisdictions is that common law jurisdictions tend to have a centralised drafting unit sometimes part of the Attorney General's office often called Parliamentary Counsel's Office (PCO). In contrast in civil law jurisdictions, drafting is decentralised and mostly done by committees comprising civil servants, academics and sometimes parliamentarians. There are other differences of course,[14] most notably in the 'first draft' of a bill, which in common law jurisdictions is usually the work of the PCO while in civil law jurisdictions it can be the work of a lawyer in the relevant ministry or an academic at the request of a minister or even the work of a private law firm.

Once again we must make a distinction between large and small jurisdictions. In large jurisdictions the first draft tends to come from the relevant government department, for example, ministry or PCO. In contrast in small jurisdictions first drafts are sometimes the work of a donor country or organisation or even the work of professional drafters who sell the same draft to different small jurisdictions. In some cases even capable and efficient small jurisdictions are simply overwhelmed by the volume of work required for the completion of a task. For example, when Cyprus had to transpose the 81,000 pages of the *acquis communautaire* into its national legal system – in view of its accession to the EU – the volume of work was such that the

---

12 See World Bank Document 'Administrative Capacity in the EU 8: Slovakia Country Report' Background Paper, World Bank Poverty Reduction and Economic Management Unit Europe and Central Asia, September 2006, at 2–3.

13 See Sir William Dale, *Legislative Drafting: A New Approach* (London: Butterworths, 1977) at 331–41.

14 See P-P. Pigeon, *Drafting and Interpreting Legislation* (Toronto: Carswell, 1988) pp. 7–11.

AG's drafting unit had to employ and train more drafters and even then some of the transposing drafts had to be written by private law firms.[15]

The Drafter and the 'Travaux Préparatoires' In recent years the useful civil law practice of attaching travaux préparatoires[16] to the final draft has become quite fashionable.[17] This extensive report contains an analysis which includes the intent of the legislators, the rationale of the legislative solution and even model laws from other jurisdictions that have been used by the drafters. In common law jurisdictions we have had the parallel development of the explanatory notes which replaced the 'explanatory memorandum' and are published alongside Acts.[18] However, unlike the travaux préparatoires which tend to be lengthy and may include detailed socio-legal explanations of the legislators intentions,[19] the explanatory notes are much shorter in length (rarely over 2–3 pages) and not considered to be authentic interpretations of the law. From a practical point of view, in common law jurisdictions the explanatory notes are written by the drafters (and revised as the bill moves through the Legislative Process) and in some jurisdictions have become stylised one-page summaries that merely state the broad intention of the law.

One point to note here is that in some small jurisdictions (or in jurisdictions where drafting takes place inside a ministry) the drafters are even expected to complete relevant Regulatory Impact Assessment (RIA) checklists or even (for minor bills) a rudimentary cost-benefit analysis.[20] This is not the case in large common law jurisdictions where RIAs are prepared by specialists in the relevant ministries.

The Legislative Process and the Drafter Irrespective of the size of the jurisdiction the drafter is at their most active during this period. For example, in the US, drafting officers assist legislators with their proposals, make the initial and middle drafts while they are also involved in the so-called *horizontal* editing of a bill. In most jurisdictions drafting officers will assist the Minister in Parliament while their bill is discussed and will also do overnight redrafts if proposed amendments are agreed

15 For details of Cyprus' effort to transpose the EU acquis and the work that Cypriot drafters had to undertake, see C. Stefanou (ed.) *Cyprus and the EU: The Road to Accession* (Aldershot: Ashgate, 2005).

16 In some civil law jurisdictions these are also known as the 'Introductory Report' The French term here is used generically to reflect the practice in civil law jurisdictions.

17 This point has also been made by, K. Patchett 'Preparation, Drafting and Management of Legislative Projects' *Workshop on The Development of Legislative Drafting For Arab Parliaments*, Beirut, pp. 3–6 February 2003, at 28.

18 See Sir Christopher Jenkins 'Bills and Acts – Explanatory Notes'. Accessed at (www.parliamentary-counsel.gov.uk/bills_and_acts/explanatory_notes_article.aspx).

19 See the *avant garde* suggestions in A. Kasemets and M-L. Liiv 'The Use of Socio-Legal Information in the Draft Acts' Explanatory Memoranda: A Precondition for *Good Governance*' 12th NISPAcee Annual Conference, CEE Countries Inside and Outside the EU: Avoiding a New Divide, Vilnius, 13–15 May 2004.

20 See the SIGMA–OECD Report where the various checklists for drafters include a list for 'Cost and Economic Impact'. SIGMA–OECD, *Law Drafting and Regulatory Management in Central and Eastern Europe*, Sigma Papers No. 15 (Paris: OECD, 1997) at 11.

by Parliament. Although drafters obviously do not take an active part in the actual decision-making they are involved with most aspects of the Legislative Process.

Policy Implementation and the Drafter

Strictly speaking, in common law jurisdictions, drafters should not be – and under normal circumstances are not – directly involved in policy implementation. When it comes to policy implementation the drafters 'involvement' is indirect and one-sided. By 'one-sided' I mean that it is usually the drafters themselves who will take an active interest in observing the implementation of a complex bill to identify possible errors or lacunae identified by enforcement agencies and the courts. By 'indirect' I mean that drafters are under a general obligation (same as all civil servants) to implement wider government policy on issues, such as human rights, gender equality or indeed the implementation of international agreements – although as a result of their position drafters could be seen as key civil servants in the implementation of broad government policy.

However, in small jurisdictions (see the example of Lesotho in the late 1990s) the drafters' membership of the civil service means that they might be called on to implement their own drafts. In fact in small jurisdictions it is not uncommon for the AG (who might also be the drafter of a particular bill) to explain policy and help ministries with the implementation of the legislation he/she had drafted. While direct involvement of the drafter with policy implementation is rare, indirect involvement is less rare, for example, drafting legislation for implementing agencies (public or private/quango) or drafters at local/regional government level who may then routinely be called upon to implement their own drafts.

For most drafters in large common law jurisdictions the mere idea that drafters might be involved in policy implementation will sound extraordinary. However, in civil law jurisdictions where the drafting of legislation is not centralised in dedicated drafting units and is the result of multi-member committees, which include civil servants from relevant ministries, the idea is not extraordinary at all.[21] If anything, it makes sense for the ministerial appointees to the drafting committee to be individuals who will later be involved in policy implementation exactly because it is prudent for them to have a very good understanding of the new law, its rationale, its details and intricacies. A good example of this practice was the involvement of Ukrainian civil servants in the drafting of money laundering legislation (2003–04). Many of the civil servants who were Members of the committee that drafted the bill were subsequently transferred to relevant implementing and enforcement agencies because they were Ukraine's *de facto* experts in the field.[22]

---

21 A possible exception here is Canada where drafting takes place at State/territory level (Legislative Counsel Office) and Federal level (where there are centralised drafting services as well as drafters in some specific ministries and the Parliament). See Department of Justice, Canada, *National Survey for Legislative Drafting Services 2002*, (Ottawa: The International Cooperation Group, 2002).

22 The Institute of Advanced Legal Studies (University of London) has had first-hand experience of Ukraine's efforts to develop expertise in drafting and had at the time a close

When it comes to policy implementation it is clear that there are differences between common law and civil law jurisdictions as well as small and large jurisdictions. What is also clear is that even though policy implementation is not the main task of drafters (always depending on the type of jurisdiction), nevertheless, it can be part of their duties as civil servants.

Policy Evaluation and the Drafter

Policy evaluation has become an important element of the policy process to the point that in some jurisdictions bills must include clauses relating to their evaluation – including expenditure specifically allocated to 'evaluation'. The need for regular evaluation is one of the main themes in modern public administration[23] and, of course, in modern computer-aided drafting evaluation of legislation is a central theme:

> Evaluation of legislation is central to the task of legislative drafting: To build a knowledge management system for legislative drafters one needs to understand how legislation compares to its alternatives.[24]

Although in large common law jurisdictions it is unusual for individual drafters to be invited to ministerial policy evaluation sessions, it is quite usual for central drafting offices, for example, PCO's or AG's chambers, to hold their own evaluation sessions either at the end of the 'political year' (usually at the beginning of the summer recess) or at the end of a particularly difficult draft. Possible exceptions are US State legislatures where drafters[25] are often invited to attend policy evaluation sessions of the legislature so that they become fully aware of legislators' concerns about a particular policy. The logic is that they will then be in a better position to make changes in the original law should the legislators decide so.

In small common law jurisdictions, especially in the developing world, things are slightly different in that policy evaluation is not always performed by the ministry – let alone the small drafting office. Yet, exactly because the drafting office is small and the drafters are multitaskers rather than pure drafters, serving the AG's chambers in different capacities, informal involvement in evaluating policy, for example,

---

relationship with the Centre for Law Reform and Legislative Drafting of the Ministry of Justice of Ukraine, which assisted in the drafting of Ukraine's money laundering legislation. See (www.ials.sas.ac.uk/postgrad/cls_uldp.htm).

23 See W. Parsons *Public Policy An Introduction to the Theory and Practice of Policy Analysis* (Brookfield: Edward Elgar, 1999). For an even more recent approach, see I. Sanderson 'Evaluation, Policy Learning and Evidence-Based Policy Making', 80 (2002) *Public Administration* pp. 1–22.

24 See A. Boer, R. Winkels, R. Hoekstra and T.M. van Engers, 'Knowledge Management for Legislative Drafting in an International Setting' in D. Bourcier (ed.) *Legal Knowledge and Information Systems: Jurix 2003: The Sixteenth Annual Conference* (Amsterdam: IOS Press, 2003) at 93.

25 In US State legislatures drafters are 'staff attorneys' often part of an Office of Legislative Legal Services, see Neal (1996) at 25.

in discussing possible amendments to existing legislation with ministerial legal services, is a regular occurrence.

In civil law jurisdictions, especially in European States with large welfare programmes, policy evaluation has been rather slow in arriving and has not always been successful.[26] As with policy implementation civil servants who took part in relevant drafting committees would probably be given preference in committees performing policy evaluation. Obviously drafting issues arising out of the implementation of a particular law would be an important element of policy evaluation. However, again, as with small common law jurisdictions, drafters' involvement in policy evaluation is a by-product of these civil servants multitasking rather than an institutionalised or formal requirement for drafters to be involved in policy evaluation. What is interesting though is that increasingly empirical studies come to the conclusion that drafters should be involved in both implementation and evaluation of policy:

> Legislative handbooks that deal with formal and technical aspects of law drafting should be accompanied by handbooks on policy development stage. Thus, the essential elements of policy development should be regulated by law and be part of the legislative handbooks, accompanied by set of standards and practical examples. Even when basic standards are set by this instrument, there is a value in developing supplemental handbooks and manuals for civil servants on tools and techniques of analysis, monitoring and evaluation, implementation, etc.[27]

Post-legislative scrutiny The concept of retrospective evaluation of legislation and 'if necessary or appropriate, the adaptation of legislation on the basis of the retrospective evaluation'[28] is not new.[29] However, although provisions for post-legislative scrutiny are present in some common law and civil law jurisdictions,[30] they are absent from most. This is a form of evaluation which is clearly of interest

---

26 See A. Schilder, *Government Failures and Institutions in Public Policy Evaluation* (The Netherlands: Van Gorcum, 2000).

27 See K. Staronova and K. Mathernova, 'Recommendations for the Improvement of the Legislative Drafting Process in Slovakia' (Budapest: OSI IPF, 2003) at 17.

28 See L. Mader, 'Evaluating the Effects: A Contribution to the Quality of Legislation' 22 (2001) 2 *Statute Law Review* at 121.

29 For example, in the UK this issue was first discussed in the early 1970s when the House of Commons Select Committee on Procedure published a report, 'The Process of Legislation' which noted the need for post-legislation committees; see House of Commons, 'The Process of Legislation', Session 1970–71, HC 538.

30 For a brief description of how other jurisdictions deal with post-legislative scrutiny, see The Law Commission, 'Post-Legislative Scrutiny A Consultation Paper' Law Commission Consultation Paper No. 178, 22 December 2005, pp. 24–9.

to drafters and one that will increase drafters' involvement in the formal evaluation of policy.

Policy Decision and the Drafter

It is an axiom in modern liberal democracies that decisions are taken by those elected. So strictly speaking appointed civil servants cannot possibly have a role in the final decision about the fate of a particular policy. When it comes to the final stage of the policy process, the legislature can only take one of three decisions: to continue, terminate or revise the policy. It goes without saying that, since termination of a policy is an implicit admission of failure by a government, policies are rarely terminated. Even when a policy has not achieved its goals the usual response of a government is to revise – often by throwing more money at the problem it is trying to address.

The decision of any government about the fate of a policy will be influenced – among others – by its formal evaluation. The drafters' input in the evaluation process might influence the final decision about a policy not so much in terms of the drafters' direct input but in terms of the drafters' input in post-legislative scrutiny or general policy evaluation as civil servants. Clearly drafters views on a policy are not going to influence the philosophy of a government's approach to policymaking. However, the views of drafters on the shortcomings of a particular bill – for instance, when the legislature invites the drafters of a bill to attend and comment on the evaluation of a specific bill – might influence individual legislators or the majority party in Parliament. In large common law jurisdictions this is highly unlikely – except for US State legislatures – unless one takes into consideration the informal interaction between drafters and high-ranking government officials. However, in small common law jurisdictions the role of the AG in the evaluation and decision about a particular policy might play a crucial role in determining its fate but once again it would be in an 'informal' capacity.

This is clearly the stage of the policy process with the weakest and practically always indirect input by drafters. Although the final decision might be influenced by the evaluation, which in turn will be affected by implementation, with the exception of the possible direct influence of the Attorney General in small common law jurisdictions I have not found evidence of drafters' involvement.

Conclusions

What this chapter attempted to show is that drafters are involved in more stages of the policy process than the often repeated legislative process. Whether or not this is warranted or ethically acceptable is a different discussion altogether. There are certainly experts who welcome and even advocate drafters' involvement with policy and substance:

> We usually consider that legistics only deals and may only deal with questions of writing in the strict sense of the term, that is: grammar, style, vocabulary, appropriate language and structure of texts. In my opinion, logistics should *also deal with the content* of the

norm; by 'content of the norm' ... The legist – the drafter – should not only man the form, but also man the content of the written norm.[31]

Similarly, there are experts who regard direct involvement of the drafter with the substance of policy as 'usurping':

> ... it is important that Parliamentary Counsel do not usurp the role of a policy maker. The interest in substantive policy is not denied. Their expertise must be conceded but they must appreciate their own limitations and they should not seek to dictate policy.[32]

Of course, there are also experts who take a more conciliatory approach:

> He [the drafter] does not make substantive policy in the sense of having the responsibility for its wisdom or of making the final decision on what is to be done and its desirability. On the other hand, in the drafting of many kinds of legal instruments the draftsman's advice on policy is often earnestly sought and properly given. The practical problem is to discharge this duty without encroaching on the prerogatives of the client.[33]

What I hope this chapter has shown is that, irrespective of one's attitude, the involvement of drafters with the different stages of the policy process is ongoing and in most instances happens in a matter-of-fact manner. What has certainly become evident is that there is no expressed wish by drafters to 'usurp' the role of elected politicians.

It is easy to argue, at this stage, that there seem to be no general rules and that each country has its own institutional idiosyncrasy. Such an argument would be too simplistic. There are obvious differences between common law and civil law jurisdictions as well as small and large jurisdictions. In small jurisdictions there is more relaxed mingling of drafters and policymakers mainly as a result of the drafters' multitasking in their capacity as civil servants. Many small jurisdictions do not have the luxury of large jurisdictions in having enough experts who can 'specialise' in their precise field and be exclusively a drafter or ministerial legal advisor, etc. Being part of the AG's chambers in small jurisdictions means that one is sometimes a drafter, sometimes a prosecutor and sometimes a government legal advisor. Similarly, being the drafter of a bill in small jurisdiction does not mean that involvement with policy-making will be reserved to the Formulation stage. Again this is 'a fact of life' for small jurisdictions and does not appear to have made a difference in the democratic processes; nor is there an outcry by elected politicians that their role is being usurped by drafters.

In contrast, large common law jurisdictions have the luxury of experts/specialists at every step of the policy process. So, it is easier – and expected – for the drafter to remain a drafter at all times without ever worrying about having to prosecute on

---

31 See P. Delnoy 'The Role of Legistics and Legists in the Determination of the Norm Content' in U. Karpen and P. Delnoy (eds) *Contributions to the Methodology of the Creation of Written Law* (Baden-Baden: Nomos Verlagsgesellschaft, 1996) at 25.

32 See Crabbe (1993) at 21.

33 See R. Dickerson, *The Fundamentals of Legal Drafting* (Boston: Little Brown, 1986) at 10.

behalf of the Crown or offer legal advice to ministries. And yet, despite the fact that the drafter can remain insulated from other stages of the policy process, in large civil law jurisdictions the drafter can be involved in more stages of the policy process often exactly because they were part of the drafting committee – which, ironically, is the reason why the drafters in large common law jurisdictions are not involved in other stages of the policy process.

Given that very little has been written about drafting and the policy process, this article showed that there is a link between the two that goes beyond the formulation stage (which ends with the legislative process). More research is required to identify specific instances of drafters' involvement with the different stages of the policy process in specific jurisdictions with a view to conducting a larger and more comprehensive comparative study which will hopefully draw some general conclusions. At the moment the only certainty is that the hypothesis that drafters consider neither policy nor substance just form has been disproven.

Index